D1481003

EMPLOYEES
AND
CORPORATE
GOVERNANCE

EDITORS

Margaret M. Blair and
Mark J. Roe

BROOKINGS INSTITUTION PRESS
WASHINGTON, D.C.

THE BROOKINGS INSTITUTION

The Brookings Institution is a private nonprofit organization devoted to research, education, and publication on important issues of domestic and foreign policy. Its principal purpose is to bring knowledge to bear on current and emerging policy problems. The Institution maintains a position of neutrality on issues of public policy. Interpretations or conclusions in publications of the Brookings Institution Press should be understood to be solely those of the authors.

Copyright © 1999

THE BROOKINGS INSTITUTION
1775 Massachusetts Avenue, N.W., Washington, D.C. 20036
www.brookings.edu

All rights reserved

Library of Congress Cataloging-in-Publication data

Employees and corporate governance / edited by Margaret M. Blair
  and Mark J. Roe.
  p.   cm.
Includes bibliographical references (p.   ) and index.

ISBN 0-8157-0944-7 (cloth : perm. paper)
  1. Producer cooperatives. 2. Management—Employee participation.
I. Blair, Margaret M., 1950— II. Roe, Mark J., 1951—
  HD3121 .E448 1999   99-6605
  658.4—dc21   CIP

9 8 7 6 5 4 3 2 1

The paper used in this publication meets minimum requirements of the American National Standard for Information Sciences—Permanence of Paper for Printed Library Materials: ANSI Z39.48-1984.

Typeset in Minion

Composition by Harlowe Typography
Cottage City, Maryland

Printed by R. R. Donnelley and Sons
Harrisonburg, Virginia

Contents

Preface

F OR REASONS EXPLAINED more fully in the introduction, I
thought, along with several colleagues at Columbia, that a
serious gap existed in American academic inquiry into corporate
governance. Corporate law academics have been using the tools of
economics and finance to analyze the triangular relationship
among the firm's shareholders, its board of directors, and one
critical labor input into the firm, namely the labor input of senior
management. We thought it was time to see whether the same
tools could be used to analyze and explain the relationships
between those three central players in corporate governance—the
shareholders, board, and managers—and the firm's employees.
The contributions to this volume, which grew out of a conference
at Columbia Law School, take up that challenge. The Sloan Foundation, through the efforts of Ralph Gomery, Jesse Ausubel, Gail
Pesyna, and Arthur Singer, has supported this conference and corporate governance research at Columbia. Margaret Blair agreed to
edit the essays with Timothy Taylor's help, two anonymous read-
ers gave us helpful feedback, and the resulting volume follows.

Mark J. Roe
Columbia Law School
September 1999

Introduction

MARGARET M. BLAIR AND
MARK J. ROE

In recent years legal and finance scholars who have studied the institutions of control and governance in large corporations have focused on the relationship between shareholders and managers, particularly on the problem of getting managers to act as faithful agents for shareholders. But little energy has gone into analyzing the role of employees in such governance. Do corporations adapt their governance structures to the type of human capital found among their employees? Do some governance structures work better in some labor markets or structures than in others? Do some labor markets affect the type of governance structure that will achieve and keep industrial peace without compromising productivity? Although human capital is widely acknowledged to be the most important asset of many firms, its role has been treated as a labor issue and not as a central concern of corporate governance.

Yet there are compelling analytic and policy reasons to care about how boardroom decisions affect employees and how employees can affect corporate governance. First, human capital is often as important as physical capital in creating value. For many firms, human capital—the ideas, skills, and organizational capabilities that employees can bring to bear on a problem, and the swiftness and flexibility with which they can deploy resources—is more important than their physical capital. Second, as a result of today's economic globalization the relevant competition for many firms and their employees may be halfway around the world, in a place where the relationships between employees and their companies may function under different legal rules and social norms. Third, boardroom decisions to close a plant, spin off a business, or merge with another company can affect the daily lives and financial security of employees; employees, in turn, may become political actors in pursuit of their own agendas. If they feel adversely affected by corporate governance institutions, employees need not be passive pawns in a corporate chess game but can try to change the institutions of corporate governance directly through contract or indirectly through courts and legislatures.

Mechanisms of Influence

Labor directly influences corporate governance structures in the United States less than it does is in some other countries. Mechanisms of influence in U.S. firms include informal internal structures, such as work teams or quality circles, by which employees influence decisionmaking on the shop floor. Employees can also organize unions, strike, seek legislation, appeal to the media, file lawsuits, negotiate individually for better terms, or leave for another job with better terms (sometimes taking critical human capital with them). In some cases, they can use control over pension fund investments in firms to influence corporate behavior. Boardroom representation is rare, however.

Employees abroad sometimes have a more formal governance role. In Germany, corporations with more than 2,000 employees must have a two-tier board, and half the seats on the upper tier, or supervisory board, must be filled by employee representatives. Works councils, which represent employees' interests at the plant level, are also a mandatory feature of German corporate governance. Japan relies more on norms than on formal law in its corporate governance structures, but major firms seem committed to lifetime employment for some employees and fill their corporate board seats with senior employees, thereby bringing employees' interests to the center of decisionmaking in corporate boardrooms.

New Contributions and Insights

This volume brings together ten essays about employee participation in corporate governance. Nine were first presented at a Columbia Law School Sloan Project conference in the fall of 1996, and the tenth, Mark Roe's essay on codetermination (chapter 6), was written apart from the conference. Several essays are about why the role of employees in corporate governance is limited in the United States and why employees have more access to corporate boardroom decisionmaking abroad. Several authors explore and seek to explain the origins or effects of three arrangements that can give employees considerable influence in the boardrooms: codetermination, as practiced in Germany; lifetime employment and enterprise union, as in Japan; and those special American situations in which employees have become significant shareholders in the corporations in which they work.

Theoretical Framework

The first four chapters in this collection lay the intellectual foundation for the overall discussion by asking why shareholders usually have the key rights of corporate control (such as the right to vote for directors and on important corporate transactions), and why employees do not typically share these rights. Greg Dow and Louis Putterman suggest in the title of chapter 1 that this question might be rephrased as "Why does capital (usually) hire labor and not vice versa?" In their discussion of the central contracting party—the party that hires the other inputs and has critical control rights—Dow and Putterman sharply distinguish between labor-managed and capital-managed firms, though they acknowledge that in practice it is not always easy to determine which input provider actually controls the firm. A traditional stock corporation, for example, may have employee representatives on the board, employees may own stock or have it held in trust for them, or employees may participate informally in decisionmaking. The far more common practice in industrial companies is for the parties that contribute financial capital, rather than employees, to have formal control, by which Dow and Putterman mean the right to choose the board and the formal authority to replace management. (This formal control may be diluted by managerial influence, a topic at the heart of recent financial and legal inquiry in the past few decades.)

The question of "why capital hires labor" is one that economists have long sought to explain in theory. Dow and Putterman group the many theories into five categories, according to the problems that worker-managed firms face: problems connected with work incentives and monitoring; wealth constraints and credit rationing for worker-owners; risk aversion and insurance market imperfections; contracting problems caused by asset specificity and investment incentives; and collective choice problems. At present, they say, anecdotal and systematic empirical evidence is insufficient to rule out any of these problems as a factor contributing to the rarity of worker-managed firms. Accordingly, they call for further empirical research to test the strength of each theory. Another point Dow and Putterman make concerns productivity in worker-managed and capital-managed firms. They find good empirical evidence to indicate that worker-managed firms often have superior productivity. This makes it all the more important, they state, to evaluate theories about the rarity of worker-owned firms, to discriminate empirically among the competing hypotheses, and to better understand the environments in which these firms flourish.

In chapter 2, Margaret Blair takes up one category of contracting problems identified by Dow and Putterman: those caused by asset specificity and investment incentives. Physical assets that are highly specific to an enterprise—in other words, that cannot be used easily outside the enterprise—are a risky investment, she notes, because their costs are sunk and not recoverable outside the firm. Investors who finance such assets will seek to protect their investment through contract and/or involvement in the firm. Many times their best protection may be to obtain control rights. Hence, according to this theory, if parties to the firm can freely contract with one another, providers of firm-specific capital will frequently end up getting control rights (unless other impediments arise).

But, Blair notes, the same line of reasoning applies to firm-specific *human* capital. Investment in skills that cannot be readily used outside an enterprise and that are not easily recoverable other than by sharing in the firm's returns will put its employees at serious risk. One might expect employees who make such investments to bargain for control rights to protect their interests. While that possibility has been noted by other theorists (including Edward Rock and Michael Wachter in chapter 4, as well as Dow and Putterman in chapter 1), most have considered it unimportant or have argued that the negative effects of employee control outweigh the benefits, or have concluded that employees can protect themselves through alternative contractual and institutional arrangements. Hence employees do not end up with control rights in the firm itself. For this reason, scholars generally treat the employee-firm relationship as a matter of labor law, outside the purview of corporate governance policy.

This standard analysis is consistent with the way most corporate and financial theorists have, in recent years, come to view a corporation: as a nexus through which participants in the firm contract with one other. Since all relationships within a firm are contractual in nature, according to this paradigm, corporation law itself is seen as a standardized solution to a central contracting problem, namely, the agency problem between shareholders and their hired managers. All other relationships are said to be governed by ordinary, negotiated contracts.

But Blair takes issue with a key assumption of this standard analysis, which is that shareholders are, and should be, the hiring party, or the "owners." This assumption (which is examined in several essays in this volume) has constrained American corporate governance scholarship by concentrating on the shareholder-management nexus. To understand why control rights have evolved as they have, she says, one needs a broader view of what a firm is, and what corporation law accomplishes.

Blair reviews several newer theories, noting that investments in knowledge, skills, relationships, and other forms of human capital can create contracting difficulties that neither arm's-length market transactions nor formal contracts can readily resolve. Where firm-specific employee investments are important, one would expect to find institutions that encourage continuity in the relationships between employees and the firm and that give employees the means to protect their stakes. Such institutions might include unions, severance pay, social norms of lifetime employment, internal job ladders, career paths, seniority rules, and direct and formal control rights. The new theories view the firm as a system of incentives or as a nexus of specific investments: in other words, as a mechanism for governing the relationships among all the participants (those who contribute labor, especially firm-specific labor, as well as those who contribute capital, especially firm-specific capital), not just the relationship between shareholders and managers. According to Blair, one of these institutional arrangements is that the law makes the corporation itself a legal entity separate from any of its participants, a fact that tends to be dismissed as unimportant by advocates of the nexus of contracts paradigm.

David Charny's discussion in chapter 3 starts with the premise that workers do participate in corporate governance, broadly defined, and that they influence management, even in mainstream, traditional, capitalist industrial firms. Three fundamental challenges arise when workers participate in governance, he states: conflicts of interest among the workers need to be resolved; workers must be kept informed so that they can provide meaningful input into management decisions; and workers must be able to make credible commitments to one another, to management, and to other participants in the firm. Charny explores the advantages and disadvantages of three governance systems that might be used to meet these challenges: "hard," "soft," and "no participation" regimes.

—Hard regimes are those that would support or make specific legal provision for institutional mechanisms or procedures by which employees would participate in governance. German corporations, for example, combine mandated social benefits, works councils, and codetermination to this end.

—Soft regimes do not explicitly mandate or enforce the mechanisms and procedures by which workers participate in management but operate through powerful social norms and traditions. Japan offers a prime example: its firms emphasize flexible work teams, job rotation, and problem solving and resource allocation on the shop floor, thereby involving employees in strategic decisions about production. In addition, unions have effectively participated in decisionmaking at higher levels of the managerial hierarchy.

—No participation regimes, epitomized by U.S. institutions, follow no particular standard of employee participation but make use of various idiosyncratic mechanisms that lead to deep employee involvement in some firms and no involvement in others.

Charny argues that industrial relations practices in all three regimes are tightly linked to corporate governance arrangements, and political cultures of each regime help sustain the various systems. He claims that all three regimes can adapt reasonably well to stresses caused by changing circumstances, such as globalization and changing technology, even if the stresses (and adaptations) differ in form, although he predicts that "soft" regimes, such as that in Japan, may have the most difficult time adjusting. Charny emphasizes the interconnectedness of institutional arrangements and suggests that it might be counterproductive to import one or a few rules or arrangements from one type of regime and impose them on another type.

Edward Rock and Michael Wachter argue in chapter 4 that employees even in standard, widely traded industrial corporations are involved in governance, but that their tasks, risks, claims, and control rights have been divided up in accordance with their specific knowledge and influence. Managers and shareholders oversee matters in which they have more specialized knowledge. Similarly, employees get claims that strike a balance between the need to motivate them and their desire to protect themselves against undiversifiable risks, whereas shareholders, who can better diversify risk, get a residual claim.

Drawing on the literature on labor economics, organizational economics, and the relevant areas of the law, Rock and Wachter argue that the division of governance tasks, risks, claims, and control rights is determined by the characteristics of the parties involved, the nature of the assets they contribute, and the transactions in which they engage. Four factors determine how the tasks, risks, claims and control rights are apportioned: the degree of asset specificity, the extent of information asymmetry, the extent of risk aversion, and the costs of drafting and enforcing explicit contracts. When the factors are similar, the authors argue, the governance arrangements tend to be similar; and, by implication, when the factors differ, legal efforts to force a uniform policy would probably be bad policy.

To demonstrate, the authors examine the arrangements in widely traded corporations. Employees of such corporations do not typically bargain for a residual claim because they are averse to the risk involved. This is not a problem for shareholders, since they can diversify their risks. Furthermore, employees do not typically participate in firm-level governance—that is, they do not have a say in the broad direction the firm should pursue, how it should invest its capital, how well executive officers are doing their jobs, or whether the corporation should be sold or restructured financially— because they lack expertise and information about these issues. But employees participate in decisions concerning wages, benefits, working conditions, terms of employment, and often the organization of work in their work units. These are areas in which they would be expected to have relevant information and expertise.

Rock and Wachter find that in closely held corporations shareholders and employees make surprisingly similar contributions in each of the four dimensions. Correspondingly, their rights, claims, and involvement in governance tend to be similar. Indeed, the authors note, shareholders' and employees' roles overlap in the closely held firm: many shareholders of small firms are firm employees, and vice versa.

German Codetermination

The authors of chapters 5 through 7 turn their attention to codetermination in Germany. German law requires large firms to have a two-tiered board, and half the seats on the upper tier, or "supervisory" board, are to be occupied by employees or their representatives. Katharina Pistor (chapter 5) analyzes the economic and political rationale for why the German government required codetermination and its consequences for corporate governance. She distinguishes between "social governance," which constrains large firms and their shareholders from exercising some of the power that they would otherwise have, and "firm governance," by which she means control of management by the owners of the company. She argues that German society sought through codetermination laws to improve the social governance of private capital, as well as to reduce worker alienation by engaging them in the firm's decisionmaking.

Although many in Germany believe this sociopolitical goal has been achieved, codetermination, Pistor notes, has raised the cost of firm governance and affected the dynamics among the three major parties involved in corporate control: shareholders, managers, and employees. Codetermination has strengthened management's hand, she argues. With membership on the supervisory board divided, management can play off the employee half against the shareholder half, to management's benefit. Anecdotal evidence suggests that the additional costs imposed by codetermination on firm governance may outweigh the benefits of social governance, although she says that codetermination cannot be made responsible for most of the inherent weaknesses in German corporate governance.

In chapter 6, Mark Roe extends these arguments, hypothesizing that codetermination may help explain why large-block shareholding persists in Germany, while securities markets—especially markets for initial public offerings (IPOs)—remain thin. Where codetermination is mandated by law, he reasons, stockholders may want the firm's governing institutions to have a blockholding "balance of power," which would be impossible to achieve in diffusely owned firms because half the supervisory board represents employees. Shareholders' "demand" for blockholding reduces the incentive of founding and large-block shareholders to sell out to a diffuse market because potentially diffuse buyers will not pay enough. Hence a good securities market does not develop, and the players have less reason than they otherwise would to build good securities distribution institutions.

Roe also suggests that having labor representatives on the board may induce German managers and shareholders to keep the supervisory board weaker than it would otherwise need to be. Board meetings are said to be infrequent, information flow to the board is poor, and the board itself is often too big and unwieldy to be effective. Instead, shareholder caucuses and meetings between managers and large shareholders substitute for effective boardroom action. Lacking a more effective board, German firms lack one control mechanism that diffuse shareholders would prefer the firm to have. One implication of Roe's thesis is that, even if other rules and institutional structures were conducive to better-developed capital markets in Germany, codetermination might lead shareholders to retain their concentrated structures and keep the board weak.

In Chapter 7, Theodor Baums and Bernd Frick take up the question of whether codetermination could be efficient, despite some arguments to the contrary (some of which were reviewed by Pistor in chapter 5). Efficiency might arise, the authors point out, if mandated rules resolved the prisoner's dilemma arising from institutional arrangements needed to support investments in firm-specific human capital, especially compressed wage structures and protection against dismissal. All firms could conceivably be better off if workers made such investments and cooperated with management. But if one firm offered a compressed wage structure and dismissal protection to encourage such investments while others pursued the traditional strategies of motivating workers through sharply differentiated wage structures and the threat of dismissal, then the firm emphasizing a cooperative culture will suffer from adverse selection: it will attract the less-motivated workers who value dismissal protection, while the best workers will go to traditional firms that pay more to its best workers. Hence a competitive market, without legally imposed codetermination rules, would inevitably end up in noncooperative equilibrium.

Even if an equilibrium with compressed pay and dismissal protection were more productive than one with more high-powered market incentives, they argue, it could unravel if it were not mandated for all firms. Firms could not always pursue the cooperative package, because their best employees might be hired away. Legally mandated codetermination could move all firms to the cooperative equilibrium, they argue, with potentially higher total output in those economies where the cooperative package is more productive than the market-based package. Given the divergent predictions of theory, then, one cannot predict with certainty whether the net effects of codetermination on firm performance and stockholder value will be positive or negative.

For insight into this issue, Baums and Frick turn to empirical evidence, namely, the impact of events leading to the promulgation of codetermination laws and court decisions on the stock prices of German firms. If the various events they identify were important, and news to investors, and if investors believed that codetermination lowered firm value, stock prices should have declined in response to those events. Although other studies have reported a negative impact of codetermination on stock price, Baums and Frick find no evidence that codetermination rules caused the equity value in German corporations to decline, a result consistent with the possibility that shareholders were not harmed by codetermination. (It is also consistent, they note, with the possibility that the effects were previously impounded into the stock price.)

Japanese Corporate Governance

In chapter 8, Ronald Gilson and Mark Roe ask whether lifetime employment facilitates investments in human capital, as conventional wisdom suggests. Most analysts in the United States have argued that lifetime
employment produces a win-win situation: the employer gets a highly
skilled employee and the employees get job security. But, Gilson and Roe
argue, a firm's commitment to job security for its employees would not, by
itself at least, protect either the firm's or the employees' investments in
human capital. Even with lifetime employment, they note, the employee is
free to leave and the employer is free to adjust salary, so lifetime employment does not, by itself, protect either's investments in human capital.

What, then, explains the heavy investment in human capital in the Japanese firm? Gilson and Roe argue that is more likely to be the "dark" side of
the Japanese firm's relationship with labor—the constriction of the external
labor market—than it is lifetime employment. Firms are prepared to pay for
human capital because employees cannot easily jump to another firm after
the employer pays up. This feature of enforced low mobility, they further
note, is not something most Americans would find appealing.

Gilson and Roe hypothesize that lifetime employment arose for both
"macro" and "micro" political reasons, rather than economic ones. At the
macro level, Japan's deep economic troubles after World War II may have
prompted conservative leaders to endorse lifetime employment as a means
of warding off socialist electoral victories. At the micro level, managers tried
to defeat unions that had become hostile after the war and win back factories from worker occupation, firm by firm, by offering lifetime employment
to a core of workers. Neither of these goals had any direct connection with
human capital training but were about reducing total worker influence,
either in elections or in the factory. But once lifetime employment was in
place as standard practice, other institutions, such as enterprise unions
(see chapter 9), emerged to support and complement it. Another complementary institution is the inside board, in which managers who win internal promotion contests end up on the firm's board.

Gilson and Roe concede that the historical record does not provide
"smoking gun" evidence that Japan's large firms agreed not to raid one
another's employees. (Again, they suggest that the constriction of the external labor market in Japan does more to protect employer investments in
human capital than does the firm's promise of a lifetime job.) At the same
time, they offer some theories as to why the parties would not advertise such

agreements, why government efforts to constrict the labor market could have been the result of the firms' influence, and why firms might on their own decide not to hire laterally. They also state that market-constricting arrangements, if they do not become consistent with a labor market equilibrium, are fragile without government enforcement.

In chapter 9 Nobuhiro Hiwatari considers whether economic forces are causing various institutional arrangements by which labor participates in corporate governance to converge. His analysis suggests they will not converge. Although local, historical, and political circumstances may have caused some arrangements to collapse, Hiwatari notes, others have emerged that are likely to prevent convergence. A case in point is the Japanese enterprise union, an institution sometimes regarded as one of the "three sacred treasures" of Japanese management (the other two being lifetime employment and the seniority wage system).

Like Gilson and Roe, Hiwatari rejects the idea that these arrangements are due primarily to a cultural predisposition toward cooperation in Japan. He finds their roots in the history of unionism in the postwar period, especially during the occupation, noting that "revolutionary unionism," the most powerful force in the earliest postwar years, was bent not just on organizing workers for gains in the workplace, but on mobilizing them politically and creating a socialist revolution. If anything, these unionists rejected cooperative approaches. Management crushed revolutionary unionism after the occupation authority's reforms and austerity in the late 1940s forced Japanese companies to face market competition, which in turn led to massive layoffs and a restructuring of Japanese industries. In the large firms, enterprise unions emerged and replaced the revolutionary unions, as workers at all levels united to cooperate with management in an effort to save their own firms and, they hoped, their jobs.

Enterprise unions have the following characteristics: membership is limited to permanent employees, blue- and white-collar workers join a single union, membership is automatic upon joining the firm, union dues are collected automatically, union officers retain their employee status during their tenure, and union sovereignty is retained at the enterprise level. Enterprise unions cooperate with firm policies, Hiwatari says, as long as the firm is "committed to employment security and provides wages and fringe benefits comparable to those offered at other large corporations in the same industry." Enterprise unionism has been credited with stabilizing employment in Japan in the past few decades and with enabling the economy to survive repeated oil and financial crises over this period with low unemployment. Hiwatari argues that the cooperation of the enterprise unions enabled some large Japanese firms to keep investing during the crises and thereby kept the firms competitive. Also important was the fact that oligopolistic export-oriented industries coordinated their investments, while fragmented industries were forced by market factors to adjust.

Employee Share Ownership

Jeffrey Gordon closes the circle in chapter 10 by returning to the idea of employee control. Like Rock and Wachter, he discusses the means by which employees participate in governance or exercise partial control rights to help protect their interests, particularly through share ownership. Although Gordon recognizes the arguments (reviewed by Dow and Putterman) against employee share ownership as a permanent arrangement, he postulates that employee stock ownership transactions might help solve at least four types of problems associated with sharp economic change in U.S. corporations: the justice questions raised by the allocation of general transition costs between shareholders and employees, inefficient bargaining over the allocation of one-time transition costs, inefficient bargaining over ongoing transition costs, and the lack of adequate structures for rapidly changing environments where "transition" costs might be a continuous part of doing business. Gordon is skeptical of the idea that employee share ownership is about justice. Rather, he shows how employee stock ownership can improve the bargaining environment between a firm and its employees, especially when the stock is granted to employees in exchange for wage and benefit concessions. His arguments apply even (and perhaps especially) in times of wrenching transitions, as in Eastern Europe and Russia. In such instances employee participation in governance as well as gain sharing may be critical to a successful restructuring.

Lessons Learned

Of the recurring themes in this volume, a central one is that institutions matter. Different institutions of governance, whether involving employees or not, have different costs and benefits, and there may be no unique, economically optimal governance arrangements. Rather, history and politics matter in explaining which institutions arise and which ones persist.

Another theme is that institutional arrangements and practices may interact to complement and support each other and thus cannot be studied in isolation. Furthermore, the institutions observed in a given nation or at a particular point in time may be partly an accident of history, rather than an optimal solution to a current economic problem. Gilson and Roe refer to this circumstance as "path dependency," a concept similar to that of multiple equilibria. Path dependency implies that an institutional arrangement may simply represent a reasonable solution to a prior problem, which in the case of governance participation in Japan and Germany happened to be a political rather than an economic one. Likewise, the general absence of standardized structures for employee participation in U.S. companies may be a product of the nation's history and political pressures. As Charny notes, the three prominent regimes ("hard" rules, "soft" rules, and no rules) simply "represent three different solutions to a set of problems common to firms in each economy." All three have adapted with more or less equivalent success to different stresses, although they may distribute the costs of adjustment in different ways.

Another theme here is that lifetime employment, codetermination, and other institutions may have been adopted to solve one problem but then had unintended costs or unintended benefits. Or, as malleable institutions evolve, the economic results may be similar to those produced by another set of institutions. To refer to the Gilson and Roe example again, Japanese firms may have adopted lifetime employment to solve a political problem, but in so doing they facilitated the rise of supporting institutions that led Japanese firms to invest in human capital and caused Japanese managers to rank employees ahead of shareholders as important constituents and beneficiaries of the activities of the firm. This arrangement, apparently beneficial for many years, may now be impeding Japan's efforts to adjust to its current financial crisis.

The chapters in this volume also have a common methodological theme: that the tools of economic and financial analysis can, when due regard is given to historical sequencing and institutional complementarities, better explain the relationships among the firm, shareholders, managers, and employees than either economic theory or historical anecdote can alone. In prior academic work, employee-related corporate governance issues have come up mostly in connection with stakeholder theory, which has not made much progress in the core inquiry into corporate governance, perhaps because purveyors of stakeholder theory have not made as much use of the intellectual discipline provided by economic theory or finance theory.

In addition, the contributors to this volume emphasize that the arrangements in place today should not be considered fixed. Corporate governance institutions have adapted before, and new historical, political, and economic pressures may precipitate other adaptations. Moreover, policy debates about reforms must not only consider economic analyses but must also be textured, contextual, and sensitive to political realities.

PART One

Theoretical Framework

1

Why Capital (Usually) Hires Labor: An Assessment of Proposed Explanations

GREGORY DOW AND
LOUIS PUTTERMAN

I n the mid–nineteenth century, John Stuart Mill argued that
once the working classes had achieved a sufficient level of education and political emancipation, the capitalist employment
relationship would be superseded by a system of voluntarily
formed producer cooperatives. In Mill's view, such an outcome
would provide "the nearest approach to social justice, and the
most beneficial ordering of industrial affairs for the universal
good, which it is possible at present to foresee."[1] Today the workers of industrialized countries are far more educated than they
were a century ago, and the adult franchise is now universal in

Both authors are grateful to the MacArthur Foundation for its support. Dow would
also like to thank the Social Sciences and Humanities Research Council of Canada and
the Swedish Collegium for Advanced Study in the Social Sciences for financial assistance. Helpful comments on an earlier draft were provided by audiences at the 1996
Allied Social Science Associations meetings, at the Columbia Law School conference
on employees and corporate governance, and at a conference on the costs of inequality sponsored by the MacArthur Foundation at the Massachusetts Institute of Technology in October 1996. All of the opinions expressed are those of the authors.
    1. Mill (1848 [1936], p. 792).

those countries. Yet Mill's prediction has shown little sign of coming to pass. Enterprises owned or run by workers have never occupied more than a small sector of any developed market economy. In this chapter, we ask why this is so.

A great many disparate explanations have been put forth on the subject of why investors, rather than workers, normally own and manage the firm. To a large extent, these stories have been advanced in an informal and unsystematic way, with little or no effort to determine where they agree or differ, or whether alternative stories even exist. This discussion takes a few modest steps toward systematizing the literature on the subject.

We begin by explaining the distinction between labor-managed and capital-managed firms, and stating a few basic facts about the incidence of labor-managed firms in developed market economies. The issue addressed next is why labor-managed firms are rare in relation to capital-managed firms in these economies. Five reasons are considered: work incentives and monitoring, wealth constraints and credit rationing, risk aversion and insurance imperfections, asset specificity and investment incentives, and collective choice problems. Attention then turns to some other hypotheses that have appeared in the literature but have not received as much attention as the "big five." The chapter concludes with some thoughts on the possibilities for empirical testing.

Defining the Labor-Managed Firm

A logical truism facing both proponents and opponents of labor-managed firms is that if capital and labor were entirely symmetric inputs in all physical and institutional respects, then it would make no difference whether the firm was run by capital suppliers using hired labor, or vice versa. Therefore, any argument to the effect that labor-managed firms are different from capital-managed firms (whether in a specific industry, or across the board) must ultimately rest on a claim about asymmetries in the nature of the two inputs. Of course, the relevant asymmetries may not be the same in all industries or time periods. Theories about labor-managed firms can be tested by how well the proposed asymmetries can account for the successes of labor-managed firms as well as their failures. For example, such theories should explain why labor-managed firms have arisen repeatedly in certain narrow market niches, such as professional partnerships and some craft-based manufacturing. They should also explain transitions from one organizational form to another, by identifying the conditions under which capitalist firms tend to sell out to their employees (Weirton Steel, Avis, United Airlines), and also the conditions under which labor-managed firms sell out to conventional investors (investment banking firms, some plywood cooperatives in the Pacific Northwest, and Avis again).

Our discussion will focus on the distinction between "capital-managed" and "labor-managed" firms. In the canonical two-input case, an equivalent distinction for our purposes is to say that capital hires labor, or labor hires capital. A common alternative approach to the problem poses the question instead as "Who owns the firm?" Thus instead of investigating the "labor-managed firm," one might examine the "worker-owned firm." In practice, it is unlikely to make much difference which of these questions is asked, for in a market economy "owning a firm" typically implies a bundle of rights that include the right to acquire revenues, to determine how the firm is operated, and to transfer ownership to others.[2] However, we emphasize management rights in our discussion because the hallmark of economic organization in firms is the assignment to one or more parties of the right to make decisions not contractually predetermined by members of the production coalition.[3] It follows that which parties come to hold this right of "residual control" is a matter of central concern.

After all, there are cases in which workers own a majority of a firm's shares through an employee stock ownership plan, but where that plan is structured in such a way that they lack the right to vote their shares. The firm in such a case is generally called "employee-owned," but it would be misleading to think of it as "labor-managed." Perhaps the most straightforward way of defining control in corporations is to ask: Who elects the board of directors? If the answer is "capital suppliers" (or some subset thereof, such as holders of common stock), then it is a capital-managed firm. If the answer is "labor suppliers" (or some subset, such as employees who have worked for the firm for more than one year), then it is a labor-managed firm.

Although in most cases it is not hard to discern who has control rights, one cannot rule out problems of ambiguity.[4] For example, employee representatives may have seats on the board of directors; or there may be informal employee participation in decisionmaking, perhaps via committees dealing with quality control, health and safety, innovation, and so on. We

2. For a more thorough exposition of this point, see Putterman (1993); Ryan (1987).

3. In this belief, we are following in the steps of such authors as Coase (1937); Williamson (1975, 1985); Grossman and Hart (1986); and Hart and Moore (1990).

4. See Rock and Wachter in this volume for an argument that both employees and capital providers typically have important—though different—control rights in firms.

sidestep some of these ambiguities by emphasizing two ideas: the importance of ultimate control, indicated by the potential ability of a group to replace top management; and the importance of formal control, as codified in corporate charters, by-laws, and similar rules of governance. However, we recognize that there is a continuum running from pure investor control to pure worker control, with numerous real-world examples falling somewhere in between.

The potential heterogeneity of capital and labor also raises several issues. For example, certain kinds of stock may carry different weights for voting purposes, or bondholders and banks may acquire control of a firm under conditions of financial distress.[5] In labor-managed firms, certain employees are entitled to participate in some decisions through complex governance procedures, but other employees—such as recent hires—may lack formal participation rights entirely. There are cases where suppliers of an input other than labor and capital have control; for example, suppliers of produce have control over some agricultural cooperatives.[6] For present purposes, we regard a firm as a pure capital-managed firm if it is controlled by suppliers of its equity finance or owners of its physical assets, by virtue of and in proportion to that role, and a pure labor-managed firm if formal control rights are shared among its suppliers of nonmanagerial and managerial labor, by virtue of and in proportion to that role. Hybrid forms clearly exist, but are most easily understood by focusing on these polar cases.

To clarify these ideas, let us explore them in the context of some potentially challenging cases of firm organization. Consider the case of partnerships. Our discussion implies that these firms may be either capital-managed or labor-managed, depending on the principle by which the right to participate in management is assigned. A real estate partnership where votes are allocated according to invested capital is a capital-managed firm. A professional partnership where votes are allocated according to the principle of one vote per partner, regardless of prior capital contributions to the firm, is a labor-managed firm. The plywood cooperatives of the U.S. Northwest provide another interesting case. In these firms, all members are entitled to participate in management, and membership is associated with the supply of labor to the firm. There is, to be sure, a market for membership where workers can purchase membership "shares" either from departing members or from the firm itself (if the existing members want to expand), and these

5. For discussion, see Aghion and Bolton (1992).
6. Hansmann (1996).

share purchases help to finance the purchase of equipment. One might therefore argue that control rights are in fact derived from the supply of capital to the firm via the purchase of membership rights. However, no member can hold more than one share, and votes are assigned on the basis of labor contributions, not on the basis of what was paid for a membership share. Thus we view the plywood co-ops as labor-managed.

A large corporation may appear to be the most straightforward case, but it poses real difficulties. In formal terms, top management is accountable to the board of directors, which in turn is elected by a majority of shareholders, which makes it a capital-managed firm. This would continue to be true even if some shareholders also supplied labor to the firm, because voting rights are determined by capital contributions, rather than labor contributions. But where the corporation poses the difficulty is with respect to the separation of ownership and control. In very large corporations with widely dispersed shareholdings, no single person or group will be able to replace the incumbent board of directors unilaterally, and the costs of organizing a majority of shareholders to do so will be high or prohibitive. Moreover, the incumbent board may often be cronies of top managers, who therefore run the firm in their own interests with little fear of outside intervention.[7] It could be argued that because the incumbent managers supply a form of labor, this firm is in fact labor-managed, albeit a case in which a very narrow subset of the firm's labor suppliers exercise managerial authority. We would reject this characterization, and instead classify corporations as a case of a capital-managed firm in which the ultimate controllers face serious obstacles in exercising their formal rights effectively.

To the extent that control is shared by a group—whether this be a group of investors or a group of workers—there will frequently be significant costs of collective action within the controlling group. These factors may well be empirically significant, and as we discuss later, they may have some bearing on the question of whether control rights are assigned to capital or labor. However, no qualitative line can be drawn between controlling groups facing large incentive problems and high collective action costs versus those facing moderate incentive problems and modest collective action costs. In any event, the history of large-scale takeovers in the United States over the last few decades indicates that the latent control rights held by shareholders are not necessarily a trivial factor in corporate governance.

7. This argument was first made prominent by Berle and Means in the 1930s, and many others have elaborated on it since.

To conclude this section, we review some basic facts about labor-managed firms in contemporary industrialized economies. While there have been many fascinating experiences with worker control in developing countries and in the former Soviet bloc and China, the institutional environment for these experiments is radically different from that in Western Europe and North America, and one must therefore be very cautious in generalizing from such experiences to cases involving developed capitalist economies. For similar reasons, we omit discussion of experiments arising in earlier periods of economic history. All of the hypotheses considered here take for granted that the relevant legal and market framework is the one characteristic of late twentieth-century capitalism.

Even within this limited sphere, labor-managed firms are a variegated phenomenon. Indeed, almost every empirical generalization about labor-managed firms seems to have some significant exception, and it is necessary to remain alert to special factors that may help to explain unusual individual cases. Such firms include professional partnerships;[8] the U.S. plywood cooperatives of the Northwest, which at their peak in the 1950s had a market share of 25 percent;[9] the numerous European worker cooperatives engaging in small-scale craft manufacturing or construction;[10] and cooperatives undertaking low-skill labor-intensive activities such as waste removal, taxi service, and reforestation.[11] An increasing number of large firms began as capitalist firms, but have made the transition to majority share ownership by employees; some well-known U.S. examples include Weirton Steel and United Airlines. Relatively few labor-managed firms engage in capital-intensive manufacturing activities. Apart from capital-managed firms bought out by their employees, the primary example is the Mondragon system of cooperatives in Spain, which includes Spain's largest producer and exporter of consumer durables.[12]

Italy's cooperative sector seems to be the largest in the West, with about 11,000 firms and 428,000 workers in 1981. This was followed by France, with about 1,300 cooperatives employing 34,000 workers in 1986, and by Spain, where the Mondragon cooperatives contributed to a sector employing 19,500 in industrial jobs alone.[13] In the European Community as a whole, over 14,000 new cooperatives employing 223,000 workers were

8. Hansmann (1990a).

9. Craig and Pencavel (1992, 1993, 1995); Pencavel and Craig (1994); Pencavel (1996).

10. Defourny, Estrin, and Jones (1985); Jones and Svejnar (1985); Estrin, Jones, and Svejnar (1987); Ben-Ner (1988a); Estrin and Jones (1992).

11. Russell (1985).

12. Bradley and Gelb (1981, 1987); Whyte and Whyte (1988); and Wiener and Oakeshott (1987).

13. Bonin, Jones, and Putterman (1993).

created during 1976–81.[14] In the United States, the plywood cooperatives had a total of about 2,600 workers in 1982, and the reforestation cooperatives had about 650 workers at that time. Britain's cooperatives had their largest presence in the clothing industry, Sweden's in small engineering firms, Italy's in construction, and France's in construction and consulting. The United States has experienced waves of cooperative formation over time, which have varied as to industry and region of concentration.[15]

Cooperatives also vary in size, from large Italian construction firms with over 2,000 workers to Mondragon industrial enterprises and U.S. plywood cooperatives averaging about 230 workers, to French construction firms averaging 60, U.S. reforestation cooperatives 29, and British clothing cooperatives averaging fewer than 10 workers. In the 1980s, individual capital accounts of members were typically worth less than $200 in the United Kingdom, $500 to $2,000 in Italy, and $1,900 to $6,000 in France, while individual capital stakes ranged up to $50,000 in the Mondragon cooperatives, and shares of U.S. plywood cooperatives sold for up to $90,000 in 1983. Financial structures and membership and voting rules varied considerably. With these introductory considerations out of the way, we can sketch out five major hypotheses that attempt to explain why capital (usually) hires labor.

Work Incentives and Monitoring

A first argument for the prevalence of capital-managed firms, which draws upon a seminal 1972 article by Armen Alchian and Harold Demsetz, begins with the premise that teamwork is often more productive than work by isolated individuals. However, it can be difficult to observe the efforts and contributions of individuals within the team. Unless rewards are tied to individual contributions, the potential productivity gains from team production will be lost because each worker will attempt to free-ride on the contributions made by others. In Alchian and Demsetz's view, the solution is to appoint a specialist who estimates the effort of individuals and sets wages accordingly. Alchian and Demsetz point out that the monitor can be deterred from shirking if the monitor is the residual claimant for the production team; that is, the monitor keeps the difference between revenues and costs.

14. Ben-Ner (1988a).
15. Jones (1984).

But why must the monitor-residual claimant be a capital supplier, rather than, for example, a team member elected democratically by workers from among their own ranks? The main rationale suggested by Alchian and Demsetz is that physical assets will be abused if their use is not monitored closely by their owner:

> An indestructible hammer with a readily detectable marginal product has zero user cost. But suppose the hammer were destructible and that care-less (which is easier than careful) use is more abusive and causes greater depreciation of the hammer. Suppose in addition the abuse is easier to detect by observing the way it is used than by observing only the ham-mer after its use, or by measuring the output scored from a hammer by a laborer. If the hammer were rented and used in the absence of the owner, the depreciation would be greater than if the use were observed by the owner and the user charged in accord with the imposed depreciation.[16]

The owner of the physical assets needed by the team thus has strong incentives to oversee their use and for this reason is a logical candidate for the job of monitoring worker effort.

This argument does leave a loose end hanging: Why not replace the capital-managed firm with a labor-managed firm where workers themselves own the physical assets and monitor their use? Indeed, Alchian and Demsetz start down this road by observing that the users of certain tools frequently own them: "Watch repairers, engineers, and carpenters tend to own their own tools especially if they are portable. Trucks are more likely to be employee owned rather than other equally expensive team inputs because it is relatively cheap for the driver to police the care taken in using a truck." The idea that worker performance usually has several dimensions, such as producing output while simultaneously maintaining equipment, has been developed in later work by Bengt Holmstrom and Paul Milgrom. These authors have sought to identify situations in which workers should own the physical assets with which they work, an arrangement that enables workers themselves to make the proper trade-offs between output and asset depreciation.[17]

It is unclear where this reasoning should stop. If asset maintenance explains the ownership of tools by individual workers such as carpenters, then perhaps large indivisible assets such as oil refineries, steel mills, or auto assembly lines should be owned collectively by the workers who use them,

16. Alchian and Demsetz (1972, p. 792).
17. Holmstrom and Milgrom (1991, 1994). See also Alchian and Demsetz (1972).

because such worker-owners would be in the best position to monitor how the physical assets are utilized. But in the spirit of the Alchian and Demsetz analytic framework, it should be pointed out that an individual worker would be inclined to overuse an asset in which that worker has only a fractional ownership stake. Thus both the free-riding problems associated with supply of effort and with the depreciation of collectively owned assets can be solved by a central monitor-residual claimant-asset owner.[18]

This story about firm organization has raised a number of theoretical and empirical issues. First, vertical monitoring by a specialist owner is not always superior to horizontal or mutual monitoring within a group of co-workers.[19] Second, it may be possible to motivate team members to behave efficiently through the use of group bonuses or penalties without monitoring individual workers, although this system can leave workers vulnerable to abuse by a dishonest employer.[20] Third, it has been shown that worker teams (or partnerships) can attain equilibria where effort levels are approximately efficient, but this result depends on the somewhat implausible assumption that there is no limit on the size of the penalties that can be imposed on individuals.[21] A fourth theoretical issue has been raised by the analysis of repeated games, which has shown that shirking can be deterred via threats of subsequent retaliation as long as all workers place enough weight on future payoffs.[22] These concerns do not necessarily overturn the Alchian and Demsetz hypothesis, but they do highlight theoretical elements of that hypothesis that remain to be spelled out.

The few bits of empirical evidence that are applicable to the hypothesis generally appear to argue against this story, at least in its standard versions. First, the Alchian and Demsetz theory would lead one to predict higher labor productivity when firms use tight central monitoring and link compensation closely with measures of individual effort contribution, as opposed to firms relying on peer monitoring and gain sharing or profit sharing to elicit effort. But there is persuasive evidence from several longitudinal data sets that the introduction of profit sharing in large capitalist

18. For similar ideas about the role of an external asset owner, see Williamson (1980); Alston and Gillespie (1989); Barzel (1989, chap. 4).

19. Putterman (1984).

20. For a proposal of group rewards or penalties, see Holmstrom (1982). For the problems posed by dishonest employers, see Eswaran and Kotwal (1984).

21. Legros and Matthews (1993).

22. On the theory of repeated games in this context, see MacLeod (1984, 1988); Weitzman and Kruse (1990); Putterman and Skillman (1992); Dong and Dow (1993). The well-known Folk Theorem (Fudenberg and Tirole, 1991, chap. 5) shows that a great many equilibria can arise in repeated games, including everything from Pareto efficient allocations to highly inefficient traps in which all workers shirk in every period.

firms increases labor productivity by about 4–5 percent.[23] Perhaps these findings can be limited to certain conditions or explained by a differing chain of causality—for example, perhaps firms expecting an exogenous increase in labor productivity are more likely to introduce profit sharing— but the finding is prima facie evidence against the Alchian and Demsetz hypothesis.

There is also econometric evidence suggesting that labor-managed firms do not have severe problems with labor productivity and may perform rather well on this dimension.[24] Indeed, increased mutual monitoring and a tendency to use fewer supervisors are common characteristics of worker-managed and profit-sharing firms.[25] Of course, there may be a selection problem here: perhaps labor-managed firms emerge only in situations where the incentive problem is minor, and the general dearth of labor-managed firms is still attributable to incentive effects. However, this objection is far-fetched for cases where capital-managed firms and labor-managed firms operate in the same industry and use similar production techniques, as in the U.S. plywood industry or European construction cooperatives.

Finally, it is unclear whether the incentive hypothesis can adequately explain the distribution of capital-managed firms and labor-managed firms across industries. It seems that labor-managed firms are less common in capital-intensive activities, and it could be argued that firms in an industry where production involves large, indivisible assets are especially vulnerable to equipment abuse, and might therefore require close monitoring of worker behavior by asset owners. It does appear that workers are paid more (other things equal) in capital-intensive industries, and it has been suggested that these may be efficiency wage payments intended to deter misuse of valuable equipment. But this evidence is ambiguous. It could also be that workers in capital-intensive industries are paid more out of a desire to reduce labor turnover and to keep specialized equipment fully utilized, or that workers may capture some of the quasi rents associated with such assets.[26]

Ideally, one would like to have evidence that capital-managed firms are more common in industries where abuse of physical assets by workers is more costly and less readily detected, rather than evidence that capital-

23. Kruse (1993) obtains such a result for U.S. data; Wadhwani and Wall (1990) for U.K. data; and Jones and Kato (1995) for Japan.

24. Estrin, Jones, and Svejnar (1987); Craig and Pencavel (1995).

25. Weitzman and Kruse (1990); Bonin, Jones, and Putterman (1993).

26. Holmstrom and Milgrom (1991) suggest the role of efficiency wages in deterring equipment abuse. However, MacLeod and Malcomson (1998) explain similar wage differentials as responses to the need to keep equipment fully utilized.

managed firms tend to arise when physical assets are large and indivisible, or where capital is an important cost item in relation to labor. Then, a convincing theory would explain why the free-rider problems associated with asset maintenance in a team setting are more readily handled by outside asset owners, as compared with the alternative of collective asset ownership and peer monitoring by the users themselves. For the latter purpose, it would be helpful to have evidence indicating that vertical hierarchical monitoring was in fact less costly than horizontal peer monitoring. Along the same lines, one would like to have evidence that capital-managed firms are more common when vertical monitoring of effort or asset use is relatively cheaper, for industries with a given degree of capital intensity. We are not aware of systematic empirical evidence on these predictions.

Worker Wealth and Credit Markets

Perhaps the most common explanation for the rarity of labor-managed firms is that workers tend to be poor and therefore cannot finance the creation of firms that they themselves own. In principle, of course, workers might borrow the required funds, but the information problems that banks would face in sorting out which groups of prospective worker-owners are deserving of credit are formidable. In any event, lenders are unwilling to finance a firm entirely by debt. Some equity is needed to signal lenders that the borrower will not shirk or take excessive risks and leave creditors holding the bag. In addition, workers may prefer to diversify their portfolios, rather than to invest a heavy share of their assets in their own company.[27] However, we defer discussion of risk and diversification until the next section and will focus here only on workers' difficulties in raising capital.

The worker wealth hypothesis is complementary to some ideas about work incentives. One idea about worker incentives was that teams could approximate efficient effort levels to any desired degree if individual liability was unlimited. But when worker wealth is limited and there is no way to impose fines or other penalties of the required size, it may be desirable to use costly monitoring, or to bring in an outside manager to impose group penalties. Thus the justification for a capital-managed firm may be seen as a combination of the need to monitor effort combined with an unequal wealth distribution and imperfect financial markets.[28]

27. See Bowles and Gintis (1990, 1993a, 1993b, 1996).
28. Legros and Newman (1996). Similarly, Newman (1994) shows that employment relationships are more prevalent in relation to self-employment when capital markets are more imperfect, and when the wealth distribution is more unequal.

A somewhat different story about interactions between wealth and effort incentives is provided by Mukesh Eswaran and Ashok Kotwal, who argue that capitalists run firms owing to a conjunction of two factors: the limited personal wealth of entrepreneurs and the temptation for entrepreneur-borrowers to substitute inputs financed by loans for their own effort in the production process.[29] One way to interpret this notion is that it generalizes the idea of incentives to avoid equipment abuse: just as there is a danger that workers will substitute machine services for their own effort (unless monitored), there is a danger that workers or entrepreneurs will substitute borrowed funds for their own effort. But this scenario leads to the conclusion that lenders will integrate the roles of financier and entrepreneurial decisionmaker, a prediction that is open to argument. While there are certainly examples of this phenomenon—for example, the managerial role played by venture capitalists in small start-up firms—this mechanism seems implausible as a general explanation of why workers do not run firms. It does not take into account that even an integrated lender-manager cannot avoid the incentive problem of monitoring effort (and equipment abuse) at the level of the shop floor. Moreover, in large publicly traded corporations it is not correct that investors participate in day-to-day entrepreneurial activities, much less in shop-floor labor.

The worker wealth hypothesis also has implications that go beyond interactions with work incentives. Let us broaden the interpretation of capital supply so that it includes the supply of financial capital, not just the services of preexisting physical assets such as machinery. The worker wealth hypothesis applies whenever capital is needed to finance a production process where inputs must be purchased today to generate output tomorrow. Of course, the size of working capital requirements depends on the scale and capital intensity of the production process, as well as various auxiliary considerations: Can physical assets be leased? Can they be bought and resold on competitive secondhand markets? Or are the assets highly specialized to a particular firm? These issues, which revolve around the question of asset specificity, will be addressed in the next section. For present purposes, we simply take it for granted that the firm must finance some outlays before it receives the resulting revenues.

Workers might be limited in the quantity of credit they can obtain in the credit market for two main reasons, corresponding to problems of moral hazard and adverse selection.[30] The moral hazard problem is that

---

29. Eswaran and Kotwal (1989).
30. Stiglitz and Weiss (1981).

the worker-borrower will engage in behavior that imposes costs on the capitalist-lender, after the loan contract is in place. For instance, the borrower may choose excessively risky projects, in the recognition that upside returns go mainly to the borrower as residual claimant, while downside losses are inflicted mainly on the lender, assuming the borrower can declare bankruptcy or has limited personal liability for losses due to low personal wealth.[31] This argument also suggests that lenders may prefer to deal with undemocratic firms having a single dominant owner because it is easier to influence the policies of such firms, either by preventing the adoption of excessively risky projects, or by inducing worker-managers to take sufficient risks.[32]

The moral hazard problems that make it difficult for workers to raise sufficient capital are worsened by asymmetries between different types of capital: physical and financial capital are (relatively) easily shifted among alternative owners whereas human capital is not. The human capital of workers is inalienable, so that workers can always walk away from failing investment projects, and the lender cannot recover its money.[33] More generally, the absence of indentured servitude and debtor's prisons is a crucial institutional feature of modern capitalism![34] Of course, in some cases it may also be hard to use certain physical assets as collateral on loans, especially if the relevant assets have a large sunk cost element and few alternative uses. This problem will be taken up in the later discussion of asset specificity.

In the case of adverse selection, the other main difficulty in credit markets, the danger is not that borrowers will shift risk to the lender after the loan contract has been signed, but rather that lenders cannot predict beforehand with accuracy what the borrowers' probability of repayment will be. However, lenders know that low-risk borrowers will only be willing to pay low interest, while high-risk borrowers will be willing to promise to pay higher interest—although they may later default. Standard analysis shows that this situation can lead to an equilibrium wherein lenders respond to this information problem by limiting the quantity that they are willing to lend at the market interest rate, and that as a result some borrowers are unable to raise funds for good projects.[35] To be sure, high-quality borrowers in an equilibrium of this kind have incentives to signal their true type in various ways. One common form of signaling is for borrowers to invest

31. Hansmann (1988).
32. Gintis (1989); Bowles and Gintis (1993a, 1993b).
33. Hart and Moore (1994).
34. FitzRoy (1980).
35. Stiglitz and Weiss (1981); Stiglitz (1987).

some funds of their own as a way of conveying their confidence in the merits of the project to lenders. But this solution is costly and will not work if
workers have desirable projects but limited personal wealth. An alternative
remedy is for lenders to screen loan applicants by investigating proposed
investments—but this is also costly. For such reasons, market equilibria
involving adverse selection may be quite inefficient.[36]

The worker wealth hypothesis has some empirical support. Most labor-
managed firms are financed by the savings of worker-members and retained
earnings.[37] This fact is compatible with the idea that labor-managed firms
lack access to credit markets, though much the same thing could probably
be said for small capital-managed firms, and data that could be used to contrast the cost of external capital to capital-managed firms and labor-
managed firms are lacking. A lack of worker wealth or ability to raise capital
is also consistent with the fact that labor-managed firms tend to avoid
capital-intensive industries as well as industries with significant scale
economies, where absolute financing requirements are large.

However, there are also empirical objections to the worker wealth
hypothesis. If wealth is really the binding constraint on the formation of
labor-managed firms, one might expect to see more workers setting up their
own firms using whatever personal wealth they do possess. For instance,
professional athletes might buy the sports franchises that employ them; or
film and television stars could own production companies. Such arrangements are not unknown, but the point is that they could be more common. Moreover, workers without much personal wealth may collectively
control large pools of capital through union pension funds, which can
sometimes exceed the financial requirements of firms, or even entire industries where such unions are active. The straightforward response is that
workers may be risk averse, and prefer not to put all their eggs in one basket.
This suggests that the credit rationing story does not suffice as an explanation on its own but needs to be supplemented by considerations of risk
aversion and imperfect insurance markets, which will be addressed in the
next section.

Another objection is that failing capital-managed firms are increasingly
often bought out by their employees.[38] To the extent that these buyouts
involve external financing, this raises a question: If workers can buy failing
firms, why can they not persuade lenders to finance a buyout before the firm

36. In particular, they may fail even second-best efficiency tests, as shown by Mas-Colell,
Whinston, and Green (1995, chap. 13).
37. Bonin, Jones, and Putterman (1993).
38. Ben-Ner and Jun (1996).

is on the brink of bankruptcy? It may be true that workers in these cases have relied mainly on their own savings or union resources, which were sufficient to buy out the firm once it entered a period of financial distress but would not have been enough to buy the firm under more prosperous circumstances. However, if there is substantial financial participation by private lenders in employee buyouts, especially in the absence of loan guarantees or other government subsidies, this would have to count as evidence against the notion that workers have difficulty raising capital. Hence a potentially productive line of empirical investigation would be to examine the nature of the financing arrangements for actual employee buyouts.

A final problem is more theoretical than empirical. If the main obstacle to employee buyouts is the wealth constraint, and if a firm could be run more efficiently by workers, then presumably there would be an opportunity for mutual gain by having the current owners of capitalist firms find ways to help workers overcome their financing constraints. For instance, existing owners could gradually convey shares of common stock to employees in exchange for wage deductions, until employees as a group held a voting majority of shares. Essentially this same mechanism is used now to finance employee contributions to employee stock ownership plans, although the fraction of firm stock held by such plans usually falls well short of a majority and workers do not normally have the right to vote the stock held in their names. To be sure, such a transfer of ownership to workers would entail bargaining between workers and owners, but similar problems must be resolved whenever one firm buys out another. One might even expect that it would be easier to value a firm's assets than in conventional acquisitions and mergers, because in the case of a worker takeover both management and the prospective worker-owners would have firsthand information about the strengths and weaknesses of the enterprise.[39] These observations suggest that the wealth constraint may be most significant at an early stage in the life cycle of a firm, while other factors tend to become more important obstacles to labor-managed firm conversion after the firm is well established.

Risk Aversion and Insurance

A third popular explanation for the prevalence of capitalist firms is that workers are typically more risk averse than investors, either because work-

---

39. However, Ben-Ner and Jun (1996) argue that informational asymmetries play an important role in employee buyouts of failing capitalist firms.

ers are less able to diversify across firms or because they are less wealthy. One common argument along these line runs as follows. Because workers are risk averse, they want fairly steady wages, rather than a share of the profits of the firm, which could be zero or quite volatile. But since they do not share the profits of the firm, workers no longer have the proper incentives to exert effort or to make managerial decisions, because losses are disproportionately borne by others. Pay incentive schemes attempt to reduce this problem, but it is not possible to overcome it completely. The alternative is to shift control rights from workers to the party who takes the risks and assures the workers of relatively steady compensation.

By itself, this story does not explain why the party who insures workers and makes managerial decisions must also be a capital supplier for the firm, rather than, say, a wealthy outsider who happens to be less risk averse. We can fill this gap with an auxiliary assumption inspired by the Alchian and Demsetz concern with equipment maintenance: capital suppliers already have an interest in safeguarding the value of their assets, and for this reason would want to monitor the activities of workers. The same monitoring activities would be valuable for the party who is assuring workers of steady wages and wants to monitor their effort; hence it makes sense to bundle the function of capital supply with that of insurance provider. We thus arrive at the capital-managed firm, where workers are paid a fixed wage and capitalists run the production process.[40]

This explanation has at least one theoretical loophole. It will not generally be optimal to provide workers with full insurance; that is, to guarantee that they receive completely fixed wages regardless of any other factor, including effort.[41] But whenever workers continue to bear some residual risk, they will have some stake in how the firm is managed. With partial insurance, it is not obvious whether workers or insurers should exercise control rights, or whether control of the firm should be shared in some way. Presumably, the more risk averse workers are, the more insurance they will desire, and the more likely it is that the insurer rather than the workers will have control. But this matter requires further analysis.

One variant of the risk-aversion hypothesis is intertwined with the difficulties that workers are likely to have in financing the firm themselves, as described in the previous section. The argument begins with the idea that prospective borrowers must first commit some amount of equity financing

40. Elements of this story trace back to Frank Knight (1964) and have been developed by several more recent authors (Meade, 1972; Kihlstrom and Laffont, 1979; Dreze, 1989).

41. This is a standard result in principal-agent theory: see Sappington (1991); or Mas-Colell, Whinston, and Green (1995, chap. 14).

to the firm if they wish to obtain credit, as a signal that they believe in the project. But outsiders who lack control rights would be unwilling to make such equity investments, since they cannot safeguard their investment adequately. (An important exception occurs when control is held by other investors having parallel interests, as in the large corporation; a small investor can then free-ride on the monitoring and control activities of larger shareholders.) If control rights must be confined to equity suppliers for this reason, then firms cannot be worker controlled unless workers provide equity investments as well as labor, and workers may not be able to do this because of liquidity constraints or may not wish to do it because of risk aversion. However, few workers choose to invest all of their assets in their employer—indeed, investing your financial capital with your employer would mean that you have all of your financial and human capital in the same venture!—which implies that risk aversion and a desire for diversification are critical.[42]

The risk-aversion framework can account for the fact that labor-managed firms do not often appear in capital-intensive sectors of the economy, because workers would then have to make large equity investments that would force them to forgo diversification. On the other hand, the kinds of industries in which labor-managed firms thrive are not necessarily characterized by low risk, compared with industries in which capital-managed firms prevail. For example, the worker-owned plywood firms of the Pacific Northwest face large fluctuations in input and output prices but nonetheless have survived and attracted new members for most of this century.[43] These labor-managed firms exhibit greater employment stability than similar capital-managed firms, absorbing fluctuations in the market environment through variations in earnings rather than layoffs.[44] It may be that the prolonged coexistence of labor-managed firms and capital-managed firms in the plywood industry represents a situation in which workers with greater tolerance for risk gravitate toward the cooperatives, while those who are more risk averse take jobs in conventional mills.[45] However, transferring control rights from shareholders to the work force does not inevitably result in increased risk for workers, since workers in a labor-managed firm

---

42. This is the explicit argument of Putterman (1993), following closely on that of Meade (1972), and sharing a close kinship with the analyses of Neuberger and James (1973); Schlicht and von Weiszacker (1977); and Gui (1985). Bonin, Jones, and Putterman (1993) view it as the most plausible explanation for the rarity of worker control.

43. Hansmann (1990a).

44. Pencavel and Craig (1994).

45. Pencavel (1996).

are not vulnerable to unilateral decisions benefiting shareholders at the expense of worker interests; for instance, labor-managed firms are unlikely to sacrifice labor rents by shifting operations to Malaysia, whereas in certain situations a capitalist firm would do so.[46]

A sophisticated elaboration of the risk-aversion hypothesis would thus need to incorporate: the lessened risks to current income under a conventional wage contract; the reduced risk of layoff when workers have control; and the fact that in the labor-managed firm, the decision about how to absorb risk is made by workers themselves. It could be that workers with relatively specific skills (including skills specific to an industry, such as plywood) who are employed in highly cyclic industries stand to gain more from the stable employment offered by labor-managed firms. In this view, risk aversion tilts the balance toward capitalist firms when: (a) workers are poor; (b) their skills are not specific; (c) firms require relatively large amounts of equity financing per worker; and (d) layoff risks in a capitalist firm are low.

Still, the risk-aversion hypothesis can be called into question to some extent by various other findings on profit sharing, on compensating wage differentials, and on the structure of agricultural wage contracts. At first glance, the increasing popularity of profit-sharing plans in capitalist firms[47] represents an anomaly under the risk-aversion hypothesis, since these plans presumably expose employees to a higher level of income or asset risk than conventional wage contracts.[48] Of course, if profit sharing has sufficiently large productivity benefits, workers could be paid wages that are high enough to compensate for their added risk, while still leaving some residual gain for investors.

The literature on compensating wage differentials is relevant to the risk-aversion story, too. If risk aversion were the major factor driving choices of organizational form, then this factor should be important in explaining the nature of employment contracts within capitalist firms. For example, firms in industries in which layoffs are costly to employees and occur with high probability should pay their employees a wage that includes a suitable risk premium. There is some evidence that wages incorporate a risk premium for jobs involving serious hazards to life, but evidence that

---

46. Miceli and Minkler (1995).

47. See Kruse (1993),

48. Indeed, when random shocks are due to economy-wide business cycles rather than specific to individual firms, it can be shown that profit sharing enables workers to shift consumption toward more probable states of the world, and that capitalist firms will undersupply opportunities for profit sharing. See Dow and Skillman (1994).

wage differentials are associated with uncertainty about earnings or hours of work is considerably weaker.[49]

Finally, there is an extensive literature on the role of risk aversion as a determinant of agricultural contracting arrangements. Having tenants pay a fixed rent to the landlord maximizes their incentives, but at the cost of exposing workers to all of the technological and market risks connected with farming. The alternative of paying tenants a fixed wage minimizes their risk, but also minimizes their incentives (or maximizes the cost of supervision). Sharecropping, in which tenants pay a fixed percentage of what they produce to the landlord, by contrast preserves some work incentives while shifting some risk onto the landowner. However, recent empirical work casts doubt on this story, suggesting that the riskiness associated with particular crops or farm locations has little or no power to explain the contractual arrangements observed in North American agriculture.[50] The alternative hypothesis is that the form of agricultural contracts is more often determined by the potential damage to the land that could be done by nonowning farmers—a story analogous to the equipment abuse problem described earlier. However, no parallel evidence yet exists for the manufacturing sector.

Asset Specificity and Investment Incentives

A fourth explanation for the prevalence of the capital-managed firm is that labor-managed firms have difficulty coping with highly specialized physical assets. Suppose that physical assets are firm-specific and would have a much lower value in any alternative use, while workers have generic skills for which there is a competitive market. In a labor-managed firm workers could then use their control rights after the physical capital investment is made to capture some payments that would otherwise go to capital suppliers. If capital suppliers anticipate that workers will use their control rights in this way, they will be reluctant to invest in firm-specific physical assets in the first place.[51] The capital-managed firm avoids these problems by awarding control rights to the firm-specific input. Thus capital-managed firms will emerge when physical assets are specific while human capital is not, and

---

49. Murphy and Topel (1987, p. 130) report that an increase of one standard deviation in the variance of annual weeks worked (4.75 weeks) requires compensation in average annual earnings of only about $45. Further references on compensating differentials appear in Filer (1993).
50. Allen and Lueck (1999).
51. Dow (1993a).

labor-managed firms should emerge in equilibrium when human capital is specialized but physical assets are generic.

The asset specificity hypothesis also appears in another variation, attributable to Sanford Grossman, Oliver Hart, and John Moore.[52] One of its key assumptions is that contracts are incomplete and that property rights give asset owners the ability to exercise "residual rights of control." In other words, asset owners have the right to make any remaining decisions about asset use that have not been explicitly contracted away. If the benefits or costs of noncontractible managerial decisions accrue mainly to capital suppliers, while the payoff to labor suppliers is not sensitive to these decisions, then the capital-managed firm is the efficient form of organization.[53] The converse situation would imply that the labor-managed firm is superior.

It is not immediately obvious how to get from these results to empirical predictions about the prevalence of capital-managed firms and labor-managed firms. But suppose the productivity or future value of some specialized physical asset is particularly vulnerable to managerial decisions within the firm. Then capital-managed firms are more likely to arise when physical assets are specific. Similarly, if investment in specialized machinery is more important to productivity than investment in worker skills, giving control rights to capital will be desirable because this puts capitalists in a better bargaining position and increases the return from investments in machinery. Conversely, if the productivity of specialized human capital skills is very sensitive to managerial decisions, or investments in such skills are more important than noncontractible investments in physical assets, it is more efficient to give control to workers.

All of the models described thus far take it for granted that capital and labor are to be supplied by separate individuals. But there is an obvious solution to the problems associated with asset specificity: have workers own the specialized physical assets required for production, which eliminates any bargaining over the streams of payments from such assets. Indeed, when two sets of complementary physical assets are involved, it is routine to propose that ownership be combined via vertical integration.[54] The question then is, what problems might arise if workers did indeed collectively own the firm's physical capital stock?

---

52. See Grossman and Hart (1986); Hart and Moore (1990). Informal expositions can also be found in Hart (1989, 1991), and a broad survey is provided by Hart (1995).

53. For a proof, see proposition 1(B) in Grossman and Hart (1986).

54. Klein, Crawford, and Alchian (1978); Williamson (1975, 1985); Grossman and Hart (1986); Hart and Moore (1990).

The first problem is that workers would have to finance this ownership, which could be particularly difficult when assets are highly specialized. Oliver Williamson has argued that generic assets can be financed by debt, because assets with many alternative uses can serve as collateral for loan contracts, while firm-specific assets need to be financed largely by equity, since assets with a large sunk cost component are not easily redeployable elsewhere and hence cannot collateralize a loan.[55] This can be viewed as a refinement of either the worker wealth or the risk-aversion hypothesis, depending on whether one emphasizes worker difficulties in raising funds or lack of diversification as the key obstacle to collective worker ownership. The twist here is Williamson's claim that redeployable assets can be financed by debt, so that only firm-specific assets pose problems for worker ownership. It remains necessary, however, to forge a link between financing and control rights. Williamson does this by asserting that suppliers of equity capital will need representation on the board of directors, because if the directors of the firm were worker representatives, for example, the firm's employees might waste equity resources on projects of dubious value. Notice that this argument closely parallels the proposition that equity investors will tend to have control rights so as to avoid the incentive problems that would arise if control rights were held by some other party.

This line of argument raises several issues. First, it is unclear why equity investors have a greater need for safeguards against managerial abuse than employees. After all, investors can easily sell off their shares if dissatisfied with the firm's policies, while the fate of employees is more tightly linked to the fortunes of the firm for which they work. Moreover, one could argue that investors as a class are protected by reputational mechanisms even in the absence of formal control rights; for example, the discretionary payment of dividends by corporations is plausibly motivated by reputational factors. Reputational effects may also operate through the managerial labor market or discipline imposed by the market for corporate control.[56] However, it may still be true that the limited control right of electing directors at an annual meeting is a necessary prerequisite for these other disciplinary mechanisms to work well. Reputational sanctions are not foolproof, and hence backup systems such as takeover may sometimes be necessary. Furthermore, even if an individual investor stands to lose only a small amount of money through managerial opportunism, the aggregate losses to shareholders as a group can be quite large.

55. Williamson (1988).
56. See Fama (1980) on the managerial labor market and Manne (1965) on corporate control. For more on these matters, see Putterman (1987, 1988a).

A rather different argument ignores the financing issues emphasized by Williamson, takes collective worker ownership of physical assets for granted, and studies the conditions under which labor-managed firms will have proper incentives for investment in these physical assets. We place this approach under the heading of "asset specificity" because generic assets presumably do not need to be collectively owned in the first place. Leasing should be reasonably simple for generic assets. The key question here is whether labor-managed firms will be willing to sacrifice current wages for internal capital accumulation.[57] Members of the labor-managed firm will not benefit from investment returns accruing after their planned departure from the firm, owing to relocation or retirement, for instance. This has come to be known as the "horizon problem." A closely related idea is that current members of a labor-managed firm will be reluctant to make new investments that will require them to admit new workers, if these new members will share on an equal basis in the returns from earlier investments. This is termed the "common property problem." Neither of these problems arises in a capitalist firm, because stockholders can capture expected future returns by selling their shares to new owners.

The horizon problem attracted considerable attention in the literature on labor-managed firms of the early 1970s. Jaroslav Vanek, a booster of the worker management idea, concluded that combining individual capital ownership with democratic worker management was critical to the success of labor-managed firms, and that the absence of such arrangements explained the past failures of cooperative experiments. While Vanek and others favored an "individual capital accounts" approach, along the lines of Spain's Mondragon cooperatives,[58] others noted that the horizon and common property problems can be eliminated, at least in principle, by creating a market for membership rights in the labor-managed firm.[59] Such a market allows departing members of the labor-managed firm to recoup the present value of investments when the membership right is sold, just as a stock market capitalizes the stream of investment returns from a capitalist firm. When the labor-managed firm expands and requires additional workers, new members would pay a price to the current members in return for the right to participate in any existing or future stream of investment returns. The

57. Questions about the investment incentives of labor-managed firms were first raised by Pejovich (1969); Vanek (1970, 1977a, 1977b); Furubotn and Pejovich (1970); Furubotn (1976); and Jensen and Meckling (1979).

58. See also Ellerman (1984).

59. Dow (1986).

alleged asymmetry between capital-managed and labor-managed firms with respect to investment behavior therefore disappears.

However, there seem to be deeper asymmetries between inputs of capital and labor that make markets for labor-managed firm membership at best an imperfect substitute for the capitalist stock market. Most workers hold only one job at a time and move between jobs infrequently. For this reason, the market for membership in any given labor-managed firm is likely to be thin. Moreover, the bargaining process between incumbent members and new applicants is likely to be complicated because the new applicants may know little about the firm's future prospects, while existing members may know little about the true abilities of the applicant. By contrast, capitalist stock markets allow for extensive diversification across firms and permit virtually instantaneous and anonymous trading, which leads to thick markets with well-defined competitive prices for the shares of each firm. Information problems are at worst one-sided (investors cannot be certain about the future profitability of the firm), rather than two-sided (the firm will generally be indifferent toward the characteristics of individual buyers of its stock). Those informational asymmetries that remain are mitigated by the presence of some informed traders in the market, so that a substantial amount of information about the firm is built into its market price.

Membership markets for labor-managed firms can run into further complications. Because labor is a highly heterogeneous input, incumbent members of the labor-managed firm have a direct personal interest in any transaction between departing members and their replacements. One might expect incumbent members to demand a right of first refusal when a membership is sold (that is, the right to buy back the departing member's share and then sell it to an applicant of their choice), or some power to veto sales to undesirable newcomers, since the departing member could impose large costs on incumbents by selling to the wrong replacement worker. But while transactions in a membership market for the labor-managed firm involve complicated multilateral bargaining problems, small transactions in the stock market are of negligible importance to third parties, because financial capital is homogeneous. Hence similar problems do not arise for a capital-managed firm with widely dispersed share ownership.

Suppose now that the market price of labor-managed firm membership is systematically lower than the present value actually enjoyed by members. This would be true, for instance, if information problems prevent the current members of "good" firms from extracting the full value of membership to new applicants up front, because new applicants cannot be certain that the firm is a good one. Then labor-managed firms will invest less in collectively owned assets and grow more slowly than similar capital-managed firms.[60] Indeed, there may be perverse incentives for current workers in the labor-managed firm to sell out to capitalist investors, even if the aggregate surplus generated by a labor-managed firm exceeds the total surplus generated by a capital-managed firm. The reason is that a transformation to the capital-managed firm enables current members to appropriate a larger present value at the expense of prospective future labor-managed firm members who will not obtain equally large rents upon joining a capital-managed firm.

Here the underlying forces are asymmetries between capital and labor inputs having to do with nondiversifiability and the costs of job switching that ultimately lead to disincentives for investment by labor-managed firms with collectively owned assets. This complex causal chain has not been fully worked out at the level of formal theory, much less integrated with the other potential explanations involving work incentives, wealth constraints, and risk aversion. However, some of these other factors can also be viewed as impediments to membership markets in a labor-managed firm, which indirectly will reduce the investment incentives of such firms. For example, worker wealth constraints and borrowing limitations interfere with the ability of workers to finance an up-front membership fee paid to the labor-managed firm, and if diversification is desirable, workers will be reluctant to pay for membership rights in their firms. The causal story sketched here, emphasizing the information problems of membership markets, is thus complementary to earlier hypotheses, although it could also stand alone as an alternative.

Markets for membership in labor-managed firms are even rarer than labor-managed firms themselves. The only reasonably prominent instance of a functioning membership market seems to be the case of the plywood cooperatives in the U.S. Pacific Northwest.[61] There is evidence that membership shares in these cooperatives are underpriced, although there is no way of knowing whether this reflects risk aversion, information problems in the process of negotiating membership prices, or other factors. It has also been claimed that the plywood co-ops use less capital-intensive production methods than their capitalist counterparts, perhaps owing to underinvestment in collective assets, but this finding remains controversial.[62]

---

60. Dow (1993b).

61. Craig and Pencavel (1992); Pencavel and Craig (1994).

62. See Berman and Berman (1989) for the claim. However, Pencavel (1996) indicates that findings of lower capital intensity are sensitive to the manner in which labor inputs are measured.

The predictions outlined in this section are broadly consistent with the actual distribution of labor-managed and capital-managed firms across industries. In particular, hypotheses relating to asset specificity and investment incentives can explain why we often see labor-managed firms in small-scale labor-intensive activities, where there is little if any need for specialized physical assets.

Some problems remain, however. First, it is necessary to explain how most real labor-managed firms survive without relying on an explicit market for membership rights. Perhaps these labor-managed firms do not require strong investment incentives, either because they engage in labor-intensive activities or because the relevant physical assets can be leased. It is also possible that real labor-managed firms have devised mechanisms that effectively substitute for explicit membership markets, such as individual capital accounts for each worker-owner (a concept used by the Mondragon cooperatives in Spain). One would anticipate that as asset specificity grows in importance, those labor-managed firms that do succeed will have to devise effective procedures whereby individual members can capitalize the future returns from collective investments. One would also anticipate that, to the extent that these procedures function imperfectly, collective asset ownership would support higher rates of investment in specialized plant and equipment when expected membership turnover is lower—that is, when most workers are young and/or immobile—so that the horizon problem is minimized. We do not know at present whether these predictions are correct.

Another series of empirical tests can be proposed on the basis of the idea that a labor-managed firm should be able to lease general-purpose assets, even if it must purchase more specific assets. This implies that capital intensity per se, or absolute scale, should not be a crucial predictor of organizational form. Only assets with a large sunk cost component should play a causal role. There does appear to be some casual evidence to suggest that generic assets are not a major stumbling block for labor-managed firms. Labor-managed firms in the transportation sector, such as United Airlines, use general-purpose assets—aircraft—for which there are extensive secondhand and leasing markets. An empirical agenda along these lines might begin by constructing estimates of the relative importance of sunk costs for the physical assets used in a cross-section of industries, and then investigate whether those industries with a higher sunk cost component had a lower incidence of labor-managed firms. Such cross-industry measures of asset specificity have been devised by economists in the areas of industrial organization and international trade.

Another concern is how to handle specific human capital. Various work suggests that labor-managed firms are more likely to arise when human capital is more specialized to the industry or the firm, holding the level of physical asset specificity constant.[63] This proposition is testable, at least in principle. It is unclear whether the asset specificity hypothesis is consistent with casual observation in this case. After all, labor-managed firms are quite common in the professions, but doctors, lawyers, and other professionals would seem to have rather generic skills. One could argue that such people accumulate a large stock of firm-specific experience over time through learning-by-doing or by investing in relationships with clients and colleagues, but this story has an ad hoc flavor. Good cross-industry measures of human asset specificity would be even harder to construct than similar estimates of physical specificity, but in principle this provides another avenue for testing (some variants of) the asset specificity hypothesis.

Collective Choice and Managerial Decisionmaking

The fifth argument for the predominance of capital-managed firms grows from a small but important literature arguing that labor-managed firms have trouble reaching collective decisions because worker objectives tend to be more heterogeneous than those of capital suppliers: that is, capital suppliers care about maximizing the present value of profits, but workers have diverse attitudes toward effort, risks to income, job security, safety, social atmosphere, and other features of the workplace. Therefore, it is more difficult or costly for labor-managed firms to reach managerial decisions in an effective and timely way, which puts these firms at a disadvantage in relation to their capital-managed competitors. One variant stresses the transaction costs of collective choice, while another is concerned with the relative stability of alternative organizational forms.

The most prominent author concerned with transaction costs of collective decisionmaking in firms is Henry Hansmann, who suggests that the heterogeneity of worker preferences increases the cost of reaching managerial decisions in labor-managed firms.[64] The nature of these costs depends upon the particular decisionmaking mechanism used. If decisions are reached through bargaining, then one could begin with the fact that bar-

63. See Williamson (1980, 1985). Dow (1993a) focuses on the industry level, while Grossman, Hart, and Moore in their various writings focus on the firm level.

64. Hansmann (1988, 1990a, 1990b, 1996). See also Benham and Keefer (1991); Milgrom and Roberts (1992, pp. 562–63).

gaining is often costly under incomplete information.[65] If decisions are reached through voting, there is the usual problem of "voting cycles": it could be that for any possible decision, there is some other decision preferred by a majority of voters.

There are various ways to avoid these problems, but such measures have costs of their own. For instance, the firm could screen incoming firm members to ensure continued uniformity of preferences; it could eschew an extensive division of labor, large skill differentials, or large wage differentials; or it could remain at a suboptimal scale to limit the size of the decisionmaking group. Yet another solution is to restrict the scope of enterprise democracy in some way. This could be done by limiting the opportunities for workers to place new proposals on the agenda; by introducing representative rather than direct democracy; by disenfranchising certain groups with interests different from those of the controlling group (such as clerical workers or janitorial staff in a professional partnership); or by appointing a leader with dictatorial powers. In every case, however, the underlying concept is that it is in some sense more difficult for workers as a group to aggregate their preferences in a commonly agreed-upon way than for capitalists as a group. Pinhas Zusman has made a start at specifying these transaction costs in more detail, suggesting that collective choice rules in firms will minimize the sum of bargaining costs and the members' risk premia.[66] He illustrates these ideas with an example involving three workers and two dimensions of choice.

The other variant of the collective choice argument focuses on the potential instability of firms managed by workers. Mixed patterns of share ownership, where both workers and external investors have voting rights proportional to their shares, are often unstable when trading in shares is unrestricted.[67] The key problem is that majority voting can be used to redistribute firm profit away from a minority of shareholders, and that majorities can be ever-shifting. This problem is closely related to that of voting cycles discussed earlier. Gilbert Skillman and Gregory Dow focus on the reasons for preference heterogeneity among workers, and the underlying reasons why a labor-managed firm may be unstable when individuals are free to sell their ownership shares (and hence their votes).[68] In their model, a firm's total capital requirement can be met by having many investors each

65. Kennan and Wilson (1993).
66. Zusman (1992).
67. Ognedal (1993). Somewhat surprisingly, Ognedal finds that initial control by workers is a necessary condition for a stable pattern of mixed ownership.
68. Skillman and Dow (1998).

contribute a small amount of capital, and this leads investors to support profit maximization unanimously. However, a worker typically supplies a significant amount of labor time to a single firm, and therefore workers will have heterogeneous preferences toward managerial decisions by that firm. Skillman and Dow conclude that the labor-managed firm is an unstable mode of organization: capitalist investors can offer to buy out the worker-owners of labor-managed firms on terms that 51 percent of the existing membership will accept. But because of the asymmetry in the divisibility of capital and labor inputs, workers are not symmetrically able to buy out capitalist firms.

In passing, it should be noted that both Hansmann's argument and that of Skillman and Dow exemplify the earlier idea that the differing observed incidence of capital-managed firms and labor-managed firms in the economy should be traced back to underlying asymmetries in the nature of the two factors of production. In the context of collective choice, two differences between capital and labor figure prominently. First, workers must be physically present at their jobs, but this is not true for capital suppliers. The fact that "workers have to be there" accounts for much of the heterogeneity in worker concerns identified by Hansmann. Second, it is much more difficult for workers to diversify across jobs than for capitalists to diversify their portfolios across firms, and inputs of financial capital are more readily divisible across investors than inputs of labor time across workers. Skillman and Dow rely heavily on factors of this sort in explaining why capitalists would have homogeneous preferences in equilibrium, while workers would not.

There is some empirical evidence to support the idea that collective choice is relatively costly for worker-controlled firms.[69] As already noted, labor-managed firms can limit the severity of collective choice problems by staying small, by carefully screening members, or by using techniques to control the agenda. All of these phenomena are observed in actual worker cooperatives. Moreover, existing labor-managed firms often have a limited division of labor among members, with rather undifferentiated skills and task assignments, and membership rights are often restricted to a relatively homogeneous subset of the work force, with others functioning as hired employees. It is less clear that the higher costs of collective choice in a labor managed firm can account for other important patterns, such as the observation that labor-managed firms are unlikely to arise de novo in capital-

69. Hansmann (1990a); Benham and Keefer (1991).

intensive industries, or in industries where physical asset specificity is important, holding constant other relevant factors such as firm size.

We are not aware of evidence bearing directly on the issue of collective choice in a labor-managed firm leading to unstable ownership. There are, of course, many cases in which capital-managed firms have been converted to labor-management through worker buyouts; we have already mentioned United Air Lines, Weirton Steel, and others.[70] There are also cases in which labor-managed firms have sold out to private investors, as in some plywood cooperatives and investment banking partnerships. However, the models described in this chapter do not attempt to explain the reasons for such transformations; rather, they make claims only about the circumstances under which specific organizational forms will persist in equilibrium.[71]

Other Stories about the Dominance of Capitalist Firms

The five hypotheses just discussed have received the most attention in the literature, and we believe that each of them possesses logical coherence and at least some empirical plausibility. But various other stories can be found as well. Our cursory sampling of these hypotheses is not meant to imply that they are trivial or wrong, only that they either have not received as much attention in the literature, have not been developed in as much detail, or are in some way dependent upon ideas already discussed.

Inefficient Supply and Demand Responses by Labor-Managed Firms

The earliest analyses of the labor-managed firm assumed that such firms would maximize net income per worker. The large literature based on this assumption shows that except under long-run competitive conditions, firms seeking to maximize income per worker will not behave in the same way as profit-maximizing firms.[72] Specifically, such firms have incentives to limit the total number of workers in order to drive up per capita income. This may generate such results as an unduly inelastic response of supply to

70. For the United Air Lines case, see chapter 10 by Gordon in this volume.

71. Perhaps the most useful attempt to address the problem of organizational transformation is that of Ben-Ner and Jun (1996), who study worker buyouts of failing capitalist firms. However, their model deals with bargaining under conditions of private information rather than voting mechanisms, and hence focuses on issues somewhat distinct from those considered here.

72. For early work, see Ward (1958); Domar (1966). For a summary of this literature, see Bonin and Putterman (1987).

changes in price (sometimes even backward-bending), a reluctance to bring in new members when market conditions improve, and an inefficient allocation of labor across firms. It has been argued that these inefficiencies make the labor-managed firm a poor competitor compared to the capital-managed firm.

We have two main reasons for treating such inefficient supply and demand behavior as only a weak explanation of the relative rarity of labor-managed firms. First, the severity of these problems has often been questioned and remains a subject of empirical debate.[73] In any case, the theory has been developed more as a normative tool for assessing the desirability of the labor-managed firm, rather than as an explanation in positive terms for why labor-managed firms are not more numerous. The distinction here is similar to the difference between saying that capitalist monopolies are inefficient and predicting on this basis that they will not exist.

Second, the inefficiencies described by these theories disappear in the presence of a perfectly competitive market for membership in the labor-managed firm, which can play the same allocative role as the labor market in a capitalist economy.[74] For this reason, the literature does not offer an explanation for the rarity of labor-managed firms unless one appends a story about the sources of imperfection in labor-managed firm membership markets as discussed earlier. But given such a story, the literature on reactions of labor-managed firms to price changes can be interpreted as tracing out some consequences that flow from underlying defects in the membership market.

Organizational Life Cycles

It has been argued that successful labor-managed firms tend to change into capital-managed firms over an organizational life cycle.[75] The key idea is that in profitable labor-managed firms, incumbent members prefer to expand by hiring new employees at their external opportunity wage, rather than bringing them in as full members who will share equally in the profits of the firm. Again, this problem disappears if there is a smoothly functioning market for labor-managed firm membership, since then a new applicant is obliged to pay a price to incumbent members that precisely offsets the loss incurred by existing members when they share profits with their new col-

---

73. Berman and Berman (1989); Pencavel and Craig (1994).
74. Sertel (1982); Dow (1986, 1993b, 1996); Fehr (1993); Kleindorfer and Sertel (1993).
75. Miyazaki (1984); Ben-Ner (1984, 1988b).

league. Thus we are again driven back to our earlier questions about the sources of friction in the market for membership in labor-managed firms.

Organizational Reputation

Perhaps investors should manage firms for reputational reasons. The idea is that a firm's reputation for selling quality goods or treating suppliers fairly is a valuable commodity in a world where contracts can never be fully complete. The value of this reputation can be severely damaged by managerial decisions aimed at reaping gains from short-term opportunism. Such inefficient decisions are less likely to occur if the controllers of the firm can easily sell their positions to replacement controllers when they leave the firm. The incumbent decisionmakers will then take into account the full present value of the firm's reputation, since they will be concerned about the price at which the firm (or their positions in it) can be sold in the future. Paul Milgrom and John Roberts argue that this is more likely if control rights are assigned to equity investors than workers, since the latter have to change jobs to transfer their claims on the firm.[76]

This can be recognized as a variant of the "horizon problem" discussed earlier, where we indicated that such intertemporal investment problems can be eliminated by means of a labor-managed firm membership market. In effect, Milgrom and Roberts are arguing that such membership markets are an imperfect substitute for conventional capitalist stock markets in reputational respects. Apart from the distinctive focus on firm reputation, the key issues are therefore similar to those addressed earlier.

Appropriation of Entrepreneurial Rents

It has been argued that entrepreneurs can more easily capture the rents from innovation by establishing a capital-managed firm than a labor-managed firm.[77] The potential problem is obvious: an innovator would be obliged to share subsequent profits with the worker-partners, while in the capital-managed firm employees could be hired at a competitive wage rate and all the rents would flow to the entrepreneur-owner. Moreover, if one tries to sell membership rights to workers, there is a severe informational problem: How do prospective labor-managed firm members know that the entrepreneur's idea is as valuable as the entrepreneur claims? In a sense,

---

76. Milgrom and Roberts (1992, pp. 331–32).
77. Marglin (1974, 1982).

this is the most extreme version of an information-based problem in setting up markets for membership in labor-managed firms. Finally, any entrepreneur who considers trying to demonstrate the value of an innovation must be concerned that expanding the number of people who have access to a valuable idea will increase the number of prospective competitors. Thus an entrepreneur has an incentive not to reveal the value of the idea to others. In the capital-managed firm, by contrast, the entrepreneur need not convey the new idea to any other individual; the entrepreneur can simply hire labor on a competitive market and take direct control of the production process. It may also be that while the aggregated returns to innovation are significant to the entrepreneur, they would be too small to exceed the attention threshold of individual workers if widely shared.[78]

While proprietary capital-managed firms may well have an advantage over labor-managed firms in appropriating the gains from innovation, we are unsure about the generality of this factor. At least at first glance, it seems more relevant for the process of starting up a new firm than for issues of long-run organizational equilibrium. Once a capitalist firm becomes large and well-established, it is less clear why a worker buyout would not succeed, or why a labor-managed firm could not replicate the entrepreneurial incentives operating within large publicly traded corporations.

This hypothesis does have empirical content. For instance, it predicts that capital-managed firms will be common in industries characterized by a high degree of technological innovation, and that labor-managed firms will tend to appear in industries with stable, long-established production methods. Although this prediction seems compatible with the existence of worker cooperatives in the plywood, clothing, construction, and reforestation fields, and with the observed prevalence of professional partnerships, we are not aware of attempts to test the proposition systematically. It is also unclear whether such a prediction is compatible with the widespread use of profit and equity sharing by high-tech firms.[79]

Macroeconomic Externalities

We close this section by sketching a hypothesis developed by David Levine and a number of others.[80] Under this hypothesis, participatory capitalist firms that have a practice of retaining workers during recession are at a disadvantage in an economy consisting largely of less participatory firms

78. Putterman (1982).
79. Smith (1988).
80. Levine and Tyson (1990); Levine (1993, 1995); Levine and Parkin (1994).

that lay workers off when aggregate demand falls. A parallel and perhaps even sharper argument can be constructed for firms that are fully labor-managed.[81] Suppose labor-managed firms maintain the size of their existing work forces when demand falls, because members prefer to absorb demand fluctuations through earnings adjustments rather than by defecting to the outside labor market (or by expelling colleagues). The practice of maintaining membership will be costly to the firm if recessions are long and deep, and may even threaten the survival of the enterprise. On the other hand, suppose capital-managed firms use a compensation scheme where nominal wages remain fixed over the business cycle, and reductions in demand are absorbed through layoffs. If capital-managed firms are the dominant organizational form, their employment practices will aggravate the business cycle for standard macroeconomic reasons relating to wage rigidity, leading to longer and deeper recessions than in a world where labor-managed firms are the dominant mode of organization. We thus have the possibility of multiple equilibria: if capital-managed firms are already dominant, then labor-managed firms may not be viable, but if labor-managed firms were already widespread, the resulting dampening of the business cycle might enable individual labor-managed firms to thrive.

The microeconomic foundations for this story are not yet fully developed, especially in relation to labor-managed firms. However, we believe that the role of external effects across differing organizational forms is an important and insufficiently explored topic. Such externalities, which could operate through capital and labor markets as well as through the macroeconomic demand effects outlined above, may undermine the prospects for labor-managed firm viability in ways not captured by our present focus on industry characteristics. It may not be enough to attempt to specify the advantages or disadvantages of capital-managed and labor-managed firms in isolation. Rather, one must study the equilibrium distribution of firms within the economic system as a whole to spot potentially important feedbacks at the system level.

Conclusion

The question of why most production in market economies occurs in firms in which capital suppliers, rather than labor suppliers, exercise managerial control is not only of deep intellectual interest, but also of substantial pol-

---

81. Levine (1993).

icy import. Examples of relevant policy issues include whether to encourage employee stock ownership or profit-sharing plans by means of taxes or subsidies, proposed changes in corporate governance to promote European-style codetermination, or various forms of governmental encouragement for employee buyouts of failing capitalist firms.[82]

The ability of economists to offer constructive advice on all of these matters would be immensely strengthened if the economics profession could provide a well-supported explanation for the prevalence of capitalist firms. However, as this discussion has shown, a multitude of different answers has been suggested, but there is at present no consensus on the matter, and very little headway has been made in settling the issue empirically. By this point, the need for additional theoretical refinement is perhaps all too clear. Many of the hypotheses reviewed here have advanced only slightly beyond the level of casual storytelling buttressed by casual empiricism. But a deeper problem in our view is that the task of systematically testing rival hypotheses against the data has been postponed much too long. A reasonable first step in this direction would be to identify proxy variables suggested by one or more of our five major hypotheses that are correlated with the incidence of capital-managed firms or labor-managed firms. One could then carry out econometric tests on samples of firms within a given industry, or on a multi-industry sample that contained information on the prevalence of worker control across industries, or on firm-level data with controls for industry effects.

This research agenda will not be easy to implement. At a theoretical level, the available hypotheses are often fuzzy on causal details and potential interactions between factors. Different hypotheses sometimes have parallel empirical implications. It is not always obvious what the relevant proxy variables would be. The required data may not exist in any convenient form. Despite this list of woes, we believe that the questions raised here warrant more attention from empirical researchers than they have so far received. Indeed, one goal of this chapter is to make some progress in systematizing the issues and in bringing into mutual confrontation ideas that have often been proposed in isolation from one another. But empirical research will ultimately be needed to determine which causal factors have the greatest influence on the allocation of control rights within the firm.

---

82. For an overview of the policy issues at stake, see Blair (1995) and Levine (1995).

References

Aghion, Philippe, and Patrick Bolton. 1992. "An Incomplete Contracts Approach to Financial Contracting." *Review of Economic Studies* 59 (July): 473–94.

Alchian, Armen A., and Harold Demsetz. 1972. "Production, Information Costs, and Economic Organization." *American Economic Review* 62 (December): 777–95.

Allen, Douglas W., and Dean Lueck. 1999. "Risk-Sharing and Agricultural Contracts." *Journal of Law, Economics, and Organization.* Forthcoming.

Alston, Lee J., and William Gillespie. 1989. "Resource Coordination and Transaction Costs." *Journal of Economic Behavior and Organization* 11 (March): 191–212.

Barzel, Yoram. 1989. *Economic Analysis of Property Rights.* Cambridge University Press.

Benham, Lee, and Philip Keefer. 1991. "Voting in Firms: The Role of Agenda Control, Size and Voter Homogeneity." *Economic Inquiry* 29 (October): 706–19.

Ben-Ner, Avner. 1984. "On the Stability of the Cooperative Type of Organization." *Journal of Comparative Economics* 8 (September): 247–60.

———. 1988a. "Comparative Empirical Observations on Worker-Owned and Capitalist Firms." *International Journal of Industrial Organization* 6 (March): 7–31.

———. 1988b. "The Life Cycle of Worker-Owned Firms in Market Economies: A Theoretical Analysis." *Journal of Economic Behavior and Organization* 10 (October): 287–313.

Ben-Ner, Avner, and Byoung Jun. 1996. "Buy-Out in a Bargaining Game with Asymmetric Information." *American Economic Review* 86 (June): 502–23.

Berle, Adolf A., and Gardiner C. Means. 1968. *The Modern Corporation and Private Property,* Rev. ed. New York: Harcourt, Brace and World. [First ed. 1932, Macmillan.]

Berman, Katrina V., and Matthew D. Berman. 1989. "An Empirical Test of the Theory of the Labor-Managed Firm." *Journal of Comparative Economics* 13 (June): 281–300.

Blair, Margaret. 1995. *Ownership and Control: Rethinking Corporate Governance for the Twenty-First Century.* Brookings.

Bonin, John, Derek Jones, and Louis Putterman. 1993. "Theoretical and Empirical Studies of Producer Cooperatives: Will Ever the Twain Meet?" *Journal of Economic Literature* 31 (September): 1290–1320.

Bonin, John, and Louis Putterman. 1987. *Economics of Cooperation and the Labor-Managed Economy, Fundamentals of Pure and Applied Economics.* New York: Harwood Academic Publishers.

Bowles, Samuel, and Herbert Gintis. 1990. "Contested Exchange: New Microfoundations of the Political Economy of Capitalism." *Politics and Society* 18 (June): 165–222.

———. 1993a. "The Revenge of Homo Economicus: Contested Exchange and the Revival of Political Economy." *Journal of Economic Perspectives* 7 (Winter): 83–102.

———. 1993b. "The Democratic Firm: An Agency-Theoretic Evaluation." In *Markets and Democracy: Participation, Accountability and Efficiency,* edited by Samuel Bowles, Herbert Gintis, and Bo Gustafsson, chap. 2. Cambridge University Press.

———. 1996. "The Distribution of Wealth and the Assignment of Control Rights in the Firm." Unpublished manuscript, Department of Economics, University of Massachusetts.

Bradley, Keith, and Alan Gelb. 1981. "Motivation and Control in the Mondragon Experiment." *British Journal of Industrial Relations* 19 (July): 211–31.

————. 1987. "Cooperative Labour Relations: Mondragon's Response to Recession." *British Journal of Industrial Relations* 25 (March): 77–99.

Coase, Ronald H. 1937. "The Nature of the Firm." *Economica* 4 (November): 386–405.

Craig, Ben, and John Pencavel. 1992. "The Behavior of Worker Cooperatives: The Plywood Companies of the Pacific Northwest." *American Economic Review* 82 (December): 1083–1105.

————. 1993. "The Objectives of Worker Cooperatives." *Journal of Comparative Economics* 17 (June): 288–308.

————. 1995. "Participation and Productivity: A Comparison of Worker Cooperatives and Conventional Firms in the Plywood Industry." *Brookings Papers on Economic Activity—Microeconomics* : 121–74.

Defourny, Jacques, Saul Estrin, and Derek C. Jones. 1985. "The Effects of Workers' Participation on Enterprise Performance." *International Journal of Industrial Organization* 3 (June): 197–217.

Domar, Evsey D. 1966. "The Soviet Collective Farm as a Producers' Cooperative." *American Economic Review* 56 (September): 734–57.

Dong, Xiao-yuan, and Gregory Dow. 1993. "Does Free Exit Reduce Shirking in Production Teams?" *Journal of Comparative Economics* 17 (June): 472–84.

Dow, Gregory. 1986. "Control Rights, Competitive Markets, and the Labor Management Debate." *Journal of Comparative Economics* 10 (March): 48–61.

————. 1993a. "Why Capital Hires Labor: A Bargaining Perspective." *American Economic Review* 83 (March): 118–34.

————. 1993b. "Democracy versus Appropriability: Can Labor-Managed Firms Flourish in a Capitalist World?" In *Markets and Democracy: Participation, Accountability and Efficiency,* edited by S. Bowles, H. Gintis, and B. Gustafsson, chap. 11. Cambridge University Press.

————. 1996. "Replicating Walrasian Equilibria Using Markets for Membership in Labor-Managed Firms." *Economic Design* 2 (November): 147–62.

Dow, Gregory, and Gilbert Skillman. 1994. "Profit Sharing and Risk Sharing." Unpublished manuscript, Department of Economics, Simon Fraser University.

Dreze, Jacques. 1989. *Labour Management, Contracts and Capital Markets: A General Equilibrium Approach.* Oxford: Basil Blackwell.

Ellerman, David P. 1984. "Theory of Legal Structure: Worker Cooperatives." *Journal of Economic Issues* 18 (September): 861–91.

Estrin, Saul, and Derek C. Jones. 1992. "The Viability of Employee-Owned Firms: Evidence from France." *Industrial and Labor Relations Review* 45 (January): 323–38.

Estrin, Saul, Derek C. Jones, and Jan Svejnar. 1987. "The Productivity Effects of Worker Participation: Producer Cooperatives in Western Economies." *Journal of Comparative Economics* 11 (March): 40–61.

Eswaran, Mukesh, and Ashok Kotwal. 1984. "The Moral Hazard of Budget-Breaking." *Rand Journal of Economics* 15 (Winter): 578–81.

————. 1989. "Why Are Capitalists the Bosses?" *Economic Journal* 99 (March): 162–76.

Fama, Eugene F. 1980. "Agency Problems and the Theory of the Firm." *Journal of Political Economy* 88 (2): 288–307.

Fehr, Ernst. 1993. "The Simple Analytics of a Membership Market in a Labor-Managed Economy." In *Markets and Democracy: Participation, Accountability and Efficiency,* edited by Samuel Bowles, Herbert Gintis, and Bo Gustafsson, 260–76. Cambridge University Press.

Filer, Randall K. 1993. "The Search for Compensating Differentials: Is There a Pot of Gold After All?" Working Paper 41. Center for Economic Research and Graduate Education, Charles University, Prague (North American distribution by University of Pittsburgh).

FitzRoy, Felix. 1980. "Notes on the Political Economy of a Cooperative Enterprise Sector." In *The Political Economy of Cooperation and Participation*, edited by Alasdair Clayre. Oxford University Press.

Fudenberg, Drew, and Jean Tirole. 1991. *Game Theory*. Cambridge, Mass.: MIT Press.

Furubotn, Eirik. 1976. "The Long-Run Analysis of the Labor-Managed Firm: An Alternative Interpretation." *American Economic Review* 66 (March): 104–23.

Furubotn, Eirik, and Svetozar Pejovich. 1970. "Property Rights and the Behavior of the Firm in a Socialist State: The Example of Yugoslavia." *Zeitschrift für Nationalökonomie* 30 (3–4): 431–54.

Gintis, Herbert. 1989. "Financial Markets and the Political Structure of the Enterprise." *Journal of Economic Behavior and Organization* 11 (May): 311–22.

Grossman, Sanford, and Oliver Hart. 1986. "The Costs and Benefits of Ownership: A Theory of Vertical and Lateral Integration." *Journal of Political Economy* 94 (August): 691–719.

Gui, Benedetto. 1985. "Limits to External Financing: A Model and an Application to Labor-Managed Firms." *Advances in the Economic Analysis of Participatory and Labor-Managed Firms*, 1: 107–20. Greenwich, Conn.: JAI Press.

Hansmann, Henry. 1988. "Ownership of the Firm." *Journal of Law, Economics, and Organization* 4 (Fall): 267–305.

———. 1990a. "When Does Worker Ownership Work? ESOPs, Law Firms, Codetermination, and Economic Democracy." *Yale Law Journal* 99 (June): 1749–816.

———. 1990b. "The Viability of Worker Ownership: An Economic Perspective on the Political Structure of the Firm." In *The Firm as a Nexus of Treaties*, edited by Masahiko Aoki, Bo Gustafsson, and Oliver Williamson, 162–84. London: Sage Publications.

———. 1996. *The Ownership of Enterprise*. Belknap Press of Harvard University Press.

Hart, Oliver. 1989. "An Economist's Perspective on the Theory of the Firm." *Columbia Law Review* 89 (November): 1757–74.

———. 1991. "Incomplete Contracts and the Theory of the Firm." In *The Nature of the Firm: Origins, Evolution, and Development*, edited by Oliver Williamson and Sidney Winter, 138–158. Oxford University Press.

———. 1995. *Firms, Contracts, and Financial Structure*. Oxford: Clarendon Press.

Hart, Oliver, and John Moore. 1990. "Property Rights and the Nature of the Firm." *Journal of Political Economy* 98 (December): 1119–58.

———. 1994. "A Theory of Debt Based on the Inalienability of Human Capital." *Quarterly Journal of Economics* 109 (November): 841–79.

Holmstrom, Bengt. 1982. "Moral Hazard in Teams." *Bell Journal of Economics* 13 (Autumn): 324–40.

Holmstrom, Bengt, and Paul Milgrom. 1991. "Multitask Principal-Agent Analyses: Incentive Contracts, Asset Ownership, and Job Design." *Journal of Law, Economics, and Organization* 7 (special issue): 24–52.

————. 1994. "The Firm as an Incentive System." *American Economic Review* 84 (September): 972–91.

Jensen, Michael, and William Meckling. 1979. "Rights and Production Functions: An Application to Labor-Managed Firms and Codetermination." *Journal of Business* 52 (October): 469–506.

Jones, Derek C. 1984. "American Producer Cooperatives and Employee-Owned Firms: A Historical Perspective." In *Worker Cooperatives in America,* edited by Robert Jackall and Henry Levin, eds., 37–56. University of California Press.

Jones, Derek C., and Takao Kato. 1995. "The Productivity Effects of Employee Stock-Ownership Plans and Bonuses: Evidence from Japanese Panel Data." *American Economic Review* 85 (June): 391–414.

Jones, Derek C., and Jan Svejnar. 1985. "Participation, Profit-Sharing, Worker Ownership and Efficiency in Italian Producer Cooperatives." *Economica* 55 (November): 449–65.

Kennan, John, and Robert Wilson. 1993. "Bargaining with Private Information." *Journal of Economic Literature* 31 (March): 45–104.

Kihlstrom, Richard E., and Jean-Jacques Laffont. 1979. "A General Equilibrium Entrepreneurial Theory of Firm Formation Based on Risk Aversion." *Journal of Political Economy* 87 (4): 719–48.

Klein, Benjamin, Robert Crawford, and Armen Alchian. 1978. "Vertical Integration, Appropriable Rents, and the Competitive Contracting Process." *Journal of Law and Economics* 21 (October): 297–326.

Kleindorfer, Paul R., and Murat R. Sertel. 1993. "The Economics of Workers' Enterprises." In *Economics in a Changing World,* edited by Dieter Bos. New York: St. Martin's Press.

Knight, Frank. 1964. *Risk, Uncertainty, and Profit.* New York: A. M. Kelley.

Kruse, Douglas. 1993. *Profit Sharing: Does It Make A Difference?* Kalamazoo, Mich.: W. E. Upjohn Institute for Employment Research.

Legros, Patrick, and Steven Matthews. 1993. "Efficient and Nearly-Efficient Partnerships." *Review of Economic Studies* 68 (July): 599–611.

Legros, Patrick, and Andrew F. Newman. 1996. "Wealth Effects, Distribution and the Theory of Organization." *Journal of Economic Theory* 70 (August): 312–41.

Levine, David I. 1993. "Demand Variability and Work Organization." In *Markets and Democracy: Participation, Accountability and Efficiency,* edited by Samuel Bowles, Herbert Gintis, and Bo Gustafsson, 159–75. Cambridge University Press.

————. 1995. *Reinventing the Workplace: How Business and Employees Can Both Win.* Brookings.

Levine, David I., and Richard J. Parkin. 1994. "Work Organization, Employment Security, and Macroeconomic Stability." *Journal of Economic Behavior and Organization* 24 (August): 251–71.

Levine, David I., and Laura Tyson. 1990. "Participation, Productivity, and the Firm's Environment." In *Paying for Productivity,* edited by Alan Blinder, 183–243. Brookings.

MacLeod, W. Bentley. 1984. "A Theory of Cooperative Teams." CORE Discussion Paper 8441. Université Catholique de Louvain.

————. 1988. "Equity, Efficiency, and Incentives in Cooperative Teams." In *Advances in the Economic Analysis of Participatory and Labor-Managed Firms,* edited by Derek C. Jones and Jan Svejnar, 3: 5–23. Greenwich, Conn.: JAI Press.

MacLeod, W. Bentley, and James Malcomson. 1998. "Motivation and Markets." *American Economic Review* 88 (June): 388–411.

Manne, Henry. 1965. "Mergers and the Market for Corporate Control." *Journal of Political Economy* 73 (April): 110–20.

Marglin, Stephen. 1974. "What Do Bosses Do? The Origin and Function of Hierarchy in Capitalist Production." *Review of Radical Political Economics* 6 (Summer): 60–112.

———. 1984. "Knowledge and Power." In *Firms, Organization and Labour,* edited by Frank Stephen, chap. 9. London: Macmillan.

Mas-Colell, Andreu, Michael D. Whinston, and Jerry R. Green. 1995. *Microeconomic Theory.* Oxford University Press.

Meade, James. 1972. "The Theory of Labour-Managed Firms and Profit-Sharing." *Economic Journal* 82 (supplement): 402–28.

Miceli, Thomas, and Alanson J. Minkler. 1995. "Transfer Uncertainty and Organizational Choice" *Advances in the Economic Analysis of Participatory and Labor-Managed Firms,* 5: 121–37. Greenwich, Conn.: JAI Press.

Milgrom, Paul, and John Roberts. 1992. *Economics, Organization, and Management.* Englewood Cliffs, N.J.: Prentice-Hall.

Mill, John Stuart. 1848 [1936]. *Principles of Political Economy.* London: Longmans, Green.

Miyazaki, Hajime. 1984. "On Success and Dissolution of the Labor-Managed Firm in the Capitalist Economy." *Journal of Political Economy* 92 (October): 909–31.

Murphy, Kevin M., and Robert H. Topel. 1987. "Unemployment, Risk, and Earnings: Testing for Equalizing Wage Differences in the Labor Market." In *Unemployment and the Structure of Labor Markets,* edited by Kevin Lang and Jonathan S. Leonard, chap. 5. New York: Basil Blackwell.

Neuberger, Egon, and Estelle James. 1973. "The Yugoslav Self-Managed Enterprise: A Systemic Approach." In *Plan and Market: Economic Reform in Eastern Europe,* edited by Morris Bornstein, 245–84. Yale University Press,

Newman, Andrew F. 1994. "The Capital Market, Inequality and the Employment Relation." Unpublished manuscript, Department of Economics, Columbia University.

Ognedal, Tone. 1993. "Unstable Ownership." *Markets and Democracy: Participation, Accountability and Efficiency,* edited by Samuel Bowles, Herbert Gintis, and Bo Gustafsson, 248–59. Cambridge University Press.

Pencavel, John. 1996. "What Has Been Learned about Worker-Owned Firms from the Plywood Co-ops of the Pacific Northwest?" Unpublished manuscript, Department of Economics, Stanford University.

Pencavel, John, and Ben Craig. 1994. "The Empirical Performance of Orthodox Models of the Firm: Conventional Firms and Worker Cooperatives." *Journal of Political Economy* 102 (August): 718–44.

Pejovich, Svetozar. 1969. "The Firm, Monetary Policy and Property Rights in a Planned Economy." *Western Economic Journal* 7 (September): 193–200.

Putterman, Louis. 1982. "Some Behavioral Perspectives on the Dominance of Hierarchical over Democratic Forms of Enterprise." *Journal of Economic Behavior and Organization* 3 (June–September): 139–60.

———. 1984. "On Some Recent Explanations of Why Capital Hires Labor." *Economic Inquiry* 22 (April): 171–87.

————. 1987. "Corporate Governance, Risk-Bearing and Economic Power: A Comment on Recent Work by Oliver Williamson." *Journal of Institutional and Theoretical Economics* 143 (September): 422–34.

————. 1988a. "Asset Specificity, Governance, and the Employment Relation." In *Management under Differing Labour Market and Employment Systems,* edited by G. Dlugos, W. Dorow, and K. Weiermair. Berlin: Walter de Gruyter.

————. 1988b. "The Firm as Association versus the Firm as Commodity: Efficiency, Rights, and Ownership." *Economics and Philosophy* 4 (October): 243–66.

————. 1993. "Ownership and the Nature of the Firm." *Journal of Comparative Economics* 17 (June): 243–63.

Putterman, Louis, and Gilbert Skillman. 1992. "The Role of Exit Costs in the Theory of Cooperative Teams." *Journal of Comparative Economics* 16 (December): 596–618.

Russell, Raymond. 1985. "Employee Ownership and Internal Governance." *Journal of Economic Behavior and Organization* 6 (September): 217–41.

Ryan, Alan. 1987. "Property." In *The New Palgrave Dictionary of Economics,* edited by John Eatwell, Murray Milgate, and Peter Newman, 1029–31. New York: Stockton Press.

Sappington, David E. M. 1991. "Incentives in Principal-Agent Relationships." *Journal of Economic Perspectives* 5 (Spring): 45–66.

Schlicht, Ekkehart, and Carl von Weizsacker. 1977. "Risk Financing in Labour-Managed Economies: The Commitment Problem." *Z. ges. Staatswiss.* 133 (1), special issue, 53–66.

Sertel, Murat R. 1982. "A Rehabilitation of the Labor-Managed Firm." In *Workers and Incentives,* chap. 2. Amsterdam: North-Holland.

Skillman, Gilbert L., and Gregory K. Dow. 1998. "Collective Choice and Control Rights in Firms." Discussion Paper 98-8. Department of Economics, Simon Fraser University.

Smith, Stephen C. 1988. "On the Incidence of Profit and Equity Sharing: Theory and an Application to the High Tech Sector." *Journal of Economic Behavior and Organization* 9 (January): 45–58.

Stiglitz, Joseph E. 1987. "The Causes and Consequences of the Dependence of Quality on Price." *Journal of Economic Literature* 25 (March): 1–48.

Stiglitz, Joseph, and Andrew Weiss. 1981. "Credit Rationing in Markets with Imperfect Information." *American Economic Review* 71 (June): 393–410.

Vanek, Jaroslav. 1970. *The General Theory of Labor-Managed Market Economies.* Cornell University Press.

————. 1977a. "The Basic Theory of Financing Participatory Firms." In *The Labor-Managed Economy: Essays by Jaroslav Vanek.* Cornell University Press.

————. 1977b. "Some Fundamental Considerations on Financing and the Form of Ownership under Labor Management." In *The Labor-Managed Economy: Essays by Jaroslav Vanek.* Cornell University Press.

Wadhwani, Sushil B., and Martin Wall. 1990. "The Effects of Profit Sharing on Employment, Wages, Stock Returns and Productivity: Evidence from U.K. Micro Data." *Economic Journal* 100 (March): 1–17.

Ward, Benjamin. 1958. "The Firm in Illyria: Market Syndicalism." *American Economic Review* 48 (September): 566–89.

Weitzman, Martin, and Douglas Kruse. 1990. "Profit Sharing and Productivity." In *Paying for Productivity,* edited by Alan Blinder. Brookings.

Whyte, William F., and Kathleen K. Whyte. 1988. *Making Mondragon: The Growth and Dynamics of the Worker Cooperative Complex*. Ithaca, N.Y.: ILR Press.

Wiener, Hans, with Robert Oakeshott. 1987. *Worker-Owners: Mondragon Revisited*. London: Anglo-German Foundation for the Study of Industrial Society.

Williamson, Oliver. 1975. *Markets and Hierarchies*. New York: Free Press.

————. 1980. "The Organization of Work." *Journal of Economic Behavior and Organization* 1 (March): 5–38.

————. 1985. *The Economic Institutions of Capitalism*. New York: Free Press.

————. 1988. "Corporate Finance and Corporate Governance." *Journal of Finance* 43 (July): 567–91.

Zusman, Pinhas. 1992. "Constitutional Selection of Collective-Choice Rules in a Cooperative Enterprise." *Journal of Economic Behavior and Organization* 17 (May): 353–62.

2

Firm-Specific Human Capital and Theories of the Firm

MARGARET M. BLAIR

To a casual observer, the relationship between a firm and its employees would seem to be a central, perhaps defining, feature of the firm itself. Yet the tendency among economists and legal theorists has been to study the nature of the firm, as well as the property rights and governance structure associated with it, separately from the structure and terms of relationships with and among the employees of firms. The main exception has been work that focuses on one subset of employees—managers—and uses principal-agent analysis to explore the relationship between managers (understood to be the agents) and shareholders (understood to be the principals). This view is premised on an underlying assumption that "the firm"

I am grateful to Gabriel Loeb and Hannah Zwiebel for research assistance on this essay; to Bengt Holmstrom, Victor Goldberg, Greg Dow, Louis Putterman, David Ellerman, and Mark Roe for comments and feedback; and to the Alfred P. Sloan Foundation, Pfizer Inc., and an anonymous donor who provided grants to the Brookings Institution to help support this research. An earlier version of this paper was presented at the Columbia Law School conference on employees and corporate governance. The opinions expressed and all errors of fact and of judgment are those of the author and are not to be attributed to Brookings, its officers or trustees, or to any of those who have helped to fund the research.

is basically a bundle of assets that belongs to shareholders but is managed for them by hired managers.

But an alternative view—in which the relationships among the people who participate in the productive activity of firms are at the heart of the definition of the firm itself—is beginning to take shape in economic theory. This alternative view has not yet fully crystallized and has so far had little influence on the legal debate about corporate governance. These evolving ideas about the nature of the firm and the role played by investments in "human capital," especially by the people involved in the firm, are the subject of this chapter. Its central thesis is that this new view of the firm should be incorporated into the legal debate on corporate governance.

The legal debate in recent years has relied heavily on a contractarian view, which treats the firm as a "nexus" through which all the various participants in the productive enterprise contract with each other, either explicitly or implicitly. Although the "nexus of contracts" view would seem to focus on the relationships among all the participants in the firm, most legal scholars have emphasized one relationship—that between shareholders and managers—above all others. A somewhat different approach can be seen in what is known as the entity view, which came to prominence during the middle decades of the twentieth century. It holds that, under the law, a new entity, with status as a separate legal "person," is created when a corporation is formed. But advocates of the nexus approach reject this idea and would analyze firms as devices by which shareholders (as principals) contract with managers (as agents). Drawing on the new economic thinking about the nature of the firm, I argue that the entity view of the firm should be brought back to center stage in the law because the legal device of creating a separate juridical person may be an important mechanism for protecting enterprise-specific investments made by all participants in the firm, including both employees and shareholders.

Some Theoretical Background

A growing body of economic theory suggests that specialized investments—investments whose value in a particular enterprise greatly exceeds their value in alternative uses—play a critical role in determining the boundaries of firms and the allocation of risks, rewards, and control rights within firms. According to the theory, such investments need appropriate incentives and protections, and in particular, there are incentive benefits that flow from assigning control rights over the assets of a firm, or over the firm itself, to parties who make such investments. Much of the earlier literature on specific investments, however, referred primarily to physical or other alienable capital.

The exception has been in labor theory, which for decades has recognized the importance of firm-specific human capital. Nonetheless, theories of the firm have done little until recently to address the problems raised by such investments. Before considering how firm-specific investments have been treated in the theory of the firm, then, it is useful to review what labor theorists have said about investments in firm-specific "human capital."

Labor Theory

In 1964 Gary Becker coined the phrase "human capital" to refer to the idea that much of the skill and knowledge required to do a job could only be acquired if some "investment" was made in time and resources. Becker considered the implications of the fact that some of the knowledge and skills acquired by employees have a much higher value in a given employment relationship than they do in other potential relationships. Such specialized knowledge and skills may often be productivity enhancing, he argued, and are therefore likely to be an important part of the employment relationship in practice. But, he noted, they introduce a complication into simple models of wages, investments in training, and other terms of the employment relationship. In particular, the labor services of employees with specialized skills can no longer be modeled as undifferentiated, generic inputs, for which equilibrium price (wages) and quantity (number of employees or number of hours of work) are determined by the intersection of supply and demand curves. Once employees are understood to have specialized skills, it matters which employee does what job for what firm. Furthermore, "if a firm had paid for the specific training of a worker who quit to take another job, its capital expenditure would be partly wasted, for no further return could be collected. Likewise, a worker fired after he had paid for specific training would be unable to collect any further return and would also suffer a capital loss." Where investments in specific skills are important, Becker reasoned, it is no longer a matter of indifference "whether a firm's labor force always contained the same persons or a rapidly changing group."[1]

Although Becker's primary interest was the economic incentives for investments in training and education, along the way he introduced a concept that provides a rationale for long-term relationships between firms and

1. See Becker (1964, p. 21).

their employees. Peter Doeringer and Michael Piore built on this insight to develop their theory of internal labor markets. They argued that investments by firms in specialized training encourage firms to put in place other institutional arrangements designed to stabilize employment and reduce turnover. The organizational stability that results from these practices in turn facilitates further development of specific skills. Doeringer and Piore further argued that the use of mass-production technology, with its detailed division of labor, requires specialized skills and makes stable employment relationships more important.[2]

Becker also argued that employees and employers would be likely to split both the costs and returns from specialized training, to provide an incentive for both parties to stay in the relationship.[3] This means that employees would typically earn less than their opportunity cost during the early stages of their employment relationship (while they were in training, for example), and more than their opportunity cost later in the relationship. An earnings pattern like this would produce an "upward sloping wage-tenure profile," an empirical regularity that labor economists before Becker had observed, and that work by subsequent scholars has documented extensively.[4] Consistent with the "firm-specific human capital" hypothesis, labor economists have also observed that long-tenured employees typically earn quite a bit more than their short-run opportunity cost. This empirical pattern is confirmed through studies of layoffs, which show that long-tenured employees laid off through no fault of their own (as a result of plant closings, for example) typically earn 15 to 25 percent less on their next jobs.[5] These estimates and others in related work suggest that the aggregate

2. See Doeringer and Piore (1971). Jacoby (1990) questions this conclusion. Though he concedes that empirical evidence supports a shift from the late 1800s to at least the mid-1970s toward greater job stability, he argues (p. 323) that "there is little evidence that the shift resulted from a growing reliance on firm-specific techniques or skills. In fact, the evidence suggests that the opposite was true: that technology and job skills became less, rather than more firm-specific over time."

3. Hashimoto (1981) subsequently provided a formal model suggesting that the division of the costs and returns from training would be split according to a formula that was a function of the relative probabilities of layoffs versus quits, and the costs of evaluating and agreeing on both the worker's productivity in the firm and his opportunity cost, or potential productivity in an alternative firm.

4. For recent contributions to this literature, see Topel (1990, 1991).

5. These are conservative estimates. Topel (1990) found that the losses of displaced workers ranged from an average of 14 percent for all displaced workers in his study to 28 percent for workers with 10 or more years of service. Jacobson, LaLonde, and Sullivan (1993) found that earnings losses persisted, so that even six years after displacement, workers who had six or more years of service in their previous job were still earning 25 percent less than comparable workers who had not lost their jobs.

returns to investments in firm-specific human capital could represent as much as 10 percent or more of the total wage bill of the corporate sector, a figure that is of the same order of magnitude as all of corporate profits.

Although wages do seem to rise with tenure, and wages of long-tenured employees often exceed short-run opportunity costs, this evidence does not persuade all labor economists that employees acquire substantial amounts of firm-specific human capital. Perhaps other features of the labor market could account for these empirical regularities. For example, labor market models that emphasize a process of searching for an especially good job "match" also predict low wages at the start, which will rise if the match is a good one. Similarly, in "efficiency wage" models, employees are induced to perform well by making it costly for them if they get laid off, generally by paying them more than their opportunity cost—that is, the wage in their next-best job. In such cases, employees have something of substantial value at risk in the firm that can be expropriated by the employer, or that can be lost altogether if the employees lose their jobs with their current employer. These other explanations for a rising wage-tenure profile also imply that labor markets would exhibit involuntary unemployment; hence they have figured prominently in the debate about the extent to which labor markets clear.[6] But these alternative theories do not generally rule out the possibility that firm-specific human capital is an important factor in determining the structure of many employment relationships. Indeed, most labor economists believe such investments are important in many situations.

Knowledge and skills that are specialized to a given enterprise, as well as effort that has been put forth toward the goals of the enterprise, are "assets" at risk in much the same way that equity capital is at risk once it has been committed to a given enterprise. As such, they inevitably present a contracting problem for the employee and the firm. If the firm compensates the employee up front and fully for the costs of expending the effort, or developing and using such assets, the employee could, in principle, take the compensation and walk out the door, depriving the firm of a return on its investment.

Suppose, however, that the firm does not fully compensate the employee up front, but instead pays a lower wage at first, with a promise of a higher wage later. That employee would then have a stake in the firm that is unrecoverable except as payments are made to the employee out of the economic

---

6. For a summary of arguments on the efficiency of nonmarket-clearing wages, see Krueger and Summers (1988); Weiss (1990). For evidence on nonmarket-clearing wages and employment practices, see Katz and Summers (1989); Dickens and Lang (1993).

surplus generated by the relationship in the future. This stake is very diffi-cult to protect by means of explicit contracts. On one side, the firm cannot enforce a contract that requires the employee to stay and utilize those skills in the firm. On the other, because the skills and special effort in question are likely to be hard to define, let alone measure, the employee cannot enforce a contract that requires the firm to pay for the special effort expended, or the development and use of special skills.

In general, the lesson from labor theory has been that employee invest-ments in firm-specific human capital cannot be well protected by explicit and complete contracts. Other institutional arrangements are needed, and those arrangements often have the effect of tying the fortunes of the employee together with those of the firm.

Theories of the Firm

In early thinking about the nature of the firm, Ronald Coase focused on the reason that a hierarchical relationship, with some individuals having the authority to make decisions about how people and resources are used, might be substituted for market transactions. "Outside the firm," Coase wrote, "price movements direct production, which is coordinated through a series of exchange transactions on the market. Within a firm, these market transactions are eliminated and in place of the complicated market struc-ture with exchange transactions is substituted the entrepreneur/coordina-tor, who directs production."[7] The general argument is that the central authority figure in the relationship can in some cases coordinate activities more efficiently than individual input providers could if they were all con-tracting with each other separately.

From Coase's initial insight, economists took the theory of the firm in two different directions. One approach has been to focus on circumstances in which it might be less costly to organize production within a firm. A central question here is what factors might increase the "transactions costs" of organizing activities through market transactions. One answer that has been given particular attention is investments in specialized assets. The second approach stresses the importance of joint production technologies, in which the firm provides a mechanism for measuring and rewarding the productivity of interacting team members.

TRANSACTIONS COSTS THEORY. Oliver Williamson has identified several features of transactions that make it costly to trade in impersonal, arm's-

7. See Coase (1937, p. 19).

length markets. Where these features apply, he suggests, transacting parties might choose to administer such transactions through hierarchical governance arrangements.[8] One key feature is what he called the "asset-specificity" of investments, which refers to the degree of difficulty in redeploying assets to other uses. Other features that encourage hierarchical administration rather than market transactions, according to Williamson, include the longevity of the asset (to what extent will it generate its return over time?); the uncertainty and complexity of the transaction, a problem which is exacerbated when assets are long-lived; the "bounded rationality" of the transacting parties, which makes it impossible for them to anticipate all possible outcomes and complications and to write "complete" contracts that specify what is to happen under each scenario; and the tendency of transacting parties to be "opportunistic." Of these reasons, asset specificity can be seen as central, since assets that can be readily redeployed are (by definition) not at risk in a given relationship. It is only when assets are specific that the problems of longevity, uncertainty and complexity, bounded rationality, and opportunism become important.

Williamson's work spawned a literature on the contracting problems that arise when assets are specific. Benjamin Klein, Robert Crawford, and Armen Alchian, for example, argued that when two contracting parties each make investments that are specific to their relationship, either party can attempt to expropriate the returns from those investments by threatening to "hold up" the other party in the enterprise.[9] The potential "hold-up" problem, they speculated, would encourage the contracting parties to integrate their operations vertically; that is, the supplier would acquire the customer, or vice versa. Suppose one party owns a coal mine, and the other party owns a power plant built at the mouth of the coal mine and designed to use coal from the mine. Then the two parties would probably find themselves in frequent disputes about the price and terms on which the coal is to be sold to the power plant. But if a single party owns both the mine and the power plant, this owner would maximize the joint return and would not waste resources haggling over the terms of trade between the two units.

Empirical research that has attempted to test the Williamson and Klein, Crawford, and Alchian hypotheses has generally confirmed that firm-specific investments are important in determining ownership structure and degree of vertical integration. But this research has taken an interesting twist, which implies that firm-specific investments in human capital may be a more important reason for corporate integration than firm-specific investments in physical capital.

8. See Williamson (1975, 1985).
9. See Klein, Crawford, and Alchian (1978).

Kirk Monteverde and David Teece have studied parts production in the automobile industry to ask under what circumstances firms might choose to undertake production in-house rather than contracting production out to a supplier.[10] They argue that vertical integration might not be necessary if the specialized assets used in production of the parts include only physical capital, such as tools or dies. The hold-up problem, in this case, can be avoided if the automobile assembly company owns the specialized tools and leases them to the contractor who produces the parts. Such arrangements, which Monteverde and Teece refer to as "quasi integration," are commonly observed in auto parts production. But where the specialized investment involved in producing the parts is in nonpatentable know-how and skills, Monteverde and Teece argue that quasi integration will no longer solve the hold-up problem. They speculate that full integration will be required to minimize the transactions costs. Similarly, Scott Masten, James Meehan, and Edward Snyder find that, in regressions in which both investments in specialized knowledge and investments in specialized equipment are used to explain vertical integration, investments in specialized knowledge have much more explanatory power.[11]

However, none of these authors offer much insight into why and how organizing production within a firm solves the hold-up problem associated with firm-specific investments by multiple parties, nor which of several participants in an enterprise should ideally be the "owner" of an integrated enterprise. Sanford Grossman and Oliver Hart address this issue.[12] Grossman and Hart's model considers a situation in which participants in an enterprise must make firm-specific investments that are very difficult or impossible to define in enforceable contracts. Their model leads to the conclusion that the ownership rights in the firm should go to the party whose firm-specific investments add the most value to the enterprise but are the most difficult or impossible to contract over. Ownership rights over the firm provide some assurance to the party who must make these investments that its claim to a share in the rents generated by the investments will not be expropriated by the other participants.

Lurking in the background of these transaction cost arguments for why a firm exists is the assumption that a firm is a fairly well-defined entity whose interests are simply an extension of the interests of its owners. By this assumption, employees are contracting with the firm but are not, them-

10. Monteverde and Teece (1982a, 1982b)
11. See Masten, Meehan, and Snyder (1989).
12. See Grossman and Hart (1986).

selves, part of it. Under the terms of the Grossman and Hart theory, for example, firms are defined as bundles of assets under common ownership, where ownership implies control over the use and disposition of the assets.[13]

The tendency in the transactions cost literature has been to recognize that firm-specific human capital raises similar questions, but then to side-step the implications of these questions for corporate governance. Williamson identifies some features of organizations, such as team accommodations, informal process innovations, and knowledge of codes and procedures, that tend to make incumbents more valuable to employers than workers hired on spot markets might be. He points out that transactions in which investments in specific human capital are important must include some sort of safeguard for those investments, noting in particular that in such transactions, "continuity between firm and worker are valued." Firm-specific human capital, he says, must be "embedded in a protective governance structure lest productive values be sacrificed if the employment relation is unwittingly severed."[14]

However, Williamson then devotes little attention to identifying the "protective governance structures" that should exist in relationships between employees and firms that employ them. To be sure, he mentions severance pay and forms of job security as possible mechanisms for encouraging and protecting worker investments in firm-specific skills, and pensions as a mechanism for providing incentives that discourage employees with specialized skills from quitting. He also points out that collective bargaining through unions and "internal governance structures" (such as grievance procedures and pay scales) can help in providing a protective governance structure for idiosyncratic investments in skills by workers, although he notes that unions, with their bent toward egalitarianism, may not be the best institutions for arranging pay structures that will differ across workers according to their degree of firm-specific human capital.[15] These and other mechanisms for encouraging investment in firm-specific human capital will be discussed in more detail later in the chapter. The point here is that it is something of a leap to assume that these protections are fully adequate to

---

13. Economists have not necessarily agreed on the key economic features of "ownership." Hart and Moore (1990), for example, emphasize that ownership implies the ability to exclude others from the use of assets. According to Wiggins (1991, p. 615), shared ownership means that the owners are compensated out of a common stream of residual payments that are left over after contractual payments are made.

14. See Williamson (1985, pp. 242–43).

15. See Williamson (1985, pp. 246–47, 254–56, 265). See also Williamson, Wachter, and Harris (1975).

protect employees who make firm-specific investments. This assumption is implicit, for example, in Williamson's analysis of the transactions cost benefits of corporate governance arrangements that give the right to elect board members only to shareholders, rather than (or in addition to) other constituents: "Stockholders as a group bear a unique relation to the firm," he asserts. "They are the only voluntary constituency whose relation with the corporation does not come up for periodic review. . . . Stockholders . . . invest for the life of the firm, and their claims are located at the end of the queue should liquidation occur."[16]

This line of thinking follows in the tradition of labor theorists, discussed earlier, that makes a hermetic separation between labor market relationships and corporate governance. But firm-specific investments in human capital cannot be redeployed (by definition), and thus employees too are invested for life. Employees can deprive the firm of their firm-specific skills, but they cannot benefit from doing so, since these skills (by definition) have less value elsewhere. Those who make firm-specific investments in human capital are presumably expecting to be compensated from the future productivity of those investments; that is to say, from a share of the future "residual" income, or economic surpluses, of the firm. Despite their reliance on the continuing relationship with the firm, however, employees have no explicit future claim on the firm—at least not solely by virtue of their employment relationship, though employees may also be shareholders, and in Germany, employees' pension claims may be tied to the long-term success of their firms. Although we do not have precise estimates of the aggregate value of investments in firm-specific human capital, it is surely large, and possibly of the same order of magnitude as the aggregate value of equity capital. This recognition of the potential importance of firm-specific human capital, soon followed by an implicit denial that it should have anything to do with actual corporate governance such as voting for board members, has been echoed by numerous legal scholars, especially advocates of a contractarian theory of the firm.[17]

TEAM PRODUCTION. A second main justification for the existence of the firm is to organize team production. Armen Alchian and Harold Demsetz characterize team production as "production in which (1) several types of resources are used and (2) the product is not a sum of separable outputs of

16. Williamson (1985), pp. 304–05.
17. See, for example, Romano (1996, p. 3).

each cooperating resource, . . . [and] (3) not all resources used in team production belong to one person."[18] The problem raised by team production, according to Alchian and Demsetz, is one of metering output (where the output of any one individual is not separable from the output of teammates), and issuing rewards in ways that will motivate team members to exert effort. Advantages arise from team production if the team members can accomplish more by working together than by working separately. If this extra productivity exceeds the cost of monitoring and motivating team members to exert effort, then team production will be chosen over individual production methods. Alchian and Demsetz go on to argue that, where team production is preferred, the metering and reward problem can be solved by having one team member specialize in monitoring, and by giving that individual both the authority to hire and fire team members, and a claim on the earnings from the enterprise net of payments to providers of other inputs, who are assumed to be paid their opportunity cost.

This story purports to provide an explanation for capitalist ownership and control of firms. Taken by itself, however, it offers no particular reason why the membership of the team could not change from day to day, or hour to hour. In fact, Alchian and Demsetz state that "long-term contracts between employer and employee are not the essence of the organization we call a firm." They argue, rather, that the relationship between firm and employee is equivalent to a series of short-term contracts: "The employer is continually involved in renegotiation of contracts on terms that must be acceptable to both parties."[19] But in large corporations, fairly long-term relationships are the norm rather than the exception. So their story seems, at best, incomplete, for explaining the actual way that large corporations typically operate.

The original Alchian and Demsetz story can be improved by allowing for investments in firm-specific human capital, or other factors that might make it advantageous to keep a particular team working together. Demsetz himself has moved in this direction in more recent work. An important aspect of the "nexus of contracts" that make up a firm, he says, "is the expected length of association between the same input owners. . . . Do the contractual agreements entered into contemplate mainly transitory, short-term association, which in the extreme would be characterized by spot market exchanges, or do these agreements contemplate a high probability of

18. See Alchian and Demsetz (1972, p. 779).
19. See Alchian and Demsetz (1972, p. 777).

continuing association among the same parties? The firm viewed as team production exhibits significant reassociation of the same input owners."[20]

Demsetz goes on to define a firm as "a bundle of commitments to technology, personnel, and methods, all contained and constrained by an insulating layer of information that is specific to the firm, and this bundle cannot be altered or imitated easily or quickly."[21] In team production with specific human capital, then, the human capital is worth more when applied together with the human capital of the other team members than it is when applied alone, and the productivity of a particular individual depends not just on being part of a team, but on being part of a particular team engaged in a particular task. If it matters who is on the team, this complicates the original Alchian and Demsetz story, because it is no longer clear that team members who invest in specialized skills and who know they are especially valuable when deployed with this particular team will be willing to accept only their (short-run) opportunity cost in wages. Hence it is no longer obvious that the monitor will be able to collect all of the economic surplus from the enterprise.

However, Alchian and Demsetz's story focuses attention on the contracting relationships among the participants within firms and provides an explanation for hierarchical structures. From that beginning, numerous other authors have addressed the contracting problem between so-called principals—the entrepreneur or central capitalist authority figure in Alchian and Demsetz's story—and "agents."

In principal-agent models, employees are viewed as agents of the firm, and the managers of firms are viewed as agents of the shareholders. The contractual problem is to design the terms of a particular relationship in a way that will encourage the agent to make decisions and otherwise behave in ways that benefit the principal. Michael Jensen and William Meckling introduced the principal-agent approach to the theory of the firm in their classic 1976 article in which they proposed that the firm should be viewed as a contracting mechanism between providers of equity capital (the principals) and managers (the agents) designed to minimize the agency costs of this relationship. Jensen and Meckling argued that organizations "are simply legal fictions which serve as a nexus for a set of contracting relationships among individuals."[22]

Jensen and Meckling are thus generally credited as the source of the view of the firm as a "nexus of contracts," and their notion of firms has been

20. Demsetz (1991, p. 170).
21. Demsetz (1991, p. 165).
22. Jensen and Meckling (1976, p. 310).

taken into the legal literature on corporate governance in support of a contractarian (rather than an entity) theory of firms. More important for the present discussion, it has often been imbued with normative status, as a statement about whose interests managers are supposed to serve. In recent years, principal-agent models have also been influential in research on labor relations in firms. But the corporate governance and labor relations literatures have typically remained rather separate.

The canonical principal-agent problem involves a transaction between two parties, one of whom must take an action that affects the other. For some reason, however, the principal cannot compensate the agent directly for the action itself, perhaps because the action itself is not observable to the principal, or perhaps because the principal does not have the information or knowledge necessary to evaluate the action. It must also be true that the consequences or observable output of the agent's action is not a determinate function of the action taken by the principal; otherwise, it would be possible for the principal to infer the action taken by observing the consequences. Instead, in the principal-agent problem, the output is assumed to be a stochastic function of the agent's action, or it is assumed to be measured with error. Since the principal cannot pay the agent for the action, the problem for the principal is to base the fee schedule on the observable factors in a way that gives the agent incentives to choose actions that benefit the principal.

The typical situation that arises is that the agent is risk averse and thus worried that because of bad luck or bad measurement, output will appear low to the principal, and the result will be a low level of payment. (If the agent is not risk averse, and if the potential losses from bad luck or bad measurement are counterbalanced by potential gains from good luck or good management, then the optimal contract is simply to pay the agent whatever the observed output is.) With a risk-averse agent, the optimal incentive structure will share the risks between the agent and the principal; for example, the principal might agree to pay a minimum wage regardless of the outcome, plus some fraction of realized output. The sharing of risks gives a risk-averse agent higher utility than if the agent bore all of the risks, but because the agent is receiving only a fraction of output, the incentive of a risk-sharing contract is less powerful than would be the case if the agent received all of the output.

Another device that can be used to induce effort by the agent is a flat fee, accompanied by a threat of termination if the agent is caught shirking. Risk-sharing fee schedules have been discussed extensively in the literature on incentive compensation systems for corporate executives, while flat fees accompanied by a threat of termination are cited in the literature on the market for corporate control as a mechanism for inducing managerial effort as well as in labor theory, where they form the basis of "efficiency wage" theories.

In some ways, the problem raised by investments in firm-specific human capital is analogous to the principal-agent problem. The employee must take some action—for example, acquire some skills, accumulate some special knowledge, exert some special effort, develop some special relationships with co-workers—which the firm cannot directly measure and for which it cannot directly compensate the employee. The firm can only observe (perhaps imperfectly) the outcomes of such investments. As Kenneth Arrow has noted, "The employment relation in general is one in which effort and ability acquired through training and self-improvement are hard to observe."[23] Steven Wiggins stresses the similarities between the principal-agent problem and the problem of firm-specific investments: whenever "one party performs first, he effectively makes an investment specific to the trading relationship; he invests in a specific asset. After investment, he relies on the other party to perform. The problem is that the second party can only make limited commitments to follow through."[24]

But the canonical principal-agent problem is different from the firm-specific investment problem in a critical way: it is asymmetric. In the canonical principal-agent problem, there is an implicit assumption that, once the fee schedule has been determined, the actions of the principal have no further effect on the outcome of the variable to which the fee schedule is tied. The outcome is realized, the fees that were promised to the agent are determined as a function of that outcome, and the agents are promptly paid. Thus some strong assumptions about the credibility of the parties and the enforceability of the arrangement are embodied in the simple principle-agent story.[25]

In the case of firm-specific investments, however, actions of both parties can affect the payoff from the investment. The employee takes an action that affects the payoff for the firm, but the firm, in turn, can take actions that not only affect the fee that the employee gets, but that affect the stream of rents and quasi rents generated by that action. For example, the firm can decide to close the plant where the employee works, and suddenly there

---

23. See Arrow (1985, p. 39).

24. Wiggins goes on to suggest that firms, contracts, and government regulations can be alternative mechanisms for solving these problems. See Wiggins (1991, p. 604).

25. Wiggins (1991, pp. 646–47).

is no opportunity for the payoff to be realized. Or the shareholders can sell the firm to someone else who can fire the manager or dismantle the firm.[26]

Principal-agent models have been useful in delineating certain kinds of contracting problems. If firm-specific human capital is an important input in corporate enterprises, however, the classical principal-agent model may be too one-sided to describe the fundamental features of the employment relationship, or of the nature of the firm itself.

Contracting Problems Raised by Firm-Specific Human Capital

Firm-specific capital is indeed central to theories about the nature of the firm. It has bearing on both transactions costs and team production problems. Although considerable thought has been given to how ownership structures might be arranged to protect investments in firm-specific physical capital, less has been said about how contracts might be drawn up or other institutional arrangements might be made to protect firm-specific human capital.

Much has been made of the idea that the corporate form facilitates a division of labor in which managers specialize in decisionmaking and outside investors specialize in risk-bearing.[27] This approach, however, essentially ignores the risks borne by employees with firm-specific human capital. An investment in firm-specific human capital can be risky not only because of potential hold-up problems and the associated risk of expropriation, but also because a particular skill may no longer be as useful in a given firm, or the firm itself may do poorly while the economy does well, or the entire economy may do poorly. Outside shareholders might be able to draw up contracts that can protect employees to some extent from some of these risks, but surely not from all of them. Employees, inevitably, will also bear some of the enterprise risk.

Numerous scholars have argued that employees are protected from the risks of expropriation by the fact that the firm must be concerned about its reputation for fairness. A good reputation enables it to contract on favorable terms with other employees in the future. Oliver Williamson writes:

---

26. Becker (1964, p. 21) was clearly aware of this problem. The point is also close to that made by Shleifer and Summers (1988) in their critique of hostile takeovers, arguing that such takeovers may create value for the new owners by breaching the implicit contracts with employees and other stakeholders put in place by previous management. Although Shleifer and Summers do not appeal explicitly to investments in firm-specific human capital, such investments would be one explanation of the quasi rents that are supposedly up for grabs in their story.

27. For the classic article that makes this argument, see Fama and Jensen (1983).

Employers who have a reputation for exploiting incumbent employees will not thereafter be able to induce new employees to accept employment on the same terms. A wage premium may have to be paid; or tasks may have to be redefined to eliminate the transaction-specific features; or contractual guarantees against future abuses may have to be granted. In consideration of those possibilities, the strategy of exploiting the specific investments of incumbent employees is effectively restricted to circumstances where (1) firms are of a fly-by-night kind, (2) firms are playing end games, and (3) intergenerational learning is negligible.[28]

In practice, employees are also not given significant protections against the risks of decline in the value of their firm-specific skills. It is difficult to imagine how such protection could be provided in any company over an extended period of time, as long as the company retains ultimate power to deny wage raises or to terminate employment altogether. Indeed, it is much harder to enforce "fairness" in an employment agreement whose terms can be renegotiated as business conditions facing the firm vary. As Paul Milgrom and John Roberts note: "The firm's management may be tempted to exaggerate financial difficulties in order to justify paying lower wages to workers."[29] On the other hand, totally insulating employees against risks might discourage them from doing the things that are under their control to pull resources out of lower-value investments and move them to higher-value investments, by retraining, for example.

Some of the disincentive effects of mechanisms that shelter employees from the risks inherent in making specialized investments could possibly be counteracted with intensive monitoring. But the monitor must focus on the measurable dimensions of performance, which might lead employees to focus on those "monitored" dimensions to the exclusion of nonmeasurable dimensions that may also be important to productivity.[30] Ultimately, attempting to monitor investments in firm-specific human capital would present such severe problems of measurement, verification, and evaluation that it would probably be ineffective.

Yet another contracting problem raised by investments in human capital is how to understand and quantify all the forms that the returns to those investments can take. Whereas the returns to physical capital investments can generally be measured in monetary terms, some of the returns to invest-

28. Williamson (1985, p. 261). For another example, see Milgrom and Roberts (1992, p. 331). For a general discussion of the role of norms, reputation, and corporate culture, see Kreps (1990).

29. See Milgrom and Roberts (1992, p. 334). For a good summary of risk-sharing issues in implicit employment contracts, see also Rosen (1985).

30. See Holmstrom and Milgrom (1991).

ments in human capital may take other forms. For example, human capital may not depreciate with use, but may, instead, appreciate. Knowledge and skills that are used may build on themselves and become more valuable. If so, the returns to tenure may go well beyond just the returns from skills accumulated up to a particular point in time, and by extension, the losses from premature job separations may be even larger than that implied by immediate losses in workers' incomes. An employment relationship may include a component that is like an option. If the employee stays with the present employer, the employee will have an opportunity to acquire skills tomorrow that build on the skills acquired through today. Those skills would generate an additional stream of returns on top of the stream of returns from the skills accumulated through today. If the employment relationship is prematurely severed, that option value is lost.

The complex nature of the returns to human capital may make it impossible, Milgrom and Roberts note, "to identify any individual or group that is the unique residual claimant [in a firm], or, indeed, to identify the benefits and costs accruing to any decision and so compute the residuals."[31] The difficulty of computing and assigning residuals complicates the problem of bargaining between any employee and the firm over the allocation of residual claims, or over any scheme of payments that might be devised to encourage both parties to the relationship to take into account the impact of decisions by one on the other. In sum, work on theories of the firm also tends to imply that explicit contracting cannot be used effectively to protect firm-specific investments in human capital by employees.

Institutional Arrangements That Address Contracting Problems

Since the contracting problems surrounding investments in firm-specific human capital are so pervasive, it should not be surprising to find that providers of human and financial capital have developed noncontractual mechanisms for encouraging and protecting firm-specific investments. Some of these mechanisms have been studied by labor economists and versions of them are found in most large corporations. In general, however,

---

31. See Milgrom and Roberts (1992, p. 315). For a general discussion of a related problem with team production, the problem of allocating returns from team efforts in ways that discourage "free riding" by individual members of the team, see also Holmstrom (1982).

they have not been linked with the institutional nature of the firm itself, or with corporate governance.

Customs and practices that encourage long-term employment relationships have a variety of benefits that support, or are perhaps complementary to, investments in firm-specific human capital. According to Milgrom and Roberts, some of these benefits include "an increased opportunity to invest profitably in firm-specific human capital, the greater efficacy of efficiency wage incentive contracts in long-term relationships, and the enhanced ability to make an accurate assessment of an employee's contributions to long-term objectives by monitoring performance over a longer period of time."[32] Long-term relationships also encourage the development of reputations. After all, good reputations are more valuable the longer the time-horizons of the contracting parties, so that in a longer-term relationship, both sides to any given transaction within that relationship will have stronger incentives to perform fully.

Job Ladders, Career Paths, and Seniority Rules

Career paths and job ladders are said to be important mechanisms for encouraging employees to make investments in firm-specific human capital and for ensuring that the firm shares the rents generated by those investments with employees.[33] Seniority rules are a related mechanism that provides some protection for employees from the possibility that the firm will renege on its implicit agreement to compensate the employee for his or her firm-specific investments by paying them a higher wage during their later years, perhaps even a wage that exceeds their productivity during those years. Seniority rules protect the high-tenured worker by requiring the firm to lay off low-tenured workers first.

Both seniority rules and job ladders help ensure that the employee will be appropriately compensated for making firm-specific investments over time. Of course, such promises would have no incentive benefit if employees did not believe that the employing organization would continue to exist over the relevant period. So these mechanisms are not useful by themselves but must be embedded in a relationship that is understood to be for the long term, with an entity that is long-lived.

---

32. See Milgrom and Roberts (1992, p. 363). The classic discussion of the role played by long-term employment relationships is Doeringer and Piore (1971).
33. For example, Koike (1990); Prendergast (1993).

Unionization

One effect of unions is to protect employees from actions such as dismissal (except "for cause"). Other terms in the typical collective bargaining agreement in turn help prevent firms from driving out unwanted employees without actually dismissing them. These take the form of rules designed to safeguard wages, benefits, and job assignments, as well as to protect against layoffs. However, these sorts of protections impose rigidities that can have negative implications for efficient adaptation to changed circumstances.[34] But these costs must be weighed against incentives for long-term investment in firm-specific capital (and other benefits) that union agreements may provide.

"Hostages" or Performance Bonds

A "hostage" is something of value that is pledged by one party to a transaction and that will be forfeited to the other party if the first party fails to perform according to the contract. One version of the efficiency wage argument, for example, is based on a hostage argument: that is, workers accept wages that are lower than their opportunity cost in the early years of their employment relationship, and this serves as a commitment by the worker to stay with the firm and to be repaid later with wages that are higher. Another version of the hostage argument is the "performance bond," in which an employee posts a bond upon being hired that must be forfeited if the employee were to leave or to underperform. The administration and enforcement of performance bond agreements, however, requires that third parties be able to observe and verify certain measures of performance and certain triggering events. Hence performance bonds by themselves seem to be poor candidates for solving the contracting problems presented by the accumulation of specialized human capital unless they are embedded in institutional arrangements that also foster trust or that make reputations valuable.

Hostages provided by the employer include severance pay commitments and their gilt-edged cousins, golden parachutes; these make it costly for the employer to sever the employment relationship. Penalties for certain kinds of changes in the contract terms may perform a similar function. Milgrom and Roberts argue, for example, that employment contracts might be designed to impose a penalty of some sort on the employer for invoking

34. See Epstein (1985, p. 147); Klein, Crawford, and Alchian (1978).

a claim of hard times in an effort to negotiate lower wages, so that the employer will not be tempted to use this claim frivolously in negotiations.[35]

Corporate Culture, Norms, and Goals

"Workable principles and routines . . . create shared expectations for group members," as Milgrom and Roberts note. The advantages of such principles are that they "help guide managers in making decisions," provide "a set of clear expectations for everyone in the organization," and "provide a set of principles and procedures for judging right behavior and resolving inevitable disputes."[36] According to David Kreps, these aspects of corporate culture may serve as "focal points" around which participants in the firm can arrive at stable patterns of interacting that are Pareto superior to patterns they might lapse into without the benefit of the common norms.[37] Hence corporate culture can help support investments in firm-specific human capital by fostering trust.

Corporate culture, itself, can also be seen as part of the firm-specific capital of the firm, the organizational capital, as it were. Richard Nelson and Sidney Winter argue that the knowledge of how to do things is often implicit in the routines that make up the daily activities of the people in the firm.[38] As such, this knowledge is neither articulable nor alienable but is embodied in the people and in their relationships to each other. Another similar mechanism, Sanford Jacoby writes, is the "socialization at the workplace itself, which relies on consensual methods of inculcating norms and goals, such as ideologies or authority that must be seen as legitimate if they are to be persuasive."[39]

Ownership and Control Rights

Yet another noncontractual mechanism for protecting specific investments is "ownership," or "property rights." Oliver Hart and others remind us that "ownership" involves possession of "residual" control rights, the rights to make all decisions (at least those that have not been delegated to others by contract) and receive whatever is left over after all payments specified by

35. Milgrom and Roberts (1992, p. 334).
36. Milgrom and Roberts (1992, p. 265).
37. Kreps (1990) provides an extensive analysis of the role of corporate culture using game-theoretic arguments.
38. Nelson and Winter (1982).
39. Jacoby (1990, p. 332).

contract have been paid. In particular, Hart has noted, "ex post residual rights of control will be important because, through their influence on asset usage, they will affect ex post bargaining power and the division of ex post surplus in a relationship. This division in turn will affect the incentives of actors to invest in that relationship." On these grounds, Hart has argued that "cospecialized" assets should be owned in common. If they are not, then the separate parties who own each asset will have reason to fear that the other parties will expropriate an unduly large share of the rents earned by the assets and will tend to underinvest.[40]

But, of course, neither the firm, nor any other participant in the enterprise that the firm directs, can "own" the human capital that may be cospecialized with the other assets of the firm. Where firm-specific human capital is important, then, arguments about the role played by property rights might in some cases point toward employee control of the enterprise, or at least participation in management, rather than capitalist ownership and control. In noting the advantages of the partnership form of organization, for example, Milgrom and Roberts point out that "human capital is not easily tradable, and if the residual returns on that capital belong to the humans who embody it, then the usual arguments about ownership rights suggest that the residual control should be assigned to them too."[41] There are several possibilities for assigning a share of ownership and control rights to labor, ranging from equity ownership by employees to labor participation in management to direct labor ownership of firms.

Compensating employees with equity stakes in corporations might foster and protect investments in firm-specific human capital. Equity ownership by employees serves as a kind of hostage, helping to make the firm's promise to share in the rents credible. It also gives employees some control rights (by virtue of their equity holdings rather than by virtue of their status as employees), while at the same time helping to align their interests with those of outside equity holders. And if equity claims are substituted for the wage premium that firm-specific human capital supposedly earns, the wages will come closer to reflecting opportunity cost and thereby send the correct economic signals to decisionmakers within the firm to guide hiring and firing decisions. There is substantial evidence that the use of equity-based compensation systems is growing in U.S. corporations, although no

---

40. See Hart (1989, pp. 1757–74, longer quotation from p. 1767).

41. See Milgrom and Roberts (1992, p. 523). For discussions of employee ownership as a mechanism for protecting investments in firm-specific human capital, see also Putterman and Kroszner (1996, p. 20); Blair (1995).

definitive empirical studies have linked employee ownership in publicly traded firms to investments in firm-specific human capital.[42]

Direct labor participation in management is more common in Japan and Europe, where corporate governance systems seem to feature institutional arrangements that provide mechanisms by which employees are given a direct voice in management. Japanese scholars, especially, have credited these arrangements with providing incentives and protection for employee investments in firm-specific human capital.[43] Germany's codetermination system has also attracted attention in this regard.

As an empirical matter, employee-controlled industrial firms remain rare.[44] However, a number of scholars were inspired by the Yugoslavian experiment with labor-managed firms in the 1960s to consider the advantages and disadvantages of organizing production in this way. This produced a lively academic debate in which some neoclassical economists argued that employee-controlled firms would be inefficient for a variety of reasons: for example, such firms would supposedly maximize net revenues per worker rather than profits, would not have the right incentives to maintain their physical capital adequately, or would be inefficient because hierarchies are needed for efficient processing of large amounts of information.[45] Other scholars have answered these criticisms by pointing out that, in each case, the supposed inefficiencies are a product of peculiar modeling assumptions made by the critics.[46] But absent obvious legal restrictions against such firms, economists generally take their rareness or absence to mean that this form is not economically viable for a variety of reasons. For example, Henry Hansmann has argued that the disadvantages of collective decisionmaking by heterogeneous employees might easily outweigh the advantages of common ownership of the capital and labor inputs.[47] According to others, the fact that capitalists have more wealth and

42. For the most comprehensive evidence of the growth of employee ownership in publicly traded firms, see Blasi and Kruse (1991). See also Blair and Kruse (1999).

43. See, for example, Aoki (1988).

44. One could argue that partnerships, which are a common organizational form in law, accounting, consulting, advertising, and other professional services, are a type of employee-controlled firm. An interesting question for corporate governance scholars is why firms in such fields are typically organized as partnerships, whereas industrial firms are typically organized as corporations.

45. The first of these arguments is made by Vanek (1970, 1977) and Meade (1972); the second by Jensen and Meckling (1979), and Furobotn and Pejovich (1974); and the third by Williamson (1975, 1985).

46. For example, see Putterman (1984); Wolfstetter, Brown, and Meran (1984); Ellerman (1986); Dow (1993).

47. Hansmann (1996). For further discussion of possible problems of employee-owned firms, see chapter 1 in this volume.

better access to credit markets than workers do, and the fact that capitalists can diversify risks better than workers can, also argue against employees having a sizable share of their personal wealth in equity stakes in the firms where they work.

New Thinking about the Theory of the Firm

The idea that the firm is a nexus of contracts was a significant insight that helped get scholars thinking about the terms of the relationships among the various participants in firms. But in probing the nature of corporations and corporate governance it is not enough to look only at relationships between shareholders and managers and to assume that employment relationships are a separable topic. The role played by investments in firm-specific human capital and the problems raised by that role suggest that the nature of the employment relationship is central to the nature of the institutional arrangements that are the essence of modern, large corporations.

Economic theorists are now begining to acknowledge the complex nature of the way employees participate in firms. Hence a few have even defined firms as institutional arrangements developed to elicit contributions by employees to the joint productive effort of the enterprise. If the full range of contributions needed could be adequately elicited through market relationships or explicit contracts, perhaps they would be. But the very fact that they cannot is what calls forth complex organizational forms such as modern corporations. Current theory offers several suggestions for dealing with this complexity.

The Firm as a System of Incentives

Holmstrom and Milgrom view firms as systems of incentives. They propose a multitask principal-agent model to address the problems that arise when the tasks the worker is supposed to do are multidimensional, and performance is difficult to measure in some or all of those dimensions. When agents must perform a number of tasks, and their choices about effort and allocation of their time can affect many dimensions of the firm's performance, high-powered incentive structures that reward performance in some dimensions, but neglect performance in other dimensions, can greatly distort the behavior of the agent.[48]

48. See Holmstrom and Milgrom (1991).

Of course, a key feature that distinguishes agents who are "in" the firm from agents who are on the outside and merely contracting with the firm is the structure of the compensation agreement. Their model explores why "the attributes of an employment relationship differ in so many ways from the attributes of a contractor relationship." Compensation for contractors generally provides for task-specific payments, with all risks of nonperformance borne by the agent, whereas with employees, such risks are generally pooled and borne collectively by the firm itself, so that the agent is paid a regular wage or salary for the duration of employment, regardless of the actual tasks performed. The Holmstrom and Milgrom model implies that, under certain conditions, an optimal incentive structure "may require the elimination or muting of incentives which in a market relationship would be too strong." Thus, they conclude, "the use of low-powered incentives within the firm, although sometimes lamented as one of the major disadvantages of internal organization, is also an important vehicle for inspiring cooperation and coordination."[49]

In comparing the terms on which in-house insurance sales agents typically operate to the terms on which independent sales agents typically operate, for instance, Holmstrom and Milgrom note that employment relationships typically involve lower-powered incentives (such as a fixed base salary and lower commissions), ownership of key assets by the employer (rather than by the employee), and more restrictions on the mode of operation of the employee. They find that the choice between structuring the relationship as an employment one, versus structuring it as one of an independent contractor type, appears to be driven by the relative ease or difficulty of measuring key aspects of performance, more than by the extent of investments in firm-specific human capital.

But it seems unlikely that this factor drives this choice in all occupations. Consider production line workers. Assembly line workers who work on large, highly capital-intensive automated assembly lines are typically paid hourly wages, and a variety of other institutional arrangements are used (such as pension funds and collective bargaining) to discourage turnover. By contrast, workers in garment factories are more likely to be paid piece rates, turnover rates are often high, and there are fewer institutional arrangements designed to reduce turnover. In other words, apparel workers are often compensated and treated more like subcontractors than employees. In both cases, the activities of the worker should be very easy to measure. But in the garment factory, individual workers can set their own

49. Holmstrom and Milgrom (1994, pp. 988–89).

pace at separate sewing machines, whereas in large automated factories, individual workers must learn to function at a pace set for them by the machines and by the other members of the team. Holmstrom and Milgrom's model might be used to test the hypothesis that the differences in compensation systems and institutional arrangements between, say, auto factory workers and garment factory workers, are accounted for by the fact that workers on automated assembly lines must make a higher level of investment (that is, exert more "effort") in learning to work with the particular equipment in the factory and with the particular teammates on the assembly line.

Holmstrom and Milgrom show the importance of considering the whole mix of incentives facing employees. Instead of seeing firms as "bundles of assets," they look at them as constellations of institutional arrangements designed to provide appropriate incentives where cooperation and coordination are especially important.

Their modeling approach falls within the principal-agent paradigm, however, and, as is generally the case with principal-agent models, it does not take into account the incentives facing the principal to renege on the promised payment scheme, or to alter the job design in ways that reduce the payoff to the agent after firm-specific investments have been made. The model also does not explain two other features that distinguish the employment relationship from the independent contractor relationship, features that have been cited as evidence that investments in firm-specific human capital are important. These are the longevities typically observed in the employment relationship in relation to independent contracting relationships and the wage premia associated with tenure.

The Firm as a Nexus of Specific Investments

According to Raghuram Rajan and Luigi Zingales, a firm should be defined not as a nexus of contracts, but as a "nexus of specific investments." Rajan and Zingales use an optimal-contract model that is similar to, and builds on, the approach used by Grossman and Hart discussed earlier.[50] Their approach is reminiscent of that used by Aoki, who defined the firm as "an enduring combination of firm-specific resources" and argued that firms

50. Rajan and Zingales (1996). A version of this paper has been published as "Power in the Theory of the Firm," *Quarterly Journal of Economics* (1998), pp. 387–32. In the published version, the authors define a firm as "a collection of commonly owned critical resources, talents, and ideas, and also the people who have access to those resources" (p. 405). The published version compresses some important arguments that I want to emphasize in this discussion.

should be regarded as combinations of specific labor and capital, and that management should be viewed as mediating between these two interests in making decisions about output levels, investments, and the sharing of firm-level rents.[51]

In the Rajan and Zingales model, the enterprise requires a physical asset that is specific to the enterprise and two individuals. The total productivity of the enterprise will be maximized if both individuals make specific investments in human capital. But each individual must have access to the physical asset in order to "specialize." If either individual fails to specialize, an unspecialized outsider can be substituted for that individual without loss of total productivity.

Rajan and Zingales distinguish between "ownership" and "power." In their model, "ownership" of the enterprise gives the owner the right to exclude other individuals from access to the physical asset and the right to sell the physical asset to some third party. These rights give the "owner" significant "power" in bargaining over the eventual distribution of rents. But participants can also acquire "power" in another way. Investment by either individual in firm-specific human capital also gives that individual bargaining power in the relationship, because his investment in human capital means that there will be more total rents to share if he stays in the coalition and uses his human capital in the enterprise.

Other economists have argued that ownership of the physical asset increases the incentive for the owner to make the optimal investments in human capital.[52] But, Rajan and Zingales point out, ownership of the physical asset also enables the owner to sell the asset, or to share in the rents from the enterprise even if he fails to make firm-specific investments. Hence ownership rights over the physical asset have a doubled-edged effect in this model. They increase the owner's bargaining power and therefore increase his incentive to "specialize" by assuring him that his share of the rents generated by the enterprise will not be expropriated. But they also raise the owner's opportunity cost of specializing, since the owner can extract rents even without specializing.

If the negative effects of ownership by either individual dominate the positive incentive effects, Rajan and Zingales show that the optimal investment decisions and production levels cannot be achieved if either of the two potential "specializers" owns the physical asset. But remarkably, if the physical asset is owned by an otherwise passive third party, optimal investment

---

51. Aoki (1984, p. 119).

52. For example, this argument is made by Grossman and Hart (1986); and Hart and Moore (1990).

decisions and production levels can still be achieved. In this situation, the two individuals who want to participate in the firm would form a coalition and bid collectively for access to the asset, and the right to use the asset in production. Third-party control over the physical asset helps encourage both individuals to make the optimal firm-specific investments, because it, in effect, enables the two individuals to make binding commitments not to use control over the asset strategically to extract rents from the other individual.

Rajan and Zingales have thus come full circle to the importance of team production, as stressed by Alchian and Demsetz, and the need for a third party to monitor the inputs of the team members. But because they assume that the individual members of the team are not generic inputs, but, rather, specialists who make decisions to invest in learning things that only have value when used by this particular team, they reach a very different conclusion about the division of rents from team production, as well as about the role played by the third-party "monitor."

Rajan and Zingales's third party has no special knowledge or insights about how the work is divided up between the two individuals in the coalition, nor how they divide up the rents. Their third party is assumed to get an arbitrarily small fraction of the total rents, and the party's only task is to select from among multiple coalitions bidding for access rights to the physical assets. The third party naturally selects the coalition that will produce the highest total rents, the bulk of which go not to the third party monitor (as in Alchian and Demsetz), but to the coalition members who have invested in specialized human capital. "Before investment [in specialized human capital] takes place, the firm is defined by who holds the ownership rights to the physical assets that are required for production and by who is given access to the physical assets," Rajan and Zingales argue. "After specific investment has been undertaken, the firm is defined by the ownership of the physical assets and the power that accrues to those who have made specific investments."

Rajan and Zingales interpret their "third-party owner" as providing an explanation for "ownership" of firms by passive outside investors, or shareholders. But this is a highly implausible interpretation. The third-party "owner" in their story is restricted to receiving an arbitrarily small return because that party does not provide anything critical to production. That role could be played by anyone except, notably, any of the active participants in the enterprise, or any participant who contributes something critical. Instead, the role of the third party is to keep control of the assets out of the hands of any of the active participants in the firm, precisely so that those active parties will not use control over the assets to gain strategic advantage for themselves at the expense of the other participants and thereby cause the coalition to fall apart. An alternative, and more plausible, interpretation of Rajan and Zingales's work might be that it provides insight into the role played by creating a separate legal entity under the law (the corporation), which acts as the repository of all the property rights over assets used in production, and over output, and assigning decision rights over this legal entity to an independent board of directors with fiduciary obligations to their firms.[53]

Future Directions

Rajan and Zingales have taken a significant step toward integrating models of the employment relationship and the associated incentive issues raised by investments in firm-specific human capital into a theory of the firm. But their model is still limited by the fact that it follows the two-period structure of most bargaining models.[54] In such models, contracts are written, investment decisions are made, production proceeds, and rents are realized and divided up. There is no second round, let alone third or fourth or more rounds, so that there is no place in the model for reputations to be built up, or for learning from experience, or for investments made in previous rounds to expand the options for the participants in subsequent rounds.

Models that have such features can become intractable very quickly. They are plagued by multiple equilibria and are often very sensitive to assumptions about who has what information when.[55] Nonetheless, the basic insight from infinitely repeated game models is that the chance to benefit from a relationship in the future can mitigate tendencies that parties to the relationship might have in the present to attempt to expropriate short-run returns.

From the perspective of repeated games, each act of self-restraint on the part of participants in the firm can be seen as a "firm-specific investment" whose value can be realized if the coalition stays together, but not if it falls apart. The cumulative result of a large number of such acts of self-restraint

---

53. Blair and Stout (1999) develop this idea in further detail.

54. Technically, there are three periods in the Rajan and Zingales (1996) model, but that is because they have made the decisions by the two individuals to specialize sequential instead of simultaneous.

55. For an interesting discussion of these issues, see Kreps (1996).

could represent a sizable investment in a type of firm-specific human capital that one might call "trust" or "culture." The firm can be viewed as a nexus of these investments, and for the full value of the investments to be realized, key participants in the firm must be kept involved. Moreover, it may be necessary for the "firm" that comprises this coalition of individuals and specific investments to have a permanent legal status separate from any of the participants, to be the repository of the reputational capital and the key property rights.

Implications

Scholarly work on the theory of the firm, both in law and in economics, has perhaps fixed too long on one particular relationship (between shareholders and managers) and on one approach to modeling corporate relationships (the principal-agent approach). The implicit assumption behind this approach has been that a firm is a bundle of assets that belongs to shareholders, so that the only relationship that matters is that between the owners of the assets and the managers hired to manage them. More sophisticated analyses have acknowledged the importance of other relationships but have overlooked their significance for corporate governance questions by assuming that they are all governed by nice, neat, complete contracts, contracts that effectively motivate participants to contribute their ideas, or skills, or effort, and either protect them from risks in the enterprise or completely compensate them for the risks that they bear.

Interest is now turning to actual contracting difficulties and alternative models that address more directly the complexities of the human input into corporations. These models have provided rich insights into many noncontractual institutional arrangements used to govern the relationships among a variety of participants in firms. Although these models have had little influence on legal scholarship to date, arrangements for governing the relationships among employees, and between employees and the firm, can no longer be treated as something separate from corporate governance.

In particular, contractarian legal scholars need to recognize that certain kinds of multilateral and multidimensional relationships and agreements among individuals may only be possible in a legal environment that grants separate legal status to the entity that serves as the repository of the specific investment involved in the relationship. It may be necessary for the law to assign fiduciary responsibilities to the individuals whose job is to govern this entity, whether as directors or as managers.

In other words, contractarians should reconsider the merits of an older school of legal scholarship that emphasizes that a corporation is a separate entity, and more than the sum of its parts. Under the entity view of the firm, a corporation is something apart from each of its participants, something that cannot protect itself through contract, but that needs to be protected by fiduciary duties and corporation law from possible predatory behavior by any of the parties. With a better understanding of the full and complex dimensions of the contracting problem involved in organizing production, it should be possible to develop a renewed appreciation of the "entity" view of firms in the law.

References

Alchian, Armen A., and Harold Demsetz. 1972. "Production, Information Costs, and Economic Organization." *American Economic Review* 62: 777–95.

Aoki, Masahiko. 1984. *The Co-operative Game Theory of the Firm.* Oxford: Clarendon Press.

———. 1988. *Information, Incentives, and Bargaining in the Japanese Economy.* Cambridge University Press.

Arrow, Kenneth J. 1985. "The Economics of Agency." In *Principals and Agents: The Structure of Business,* edited by John W. Pratt and Richard Zeckhauser, 37–51. Harvard Business School Press.

Baker, George, Robert Gibbons, and Kevin Murphy. 1996. "Implicit Contracts and the Theory of the Firm." Working Paper, April, 1996.

Becker, Gary S. 1964. *Human Capital: A Theoretical and Empirical Analysis, with Special Reference to Education.* New York: National Bureau of Economic Research.

Blair, Margaret M. 1995. *Ownership and Control: Rethinking Corporate Governance for the Twenty-First Century.* Brookings.

Blair, Margaret M., and Douglas L. Kruse. 1999. "Giving Employees an Ownership Stake." *Brookings Review,* Fall.

Blair, Margaret M., and Lynn A. Stout. 1999. "A Team Production Theory of Corporate Law." *Virginia Law Review* 85(2): 247–328.

Blasi, Joseph Raphael, and Douglas Lynn Kruse. 1991. *The New Owners: The Mass Emergence of Employee Ownership in Public Companies and What It Means to American Business.* New York: HarperCollins.

Coase, R. H. 1937. "The Nature of the Firm." Republished in *The Nature of the Firm,* edited by Oliver Williamson and Sidney Winter. Cambridge University Press.

Demsetz, Harold. 1991. "The Theory of the Firm Revisited." In *The Nature of the Firm,* edited by Oliver Williamson and Sidney Winter. Cambridge University Press.

Dickens, William T., and Kevin Lang. 1993. "Labor Market Segmentation Theory: Reconsidering the Evidence." In *Labor Economics: Problems in Analyzing Labor Markets,* edited by William Darity Jr., 141–80. Boston: Kluwer Academic.

Doeringer, Peter B., and Michael J. Piore. 1971. *Internal Labor Markets and Manpower Analysis.* Lexington, Mass.: D. C. Heath.

Domar, Evsey. 1966. "The Soviet Collective Farm as a Producer Cooperative." *American Economic Review* 56: 734–57.

Dow, Gregory K. 1993. "Why Capital Hires Labor: A Bargaining Perspective." *American Economic Review* 83 (March): 118–34.

Ellerman, David P. 1986. "Horizon Problems and Property Rights in Labor-Managed Firms." *Journal of Comparative Economics* 10: 62–78.

Epstein, Richard A. 1985. "Agency Costs, Employment Contracts, and Labor Unions." In *Principals and Agents: The Structure of Business*, edited by John W. Pratt and Richard Zeckhauser, 127–48. Harvard Business School Press.

Fama, Eugene F., and Michael C. Jensen. 1983. "Separation of Ownership and Control." *Journal of Law and Economics* 26 (June): 301–25.

Furubotn, Eirik G., and Svetozar Pejovich. 1974. "Property Rights and the Behavior of the Firm in a Socialist State: The Example of Yugoslavia." In *The Economics of Property Rights*, edited by Furubotn and Pejovich. Cambridge, Mass.: Ballinger.

Grossman, Sanford J., and Oliver D. Hart. 1986. "The Costs and Benefits of Ownership: A Theory of Vertical and Lateral Integration." *Journal of Political Economy* 94 (August): 691–719.

Hansmann, Henry. 1988. "Ownership of the Firm." *Journal of Law, Economics, and Organization* 4 (Fall): 267–305.

———. 1996. *The Ownership of Enterprise*. Harvard University Press. Belknap Press.

Hart, Oliver. 1989. "An Economist's Perspective on the Theory of the Firm." *Columbia Law Review* 89: 1757–74.

Hart, Oliver, and John Moore. 1990. "Property Rights and the Nature of the Firm." *Journal of Political Economy* 98 (6): 1119–58.

Hashimoto, Masanori. 1981. "Firm-Specific Human Capital as a Shared Investment." *American Economic Review* 71 (June): 475–82

Holmstrom, Bengt. 1982. "Moral Hazard in Teams." *Bell Journal of Economics* 13 (Autumn): 324–40.

Holmstrom, Bengt, and Paul Milgrom. 1991. "Multi-Task Principal-Agent Analyses: Incentive Contracts, Asset Ownership, and Job Design." *Journal of Economics and Organization* 7 (Special Issue): 24–52.

———. 1994. "The Firm as an Incentive System." *American Economic Review* 84 (September): 972–91.

Jacobson, Louis S., Robert J. LaLonde, and Daniel G. Sullivan. 1993. "Earnings Losses of Displaced Workers." *American Economic Review* 83 (September): 685–709.

Jacoby, Sanford M. 1990. "The New Institutionalism: What Can It Learn from the Old?" *Industrial Relations* 29 (Spring): 316–59.

Jensen, Michael C., and William H. Meckling. 1976. "Theory of the Firm: Managerial Behavior, Agency Costs and Ownership Structure." *Journal of Financial Economics* 3 (October): 305–60.

———. 1979. "Rights and Production Functions: An Application to Labor-Managed Firms and Codetermination." *Journal of Business* 52 (October): 469–506.

Katz, Lawrence F., and Lawrence H. Summers. 1989. "Industry Rents: Evidence and Implications." *Brookings Papers on Economic Activity: Microeconomics*, 209–75.

Klein, Benjamin, Robert A. Crawford, and Armen A. Alchian. 1978. "Vertical Integration, Appropriable Rents, and the Competitive Contracting Process." *Journal of Law and Economics* 21 (October): 297–326.

Koike, Kazuo. 1990. "Intellectual Skill and the Role of Employees as Constituent Members of Large Firms in Contemporary Japan." In *The Firm as a Nexus of Treaties,* edited by Masahiko Aoki, Bo Gustafsson, and Oliver E. Williamson, 185–208. Newbury Park, Calif.: Sage Publications.

Kreps, David M. 1990. "Corporate Culture and Economic Theory." In *Perspectives on Positive Political Economy,* edited by James E. Alt and Kenneth A. Shepsle, 90–143. Cambridge University Press.

———. 1996. "Markets and Hierarchies and (Mathematical) Economic Theory." *Industries and Corporate Change* 5(2): 561–95.

Krueger, Alan B., and Lawrence H. Summers. 1988. "Efficiency Wages and Inter-Industry Wages Structure." *Econometrica* 56 (March): 259–93.

Masten, Scott E., James W. Meehan, and Edward A. Snyder. 1989. "Vertical Integration in the U.S. Auto Industry: A Note on the Influence of Transaction Specific Assets." *Journal of Economic Behavior and Organization* 12 (October): 265–73.

Meade, J. E. 1972. "The Theory of Labor-Managed Firms and of Profit Sharing." *Economic Journal* 82 (March supplement): 402–28.

Milgrom, Paul, and John Roberts. 1992. *Economics, Organization and Management.* Englewood Cliffs, N.J.: Prentice-Hall.

Monteverde, Kirk, and David J. Teece. 1982a. "Supplier Switching Costs and Vertical Integration in the Automobile Industry." *Bell Journal of Economics* 13 (Spring): 206–13.

———. 1982b. "Appropriable Rents and Quasi-Vertical Integration." *Journal of Law and Economics* 25 (October): 321–28.

Nelson, Richard R., and Sidney G. Winter. 1982. *An Evolutionary Theory of Economic Change.* Harvard University Press (Belknap).

Prendergast, Canice. 1993. "The Role of Promotion in Inducing Specific Human Capital Acquisition." *Quarterly Journal of Economics* 108 (May): 523–34.

Putterman, Louis. 1984. "On Some Recent Explanations of Why Capital Hires Labor." *Economic Inquiry* 22 (April): 171–87.

Putterman, Louis, and Randall S. Kroszner. 1996. "The Economic Nature of the Firm: A New Introduction." In *The Economic Nature of the Firm: A Reader,* 2d ed., edited by Putterman and Kroszner, 1–31. Cambridge University Press.

Rajan, Raghuram G., and Luigi Zingales. 1996. "Power in a Theory of the Firm." Working Paper.

Romano, Roberta. 1996. "Corporate Law and Corporate Governance." Paper prepared for Conference on Firms, Markets and Organizations, University of California at Berkeley, Haas School of Business.

Rosen, Sherwin. 1985. "Implicit Contracts: A Survey." *Journal of Economic Literature* 23 (September): 1144–75.

Shleifer, Andrei, and Lawrence H. Summers. 1988. "Breach of Trust in Hostile Takeovers." In *Corporate Takeovers: Causes and Consequences,* edited by Alan J. Auerbach, 33–56. University of Chicago Press.

Topel, Robert C. 1990. "Specific Capital and Unemployment: Measuring the Costs and Consequences of Job Loss." In *Studies in Labor Economics in Honor of Walter Y. Oi,* edited by Allan H. Meltzer and Charles I. Ploser, 181–214. Amsterdam: North Holland.

———. 1991. "Specific Capital, Mobility, and Wages: Wages Rise with Job Security." *Journal of Political Economy* 99 (February): 145–76.

Vanek, Jaroslav. 1970. *The General Theory of Labor-Managed Market Economies.* Cornell University Press.

———. 1977. "The Basic Theory of Financing of Participatory Firms." In *The Labor-Managed Economy: Essays by Jaroslav Vanek,* edited by Vanek, 186–98. Cornell University Press.

Ward, Benjamin. 1958. "The Firm in Illyria: Market Syndicalism." *American Economic Review* 48: 566–89.

Weiss, Andrew. 1990. *Efficiency Wages: Models of Unemployment, Layoffs, and Wage Dispersion.* Princeton University Press.

Wiggins, Steven N. 1991. "The Economics of the Firm and Contracts: A Selective Survey." *Journal of Institutional and Theoretical Economics* 147 (December): 603–61.

Williamson, Oliver E. 1975. *Markets and Hierarchies: Analysis and Antitrust Implications.* New York: Free Press.

———. 1985. *The Economic Institutions of Capitalism: Firms, Markets, Relational Contracting.* New York: Free Press.

Williamson, Oliver E., and Janet Bercovitz. 1996. "The Modern Corporation as an Efficiency Instrument: The Comparative Contracting Perspective." In *The American Corporation Today,* edited by Carl Kaysen. Oxford University Press.

Williamson, Oliver E., Michael L. Wachter, and Jeffrey E. Harris. 1975. "Understanding the Employment Relation: The Analysis of Idiosyncratic Exchange." *Bell Journal of Economics* 6 (Spring): 250–80.

Wolfstetter, Elmar, Murray Brown, and Georg Meran. 1984. "Optimal Employment and Risk Sharing in Illyria: The Labor Managed Firm Reconsidered." *Journal of Institutional and Theoretical Economics* 140: 655–68.

3

Workers and Corporate Governance: The Role of Political Culture

DAVID CHARNY

The relation of workers to corporate governance generally has been analyzed by considering firms in which workers have exclusive or predominant managerial power, or in the extreme case, firms that workers own directly. Here, I take a different approach. My goal is to explore the relationship between worker influence and structures of corporate governance in firms where workers are one of several constituencies that exert managerial power. Clearly, this is a far more pervasive structure than worker predominance or outright ownership. Moreover, there are important links between the structures by which workers exert managerial power and the general system of corporate governance.

Of particular interest here is the diversity, across industrial economies, of the regimes that govern workers' exercise of managerial power. I distinguish three stylized types: "hard," "soft," and "no-participation" regimes. "Hard" regimes rest on a foundation

This paper was written during my 1995–96 term as Olin Fellow, Columbia Law School, and presented at the Columbia Law School conference on employees and corporate governance. I am grateful to the Olin Program at Columbia Law School and the Sloan Foundation for financial support, and to Columbia Law School for its hospitality.

91

of legally mandated and regulated mechanisms for worker participation in corporate governance. The paradigm case is Germany. "Soft" regimes work through mechanisms that are not explicitly mandated by the legal order (nor by legally enforceable contracts); the law neither spells out explicitly what the mechanisms should look like nor enforces whatever background understandings do exist. The paradigm case is Japan. Both "hard" and "soft" regimes differ again from regimes in which mechanisms for participation are exceptional among firms, or at least, in which there is no standard model for participation. The United States, among industrialized countries, is most representative of these "no-participation" regimes.

These regimes represent three different solutions to a set of problems common to firms in each economy. If corporate governance structures that give managerial power to workers are to contribute to the value of the firm, they must provide ways for workers to resolve conflicts of interest among themselves, and for workers and managers to make credible commitments to each other. Each alternative—hard, soft, or no participation—appears to satisfy the institutional requirements for conflict resolution and credible commitment. Furthermore, each adapts effectively to changes in industrial and economic conditions. In particular, I analyze how the alternative structures for participation in governance have responded to recent transformations of work organization ("new production methods") and of welfare-state entitlements. Unlike many recent commentators, I doubt that the disparate corporate governance systems will converge rapidly, as each offers a set of counterbalancing advantages and disadvantages specific to the social systems in which they are embedded. I suggest, however, that, in current economic circumstances, "soft" worker-managerialist systems will tend to degenerate (or progress?) toward a no-participation regime.

In any comparison of how these three regime types operate, a notion of "culture" must play a crucial role. For the analysis here, "culture" refers to the influence of shared beliefs and of social norms on the conduct of the firm's participants. The point is to provide an explanatory model richer than could be built from an austere rational-actor interpretation of participants' conduct, but without falling into merely ad hoc explanations. In particular, cultural influences within the firm—embodied in or mediated through the structures of corporate governance—can induce firm participants to cooperate in situations where it might not appear individually rational for each of them to do so; meanwhile, the background political culture influences firm participants indirectly, by establishing social welfare entitlements that affect governance at the firm.

The Analytic Problem: Can Workers
Exercise Managerial Power Effectively?

The simplest and most familiar models of the large investor-owned firm, in which shareholders hire managers to be their agents, leave no room for employees to exercise managerial power. In these models, managers are responsible solely to shareholders. Managers deal with workers either by drawing up explicit contracts that specify workers' tasks and compensation or by retaining discretion to tell workers what to do. The influence of these conceptions is seen, for example, in the tendency, at least among American analysts, to separate corporate governance—and particularly corporate law—from the structure of labor relations. This remains clearly reflected in the curricular structure and the divisions of academic labor in most law schools. Corporate governance—with management viewed as representatives of residual claimant interests of investors or of managers' interests themselves—is defined independently of the range of possible relations to workers. The typical assumption is that, whatever the management structure, the firm's actions in relation to workers will be largely the same.[1]

Within this framework, workers can exercise managerial power only by owning the firm, or by inducing owners to appoint workers' representatives as managers. The literature has focused on worker-owned firms, as it would be unlikely—within this framework—for owners to hire, as managers, workers who have interests directly contrary to those of the owners. But worker ownership itself proves equally anomalous in the conventional framework. From the perspective of the manager- and shareholder-dominated firm of the industrialized American economy, these worker-owned and managed firms appear as mutants, strange variations of the familiar species of the large industrial firm. They stride across the vast industrial veldt as occasional exotica, or thrive in their own, idiosyncratic economic niches. The literature often takes one on a sort of global tour, with stopovers at such diverse and picturesque locales as the plywood cooperatives of the Pacific Northwest, the refuse collectors of San Francisco, the Mondragon enterprises of the Basques, and the Israeli kibbutzim. On more familiar terrain, the literature emphasizes that, even within the advanced industrial economies, some economic niches seem to foster, or at least

---

1. An exception in the literature has been the recognition of links between industry structure and outcomes of union bargaining, particularly, the suggestion that firms sheltered from competition would buy labor peace by sharing monopoly gains with workers.

tolerate, flourishing worker- or producer-owned firms: professional firms such as investment banks, law practices, and advertising agencies; farm cooperatives; and economically troubled Fortune 500 companies that become subject to worker buyouts.

This literature is deeply interesting and raises important questions about the extent to which the more familiar forms of organization are the products of historical accident or cultural bias rather than the iron laws of efficiency or "survival of the fittest."[2] Even if one considers such examples to be deviants from a norm, the deviants can provide powerful insight into the norm. In this chapter, however, I take the somewhat different tack of exploring the interactions between corporate governance structures and worker influence on managerial decisionmaking in the "standard" model of the manufacturing firm. The focus here is on firms in which workers exert managerial power beyond the mere right to negotiate a contract, but in which the workers' power falls short of the predominant control exemplified by the worker-owned firm.

What are the mechanisms by which workers exert managerial power in these intermediate firms? Managerial power encompasses any exercise of influence over "strategic" decisions, such as those pertaining to investment, product and market scope, and basic industrial relations policy. As a subsidiary matter, the analysis includes mechanisms by which workers gain information about managerial decisions, as information sharing is an important function of worker participation mechanisms and can greatly influence the outcomes of bargains between workers and the firm.

Workers can exercise managerial power in three fora. First, workers may appoint representatives to the organs that corporate law formally recognizes as the seat of managerial power; for example, board representation may be obtained as a result of share ownership, by legislative mandates, or under the terms of a collective bargaining agreement. Second, power may be exerted at the shop or plant level, through workers' councils and worker problem-solving groups (such as "quality circles"). To some extent, decisions at lower levels cumulatively define a corporate strategy. Third, workers exert influence on strategic management decisions through contract negotiations: for example, through the provisions in a collective bargaining agreement that covers levels of investment or the amount of side-contracting or outsourcing.

---

2. See, in particular, the series of papers by Louis Putterman, including chapter 1 coauthored with Gregory Dow in this volume.

Several developments have impelled firms toward greater employee involvement in managerial decisions. One source of this new-found power comes through the traditional channel of corporate influence: share ownership, either by workers or unions directly, usually through the mechanisms of employee stock ownership plans (ESOPs) or by worker-controlled pension funds holding a portfolio of stock. At some firms, such share ownership (or influence) is explicitly tied to the workers' willingness to accede to demands for cuts in job security, wages, or benefits. At other firms, employee involvement in management is an outgrowth of the general movement toward active monitoring by financial intermediaries, among which pension funds loom large. The combination of ESOPs, some well-publicized worker buyouts, and the growing energies of unions and pension funds in seeking board influence all seem to indicate that some change is afoot, although no systematic patterns have developed as yet.

More important, workers' influence on management is strengthened by the specific expertise that innovations in production methods and technology give to shop-floor workers, and the firm's dependence on the level of effort of individual workers. These new production methods are generally taken to require a new model of employees' relation to the firm, in which teams of workers on the "shop floor"—which may now be a laboratory, client service center, or financial back office—make managerial decisions by directly solving problems as they arise, sometimes in collaboration with other teams in different parts of the firm or at other firms. This change also offers a reason why the idea of having workers participate in governance may be appealing: they have an intimate knowledge of production conditions and long-term ties to (and hence economic interest in) the firm.

In the face of these forces, however, at least three factors are taken to counsel decisively against substantial managerial power for workers.[3] First, workers may gain little benefit from participating in management: workers are thought to be in a position to protect their basic interests through expressly bargained agreements on wages, hours, benefits, and so forth, supplemented with the myriad default and mandatory background rules supplied by common, statutory, and constitutional law. Second, having workers exercise managerial power may incur high costs because of severe conflicts of interest among workers and between workers and other firm participants. Depending on their particular tasks at the firm, and their labor market options, workers will have a diverse array of interests; while shareholders—for whom managerial power is most commonly exercised—are

3. See, for example, Hansmann (1988, 1990); Williamson (1994).

generally homogeneous, with a single-minded interest in maximizing equity share value. Third, shareholders are rather poorly situated to protect their interests through contractual devices. If these constituencies were to contract, leaving workers with managerial power, workers would face powerful temptations to divert funds to themselves at the expense of value-maximizing corporate policies.

Because worker participation has the potential advantages noted above, however, it is useful to look for ways to address these three problems. The one of particular concern here is conflict of interest. Although there is doubtless a potential for conflicts of interest between subgroups of workers, and between workers and other groups, numerous governance devices are available to temper these conflicts. The structure of employee participation in management may have the important indirect (perhaps unintended) effect of serving as a mechanism for resolving such conflicts. However, we lack a well-developed analytic framework for considering when and why the partial integration of workers into managerial decisionmaking can be effective; and how such integration would be embodied in particular institutions of corporate governance. The next section develops the foundations for such a framework.

A Game-Theoretic Schema for Employees' Exercise of Managerial Power

Corporate governance structures that facilitate worker participation in managerial decisionmaking play several roles. They provide a point of entry for worker involvement in strategic management decisions. They provide a set of mechanisms by which workers or firms may coordinate workers' input so that they reach decisions that are rational for workers as a group. They may also foster workers' psychological commitment to the firm or make workers more willing to respond to managerial demands. Whichever of these goals are sought, the problem for the firm as a polity is to construct mechanisms for worker participation in the firm's strategic decisions that yield rationally acceptable results for firm participants. That is, the mechanisms must increase the value created by the firm as a whole, rather than merely generate gains for a dominant subgroup at the expense of firm value. There are two aspects to the problem: first, the interactions among workers when workers exercise managerial power; second, the interactions between workers and management.

The Problem of Coordination among Workers

Stipulate that workers have power or influence over strategic decisions of the firm, such as level of investment. For now, the exact form of influence—direct voting, election of directors, bargaining power in the negotiation of individual contracts or collective bargaining agreements, threats to breach "implicit" or gift contracts for effort or human capital investment—is unimportant. Subgroups of workers then can use their strategic power in one of two ways. The first involves diverting resources to the direct consumption benefit of the members of the group. I call this the "grab" strategy. For example, the subgroup might increase wages and benefits for itself, or give itself perks or workplace amenities, or protect its jobs in any technology-related layoff, even if it would be efficient to eliminate those jobs. Grab behavior could also stem from envy, lust for power, or a desire to "keep up with the Joneses." Alternatively, the subgroup might use its influence, not to grab benefits for itself, but to push for a cooperative strategy that would enhance the interests of workers as a group by enhancing total firm value.

The problem is pervasive, but it is particularly salient during periods of economic transformation. Suppose, for example, that a firm is considering whether to invest in a new production technology that involves a new disposition of assets and a new allocation of labor. The move to the new technology benefits workers as a group but requires cooperation among them, in the sense that all workers must, say, learn new skills, agree to make an effort in reassigned positions, or cope with unfamiliar equipment. In short, current workers are required to make a human capital investment. At the same time, workers have a partial "veto" or obstructive power over the transition, which they may use to attempt to hold up the firm for some amount of the benefits from the transition to the new production technology. But if workers attempt to hold up the firm to increase their claim on the pie, the transition may not go forward, and the workers may lose the advantage of the investment in new technologies.

The worker buyout provides another recurrent example. Characteristically, in this transaction, the firm's difficulties can be alleviated by a substantial infusion of investment. If each subgroup can invest (in the form of a wage and pension giveback to the firm), the firm can be restored to prosperity and employee jobs and pension funds salvaged. If subgroups start grabbing, however, the firm will soon cease to be a viable entity for lack of sufficient investment capital, and workers will lose their jobs and unfunded pension benefits.[4]

For analysis, one can begin with the case in which each subgroup would prefer the cooperative strategic outcome, which can only be achieved if all subgroups cooperate to achieve it. The worker subgroups then find themselves in a familiar prisoner's dilemma. All subgroups would prefer to commit themselves to the cooperative strategy, but each subgroup will prefer to pursue the "grab" strategy if at least one other subgroup prefers that strategy. Unless the subgroups can coordinate or commit themselves separately to the cooperative strategy, they will choose the less desirable "grab" strategy. Indeed, even the fear of such an outcome occurring may serve to deter them from proposing otherwise desirable investments.[5]

What prevents workers from committing to the collectively maximizing strategy? Familiar contracting and coordination problems may bar the optimal outcome. In a unionized firm in which each of several subgroups is represented by a different union, for example, the commitment would require a long-term agreement among the different unions to pursue the investment strategy. (The strategy would involve repeated investment and compensation decisions over a long period.) But because the collective bargaining agreement lasts for only a short period of time, the unions cannot recommit by simultaneously bargaining with the firm; and it is uncertain whether a contract between unions would be enforceable. More fundamentally, it would be difficult—either in a collective bargaining agreement or in a side contract among unions—to draft a set of legally enforceable terms that would cover the variety of future contingencies that may affect the optimal investment strategy and would still be sufficiently definite to be enforceable at law.

Of course, one might try to convert all workers into a single union or a single governance structure. Although this maneuver would import the problem into a unitary organization, it would not eliminate it. As a series of votes are held over time to determine this union's bargaining strategy, coalitions of subgroups might unite to seize power and pursue their own "grab" strategy, at the expense of the minority not included in the power-seizing coalition. Workers who vote for the collective-maximization strategy must also be confident that leaders will in fact pursue that strategy and withstand various interstitial pressures. Finally, since no single worker's vote

4. The situation is analogous to the "grab" that occurs among creditors when firms are close to insolvency (Jackson, 1986).

5. See, for example, Elhanan and Dekel (1992). For a model along these lines where future investment is deterred, see Rajan and Zingales (1998).

is likely to swing the union election, the familiar collective action problems may arise: that is, many workers will not find it worthwhile to become informed on the issues. In short, the unitary union or worker governance organization is no easy pathway to the collective-maximization strategy.

The payoffs that subgroups face for the choice between "grab" and collectively maximizing strategies will not always create a simple prisoner's dilemma. The irony of workers' coordination problems is that the possibility of coordination cuts several ways. Coordination may help workers agree upon a collective-maximization strategy, or it may empower a subgroup of workers to "grab," or it may allow workers to act together to block the adoption of new production methods. Conversely, the inability to coordinate may prevent grabbing or may block implementation of productive improvements, but it may also sometimes facilitate productive improvements. Consider the case of workers who can coordinate their behavior to resist a certain new production method, perhaps because it makes cognitive demands, or because of the enhanced responsibility it imposes, or because it threatens some sense of autonomy or privacy. But if workers cannot cooperate and each one fears being left behind as others learn the new production methods, then the lack of cooperation may encourage the rapid adaptation to the new method.

Coordination may also prove difficult if there are several alternative collectively maximizing strategies. Because all groups must choose a common strategy, some coordination mechanism is needed. Nonunionist American firms have no obvious institutional mechanism for identifying a common worker strategy; in other systems, unions or works councils may serve this function.

Cooperation between Workers and Management

The basic "game" here is played between management—representing variously the interests of investors and its own interests—and workers below the top management. The problem of trustful cooperation arises whenever management and labor must take joint or sequential steps that make them vulnerable to the possibility that the other party will take a noncooperative action in the next period (and when the other party's future actions cannot be secured by legally enforceable contract). Perhaps the most recurrent form of the problem in the present economy is the economically troubled firm: workers must take pay cuts or agree to increased effort to keep the company afloat, but they will do so only if they can trust management to use their efforts to increase total firm value, not to enrich management and shareholders. Correspondingly, investors will continue to fund the firm only if they believe that they can trust workers to make increased efforts and to remain loyal to the firm despite pay cuts.[6]

Both sides face a problem of trust. Management and workers must be able to commit themselves to the firm-welfare-maximizing strategy (rather than a "grab" strategy). Generally, the cooperative outcome requires that each group be willing to share information with the other and to honor their commitments to implement changes in the workplace. Although some of this conduct—particularly, disclosure by management—can be enforced by contract or background regulation, it is clearly impossible to obtain a consummate degree of cooperation by relying primarily on legal mechanisms.

The Role of Political Culture

How can these conflicts of interest among subgroups of workers and between workers and management be resolved? What I shall call the "political culture" of the firm—with direct implications for corporate governance—plays a crucial role here. Here, the term "political culture" is taken to mean the beliefs that participants in the firm share about the firm's governance and the norms that influence their behavior at the firm. Shared beliefs, in particular, may include notions about physical and social causation, or what consequences will follow upon any given action. These beliefs will affect the conduct of individuals whenever their actions are based in part on expectations about how others will act. Furthermore, culture includes an array of social norms: standards of conduct that individuals follow, even if doing so is sometimes unpleasant or costly for them, or leads to consequences they think undesirable. The rule of conduct in such cases is enforced by some nonlegal social sanction such as social disapproval, diminished reputation, internalized self-criticism or "guilt," or social systems of fines or penalties. (In particular, the force of norms may explain why perfectly rational individuals may act in ways that appear inconsistent with their direct self-interest.) The shared beliefs and norms at issue may be observed at many, if not most, firms in a particular economy; and they will often mesh in important ways with beliefs or norms pervasive in the culture

6. This dynamic is explored in detail in chapter 10 in this volume. Previous work that has identified a similar dynamic of mutual commitment in the role of unions in encouraging maximal worker commitment includes Barenberg (1993), and for a discussion of worker buyouts generally, see Hyde (1991).

at large. Consider, now, the ways in which shared beliefs and norms facilitate cooperation among firm participants even in situations where a more austere "rational actor" model of participants' conduct would predict defection.[7] Three elements of the background culture will be especially important in the labor governance contexts for achieving equilibrium in the games among workers and managers: focal points, deliberative procedures, and sanctions for defection.

A focal point is a seemingly arbitrary reference point established by convention or history and used by groups to resolve cooperation problems. Focal points may give rise to strategies that workers will follow presumptively, even unreflectively: these might consist of unarticulated conceptions built into the traditions or ideology of a workers' movement. Focal points may also suggest mechanisms for resolving conflicts when a variety of strategies are available and each is advantageous to the group.

The traditions and ideologies of workers' movements provide a rich body of effective focal points. As one example, the Italian labor movement has a long-standing commitment to exploring alternative methods of organizing the details of work—a program of thought that some have traced at least back to Gramsci and his contemporaries. Guided by this tradition, dispersed workers and small groups decided to invest in reforming workplace structures in the 1970s and 1980s. Their approach stands in sharp contrast to the gradual attenuation of these concerns in the United States, where labor has moved toward the type of postwar settlement reached by the American Federation of Labor and Congress of Industrial Organizations (AFL-CIO). Focal points may also lead groups to choose a particular mechanism to resolve conflicts when their choice of strategies are all advantageous to them. Of course, focal points may also impede cooperation rather than foster it. For example, they may define subgroups that differ sharply with each other, as in the conflicts over jurisdiction among German craft groups.[8]

Deliberative procedures are institutionalized procedures for the exchange of views, which can lead to a cooperative solution to be enforced by legal or social sanctions, or the formulation of focal points. As an example, com-

7. Important presentations of the influence of cognition and norms on rational behavior include Sunstein (1996) and Jolls (1998). For work on norms, see, for example, Charny (1990, 1996). For applications of these ideas to resolving decisionmaking conflicts in the firm, see Kreps (1992); Greif (1994). Ferejohn (1991) presents a methodological statement of the relation between culture and rational choice very close to the approach here, although his topic is rather distant from our present concerns.

8. See Kern and Sabel (1994).

pare the ways in which the German and American auto industries adapted
to new production methods.[9] When German auto workers undertook a
much-needed drastic reform of the traditional production line, they carried
out their deliberations through a complex set of intermediary institutions.
At some plants, the works councils provided a forum for discussing how to
implement new production methods in ways that minimized transition
costs while fairly allocating the burdens of job dislocation and new training.
At other plants, the plant union—sometimes speaking through works
council representatives, at other times operating independently—took the
primary role. These unions could look for intellectual and material support
from a national union movement that, among its other tasks, could conduct
extensive analyses of modes of industrial adaptation. All of this enabled
workers to play a proactive cooperative role in the adoption of new methods
of production on the shop floor, particularly by sharing information about
production processes with management, and by fairly allocating among
workers the burdens of job dislocation and retraining. In contrast, American
auto manufacturers had long resisted any form of worker involvement in
discussions of long-term investment or technology strategies, while, at the
shop-floor level, the unions focused directly on wage, benefit, and discharge
issues, rather than on issues related to the quality of work or productive
efficiency. The natural result of these narrowly channeled interests was a
greater variety of "grab" rather than maximizing behavior when faced with
the need for new production methods. Only recently, after having learned
the lessons of failed adaptation in the 1970s and early 1980s, have the
United Auto Workers and auto company managers moved toward a more
cooperative model of decisionmaking.

Sanctions for defection are a third element in the firm's culture that may
promote cooperation among firm participants. Effective sanctions are particularly important when it only makes sense to follow the collectively maximizing strategy if everyone else does so as well: the mere announcement
of a focal point will not suffice to achieve cooperation if the payoffs for a
"grab" strategy create a prisoner's dilemma. In this case, there must be some
means of punishing those subgroups that "grab" for their group rather
than pursue the collective welfare-maximizing strategy. Effective policing of
defection stabilizes the norm.

Consider the cultural norm under which pension funds in the United
States had abstained from monitoring—or at least, had not interfered with
the decisions of—the managers of the companies in the fund.[10] The fund

9. See, for example, Turner (1992); Womack, Jones, and Roos (1990).
10. For a discussion of the affirmative pressures against monitoring, see Roe (1994).

managers might gain from monitoring in those situations where it can increase the value of their fund; remember that when a company has a defined benefit plan, the employer-company garners any upside return to its pension fund over what it needs to pay its defined obligations to employee-beneficiaries. But fund managers are controlled by (indeed, are often employees of) the employer-companies whose funds they manage; and the managers of the employer-companies wish to avoid being monitored themselves. Here is where sanctioning mechanisms become important. The company managers are vulnerable to tit-for-tat retaliation: if they permit their fund managers to agitate against managers of other companies, then these companies may permit their funds to act against them. Social pressures among senior managers may also militate against close monitoring by pension funds.

In the context of labor influence on governance, similar sanctions have sustained beneficent as well as harmful forms of cooperation. The English and Swedish union movements and labor relations are a case in point. The English labor movement, on the one hand, has been described as a "sect" because its ideology reflects a high degree of individualism and voluntarism. Group cohesiveness comes from a set of strong sectarian commitments that generate a high degree of subgroup factionalism within the organization, and considerable hostility to outsiders, particularly corporate managers.[11] This is a recipe for subgroup "grab" behavior. Not surprisingly, under this regime the extent of adaptation to new production methods and of labor integration into managerial decisions had been lower in England than in the other industrialized nations. In contrast, Sweden emphasizes cooperation among its unions and integration of the unions into a single large-scale labor organization. This approach suppresses subgroup grab behavior and fosters cooperation with management and government. As discussed shortly, this strong corporatism in public policy facilitates cooperative bargaining at the firm and industry level, while the cooperative structures that emerge from such successful micro bargaining in turn strengthen the organizations that are needed for effective corporatism at the level of national policy.[12]

However, even apparently well-functioning coordination and sanctioning mechanisms among labor subgroups may break down. In Sweden, this happy set of corporatist synergies, particularly the economy-wide "solidaristic bargaining," is under threat now that substantial portions of the

---

11. Douglas (1989).

12. For discussions of the threat to Swedish-style industrial cooperation, see Kjellberg (1998); Mahon (1991).

system are being dismembered. Financial pressures at Swedish auto firms led various unions to adopt what might be characterized as a grab strategy: they sought to protect their own jobs and levels of benefits at the older plants, rather than permit investment to be channeled into more innovative operations, which might well have been more beneficial for workers as a group in the long run.[13]

Systems of Corporate Governance

Stipulate, then, that workers' exercise of managerial power requires institutions to help identify focal points, provide opportunities for deliberation, and punish potential defectors. How are these concerns to be integrated into the analysis of corporate governance systems?

Consider the structure of worker participation in strategic decision-making in Germany, Japan, and the United States. These three examples show how different structures of corporate governance work in tandem with different structures of labor relations. They also illustrate the close link between industrial relations and corporate governance, especially the importance of political cultures in sustaining various equilibria.

The German model represents legally formalized worker managerialism: the "hard" forms of worker participation in governance.[14] The workers exert managerial power through a set of institutions established by legal mandate: the law specifies their form and provides for the enforcement of the obligations that define the particular roles of workers and managers in that form. This is not to say that the form of worker participation is always mandatory; for example, German workers may choose not to have works councils, but once workers request them, they must be provided as stipulated by law. By contrast, the Japanese system embodies informal worker managerialism, or "soft" forms of worker participation in governance. In this case, a set of conventions provides avenues for worker participation, but these are not formalized by law and are not legally enforceable. The third stylized type, which I refer to as the American model (although, of course, American firms fall on a broad spectrum), provides neither formal nor informal institutional mechanisms for worker participation. This type adheres to the classical model that separates managerial power and workplace relations.

13. See Hancke (1993).
14. I borrow this term from Wolfgang Streeck (1995).

These three systems are not the only ones, of course. In Sweden, for instance, institutions providing for managerial power are formalized by law, but this is done through enforceable legal contracts between unions and firms. In other settings, such as Italy, workers have comparable institutions, such as works councils, but until recently they operated through nonlegal pressures and in less formalized regimes. Nevertheless, the labor relations and corporate governance structures in Germany, Japan, and the United States create a useful framework for discussion.

Germany: A Formalized System for Participation

The German model, as it has functioned during most of the post–World War II period, provides the basis for labor participation in managerial decisionmaking at three levels. Contracts regarding terms of compensation are negotiated industry-wide, with the social welfare state providing an important component of background compensation (the "social wage") in the form of welfare entitlement. At firms, workers' councils (abetted by relatively powerful unions) deal with plant-level enforcement of contract and legal rights and at least temper the exercise of managerial power in implementing investment decisions and determining production methods. At the top, codetermination enables the worker to have input at the high managerial level through representation on the supervisory board, and perhaps even more important, it provides access to information about managerial decisions.

Several features of Germany's tripartite system are crucial to its effective overall functioning, particularly to the resolution of various corporate conflicts of interest. Most obviously, the legal mandates behind the system, combined with the strength of unions, help ensure that management will remain committed to cooperative participation. The forum for deliberation at the plant level provides opportunities for workers and management and for subgroups of workers to exchange information and reach consensus. Worker representatives on the board—most often chosen from the members of workers' councils—supplement the strategic and managerial information available to workers as a result of their participation at the plant level.

Of course, the system does not always work smoothly. At times, German boards conduct deliberations to keep preliminary information from workers or hold meetings to reach a managerial consensus on an issue before it reaches the supervisory board, where workers' representatives can voice their views on it.[15] Furthermore, workers may be a minority on the supervisory board. Yet the German system has successfully divided the responsibility for different aspects of the workplace regime: board representation provides workers with a means of gathering information and communicating their views to the board; sector and public (legislative) bargaining resolves basic compensation issues; and councils can deal with plant-level issues of enforcement and work structure. This arrangement simplifies the agenda of issues before workers at each forum and makes it easier to arrive at a consensus. The lowest and highest rungs of the system are where workers' representatives focus on the interests of workers as a group and address issues that are unlikely to cause much conflict among subgroups. The center is where the most contentious issues are resolved—such as conflicts over the division of surplus—through forums in which each subgroup can act separately.

Japan: Participation under a Legally Informal Regime

The Japanese labor relations system, like the German system, enables workers to participate in strategic decisionmaking both at the shop floor and at the pinnacles of corporate management, but it does so largely through informal, nonlegal mechanisms.[16] Japanese industrial production methods—with their emphasis on flexible work teams, job rotation, and problem solving and resource allocation at the shop floor level—inherently require workers to make strategic decisions as part of the ongoing production process. However, labor had little presence at the higher levels of the managerial hierarchy until the economic crises of the 1970s and 1980s, when the unions insisted on having a say in the successive restructurings precipitated by the oil shocks.

From the time of the post–World War II settlement in labor relations, Japanese workers appear to have exhibited group-maximizing rather than grab behavior when participating in management decisions. One institutional reason for this is Japan's enterprise unions, which represent workers

15. Witte (1978) suggests in his study of board decisionmaking that in cases where unions and management are equally represented on the supervisory board, with a tiebreaking vote to be cast by a shareholder representative, the main effect of labor representation is to give power to the tiebreaking voter. In firms in which labor representatives constitute only a third of the board, the strong social pressures for consensus decisionmaking—particularly the worker discontent that arises from a decision that sparks a dissenting vote from the labor representatives—gives the labor representatives a power disproportionate to their voting strength

16. The account in the text is influenced in particular by Gordon (1985); Taira and Levine (1985); Aoki (1988); Sabel (1994); Nakamura and Nitta (1995).

as a group, rather than as a particular craft or assembly-line subgroup, and which also accede to an ideology that emphasizes loyalty to the firm. In effect, the union moderates wage demands in exchange for an implicit commitment by the firm to share the benefits of long-term growth through lifetime employment and through gradual wage increases keyed to seniority and increasing company profitability. This understanding has survived even when economic crises have forced the firm into reinvestment, with corresponding cuts in wages and job transfers. Job rotation and flexible promotion and transfer ladders have addressed subgroup grab problems by smoothing out subgroup differences over time; each subgroup knows that "its turn will come."

Japan has achieved this high degree of cooperation despite the absence of direct, formalized representation on boards or other senior management governance structures, and despite highly antagonistic labor-management relations at times.[17] This outcome can be attributed to several features of the Japanese corporate governance system. To begin with, the board is relatively free from direct pressure from shareholders seeking to maximize profits and is instead loyal to a loose coalition of trading partners (*keiretsu* members), corporate affiliates, banks, and other creditors. The need to elicit high levels of worker cooperation from the well-informed teams ensures a degree of responsiveness to worker input. The fact that the Japanese managerial elite—including predominantly insider boards—will admit those who have risen through the corporate ranks means that at least some board members have personal connections and familiarity with labor interests. In sum, the structure of Japan's enterprise unions resolves the problem of collective action among subgroups, while the corporate governance system permits the union, as a collective action device, to have input in strategic decisions.

American Labor and Corporate Governance

By contrast, American unions tend to be fragmented and organized around sharply defined job slots and promotion ladders. This structure yields subgroups with specific and conflicting interests. Moreover, because bargaining

17. Gordon (1998) powerfully demonstrates that the apparently cooperative equilibrium in Japanese corporate governance emerged as the product of intense and sometimes violent contestation over the terms of labor-management relations. See also chapter 8 of this volume. Although the emergent modus vivendi rejected the unions' more radical claims for security and managerial participation, and perhaps has left Japanese workers less powerful than, say, their German counterparts, the Japanese corporation's ability to "absorb elements" (Gordon, p. 202) of the workers' program helped to produce the regime described here.

is organized by industrial sector rather than by firm, bargaining strategies are more oriented toward the subgroup than the firm.

This structure of corporate governance has played an important role in limiting worker involvement with strategic decisions. In part, the ideology of managerial autonomy—well captured by Adolf Berle and Gardiner Means—has discouraged initiatives that might have increased labor involvement at the expense of managerial autonomy. Some of the most vivid examples of such behavior can be found in the post–World War II auto industry, a key industry for setting the pattern of industrial relations in the United States. For example, the auto industry structured its own pension funds—and lobbied Congress for regulation of these funds—in ways that would prevent the unions from converting workers' investments into managerial influence.[18] In addition, management refused union proposals to link moderated pay increases with management's commitment to continuous reinvestment in productive and technological improvements: such a deal would have required management to make ongoing disclosures about investment and business strategy and threatened to give workers some direct input, not only into levels of investment, but also into the particular directions of business strategy.

The structure of U.S. corporate governance also generates resistance to cooperative solutions. The hostile takeover, for example, monitors management on behalf of shareholder interests and therefore enables shareholders to profit from breaches of implicit contracts: shareholders can replace the management that made the contract with a new management that is willing to reap the profits that can be made by reneging on it. Moreover, reliance on stock price information to measure corporate performance, if it indeed breeds the "short-term" orientation of managers that is deplored by many commentators, would also discourage the development of long-term cooperative implicit contracts between workers and managers.[19] The takeover mechanism and the market as the benchmark for performance imply that managers are often brought in from outside and will often be oriented toward finance rather than production. Furthermore, the new emphasis on monitoring by large financial institutions—which has attracted much attention in the corporate governance literature—may do

18. Roe (1994).

19. These phenomena provide the background for Jeffrey Gordon's (1985) analysis of the Paramount decision and related regulatory developments, which, by restricting takeovers and supporting implicit-contract-invoking justifications for takeover defenses, would counteract the tendency noted here.

little to promote worker participation in governance: the new monitors presumably remain focused on share value and so presumably retain the standard managerial mind-set with regard to the role of workers.

Thus corporate governance structures clearly influence the possible outcomes of the games between subgroups of workers, and between workers and managers. A conducive management structure can encourage cooperative actions by providing opportunities for deliberation and for putting restraints on "grabbing" behavior.

Synergies between Public Provision of Services and Cooperation at the Firm

The standard theory of contract default would suggest that public regulation of the employment relationship and privately negotiated contract terms are direct substitutes. After all, in either case, the total wage-compensation-benefit package of the firm is presumably determined over time by a labor market equilibrium. Of course, in the absence of publicly imposed terms, workers and firms bear the costs of negotiation; but these are likely to be very small for individual workers, whose contract terms are usually offered on a take-it-or-leave-it basis. Moreover, although the public provision of social welfare goods—such as medical care—frees up the bargaining energies of unions, who must no longer bargain for these benefits from firms, public provision can affect the labor market in complex ways. It is not obvious that workers are better off with publicly provided than with employer-provided benefits.

However, once one takes into account the impact of regulatory provisions on prospects for governance, differences between public and private provision emerge. A publicly set term affects the bargaining agenda at the firm level, that is, the items that the various groups are negotiating about. For example, mandatory public terms and generous public provision spare German unions the burden of bargaining about such matters as health insurance, severance pay, and access to strategic information. The primary impact of providing such benefits publicly is not to win higher total levels of overall compensation for workers than they would obtain without regulation. Instead, public regulation alters the agenda for workers. For example, when a country provides a basic social welfare entitlement such as health care, it relieves subgroups of workers of the need to protect their own claims in this respect against other subgroups that would seek to divert resources to themselves through contract terms on these issues. Of course, if the workers can supplement the mandatory provisions, they may still do so; but this does little to weaken the agenda-setting strength of the mandatory provision. The existence of the background terms may make credible the employers' refusal to grant further concessions on these issues. Furthermore, regulations (such as the Employment Retirement Income Security Act) may either directly prohibit supplementation of the mandated benefits or tax these extra benefits more heavily. Finally, workers may be satisfied with the mandatory terms. In a sense, the terms not only serve as a focal point, but affect worker preferences by giving them a standard for the "fair" term; workers would then be willing to abstain from engaging in "grab" strategies on these issues.

Thus the public provision of certain goods resolves issues that could otherwise be subject to "grab" strategies by worker subgroups and so makes it easier for workers to unite around a collective welfare-maximizing strategy. In the cases of Germany and Japan, the public provision of social welfare services functions in tandem with workers' influence on corporate governance and with an institutionalist rather than market-oriented managerial system to produce a governance mechanism distinct from that of the United States. The tripartite interaction of these features in particular changes the structure of deliberation among workers and between workers and managers.

Problems of Adaptation

Developed economies recently have confronted several closely linked problems of large-scale industrial adaptation: disinvestment from sectors with overcapacity, as has occurred in some basic industries and manufacturing; the development of growth areas such as biotechnology and information systems; adaptation to new methods of production that emphasize teamwork and shop-floor problem solving rather than the classical "Taylor-ist" mass production; and increases in the costs of social entitlements for workers and retirees. These factors have placed enormous stress on both the formal and informal versions of the systems giving workers a role in managerial decisionmaking. How well equipped are the systems that I have analyzed to respond to these pressures for adaptation?

A great deal depends on the nature of the workers' managerial powers. In Germany, firms have found it advantageous to avoid comprehensive industry-wide negotiations when attempting to reach basic settlements on wages and benefits. Yet localized schemes, especially for retraining and relocation, have their problems, too, because of regional and sectoral differences. These pressures overload the agendas of local unions and works councils, which find themselves embroiled in conflicts among subgroups of workers that used to be preempted by comprehensive agreements. At the top—the board level—adaptation is equally difficult because of a lack of detailed information about rapid changes in production. At the plant level, the plantwide structure of the works council and its formal procedures make it unresponsive to the changes required by local team production. In short, the institutions are beset by an overloaded agenda requiring comprehensive renegotiation of work arrangements in the face of rapid changes and insufficient information. These problems erode the stabilizing focal points that had assured dispersed and potentially conflicting workers of a fair resolution of their intragroup conflicts, they disrupt the accustomed forms of deliberation, and they may lead workers to believe that acting on their more immediate interests will outweigh gains from loyalty to the established settlement. The participatory regime begins to unravel.

Since the Japanese system is less formalized, it is more difficult to suggest a possible trajectory of disintegration. It may well begin with stress on the lifetime employment system. Companies in sectors that need to reduce employment may be tempted to withdraw the lifetime commitment. In turn, workers' commitment to the firm will erode; no longer seeing themselves the eventual beneficiary of increases in firm value, workers may rationally decide that the best strategy for them is to maximize individual or subgroup interests. Reduced cooperation, in turn, would raise firm costs and increase the pressure on management to use disciplinary devices that undermine the consensual basis of worker input into managerial decisions. Another scenario for the unraveling of Japan's system begins with the growth of alternative sources of investment capital that free at least the most successful firms from the hegemony of the *keiretsu*/main bank complex, and from the managerial constraints and cross-subsidizations that it imposes. For workers, the loosening of these constraints means that management will be freer to pursue profit-maximizing and management-protective strategies that used to be constrained by main bank monitoring and *keiretsu* management. Workers, in turn, then protect themselves by engaging in grab behavior.

From the perspective of the "worker-managerialist" systems of Germany and Japan, the American system has appeared to present an enviable responsiveness and flexibility. Yet the trade-offs are clear. On the one hand, the American system does not provide direct mechanisms for information exchange or deliberation that might promote cooperative firm-value-maximizing behavior. Faced with severe threats to their jobs, income levels, or entitlement, workers with economic power and the ability to coordinate would naturally resort to "grab" strategies. On the other hand, the American system atomizes subgroups and gives workers few levers with which to exert managerial influence. Consequently, workers find themselves cooperating with managerial dictates because not keeping up in this economy risks unemployment, or reemployment at a drastically reduced wage and status. Moreover, the inability of workers to coordinate on a grand scale may limit their power to resist new production technologies, or to make hold-up demands for the surplus from productivity gains. The lesson from America, then, is that worker "cooperation" in the sense of acquiring new skills or making new "firm-specific" investments may be induced without the protective participatory devices of either "hard" or "soft" worker managerialism. In fact, under conditions of rapid change in production, "hard" or "soft" worker managerialism may become a barrier to worker cooperation.

What, then, can one make of the adaptive potential of worker managerialism in the style of Germany and Japan? To begin with, the direction of evolution may not be toward a more efficient system. Current arrangements may fall apart if managers and workers "defect" from them: defection may result in an inefficient failure to coordinate, the classic phenomenon associated with "grab" behavior among firm participants.

The important question is how the transition to new forms of production and to sectoral adjustments is to be managed to avoid such inefficiencies. Here there seem to be two broad answers: to supplement the present mechanisms with new forms of coordination on the shop floor and among work teams, or to dismantle the current mechanisms altogether, replacing them with new ones or abandoning the worker-managerialist project for the American model. The analytic problems posed by this choice are acute, because the changes that would heighten the pressure for worker participation in managerial decisions—such as the move to new production methods—also have wide-ranging, but poorly understood, implications for corporate governance.[20] The new production methods weaken the credibility of the model of the board as monitor; for example, the board may not be able to get the information it needs about ongoing changes in production processes, because it cannot identify the pertinent benchmarks or the best-informed employees. Furthermore, collaboration between firms, as well as within them, will make it more difficult to specify what a firm is maximizing, while loyalties of subgroups will become diffuse and difficult to enforce. These changes translate directly into problems for the interpre-

20. See Sabel (1996).

tation of worker involvement in managerial decisions. It will be unclear what mechanisms workers should use to exercise whatever power they have, and unclear—if the basis of worker power is improved information flows or improved cooperation—what counts as information or cooperation in the new model of the firm.

However, it would be premature to declare that the spread of new production methods, the prosperity of new high-tech sectors, or the decline of the welfare state signal the demise of such coordination mechanisms as the German codetermination system, although it probably implies a change in institutional functions. The extant institutions may provide opportunities to pool information about the success of emergent new forms of collaboration, and to reach a consensus on how to allocate the costs and benefits of transition. In these circumstances, the "hard" worker-managerial model enjoys distinct advantages over its "soft" variant. The "hard" background legal regime supplies a type of constitutional order that sets the framework in which particular adaptations may proceed: it establishes fundamental procedures that can be relied on by all participants. In contrast, under a regime of "soft" worker-managerialism, it may never be clear to the participants which aspects of the system may survive new circumstances: in this situation of ignorance, participants are more likely to defect to protect themselves.

Of course, these "constitutional" features of a "hard" system may prove to be impediments to change, particularly if viewed in the short run. In this respect, however, it is important to recall the basic lesson of contemporary American constitutional theory: fixity of basic institutions is compatible with a large-scale rethinking of their purposes and roles. Indeed, that certain basic institutions are taken as fixed may facilitate adaptation, by providing the focal points around which deliberation takes place. The current period of large-scale economic adaptation may, then, prove to be a sort of constitutional moment for the hard worker-managerialist system. This is an opportunity to rethink institutional roles, which is all the easier to do when those roles are legally fixed than when they are instantiated only in more inchoate, inarticulate understandings supplied by background social norms.

Conclusion

Perhaps the best way to synthesize the analysis is to address four central questions about corporate governance: Do workers' managerialist institutions contribute to total firm value? Are these contributions traceable to individual components of these institutions, or are they "systemic"? What predicts whether such systems will emerge? What is the role of law in constituting these systems?

Do worker-managerialist institutions contribute to total firm value? The lessons here are equivocal. At times the involvement of employees in corporate governance helps employees as a group and enhances total value created by the firm, as when subgroups agree to sacrifice subgroup gains for collective benefits. At other times, cooperation diminishes value created by the firm and may harm employees as a group, as when subgroups of workers (such as entrenched crafts) cooperate to block innovation, or when pension fund managers coordinate to block managerial monitoring. There is also a trade-off between the value-enhancing advantages of worker coordination and the greater adaptability of an atomized work force acting in relation to a management relatively free from labor-imposed constraints. It may sometimes be that the more oblique means of assuring workers a "voice," such as the diverse and largely informal channels of influence that workers have at their disposal in the Japanese industrial firm, are actually more helpful in conveying the spirit of workers as a group, while more direct channels may sometimes devolve into a cacophony of self-interested claims. Yet the more oblique means may lack the deliberative structures and resources needed to adapt to new technologies and new economic circumstances. They may lack a crucial capacity for "self-reflectiveness," for the conscious, articulated consideration of needed changes.

Of course, worker participation in management might serve other values beyond the economic consequences of income for workers or profits for the firm, such as promoting worker self-fulfillment or autonomy, or redistributing wealth. Although I have generally set these issues aside in this discussion, it is worth noting that the framework here does cast light on the types of governance structures that should be employed to serve these other ends. For example, a governance mechanism that permits one worker subgroup to exploit another (by grab behavior) would seem objectionable, within various theories of autonomy or just distribution, as well as from an efficiency standpoint. Grab behavior may also disrupt a governance system that was desirable on normative grounds other than efficiency. Ultimately, it should be remembered that these other values—even if plausibly served by worker participation in managerial decisionmaking—are not absolute, and where they do conflict with the economic consequences that I have explored here, striking a balance would be appropriate.

Should devices for worker management be viewed as "systems"? The argument developed here suggests that it generally will be ineffectual or dangerous to import a single mechanism of worker participation without its complements. A mechanism for input or information gathering may be ineffectual if not supplemented by others that permit the formation of a consensus among workers. Alternatively, the mechanism may be dangerous if adopted in organizations in which some subgroups of workers are well enough organized to foster their own interests at the expense of other subgroups of workers or other firm participants. For example, board representation for workers will have little effect if no organized group of workers either can form consensus opinions to be expressed to management, or if there is no process for disseminating the information that a board representative obtains. Or board representation may even be harmful if a subgroup can use board representation to push its own interests or to grab for itself information that gives it a bargaining advantage over other workers.

However, the analysis here also cautions against the use of "complementarity" as a model for these systemic interactions, where complementarity is understood to mean the construction of a set whose elements are given a consistent partial order.[21] In the present context, the elements of the set would be particular devices for facilitating worker participation in corporate governance, and the partial order would reflect the fact that the presence of one device would enhance the effectiveness of some other devices as contributors to firm value. The problem is that a consistent order of this type may be impossible to construct. Devices to facilitate participation may increase or decrease firm value, depending on what other devices are present. At the level of firm outcomes, the analysis seems to point to a type of indifference theorem: the forms of worker participation in corporate governance, though phenomenologically important, will not appear as net factors in firm value (in the long run) because each form of cooperation may generate offsetting interactions.

What factors predict the emergence of effective systems for worker participation in management? One implication of the analysis is that effective systems are not "constructible" in any straightforward way. Institutions of corporate governance, such as large block ownership by outside investors, representation of financial institutions on boards, or compensation

---

21. For a discussion of the basic features of complementarity models, see Milgrom and Roberts (1994). However, it seems likely that applying such models in a corporate governance context would require a somewhat different structure.

incentives for senior managers, are readily modified by a set of contracts or even by a single transaction. In contrast, the conditions for effective worker action through corporate governance require a deeper set of social adjustments. Fostering worker-oriented governance may require not only changes in regulations, but also a set of affirmative institution-building (and culture-building) measures, what, in a related context, has been labeled "norm entrepreneurship."

Is there any long-run selection mechanism that would accomplish these adjustments: that would favor "good" but not "bad" cooperation, or that would sustain some cultural equilibria but not others? One approach is rooted in the vast and at times amorphous set of speculations about cultural preconditions to various organizational forms or to industrial development, of which Max Weber is the precursor and remains the most spectacular exemplar. In this literature, patterns of workplace cooperation in Japan and Germany, in contrast to those in the United States, are traced to the greater "collectivism" of German or Japanese culture. Generalizations of this sort are repeatedly falsified by historical developments. After all, it was not long ago that the "Confucianism" of Japanese and other East Asian cultures was cited as a perhaps insuperable obstacle to development, or that American "individualism" was cited as an equally insuperable obstacle to workplace innovations that are now widespread. Moreover, such generalizations generally encounter conceptual difficulties when they attempt to explain the causal link between broad cultural norms and industrial structures: as Ernest Gellner wryly observes, Weber's analysis of Protestantism would lead one to predict that the nations of Islam would be leaders in modern industrial development. Generally, this body of argument runs into trouble because different cultures often do have a capacity to accommodate common forms of economic organization. Ultimately, one suspects that virtually any set of cultural forms that has survived for a substantial period of time over a large population will either have sufficient resources to sustain basic features of industrial and postindustrial organization—such as forms of cooperation, the capacity to induce intensely disciplined work, and cognitive sophistication—or will be able to transform itself to sustain these features.

An obverse approach has cultural or ideological influences operating at the boundaries where self-interested conduct runs out. One might say that self-interest provides for "strong" interactions and commitments, ideology only for "weak" ones. This approach can work, particularly in areas such as the regulation of financial markets, where actors are presumptively acting for profit-seeking motives and where interests of particular groups are readily identifiable.[22] In the context of worker participation in governance, however, such a distinction between strong and weak forces becomes problematic. Workers' perception of interests will depend on the range of alternatives defined by current institutional structures and by currently competing ideologies. Consequently, public policies that alter these institutional structures—by, say, promoting "high trust" via powerful unions—can alter the perception of interests as well as norms of conduct. Public institutional mandates, particularly those that modify channels of deliberation among workers, would then play a critical role in defining workers' relevant interests and available strategic moves. In particular, what seems important is that some internal or external mechanism be in place to offset the exercise of power by any entrenched subgroup. This mechanism may be, say, a regional economic development association whose assistance helps innovative efforts within the workplace. Or the mechanism may simply be the enhanced "exit" threat that results from the greater sophistication that worker training brings. These mechanisms alter outcomes, not by directly modifying governance, but by changing the threat-points in the corporate governance game.

What is the role of law in constituting worker participation systems? Does it matter whether the mechanisms for worker participation are defined and enforced by law or by nonlegal understandings and sanctions? Generally, for well-informed transactors who can form binding contracts among themselves, the imposition of legal norms may reduce the costs of forming contracts that the parties would otherwise make, but these effects are of second-order importance. In particular, parties may be largely indifferent to whether their commitments are enforced by legal or nonlegal sanctions and may rely largely on nonlegal sanctions even when legal ones are in place.[23] All of this would seem to suggest that the decision to embody governance devices in legally enforceable form is of secondary importance.

Law has an important role to play, however, in settings where the parties are poorly informed or face barriers to transactional cooperation. In particular, apparently equivalent legal and nonlegal mechanisms may work

22. Roe (1994, pp. 26–49) sees populism's hostility to large financial agglomerations as a weak ideological force that might have molded the public opinion of those who did not consult their stronger financial interests in, for example, independence from monitoring by these institutions, or, alternatively, the opportunity to profit by forming and operating them.

23. The ready ability of sophisticated parties to contract around legal norms adverse to their interests, extended to the corporate setting, provides the impetus for Black's (1990) powerful and ingenious argument about the "triviality" of corporate law.

very differently in the face of new circumstances that the parties could not have anticipated in constructing their arrangements. As I argued earlier, the advantage of legally mandated institutions is that they serve as fixed reference points for exploring future possibilities, while (if properly structured) remaining open to deliberate revision of institutional roles.

The law also plays an important role by placing limits on the voluntary contract as the source of worker governance. Even when worker governance devices would enhance firm value, the firm may not adopt them for several reasons. First, worker governance may, while increasing firm value, also permit a larger share of surplus to be diverted to workers as a group, a consequence that shareholders or managers may wish to avoid.[24] Second, it may be difficult for the firm to commit itself to governance devices over long periods of time: contracts can be revised or breached, charter provisions amended. Third, and perhaps most important, the effectiveness of worker governance devices may depend on a highly reticulated set of supportive background institutions, including intermediate institutions such as unions and financial monitors, and public institutions for social welfare entitlements. Individual firms cannot create these; they are the products of political action.

References

Aoki, Masahiko. 1988. *Information, Incentives and Bargaining in the Japanese Economy.* Cambridge University Press.

Barenberg, Mark. 1993. "The Political Economy of the Wagner Act: Power, Symbol, and Workplace Cooperation." *Harvard Law Review* 106 (May): 1391–1496.

Ben-Porath, Elchanan, and Eddie Dekel. 1992. "Signaling Future Actions and the Potential for Sacrifice." *Journal of Economic Theory* 57 (June): 36–51.

Black, Bernard S. 1990. "Is Corporate Law Trivial? A Political and Economic Analysis." *Northwestern University Law Review* 84 (Winter): 542–97.

Charny, David. 1990. "Nonlegal Sanctions in Commercial Transactions." *Harvard Law Review* 104 (December): 373–467.

———. 1996. "Illusions of a Spontaneous Order: 'Norms' in Contractual Relationships." *University of Pennsylvania Law Review* 144 (May): 1841–58.

Douglas, Mary. 1992. "Institutions of the Third Kind: British and Swedish Labour Markets Compared." In *Risk and Blame: Essays in Cultural Theory,* edited by Mary Douglas, 167–86. New York: Routledge.

Ferejohn, John. 1991. "Rationality and Interpretation: Parliamentary Elections in Early Stuart England." In *The Economic Approach to Politics: A Critical Reassessment of the*

24. This problem, as to workers' councils, is modeled in Freeman and Lazear (1995).

Theory of Rational Choice, edited by Kir Monroe, 179–305. New York: HarperCollins.

Freeman, R. B., and E. P. Lazear. 1995. "An Economic Analysis of Works Councils." In *Works Councils: Consultation, Representation and Cooperation in Industrial Relations,* edited by Joel Rogers and Wolfgang Streeck, 27–52. University of Chicago Press.

Gordon, Andrew. 1985. *The Evolution of Labor Relations in Japan: Heavy Industry, 1853–1955.* Council on East Asian Studies. Harvard University Press.

———. 1998. *The Wages of Affluence: Labor and Management in Postwar Japan.* Harvard University Press.

Gordon, Jeffrey N. 1991. "Corporations, Markets, and Courts." *Columbia Law Review* 91 (December): 1931–88.

Greif, Avner. 1994. "Cultural Beliefs and the Organization of Society: A Historical and Theoretical Reflection on Collectivist and Individualist Societies." *Journal of Political Economy* 102 (October): 912–50.

Hancke, Bob. 1993. *Technological Change and Its Institutional Constraints: The Politics of Production at Volvo Uddevalla.* Center for Science and International Affairs, Harvard University.

Hansmann, Henry. 1988. "Ownership of the Firm." *Journal of Law, Economics, and Organization* 4 (October): 267–305.

———. 1990. "When Does Worker Ownership Work? ESOPs, Law Firms, Codetermination, and Economic Democracy." *Yale Law Journal* 99 (June): 1749–816.

Hyde, Alan. 1991. "In Defense of Employee Ownership." *Chicago-Kent Law Review* 67 (Winter): 159–211.

Jackson, Thomas. 1986. *The Logic and Limits of Bankruptcy Law.* Harvard University Press.

Jolls, Christine, Cass P. Sunstein, and Richard Thaler. 1998. "A Behavioral Approach to Law and Economics." *Stanford Law Review* 50 (May): 1471–1550.

Kern, Horst, and Charles F. Sabel. 1994. "Verblaßte Tugenden: Zur Krise des deutschen Produktionsmodells." In *Umbrüche gesellschaftlicher Arbeit,* edited by Niels Beckenbach and Werner van Treeck, 605–24. Verlag Otto Schwartz.

Kjellberg, Anders. 1998. "Sweden: Restoring the Model?" In *Changing Industrial Relations in Europe,* edited by Anthony Ferner and Richard Hyman, 74–117. Blackwell.

Kreps, David M. 1990. "Corporate Culture and Economic Theory." In *Perspectives on Positive Political Economy,* edited by James E. Alt and Kenneth A. Shepsle, 90–143. Cambridge University Press.

Mahon, Rianne. 1991. "From Solidaristic Wages to Solidaristic Work: A Post-Fordist Historic Compromise for Sweden?" *Economic and Industrial Democracy* 12 (August): 295–325.

Milgrom, Paul, and John Roberts. 1994. "Complementarities and Systems: Understanding Japanese Economic Organization." *Estudios Económicos* 9 (June): 3–42.

Nakamura, Keisuke, and Michio Nitta. 1995. "Developments in Industrial Relations and Human Resource Practices in Japan." In *Employment Relations in a Changing World Economy,* edited by Richard Locke, Thomas Kochan, and Michael Piore, 325–58. MIT Press.

Rajan, Raghuram G., and Luigi Zingales. 1998. "Power in a Theory of the Firm." *Quarterly Journal of Economics* 113 (May): 387–432.

Roe, Mark. 1994. *Strong Managers, Weak Owners: The Political Roots of American Corporate Finance.* Princeton University Press.

Sabel, Charles F. 1994. "Learning by Monitoring: The Institutions of Economic Development." In *The Handbook of Economic Sociology,* edited by Neil J. Smelser and Richard Swedberg, 137–65. Princeton University Press.

———. 1996. "Ungoverned Production: The Novel Universalism of Japanese Production Methods and Their Awkward Fit with Current Forms of Corporate Governance." Unpublished manuscript.

Streeck, Wolfgang. 1995. "Works Councils in Western Europe: From Constitution to Participation." In *Works Councils: Consultation, Representation and Cooperation in Industrial Relations,* edited by Joel Rogers and Wolfgang Streeck, 313–48. University of Chicago Press.

Sunstein, Cass R. 1996. "Social Norms and Social Roles." *Columbia Law Review* 96 (May): 903–68.

"Symposium: Law, Economics, and Norms." 1996. *University of Pennsylvania Law Review* 144 (May): 1643–2339.

Taira, Koji, and Solomon Levine. 1985. "Japan's Industrial Relations: A Social Compact Emerges." Industrial Relations Research Association. University of Wisconsin, Madison.

Turner, Lowell. 1992. *Democracy at Work: Changing World Markets and the Future of Labor Unions.* Cornell University Press.

Williamson, Oliver. 1984. "Corporate Governance." *Yale Law Journal* 93 (June): 1197–230.

Witte, Eberhard. 1978. *Untersuchungen zur Machtverteilung im Unternehmen.* Verlag der Bayerischen Akademie der Wissenschaften.

Womack, James P., Daniel T. Jones, and Daniel Roos. 1990. *The Machine That Changed the World.* Maxwell Macmillan.

4

Tailored Claims and Governance: The Fit between Employees and Shareholders

EDWARD B. ROCK AND
MICHAEL L. WACHTER

L abor and capital are the two principal inputs to the firm, but their legal relationships with the firm differ sharply. Why is it that shareholders or their agents seem to have the right to call all the shots? For many years, a formalistic answer sufficed: shareholders "own" the corporation, while employees work for it, and that is why they are treated differently. But this formalistic answer merely restated the question. More recently, an answer has emerged that goes beyond formalism. According to Frank Easterbrook and Daniel Fischel, shareholders control the destiny of the firm because they are the residual beneficiaries and, as such, have the best incentives to choose projects with the highest present value.[1]

We are grateful to participants in the Columbia Law School conference on employees and corporate governance for helpful comments, and, in particular, to our commentator/ presenter, Jonathan Macey. In addition, we thank Omri Ben Shahar and Zohar Goshen for their criticism and encouragement. Unfortunately, we remain responsible for all remaining errors. This work was supported by the University of Pennsylvania's Institute for Law and Economics.
    1. Easterbrook and Fischel (1983).

This argument, although persuasive, is incomplete. Assuming that the premise of the argument is correct—that shareholders are residual beneficiaries of the firm—the question then becomes why are employees not also considered residual beneficiaries?[2] After all, if the firm does well, the employees may share in the success through higher wages, promotions, and greater job security. Although equity capital is indeed a residual claimant, it can be argued that employees also share many "residual claimant" characteristics, have invested as much as shareholders if not more, and therefore may also have good incentives for looking after the longterm health of the firm.[3] As Clyde Summers has observed:

> If the corporation is conceived . . . as an operating institution combining all factors of production to conduct an on-going business, then the employees . . . are as much members of that enterprise as the shareholders who provide the capital. Indeed, the employees may have made a much greater investment in the enterprise by their years of service, may have much less ability to withdraw, and may have a greater stake in the future of the enterprise than many of the stockholders.[4]

For many scholars of labor law, the similarity between the employees' and shareholders' positions, in contrast to their rights and powers, is the basis for an argument for greater employee involvement in both ownership and governance.[5] On the other side, many scholars of corporate law take the fact that employee ownership and formal involvement in corporate governance have not emerged, except where legally required or subsidized, as a reason to believe that greater employee ownership would be inefficient or unworkable.[6]

Both perspectives neglect critical prior analytic questions. Both views take as given that employees do not already have ownership rights of some sort, nor any significant governance role in the corporations for which they work. Moreover, both viewpoints tend to gloss over the substantial differences between shareholders of close corporations and shareholders of pub-

2. It is to this question that much of Henry Hansmann's important work on the distribution of employee ownership is directed. See Hansmann (1996).

3. See chapter 2 in this volume.

4. Summers (1982, p. 170). See also Gower (1969, pp. 10–11): " The employees are members of the company for which they work to a far greater extent than are the shareholders whom the law persists in regarding as proprietors."

5. See, for example, Gower (1969); Summers (1982); Hyde (1991, p. 183); Gould (1993); O'Connor (1993).

6. For discussions of worker ownership and corporate governance from an economic perspective, see Jensen and Meckling (1969); Hansmann (1990; 1988, pp. 291–96); Easterbrook and Fischel (1991, p. 69; 1983). For a discussion of the various explanations of the observed paucity of labor-owned firms, see Putterman (1993) and chapter 1 in this volume.

licly held corporations, taking the publicly held corporation to be the paradigm case. These assumptions are made too easily.

In this chapter, we start from the insight of modern industrial organization scholarship that four features are key to understanding the structure of the firm, contractual relationships, and the organization of industry: match-specific or relationship-specific investments, asymmetric information, risk aversion, and transaction costs.[7] We define match-specific investments as investments that are more valuable to the parties to the match than to outsiders.[8] We use the term "match-specific" investment in place of the more common "firm-specific" training for several reasons. First, the term "match investment" captures the broader range of activities that create a good partnership, including training and learning by doing, but also including adaptations to each other's styles of interaction. In addition, the term is more general and does not restrict the meaning to investments inside a firm. Finally, the term "match-specific" leads one to identify the specific asset created or improved by the parties' investments.

We use these four factors to provide an account of the relationships between the firm and its suppliers of capital and labor. We start with the problems the firm faces in its relationships with these suppliers, both in the standard case of the publicly held corporation and in the enlightening, if less commonly discussed, case of the closely held corporation. The objective is to generalize the analysis of the employment relationship to provide the basis for a comprehensive explanation of the relationships between the firm and its suppliers of capital and labor, the connections between those relationships, and the similarities and differences that emerge.

We show that ownership rights of shareholders have direct parallels, with the differences between the two parallel tracks reflecting the parties' ability to gain from investments in the match, their willingness to trade off higher return for greater risk, and their solutions to the problems of asymmetric information and transactions costs. Indeed, when one organizes the discussion around these characteristics, one finds that participants with similar industrial organization characteristics have similar claims, whether they are suppliers of labor or capital. For example, suppliers of labor are similar, in relevant respects, to suppliers of capital in close corporations, and have similar sorts of claims. However, both differ significantly from shareholders of the publicly held firm.

7. Wachter (1995).

8. In the polar case, match-specific investments have no value outside of the match. For our purposes, we do not need to limit the term to the polar case.

The chapter is divided into two main parts. The first uses a stylized model of the firm to describe the "deals" reached by the firm and its suppliers, in other words, the terms and conditions of their relationship, including income streams and governance rights. The second part relates the similarities and differences across the stylized deals to the kinds of assets in which the parties have invested and to the four factors embedded in their respective relationships (match investments, risk aversion, asymmetric information, and transaction costs).

The analysis has two important implications. First, as already mentioned, the ownership rights of shareholders have direct parallels in the employment relationship. Second, corporate (shareholder) governance is a special type of governance and has strong parallels to employee governance. The board of directors and the executive officers participate in issues about which they have the appropriate knowledge and ability to assess and affect the outcomes. Employees do the same, participating in the governance over their workplace, the area over which they have the knowledge and ability to assess and affect the outcomes. Both groups could engage in a broader set of topics, even under existing corporate structures. The fact that they do not reflects the transaction costs of participating in decisions for which they do not have the relevant information, and for which the acquisition of such information would be costly. In a sense, both groups agree to allow the other to make decisions in their area of expertise; that is, both have governance rights, but over distinct topics. Employee and shareholder governance should not be thought of as opposites, but rather as deeply complementary activities.

The Stylized Relationships

At the center of a firm are its assets and core competencies: that is, the firm's products, technology, and investment opportunities that allow it to survive in competitive markets. To take advantage of these core competencies and to maximize the value of its assets, the firm must develop relationships with suppliers of inputs, on one side, and with customers, on the other. Because the two principal inputs to the firm are labor and capital, the relationship with employees, as suppliers of labor, and shareholders, as suppliers of financial capital, have great bearing on the firm's success. The prototypical deal for employees offers them an expected stream of wage payments of indeterminate length, coupled with terms and conditions that describe the working conditions. The supplier of capital is likewise offered an expected stream of returns, and terms and conditions describing the relationship. From this perspective, the question of employee involvement in corporate ownership and governance becomes: under what circumstances is it beneficial to the relevant parties for the terms and conditions of the employment relationship to look and function more like the terms and conditions for the supply of equity capital? To explore this question, we must first describe the nature of the employee/firm problem and the owner/firm problem.

Employer/Firm Problem and Owner/Firm Problem

Labor economists distinguish between two fundamentally different labor markets. The external labor market is the market in which firms seek to fill vacancies and workers search for new jobs. Both the supply and demand sides of the external labor market have numerous parties, and neither employers nor employees have investments that are specific to the relationship. As a result, external labor markets are typically competitive. Although most firms do not rely continuously on the external labor market, some do and the option is available.[9] Temporary workers, outsourcing, and subcontracting are also examples of the external labor market, although in these cases, the subcontracting party is often a different firm.

The employment relationship within firms—the internal labor market—is different. Here, firms and workers both make investments in their match, which are lost if the relationship is terminated. These investments include identifying and training employees, and joint investments in the organization of work in a firm. Once firms and employees are tied together in the internal labor market, relevant information is asymmetrically distributed. Firms have better information about product markets, technologies, and the revenue generated by the match assets, whereas workers have better information concerning their own work effort devoted to the match and concerning their potential wage in an alternative job. As a result, the internal labor market, unlike the external labor market, is not a competitive market, in which workers must simply accept the market wage. Rather, it is better modeled as a bilateral monopoly, which offers considerable potential for strategic bargaining.[10]

Employees and firms can be expected to choose an internal labor market when the benefits it generates are sufficiently higher than those available in the external labor market that both parties are better off, even after

---

9. Wachter and Wright (1990, p. 89).
10. Wachter and Wright (1990, pp. 89–90).

deducting the costs imposed by a bilateral monopoly. From this perspective, then, the employee/firm problem can be stated straightforwardly: how can the firm and the employees structure their relationship to take advantage of the benefits available from the creation of match assets and the use of an internal labor market to enhance the value of those assets?

Analogous issues arise in capital markets in the choice between debt and equity. A debt contract has a fairly well-defined return over a pre-set period of time. By contrast, an equity investment has a more uncertain return and a seemingly more dangerous status. After all, once the firm has its equity capital, it typically does not need anything else from those investors (except perhaps more money), and the worries about opportunistic behavior by the firm are now on the side of the capital providers.

Again, the answer must be that equity capital is chosen when the benefits available from the long-term commitment of capital—from an "internal capital market," as it were—are large enough to leave both parties better off, even after the costs imposed by opportunistic behavior and attempts to monitor and prevent such behavior. The owner/firm problem can be stated in a parallel form: How can the firm and capital providers structure their relationship to take advantage of the benefits of equity capital, in an environment with considerable potential for opportunistic behavior?

How the Firm Solves Problems of Employees and Equity Suppliers

Firms, their employees, and their equity suppliers must decide whether and how to build a long-term relationship. To understand the particular solutions that have emerged, the discussion that follows will turn to the four factors that are key to understanding industrial organization in general— that is, investments in match, asymmetric information, risk aversion, and transaction costs. We rely on these same factors to explore three relationships: between employees and the firm in the internal labor market, between shareholders and the firm in the publicly held corporation, and between shareholder/employees and the firm in the closely held corporation. Table 4-1 summarizes the four central industrial organization characteristics of these relationships.

THE EMPLOYEE/FIRM RELATIONSHIP. Perhaps the defining characteristic of a firm is that employment relationships are brought inside.[11] Approximately 90 percent of private sector workers in the United States are employed in

11. Coase (1937).

Table 4-1. *Shareholders, Employers, and the*
Four Critical Industrial Organization Factors

Factor	Employees in internal labor market	Shareholders in public corporation	Shareholders/ employees in close corporation
Match investments	Large	Small	Large
Asymmetric information	Bilateral	Unilateral	Bilateral
Degree of risk bearing	High: human capital	Diversified	High: all capital
High transaction costs	Yes	Yes	Yes

nonunion firms.[12] Hence we use the nonunion sector as the foundation for our discussion of the employment relationship, although we also draw from the more explicit contracting of the union sector. We focus mainly on the persistent features relating to how compensation varies and how labor participates in firm governance. The patterns of employee compensation can be understood as describing the financial "instrument" that employees hold, while the arrangements by which employees influence firm behavior are important because they form a functional parallel to corporate governance by equity holders.

These pay, governance, and other features are typically not written down in any contract between the firm and employee, and the parties eschew any third-party enforcement. Instead, the nonunion internal labor market is self-governing. Decisions on the allocation of labor are made using a hierarchical governance mechanism, but because of the repeat-play nature of the internal labor market, the parties have broad power to administer sanctions, and information sharing takes place to allow the parties to understand the governance arrangements. Thus the internal labor market relationship, especially the nonunion internal labor market, can be described as a norm-governed relationship.[13]

12. Ehrenberg and Smith (1994, p. 448).
13. Rock and Wachter (1996).

In this stylized employment relationship, employee wages are generally stable and increase slowly, at regular fixed intervals, reflecting tenure with the firm.[14] Above-average wage increases are granted periodically. They are typically based on merit or consummate performance and are often associated with a promotion that increases the employee's responsibility. Performance is not finely and continuously measured as a function of output. Instead, promotions are based on merit as perceived and recorded by supervisors. At higher-level positions, where relatively few promotions are made and the candidate pool is large, promotions can be viewed as "tournaments," in which the few winners get promotions and significantly higher pay, while others stay in their incumbent roles.[15]

Generally, the firm ensures that earnings will be smooth in most circumstances. Employees are given sick days and personal days, when their guaranteed wage and hours are honored. If business turns down, high-tenure employees maintain their weekly earnings, and the adjustment to lower labor demand is made by laying off junior workers. In exceptional cases, if firms discharge older workers before younger workers, they typically do so through voluntary retirement mechanisms, which can be viewed as buying out the "contract" of the older worker.[16] If an employee is caught shirking, the employee is discharged rather than having wages reduced, and the general wage stability is left intact.[17]

Employees—including nonunion employees—do generally participate in the organization of work in their work units. This participation includes elements of how match-asset technology is utilized (that is, two or three folks around the machine, computer, drafting table, and the like), the speed at which work gets done, who orders whom around, seniority provisions, bumping rights, and promotion rules. The information provided is geared to improving the employee's understanding of his or her specific working environment. In these ways, employees do participate, and very actively, in topics related to their terms and conditions of employment.[18] Hereafter, we refer to this participation as employee governance.

Just as important as the patterns we do observe, however, are those that we do not observe. First, the bumping rights of employees, although intricate and well established within the workplace, virtually never extend beyond the workplace or unit. Occasionally, bumping rights are plantwide,

14. Ehrenberg and Smith (1994, p. 394).
15. Lazear and Rosen (1981).
16. Ehrenberg and Smith (1994, p. 370).
17. Wachter (1995, pp. 17–18).
18. Summers (1994, p. 126); Riordan and Wachter (1982).

but firmwide bumping rights are a rarity. Second, pay is not directly based on performance. By one estimate, 86 percent of U.S. employees are paid for their time, not their output.[19] No attempt is generally made to measure the output of employees on a continuing basis, nor to base their pay on output. Performance pay appears only in a few well-defined exceptions: executive managers who receive part of their compensation in the form of stock options, and sales workers who are frequently paid commissions. Employees do not participate in broad issues of corporate governance and are given little information about corporate strategies or plans.

The challenge is to explain the pattern of practices that are observed in the internal labor market as well as those that are not.[20] The central rationale for long- term employment attachments rests on match-specific investments. Match investments include job-specific training, learning by doing, and any other factor by means of which a firm and an employee may simply have formed a good match. The result of the investments is the parties' match assets. Since employees involved in such a match are more productive than they would be elsewhere, the match assets have more value to the investing parties than they have to outsiders.

Asymmetric information exists when it is relatively more costly for one of the parties to observe or monitor the quantity and quality of inputs, outputs, technology, or product market factors. For example, employees may have superior information about their level of work effort devoted to the match assets, while the employer has superior information about the state of the product market, technologies, and revenue generated by the match assets. Asymmetric information allows hidden actions, whereby one or another of the parties can redirect the returns on match investments to improve their own relative position at the cost of the other. A case in point would be an employee who pretends to be working hard to justify higher payout, or an employer who pretends that business prospects are poor to justify a lower one. Asymmetric information is increased by the existence of match assets since external benchmarks are of little value in measuring performance.

High transaction costs result from the repeated nature of the tasks, the long period over which they are performed, and the need for the tasks to evolve with the environment. High transaction costs are embedded in any long-term relationship. However, they are lower than the costs that would be generated by frequent use of the external labor market or, alternatively, by writing contract terms to cover all of the contingencies.

19. Ehrenberg and Smith (1994, p. 373 and surrounding discussion).

20. Our presentation in this chapter is brief since we have discussed these issues in more detail elsewhere. See Wachter and Wright (1990).

The fourth factor, risk aversion, helps explain why employees may prefer to reduce the risk associated with their earning streams. Since employees' work effort is not diversified across many firms and product markets, the variance associated with their earning streams is necessarily high.

The literature on the internal labor market has successfully used these four features to explain the persistent features of the employment relationship identified earlier.[21] Why, for example, are employees' earnings stable? Generally, the variance or risk in the productivity of match investments is borne by the employer. The first piece of the explanation is that individual employees are more risk averse than the employer. Indeed, risk aversion was one of the first reasons cited by labor economists as the rationale for the "implicit contract" between employers and employees.[22] It is widely accepted in corporate finance that the higher the risk, the greater the expected return the firm must offer to investors. The same is true when individuals are supplying labor. If a firm can offer a less risky job, that is, a job with smoothed compensation, it can offer a lower wage rate. In fact, firms in sectors with high seasonal variance, such as construction, or high cyclical variance, such as manufacturing, tend to pay a higher wage than do jobs with little cyclical or seasonal variability.

Although employees' risk aversion helps explain why earnings are smoothed, it is far from a complete explanation. For example, it does not explain why earnings are so stable, instead of perhaps just fluctuating less. Nor is risk aversion sufficient to explain why an employee who is detected shirking is typically fired, rather than penalized with a reduction in wages, or why employers typically do not reduce wages even when the relevant product market declines.

The full explanation for the high stability of earnings requires asymmetric information. Employers discharge shirkers, rather than just reduce their wages, because information about the effort of workers is asymmetric, and monitoring employees is costly. If an employer could simply declare that an employee was shirking and cut that person's wages, the employer would have an incentive to overstate the degree of shirking to hold wages down. A norm of forcing the employer to discharge workers eliminates the firm's incentive to overstate the degree of shirking, because it forces firms to lose workers in whom the firm has made investments.[23] The reason that firms typically reduce employment in response to cyclical

21. For more extended discussions from this literature, see Wachter and Wright (1990); Ehrenberg and Smith (1994); Wachter (1995).
22. Baily (1974); Azariadis (1975).
23. Wachter and Wright (1990).

changes in output, rather than adjusting wage rates, has a parallel logic. If a firm could lower wages in response to a decline in its product market, it would have an incentive to misstate the condition of its product market. By contrast, a norm of laying off workers means that the firm must reduce its output and revenues, which limits the firm's incentive to misstate information.

The four key factors explain not only the elements of the internal labor market that parties choose to adopt, but also those that they choose to avoid. Central to this discussion is the fact that firms rarely base pay directly on performance. This is important because pay for performance is akin to employee ownership: more than anything else, it holds the potential of making employees true residual beneficiaries of their investments in match and work effort. One possible explanation—but a false one—is that employees would not respond to pay incentives by increasing productivity. In fact, the empirical evidence shows that a properly designed system of incentive pay can bring productivity gains of 10–25 percent.[24] Yet one rarely finds performance pay, and employees resist it strenuously.

In part, the explanations cited in favor of earnings stability explain some of the resistance to performance pay. After all, to the extent that performance varies, performance pay introduces earnings instability. But the arguments for why performance pay is not commonly observed run deeper.

More important, performance pay mechanisms suffer from embedded problems of asymmetric information, which makes implementing them costly and uncertain. Any pay-for-performance arrangement requires the monitoring of the outputs that are realized, agreement on a formula that links outputs to pay, adjustment of that formula when the business environment or technology changes, and adjudication of disputes that arise. For most jobs, even the first task is daunting. Most employees in the internal labor market perform a series of connected tasks, and the value of the output that results from any one person's effort is difficult if not impossible to measure. Any attempt to implement such a system will take a great deal of time and effort, from both supervisors and workers. Moreover, any such system will tend to put management and workers into an adversarial relationship, since management will have incentives to understate the level of performance to hold wages down, while workers will try to take advantage of the agreement to raise wages.[25]

24. For a review of the evidence, see Mitchell, Lewin, and Lawler (1990); Kling (1995). Conversely, for a highly negative assessment of pay for performance, see Kohn (1993a, 1993b). However, note also Beer's (1993) response to Kohn. Beer agrees that managers often misuse incentive pay, but also describes situations in which pay for performance is necessary and useful.

25. Brown (1990); Mitchell, Lewin, and Lawler (1990).

The nature of the task is best illustrated by citing again the exceptional cases in which performance pay is used. The most famous example, albeit largely of historical interest today, is piecework. Piecework refers to the system in which individual employees produce discrete amounts of output, and the pay of the employee is a fraction of the value of the output. The advantages of this system are obvious: since pay is based on output, it does not require performance reviews, and it provides incentives for employees to maximize the value of their work. The main disadvantages are rooted in asymmetric information and the associated ability to manipulate the piecework formula. For example, if the compensation formula turns on the value of the output, the employer can understate the price and thereby reduce the payout. If an employee can produce outputs of inferior quality, and quality is difficult for the employer to observe, the employee can cheat on the employer.[26] If the employer has private information about technology, the employer can claim that an improvement in technology renders the output target attainable with even low effort, and then adjust the formula by reducing the payout to the employee.[27] Such incentive-based mechanisms were widely adopted during the 1920s, under the rubric of scientific management. But they became highly contentious when employers tightened the payouts, a device that employees labeled a "speedup." The problem was, and is, that the required information is asymmetrically known to the individual parties, so that neither can verify the assertions made by the other.

These problems are manageable in the case of top managers, which is why stock options form an important part of their compensation package. The problem of asymmetric information is solved in this case because the executive officers' performance or output is measured by the common stock price, and this output measure is jointly observable at low cost. Moreover, the Securities and Exchange Commission requires that firms truthfully report on their use of stock options, which means that firms and executive officers can observe and verify the payouts received by managers at other firms. The problem is only slightly more difficult in compensating the managers of subsidiaries. In these cases, managers are typically compensated by bonuses based on the subsidiaries' profits, as determined by an independent auditor.[28]

As one moves down the corporate hierarchy, however, the employee's output becomes more difficult to tie to a mutually verifiable measure, which

26. Baker (1992, p. 608).
27. Mitchell, Lewin, and Lawler (1990, p. 30).
28. Kay (1992, p. 217), drawing on the 1991 Hay Group "Executive Compensation Report."

makes it more difficult to tie pay to performance. In addition, the work effort of the individual employee becomes less highly correlated with the firm's profits, which makes stock ownership a less plausible mechanism for improving work effort.

The result for these workers is the implicit incentive pay mechanisms described earlier. The most prevalent example is the merit pay system, whereby employees are promoted and given high wage increases targeted to their higher position. Promotion pay is self-enforcing because it is difficult to manipulate to the advantage of either party. By paying higher wages to those employees who perform best, the firm provides the greatest incentive for employees to perform well. If the employer were to misuse the system by promoting more favored but less productive employees, it would have to bear the cost in forgone profits. This, plus negative reputational effects in the external labor markets, should discourage firms from unjustified favoritism.[29] Similarly, it is costly for lower-level managers to manipulate the system. The employer, by observing reduced performance, will eventually detect a promoted but inadequate employee in the managers' work group.[30]

The reluctance of employees to approve performance-based pay mechanisms is most apparent in collective bargaining negotiations, in which unions almost always attempt to minimize both the risk of earnings' variation and the extent of managerial performance reviews in setting wages.[31] Instead, unions prefer "time rates" or "standard rates" in which the wage or salary is fixed contractually, and some restrictions are placed on the ability of the firm to vary hours of work. Promotions are based mainly on seniority; a Bureau of National Affairs survey in the early 1990s showed that 73 percent of union contracts in the survey used length of service to determine progression, whereas only 27 percent used merit. The main "merit" exception is when certified training accomplishments are included (as in the case of teachers who receive higher salaries for extra years of training).[32] The employee's lifetime income is tied to the performance of the firm, but only because a growing firm will create a higher probability of seniority-based promotions. When the firm is financially troubled, the jobs of senior employees are often protected by providing "bumping" rights, whereby

29. Malcomson (1984, esp. pp. 487–88).
30. Lazear and Rosen (1981, p. 842).
31. Brown (1990, p. 180-S).
32. See Bureau of National Affairs (1992, p. 118), as referred to in Lewin and Mitchell (1995, p. 414). For more detail, see Freeman and Medoff (1984); for example, their discussion of teacher pay on pp. 126–28.

junior workers are laid off and senior workers inserted in their jobs.[33] These patterns indicate the limited attractiveness of performance or merit pay systems.

Another feature of the internal labor market is that employees seldom have a significant role in corporate governance, although they do participate in a variety of ways within the workplace; we have termed this kind of participation "employee governance."[34] One immediate hurdle here is that the lack of employee participation in corporate governance in nonunion firms may partly reflect restraints imposed by labor law, rather than employee or firm preferences. In particular, section 8(a)(2) of the National Labor Relations Act prohibits firm-employee associations other than labor unions as defined by the act. The observable governance in the nonunion sector may thus reflect legal constraints, rather than the parties' preferences.[35] In contrast to our earlier discussion, therefore, it makes more sense to begin by looking at the union sector for an unimpaired view of employees' preferences with regard to both corporate and employee governance. We then offer a parallel discussion of the nonunion sector.

Collective bargaining agreements contain explicit schedules for wages, restrain the flexibility that employers have in scheduling hours, and provide highly detailed terms covering working conditions, employment security, and nonwage benefits. They include grievance mechanisms that range from shop stewards to third-party arbitrators, all of which offer ways to exchange information. Employee governance thus appears in both the negotiation and performance of collective bargaining agreements. Strikingly, however, American collective bargaining agreements almost never provide for employee participation in decisionmaking with respect to product market strategies, capital investments, advertising, or financial capital plans, whether through board representation or any other mechanism.[36] Indeed, collective bargaining agreements typically enshrine employees' noninvolvement in such matters of corporate governance. Unlike the situation of employee governance in the workplace, there is no evidence that employ-

33. Freeman and Medoff (1984, pp. 123–26).

34. Summers (1994).

35. The legal literature suggests that the specter of section 8(a)(2) litigation is minimal, and few firms complain about it, but 8(a)(2) remains a potential issue. For an example of a successful implementation of worker participation where unfair labor practices, including violations of Section 8(a)(2), were alleged and refuted, see Powers (1988).

36. Also, as Hansmann (1990, pp. 1804–05) points out: "By adopting this strategy a union avoids some possibilities for costly internal conflict. . . . By confining themselves to such matters as wages, hours, and job classifications, unions can largely avoid the necessity of making invidious distinctions among their members. They can leave that task to management and adopt the simpler and less controversial strategy of pressing for greater equality with respect to the subjects they bargain over."

ees even implicitly cogovern with respect to these sorts of issues. Why do collective bargaining agreements steer away from such terms?

The answer lies in part in the law of collective bargaining. Under the National Labor Relations Act, employers and unions both have a duty to bargain "with respect to wages, hours, and other terms and conditions of employment."[37] As interpreted by the U.S. Supreme Court, certain topics are subject to this "mandatory bargaining," which means that parties have a statutory obligation to engage in good faith bargaining. As a descriptive matter, the terms of the typical collective bargaining agreement, as well as those topics over which the nonunion internal labor market parties develop practices, focus on the matters to which mandatory bargaining applies: wages, hours, the physical dimensions of the workplace, nonwage benefits, seniority rights, and other terms and conditions of employment.[38] Unions are permitted to raise other topics, such as investing in labor-saving machinery, liquidating assets, and other decisions that lie at the core of corporate strategy, but such topics rarely find their way into the collective bargaining agreement.

For the most part, however, collective bargaining agreements do not generally include anything other than mandatory topics because those are the topics that offer the possibility of mutually beneficial trades and are more valued by employees. In the give and take of any bargaining process, one would expect employees to place a high value on significant control over their immediate workplace environment. Similarly, one would expect firms to be more likely to cede real employee participation in topics over which employees have a capacity to affect the outcome. To employers and employees, the nonmandatory topics relate largely to matters at the core of entrepreneurial control, which are driven by product market influences and external developments in technology. In these areas, employees have little to offer that can affect the situation.[39]

In other words, in the employee-firm relationship, targeted employee governance, unlike wide-ranging governance, saves transaction costs. Each part of the internal labor market can be understood to work on its piece of the profit-maximization calculus. Given that information on product markets, technology, production strategy, and so on, is costly, the parties specialize in their own core competencies. Employee governance is targeted to getting their particular jobs accomplished. Part of effective management

37. Section 8(d), 8(a)(5) and 8(b)(3), 29 U.S.C. 158(d), 158(a)(5), and 158 (b)(3).
38. *Fibreboard Paper Products Corp.* v. *NLRB*, 379 U.S. 203 at 220–22 (1964).
39. For a full discussion of "mandatory" and "permissive" topics of bargaining under the National Labor Relations Act, see Wachter (1999). See also Hylton (1994).

is, indeed, learning to profit from the expertise that employees develop regarding their work.

THE CAPITAL/FIRM PROBLEM: THE PUBLICLY HELD FIRM. A firm can hire capital for use at its own discretion in two ways: equity and debt. Debt is capital hired pursuant to explicit and relatively simple contracts that set the term, the interest rate, and any ancillary restrictions on firm activities. Equity capital is hired in a more complicated way. It is hired for an indefinite term and receives the residual returns of the firm, that is, what is left after all the other claimants of the firm are paid off. This stream of earnings varies directly with the performance of the firm and varies more than any of the other claims on the firm's income stream. Thus when firms attempt to persuade investors to supply them with equity capital, they must find a way to reassure those investors that the residual return will not be dissipated by managers who shirk or underperform, divert resources to their own use, or choose investment objectives not directly related to the firm's profitability.

In the classic, publicly held firm, shareholders receive a combination of rights and protections in return for their investment. They have a right to receive the residual returns of the firm, either directly through dividends or indirectly through appreciation of the stock price. Shareholders have the right to elect a board of directors who have legal power to manage the firm, and who owe legally enforceable "fiduciary duties" of loyalty and care to the corporation and its shareholders.[40] Through the right to elect directors, and the directors' power to control the destiny of the firm, shareholders have an internal corporate mechanism to displace current management by replacing directors. Beyond electing directors, however, shareholders' participation is limited mainly to "extraordinary" rather than "ordinary" business matters and cannot, for example, dictate directly the firm's policies on ordinary business matters. Indeed, under the federal proxy rules, management is free to exclude any shareholder proposal that relates to such matters.[41] In addition, shareholders have the right to receive certain sorts of information and to meet and question management at an annual meeting. But, as is the case in the employment relationship, mandatory disclosure to shareholders is directly tied to issues of direct financial interest.

This set of rights and protections coincides with a market for shares that is large, liquid, and efficient. For the typical large, publicly held corpo-

40. For a transaction cost argument for why directors are elected by and expected to look out for shareholders, see Williamson (1984).
41. Rule 14a-8(i)(7).

ration, shares are widely held. Since investors know that their individual actions will have little effect on the board, it is rational for them to avoid the costs of investing in a great deal of knowledge about the firm. Shareholders generally play a small and episodic role in the governance of the corporation, implicitly delegating most decisions to the managers under the general supervision of the board. Moreover, courts do not second-guess judgments of management, except occasionally when there are conflicts of interest. Shareholders are generally not employees, although employees, in the role of investors, may own shares in the company.

Viewed in terms of our four key factors—match investments, asymmetric information, transactions costs, and risk aversion—the market in which a firm hires equity capital is fundamentally different from the internal labor market governing the hiring and utilization of labor. In internal labor markets, substantial match-specific investments are made. Indeed, that is their reason for being. By contrast, even for active investors with a relatively small number of holdings, the investments in match, although positive, are relatively small, at least when compared with the match investments made by employees in internal labor markets. Widely diversified investors in equity capital typically make only small investments in match; for an index fund, the investments in match are zero. The small or nonexistent shareholder investments in match allow shareholders to diversify their supply of capital across a wide range of firms and industries. On the other side, the firm's investments in match will also be small: they will consist of the costs of marketing shares, the costs of identifying investors (typically subcontracted to underwriters), and the costs of an investor relations program.

Asymmetric information is pervasive in equity markets, but the problem is different from that in the internal labor market. The asymmetric information problem in labor markets was bilateral: firms could not know the effort of employees with certainty; employees could not know whether the business environment was as dire as management painted. But the information problems in equity capital go only in one direction. Once the equity capital suppliers provide capital to the firm, the managers know better than the capital suppliers how hard and smart they are working, and the expected value of the assets of the firm. By contrast, one cannot identify issues of common concern on which the capital suppliers have better information than the firm and an incentive to mislead the firm.

Transaction costs in the equity capital market are high, as they were in internal labor markets; that is, a complete contract governing the appropriate managerial actions to be taken under all conditions and contingencies simply cannot be written. Suppliers of equity capital are risk averse, but, unlike suppliers of labor, they have the ability to diversify cheaply.[42]

As stated at the outset, many of the legal and economic features of the publicly held corporation can be understood and explained by the four key factors. Generally, just as high match investments foreshadow the ongoing nature of the employment relationship, low investments in match foreshadow the high turnover of the average investor's shareholdings. In the stylized publicly held corporation, the low match investments also allow suppliers of capital to diversify their holdings in order to reduce risk to the irreducible level of market risk. Mandatory disclosure requirements of the Securities and Exchange Commission reduce the managers' informational advantage and provide investors with sufficient information about their shareholdings to value the shares. More generally, monitoring by the board or large shareholders or through lawsuits can be understood to be a means of controlling the divergence of interests of management and shareholders, and a means of limiting the ability of managers to use their asymmetric informational advantage to further their own interests. Similarly, stock options for top managers can be understood to be an attempt to align the interests of managers and shareholders. The system of voting for boards of directors is important both as a means of forcing dissemination of information to shareholders and the market and as a mechanism for displacing ineffective management. Fiduciary duties provide an opportunity for judicial scrutiny of managerial conduct. These legal and institutional checks exist against a backdrop of market disciplines, which can punish poor managers and reward good ones: the product market, the managerial labor market, the market for capital, and the market for control.

THE CAPITAL/FIRM PROBLEM: THE CLOSELY HELD CORPORATION. In the early stages of a firm's development, and continuing in some firms through their existence, one typically see two types of structures that fall under the heading of "close corporation." One is the classic "mom and pop" close corporation; the other is what one might call the "Silicon Valley start-

---

42. The four factors can also be applied to debt markets. For diversified holders of debt, investments in the match are also typically small or negligible. Asymmetry of information is less of a problem for debtholders than for equity holders, because of the limited complexity of their claims and because debt will be paid first, ahead of equity, and thus the holder can worry less about managerial opportunism (except in the case where the firm is bankrupt). Transaction costs for the debtholders are low: standard form debt contracts are cheaply available. Finally, suppliers of debt capital also have the ability to express their risk aversion by diversifying cheaply.

up."[43] In both cases, the firm must persuade investors to provide capital before it is clear whether the business will succeed, in contexts in which realizing value from the business through a sale to a third party is problematic. The close corporation offers an interesting middle case that will illustrate the extent to which ownership and governance vary across the spectrum of firms and how that variety is driven by differences in underlying features.

The closely held firm has several common traits. There is substantial overlap between suppliers of capital and suppliers of labor, that is, between employees and shareholders. In the mom and pop corporation, capital is usually provided either by retained earnings, by the dominant figure in the firm, or more or less equally by the participants. In the Silicon Valley start-up, where the capital needs are often larger, capital is often provided by venture capitalists, who also participate in the running of the firm through seats on the board of directors, frequent meetings, and intensive monitoring of the operating managers.[44] There is no public market for shares and often no private market either, which means that there is no easy way out for capital providers. However, at least in the mom and pop close corporation, the liquidity problem is solved through some sort of legally enforceable agreement that an investor's stake will be bought out at prearranged terms on demand.[45] Because the remaining shareholders worry about who will come into the firm, the right to sell shares to a third party is usually limited by various sorts of consent provisions. The number of shareholders tends to be small; indeed, when corporation codes distinguish between close corporations and other sorts of corporations, they do so on the basis of the number of shareholders.[46]

Generally, the relationship between capital providers and the firm is longer for a closely held than for a publicly held firm, and there are often specific rules for contingencies such as terminating the relationship or bringing in new capital suppliers. Moreover, the suppliers of capital to closely held firms, especially mom and pop firms, are often relatively undiversified; that is to say, their human capital and financial assets are

43. There is, now, a substantial literature on the structure and governance of venture capital start-ups. See Gorman and Sahlman (1989); Barry and others (1990); Sahlman (1990); Lerner (1994, 1995); Gompers (1995); Lerner and Merges (1996). For a more comprehensive description of the "private equity" market, see Fenn, Liang, and Prowse (1995).

44. For a description of the characteristic problems and solutions in the close corporation, see Gorman and Sahlman (1989); O'Neal and Thompson (1986/1995); Barry and others (1990); Lerner (1995).

45. O'Neal and Thompson (1986/1995).

46. See, for example, Del. Code Ann. tit. 8, sec. 342(a)(1) (close corporations have thirty or fewer shareholders).

concentrated in a single firm. As a consequence of the overlap in roles and the lack of diversification, pay in such firms is based much more heavily on performance than is typical in the labor market. Also, governance covers a broad range of issues. This is in contrast to the board of a publicly held corporation, which deals with few specific issues, and unlike the limited governance by employees in the internal labor market. Because shareholders of a closely held corporation expect to be involved in the management of the business and expect a big chunk of the benefits to be received in the form of salary, employee-shareholders must ensure they do not get frozen out of management or profits. This is usually accomplished by sharholder agreements or classifying shares.[47]

Generally, in the case of Silicon Valley start-ups, the outside venture capitalist who contributes both capital and advice in exchange for an equity position is protected in various ways.[48] Managers receive stock ownership and options, so that their incentives are better aligned with those of the equity investors. Outside investors also receive preferred stock, which in the event of liquidation will be paid off before the common stock held by managers. This provision protects the investors and sharpens the incentives of managers. Venture capitalists may also require employment contracts with managers specifying situations in which management can be replaced and allowing the firm to buy back the managers' shares in such an event. Finally, venture capitalists exercise control over the firm by representation on the board of directors; allocation of voting rights; controlling access to additional financing; inspecting the company's facilities, books, and records; and limiting the ability of the company to accept capital from other sources or to enter into large contracts without prior approval.

These characteristic features of the closely held firm are best understood as mechanisms that allow the firm to maximize value, given the particular configuration of the four relevant factors. As a general matter, shareholders of close corporations (of both types) look more similar to employees with investments in match than to shareholders of the publicly held corporation. For example, both employees and shareholders of close corporations invest heavily in match. Since optimal match investments are at

---

47. O'Neal and Thompson (1986/1995).

48. For further discussion of the provisions in this paragraph, see Gorman and Sahlman (1989); Barry and others (1990); Fenn, Liang, and Prowse (1995, pp. 32–33); Gompers (1995); Lerner (1995).

significant risk, the parties choose an internal labor market-type arrangement. Without these protections, the appropriate investments would not be made and the new match asset would suffer from underinvestment. Both employees and shareholders in close corporations also face problems of asymmetric information in relation to outside shareholders. Each is undiversified, and the relationships evolve in a setting of high transaction costs (see table 4-1).

The overlapping of suppliers of capital and labor in the close corporation can be understood as a solution to pervasive asymmetry of information. The overlap provides both the entrepreneur and the capital suppliers with continuing information and an ongoing stake in the success of the venture, paralleling their continuing investments in match, and allowing the stake to be calibrated to their investments. The overlap is also driven by transaction costs. Rather than attempting the impossible task of drafting a complete contract, covering every possible future contingency between those working in a Silicon Valley start-up and those providing the capital, the overlap between employees and owners puts all the relevant players into the same room, at the same time, thereby forcing a bargaining solution. However, it is obvious that the overlap between shareholders and employees cannot be explained by risk preferences. Instead, the lack of diversification that results from overinvestment in the close corporation is a heavy cost that parties are no longer willing to pay when the asymmetry of information between insiders and outsiders becomes small enough to sell the company in an initial public offering.

This leads to another persistent, even defining, characteristic of the close corporation: the market for shares is nonexistent or very limited. This is, in part, a consequence of the fact that match-specific assets present significant problems of asymmetric information. The expected future cash flow attached to the asset is highly uncertain, especially to potential outside investors. Hence they could not be sold in an initial public offering to the outside world of diversified investors—at least not without deeply discounting the price or surrendering significant management control. This is a situation in which the importance of maximizing the value of the match-specific investment trumps diversification concerns. For a close corporation of the Silicon Valley model, the use of venture capitalists and specialist investment bankers at the later initial public offering stage provides two actors who are willing to overcome the asymmetric information problem by investing their time in learning about the asset. Indeed, experienced venture capitalists have a better track record at timing initial public offerings, from the standpoint of both the firm's and the market's readiness, so that the firm receives a larger infusion of capital for its stock.[49]

The lack of marketable shares is not just a difficulty to be overcome by a close corporation; it may also serve a positive function. The lack of a market prevents exit, except under narrowly defined circumstances, which makes credible the up-front commitment to continuing investments in match. Likewise, it reinforces a long-term relationship, thereby forcing ongoing investments in communication, information, and joint problem solving. For example, a venture capital firm is forced to help save the project when things go a little wrong, rather than selling out, cutting its losses, and taking what is known among shareholders of publicly held firms as the "Wall Street Walk." Likewise, the entrepreneur and the employees have a stronger incentive to stay with the firm. The lack of liquidity provides a partial solution to this problem, "trapping" the participants in the venture. This makes it harder for participants to threaten to leave as a way of capturing additional surplus, and it limits the ability of the entrepreneur to recruit capital from anyone other than the original venture capitalists. This issue is also handled, at least in the Silicon Valley start-up, by negotiating legally enforceable contracts that protect early investors through particular financing structures.[50] The venture capitalist typically exits the relationship when the close corporation has proved successful and graduates out of the venture capitalist phase, either by being sold or going public, or, if the prospects turn sufficiently adverse, by being sold or liquidated.

The characteristic overinvestment of shareholder/managers in the firm and their corresponding lack of diversification is both a cost of the close corporation structure and a mechanism for sharpening the incentives of all participants. It is made possible in this case—in contrast to the lack of pay for performance for employees in the public firm—by the close link between employee performance and firm performance.

The final generalized feature of the close corporation, the wide governance mandate of its board of directors, results from the overlap in the roles of capital and labor providers. In the close corporation, the owners/employees deal with both the "extraordinary" and the "ordinary" business matters. This reflects the fact that the owners/employees have the expertise of both, and therefore their governance enhances the match and is not an unnecessary transaction cost.

---

49. For evidence that younger venture capital firms take firms public more quickly and firms are more underpriced, see Gompers (1996). How venture capitalists are skilled at taking firms public at peaks in the market for initial public offerings is discussed by Lerner (1994).

50. Sahlman (1990); Gompers (1995).

Notice that in this analysis of the persistent features of close corporations, the primary factors are match-specific investments, asymmetric information, and transaction costs. The analysis does not rely on capital market problems or risk aversion to explain the persistence or distribution of close corporations. Although some problems along these lines surely exist—for example, tapping public capital markets may not make sense for some corporations because of high fixed costs—that cannot be the entire explanation for such corporations. As Silicon Valley demonstrates, the close corporation structure appears even when the assets involved are quite large and therefore the high fixed costs of public offerings relatively insignificant.

Shareholders and Employees: Tailored Ownership and Governance and the Employment Relationship

The previous section examined the relationships of employees and capital providers and the firm, and how they solve their distinctive problems. The key insight is that the standard features of the employment relationship and of corporate ownership/governance reflect the need to solve for the different arrays of issues associated with match investments, asymmetric information, transaction costs, and risk aversion. The bundle of rights associated with corporate ownership and governance is rooted in a particular type of arrangement for attracting and retaining suppliers of financial capital. Similarly, the bundle of rights associated with the employment relationship solves the corresponding problem of dealing with the suppliers of labor. There is no particular magic in these features, nor is it simple to rank one solution as preferable to another. This section compares the observed solutions in an attempt to understand how the ownership and governance stakes of employees fit with those of shareholders.

Patterns of Asset Ownership and Returns

Both shareholders and employees are variable claimants, in the sense that their earnings depend on the size or growth of the revenue stream of the firm. But these claims do not vary in the same way across employees, shareholders in the publicly held firm, and shareholders in the close corporation.

The central feature of the variable claim of equity capital—the feature that makes them "owners" of the firm—is that they are the residual claimants to the revenue stream produced by the firm as a whole. The residual claim has the highest variance of any of the claims on the firm's revenue and is a claim to the profits or losses generated by the overall assets of the firm, rather than by some subset of the firm's assets. Although the attention here is on this residual claim of equity holders, it is hardly inevitable that capital suppliers as a group receive a variable and residual stream of income; bondholders, of course, typically receive a fixed payment, except in the extraordinary circumstance of bankruptcy. Moreover, capital suppliers can also take cuts of the revenue stream with variance profiles between the two poles of equity and debt, as, for example, in the case of bonds that can be converted to stock.

The employees who are most like owners—indeed who are owners— are the senior officers of the close corporation. They are not only shareholders but are also likely to hold a controlling percentage of the company's stock. A high percentage of their total payments will therefore depend on the size of the residual earnings of the company. For this group of employees, the return to capital and labor are blended together. But, as already mentioned, when it becomes possible for the owner-employees to sell ownership shares to the public market at a price that accurately reflects the value of the asset, most choose to do so, thereby diversifying their financial assets.[51]

Next in the line of employees who have some similarity to owners are the executive officers of the publicly held corporation. Here, one must differentiate the top executive officers who work at the corporate level, are most likely to serve on or deal with the firm's board of directors, and are most likely to receive significant stock options, from other senior managers, such as division heads, who focus on a narrower set of assets. Executive officers of publicly held companies, like their counterparts in close corporations, make match-specific investments at the most aggregated level, that is, not just in the specifics of their job, but in their overall knowledge about the company and its place in the industry. But executive officers differ from the owner-managers of the close corporation in that they are far less diversified in their financial assets than the managers of a publicly held firm. Instead of acquiring direct ownership, managers of public companies typically receive stock options. A stock option has similar effects on work incentive as does direct share ownership, but it operates as a kind of halfway house between a residual claim and a variable claim. It offers the possibility of gain, if the stock price rises, but it does not impose losses directly if the stock price falls, and it allows more diversified financial holdings.

---

51. Hyde (1991, p. 173); Miyazaki (1984).

The employee, whether a lower-level manager or a production employee, differs from executive officers in fundamental ways. Executive officers and shareholders are paid on the basis of the returns generated by the firm's entire assets, whereas employees are best thought of as having an ownership claim to a disaggregated or localized match-specific asset. For the plant manager, the match investments are in the plant assets. For the production-line employee, the match investments are in the production line. These disaggregated or localized match assets, like any other asset of the firm, generate revenue streams that can be carved up into residual, variable (but non-residual), and fixed payment streams. The more the payment mechanism is based on performance (performance pay) or merit (merit pay), the more variable is the payment stream and thus the more the employees are like shareholders rather than bondholders. On the other hand, if the payment mechanism makes heavy use of seniority or standard pay, the employee is more like a bondholder. The design of the specific payment mechanism will depend on risk aversion, the employees' ability to influence the value of the match asset, the ability of the parties jointly to overcome problems of asymmetric information by observing and verifying either their labor input or the output, and the related ability to control opportunistic behavior through the design of an appropriate payment mechanism.

In union internal labor markets, employees almost always bargain for standard pay, which is based on a contractual wage rate and the number of hours of work. Pay of this kind provides the employer with almost no discretion and gives employees little incentive to work harder or smarter.[52] Although the pay of such employees is not a residual claim, it is, however, still a variable claim. The expected future payments for a standard pay employee vary with the probability of promotion, the number of overtime hours, and the possibility of layoff, all of which are variables tied to firm performance. The union employees' apparent preference for standard pay likely reflects their mistrust of employers.[53]

Employees in nonunion internal labor markets accept greater variability, since they are typically evaluated by supervisors who make qualitative decisions on the basis of merit.[54] It is difficult to compare the payments received by merit-paid employees with the payments to any capital suppliers. Merit pay is both qualitative and based on work input, while the residual claim of shareholders tends to be quantitative and output related. Merit pay is a variable payment, which makes it unlike the bondholders' claim. However,

52. Brown (1990, p. 180-S).

merit pay can be viewed as a halfway house between a bond and a stock, in which a promotion can be viewed as converting a fixed stream of payments to a position with a higher expected return (the higher wage level) plus a higher variance (the risk of failing plus the chance of further promotions). Relatively few employees receive the bulk of their earnings through performance pay, for reasons discussed earlier. But for those who do, performance pay is directly related to output and thus gives the employees a shared and direct claim on the benefits produced by the match. Even performance pay, however, does not make the employee an owner of the firm's overall assets, or even of the match asset.

Should corporations use financial incentives to motivate all employees to "work hard and smart on behalf of the owners?" From an incentive-compatibility perspective, the answer is clearly "yes." Should corporations use financial incentives in the form of stock ownership? The answer is just as clearly "no." The reason is that, as one moves down the corporate hierarchy, the performance of the employee is less linked to the overall success of the company. A typical approach here is to eschew stock ownership in the overall firm for bonuses tied to the net revenue of the specific assets that the employee can affect. For example, the division heads of a multidivision firm are usually compensated according to division performance, not firm performance.

This is the sense in which pay for performance can be considered a form of stock option in the relevant match assets, in this case, in the value created by the individual job. Like stock options, pay for performance compensates employees when output improves, whether the rise is due to working smart or hard, or just getting lucky. Similarly, it lowers compensation if the employee works less hard or gets unlucky. Pay for performance does not require employees to share in the corporation's losses if business goes very bad. In that sense, the employees are not the residual claimant on their own match investments, although they could be. The principal barrier seems to be that employees do not want to be residual claimants for the reasons discussed here, including diversification and risk aversion.

Of course, pay for performance differs from stock options in various ways. Pay for performance pays in cash, not in the company's common stock. But this difference is not material, since executive officers usually cash out stock options rather than converting them into stock. Stock options typically have a maturity of several years, whereas pay for performance has

---

53. Freeman (1982, pp. 4–5).
54. Lewin and Mitchell (1995, pp. 179–81).

a shorter duration. This may be because the match-specific assets of executives take longer to pay off, or it may be that lower-salary employees do not have the cash flow (or the ability to borrow against expected future pay) to allow performance pay to go unrealized.[55]

On the surface, stock options for lower-level employees may seem to be a way of compensating employees as if they were executive officers. Just beneath the surface, however, any likeness fades rapidly, and stock options turn out to be a poor substitute for pay for performance. Indeed, as long as employees are investing in a more localized match asset than executive officers, the closer the superficial resemblance, the worse the comparison. Since individual lower-level employees cannot affect the company's profits, there is no incentive to work harder and smarter. What makes stock options for executive officers attractive is that they are geared to the match assets of the executive officers. The hope, of course, is that employee stock ownership serves to improve productivity and performance by such indirect means as decreasing labor-management conflict and increasing employee effort, cooperation, and information sharing, but whether these effects actually occur is the subject of controversy.[56] Though such options may look quite attractive during a rising stock market, firm performance and stock value can also decline because of factors beyond a worker's control, and a decline of this kind tends to create negative perceptions about such a program of equity ownership.[57]

Rather than thinking about the U.S. economy as a place where employee ownership does not exist, it is more appropriate to recognize that there are a number of situations—most prominently, the closely held firm—in which employee ownership and governance are commonplace and serve to induce match-specific investments. Although the close corporate form works across a wide variety of firms, it is also costly, and its properties of employee ownership are unlikely to be transplantable to the fundamentally different context of the large publicly held firm.

Patterns of Governance

"Governance" refers to the variety of ways in which parties control or influence the decisions reached in an enterprise. Historically, the arguments for employee involvement in corporate governance have focused on codeter-

---

55. Kay (1992, p. 8).

56. For hopes about employee stock ownership, see Blasi (1988, p. 241); for judgments about how those hopes have turned out, see Blasi, Conte, and Kruse (1996, p. 61).

57. Levin (1985, p. 167).

mination, which refers to employee representatives on the board of directors and works councils, which offer organized employee input at the plant level.[58] We expand on this concept, suggesting that different sorts of governance devices coexist in the firm and relate to each other. This view may seem odd at first, since corporate governance is typically thought of not as a set of topics of discussion, but rather as the interaction between the board of directors, executive officers, and shareholders. But suppose that we define corporate governance in terms of the subject matter rather than the participants. These topcs include: What direction should the corporation pursue? How should it invest its capital? How well are the executive officers doing their jobs? Is there someone who could/would do it better? Should the corporation be sold? Should it file for bankruptcy?[59]

What unifies these topics, other than that they are all things that boards of directors, executive officers, and shareholders talk about? Recall, for a moment, our earlier analysis of the topics of bargaining in labor agreements. We argued that the "mandatory" topics of bargaining under section 8 of the National Labor Relations Act (as interpreted in years of court opinions) are essentially those about which discussion could be beneficial to both sides, because both sides have something to contribute.

A similar argument can be made about the scope of corporate governance. The "mandatory" topics of corporate governance, as it were, are those decided directly or delegated by the board of directors. These fall into a few broad categories. The first comprises decisions that drive the core competencies of the company: whether to enter a new market or develop a new product, whether to move or close a plant, and whether to invest in a new technology. A second group of issues relate to the payments made to shareholders: whether to pay a dividend or repurchase stock, how to raise financial capital, and whether to accept an outside offer to buy the company. These topics are the financial market counterpart to the operating decisions just mentioned. A third group of questions relate to the contractual relationship between the board of directors and the executive officers:

---

58. German law requires a form of codetermination that provides for substantial worker participation in corporate governance but requires no equity investment by workers and offers them no direct participation in net earnings. Thus the role of worker representatives to the supervisory board is mainly to gather and communicate information, while the real worker influence takes place in works councils. However, works council representatives do not "represent" the workers in any direct sense, since they are prohibited from participating actively in union-type activities such as organizing workers for action against the employer. For more discussion of German practices, see Hansmann (1993, pp. 600–05), and chapters 5, 6, and 7 by Pistor, Roe, and Baums and Frick in this volume.

59. Lorsch (1989).

compensation level for executive officers, stock option packages for directors, and whether to fire the chief executive officer. These items are the building blocks of the self-enforcing contract provisions that create the incentives for the board and executive officers to maximize profits while providing protection against opportunistic behavior.

The common link across these three categories of issues is that they involve the parties who are most informed and most motivated to solve them. They are all at a level of overview at which lower-level, but still senior, managers would not have the appropriate knowledge base and compatible incentives to resolve them. They all drive the financial returns to the shareholders, the directors, and the executive officers in the same manner that collective bargaining settles the financial returns in wages and benefits to the employees.

Although these topics are not "mandatory" topics in the same legal sense in which collective bargaining has mandatory topics, the parallel between what we are calling the "mandatory topics" of corporate governance and the mandatory topics of the National Labor Relations Act is very close. In both cases, the bargaining is confined to spheres in which both parties have something to contribute. Moreover, the nature of the statutory duty of mandatory bargaining under the National Labor Relations Act should not be overstated; after all, the statutory obligation in collective bargaining is to bargain "in good faith," not to come to any particular resolution.[60] The same is true on the corporate side. Under the duty of care, as interpreted by the courts, members of a board of directors must act with good faith and due care. Under the duty of loyalty, the courts push directors to adopt bargaining procedures that will replicate arm's-length bargaining between the conflicting interests, which may entail the use of special committees of independent directors, votes by a majority of the minority shares, or equivalent structures. In other words, the duties of care and of loyalty end up being about how bargaining should be structured and what counts as "good faith." Neither duty imposes a requirement to come to any particular conclusion.

Perhaps the most obvious feature of corporate governance is how little impact it has on the day-to-day and even year-to-year operations of the company. Corporate governance involves the big picture, the strategic direction, but little else. The continuous series of connected and complex deci-

---

60. Section 8(c) of the National Labor Relations Act, 29 U.S.C. sec. 158(c), provides that: "for the purposes of this section, to bargain collectively is the performance of the mutual obligation of the employer and the representative of the employee to meet at reasonable times and confer in good faith with respect to wages, hours, and other terms and conditions of employment, or the negotiation of an agreement, or any question arising thereunder."

sions that allow the firm to produce the product, to sell it to the customers, to hire the needed suppliers and employees, and so on is the province of middle managers without guidance from corporate governance. The operating topics of the firm are akin to the nonmandatory but permitted topics of bargaining at the unionized employee level. The operating topics could be imported into corporate governance if the board of directors and the executive officers so desired, but they generally do not. The reason that they do not choose to talk about these topics is that they have little to add, and they understand that talk has opportunity costs.

The operating topics, however, are the "mandatory" topics of the middle and senior (but not executive) officers of the company. They are mandatory not in any legal sense, but in the sense that the employer tells the relevant individuals that those decisions are part of their job. Again, this is appropriate because the appropriate senior and middle managers can best observe the factual environment, are best trained to make and carry out the decisions, and are thus best able to maximize the economic value generated by their work.

If we group senior and middle managers with employees, then the overall picture becomes clear. There are three broad groups: employees (including nonexecutive managers), executive officers, and shareholders. Discussions between the executive officers and shareholders are the conventional subject of corporate law, and cluster around those topics that are "mandatory." Discussions between executive officers and employees are the subject of labor and employment law and cluster around those topics that are "mandatory" in the union sector because of the duty to bargain under the National Labor Relations Act. In the nonunion sector they are usually handled through a system of nonlegally enforceable norms, whose substantive content is similar.

If the topics between the shareholders and the firm are considered corporate governance, the topics between the employees and firm can be called employee governance. The striking feature of corporate and employee governance is that they roughly parallel each other, and rarely overlap. The division of the relevant topics is motivated by two factors: first, that the topics bring to bear the parties' relative competencies in solving different issues; and second, that they most closely affect the parties' expected payouts. Shareholders and the firm discuss the issues related to how the total assets of the firm are organized and which new overarching investments are chosen. Employees and the firm discuss issues related to how specific assets are used and new directions in which further investments by the employer and employee would be valuable. Shareholders and employees both discuss with the firm what payments they will receive, and this discussion determines which party will be the residual claimant, which parties will be variable claimants, and which parties will prefer to minimize their risk by being fixed claimants. Whether the structure determining these payments is specified by legally enforceable contracts or by nonlegally enforceable norms, it will be worked out in such a way as to encourage productive behavior and discourage opportunism. Merit pay for employees and stock options for executive officers of publicly held companies are chosen because of their power to bring the disparate incentives of the parties into alignment.

In this view, employee governance is neither less nor more important than corporate governance. For the firm to succeed, both need to take place. Indeed, the value of the firm rests in its ability to integrate these different specialties in a way that allows each part to solve the problems it is best able to solve. Similarly, employee governance is neither less nor more restrictive than corporate governance. A firm needs to learn enough about the input of external and internal markets if it is going to maximize the size of the residual and variable payments available to the parties. Too much governance raises transaction costs and too little governance leaves the firm inadequately informed. Either way, the result would be a reduction in the residual and variable payment streams available to the input suppliers.

Indeed, a policy goal that would expand the governance of one group or another is perplexing, since it would sacrifice some part of the value created by using the firm to integrate functions. Asking line employees to work with the board of directors on determining whether a new product ought to be developed has the same merit as asking the board to work with the employees in determining how a particular product ought to be produced at the machine level. Most of the time, neither party would have any initial ideas, and would need to reserve judgment until they learned what the other party already knew. In addition, neither party would have the appropriate incentives to solve the problem because there would be no real return to offset the added work. Moreover, in some cases all parties might have inappropriate incentives and would be tempted to use their leverage in other decisions to extract concessions in other areas.[61]

The close corporation is the case in which the roughly parallel lines of corporate governance and employee governance are most likely to cross or overlap. In the close corporation, labor and capital suppliers have overlapping knowledge of the match asset. The value of the asset is either too idiosyncratic or undeveloped for the functions of the input to be divided. The

61. Williamson (1984, pp. 1206–07).

supplier of capital needs to know how the asset will be developed in the workplace before agreeing to supply equity capital. Similarly, employees will not invest in the asset unless they retain some control over the decisions made by the board of directors. In this case, neither party is willing to specialize in nonoverlapping governance.

Selling the Asset

To an important degree, then, employees are co-owners of their match-specific investments. They receive a variable share of the income stream—although not a residual stream—and, at least implicitly, cogovern the utilization of the match-specific assets. However, one might argue that to call this ownership or quasi ownership is misleading because employees cannot sell those match-specific investments and therefore do not "own" them, whatever their claims on the income streams and governance. When employees make joint investments in match, whether in training or in identifying each other, or in other ways, those investments are lost (to the employees and to the firm) if the employee leaves.

The intuition of this argument is correct: selling match-specific assets is highly problematic. This "limited alienability" feature applies to the firm and to the employee. Consider the computer programmer who leaves Microsoft for one of its competitors. The programmer brings general training to Microsoft and takes it away upon departure. But when working for Microsoft, the programmer also learns how to work with the Microsoft programming code and the Microsoft culture. One can say that the match asset generated by the joint investment of Microsoft and the programmer has value elsewhere, but only at a lower price, reflecting a combination of asymmetric information problems in valuation and lower use value. Alternatively, one can describe the investment as a combination of investment in a pure match asset (which only has value at Microsoft and is worthless elsewhere) and incremental general purpose training which the employee takes away upon leaving. One advantage of the latter description is that it treats the incremental general training as part of the employee's compensation package, part of the inducement to the employee to make the optimal investments in match.

The same problem arises when one looks at the firm's ability to sell the match-specific assets. The firm cannot easily sell these assets because if the employee can leave, then the asset has significantly reduced value. To some extent, deferred compensation and the other mechanisms that emerge to induce optimal investment in match help out; that is, the same structures that keep the employee from walking away during the life of the match asset also allow the firm to transfer those assets. Noncompetition clauses may also help prevent employees from leaving, but most firms view these protections as bordering on inadequate, although the firm can sometimes sue employees who leave for close competitors. While such mechanisms constrain exit, they do not prevent it. The situation is bilateral: just as the firm can walk away if it is willing to give up the value of the investment in match plus the reputational effects, so too an employee can walk away if willing to give up the value of personal investments in match.[62]

From this perspective, the distinctive innovation of the publicly held corporation is its success in packaging a set of investments, many of which may be match-specific, in such a way as to make the overall asset, the firm, salable to third parties, in this case, shareholders. One should not underestimate the accomplishment of packaging assets, many of them intangible, in a way that allows them to be bought and sold like grapefruit or automobiles. When assets can be packaged in a way that appeals to third-party diversified investors who need not make investments in match, they provide the firm with access to the external capital markets, with all the accompanying advantages (and disadvantages).

Of course, not all assets can be successfully repackaged: some firms are not suited to the publicly held form. Consider a close corporation that is a biotechnology start-up firm with few employees and few physical assets. In the initial stages, the biotechnology firm is at the whim of both the star biotech researchers, who have the ideas, and the venture capitalists, who have the financial capital and the management skill. If either party left at this stage, the company would be badly damaged, but so would the defecting party. Hence the match investments create a beneficial lock-in. The close corporation goes public when a sufficient amount of the match investments can be divorced from the star(s) or the initial investor/executives to overcome the holdup problem of the key players.

This treatment of the close corporation shows that the common intuition regarding the one-sided vulnerability of employees to the opportunistic behavior of the firm is not necessarily true. When an employee has substantial profitable ideas, the firm is at the mercy of that employee, as in the start-

62. The idea of match-specific capital here should be kept separate from the idea of intellectual property, which might be broadly valuable to many firms. If the innovations that the software programmer takes with him have substantial value outside the firm, indeed, if they may be worth more to others than to the innovating firm, then they are not really match assets. If this is what is going on, there will be a serious problem in inducing optimal investments in such easily stolen assets, but it is not a problem related to the sale of match assets.

up biotechnology firm. It is only after the employee has transferred the core competencies to the firm that the firm is no longer vulnerable. But in this case, the employee is not particularly vulnerable either, because the magnitude of the match investments has been reduced. Only match investments create vulnerability, because they are sunk investments. If both parties maintain ownership of the joint asset, then neither is vulnerable to the extent that they develop agreements that beneficially lock themselves together.[63]

This example of the close corporation is important, not least because of what it reveals about what it means to own a firm. Remember that the core assets of the close corporation typically cannot be sold to a third party for anything close to their value. This, in turn, creates the distinctive contracting problems that must be solved. The limited alienability of the close corporation is quite similar to the limited ability of employees with match-specific investments to sell those assets. The limit on alienability is not, in the first instance, a legal limit but a practical limit. In both cases, the assets are worth substantially more to the parties to the match than to any third party.

In the context of the firm, whatever the situation in property law more generally, easy alienability is far from being a defining characteristic of ownership. The relatively easy alienability of shares of the public corporation is a consequence of its nontrivial achievement in combining and transforming match-specific assets, and should not be thought of as a necessary feature of the ownership more broadly.

Conclusion: Parallel Tracks

We have discussed the differing sorts of variable returns and governance structures that emerge in three related and important contexts: the internal labor market, the close corporation, and the publicly held firm. The most significant features of the comparisons are the extent to which the structures can be understood as incentive-compatible solutions to the problems that face the parties in trying to maximize their joint profits; and the extent to which similar structures emerge when players manifest similar industrial organization characteristics. These similarities have several important implications.

One already finds substantial employee ownership and quasi ownership if one is careful to identify the assets about which the ownership question

---

63. For a full discussion of these issues, see Rock and Wachter (2000).

is being posed. The firm is a collection of assets, including many that are jointly created as match-specific investments by the firm and the employee. Although employees are not the residual claimants of either the match-specific assets or the total assets of the firm, one does find patterns that are close, such as merit pay (in which case the return is dependent on the observed quality of the input) and pay for performance (in which case the return is dependent on the output of the asset). That employees rarely accept a compensation package that is entirely variable is due to the presence of asymmetric information and risk aversion.

Although one does not typically find significant employee participation in corporate governance, one finds substantial employee governance over those things amenable to employee governance. That employees appear unwilling to purchase the right to corporate governance seems to parallel the situation in corporate governance, where shareholders do not participate in the day-to-day decisions that directly affect the use of the match assets of the employees. Thus employee and corporate governance are nonoverlapping, each participating in those matters about which they are most informed and in which their payment streams are most likely to be directly affected. This result is not dictated by legal regulation: just as there are few legal impediments to micromanagement by the board of directors, so, too, there are few legal impediments to employee bargaining over issues that lie at the core of entrepreneurial control.

From this perspective, employees and shareholders in publicly traded corporations appear to be on parallel tracks. With regard to their match-specific assets, employees' ownership, governance, and alienability rights are very similar to those of the shareholders, although the parties seek different packages of returns and risks. Shareholders participate little in the life of the match assets and allow their interests to be protected by their agents, the senior executives of the company. Employees, on the other hand, participate little in the life of the overall company assets. Employees reveal their risk aversion by choosing to be variable, rather than residual, claimants over their match assets, whereas investors reveal their risk aversion by accepting the increased risk of residual claimants, while remaining passive and diversifying their risks at the portfolio level.

The metaphor of the parallel tracks in the publicly traded corporation is supported by the pattern that emerges in the close corporation. Wide governance in the close corporation emerges because the owner/managers have shared expertise in both sets of "mandatory" topics, and their mix of variable and residual payment streams are more broadly at risk. These juxtapositions are important because they show that the more sharply specified concepts of ownership and governance that we find in the publicly held corporation and that provide the traditional model for thinking about employee ownership and employee involvement in corporate governance are peculiar to that form.

There is no particular magic in the style of ownership and governance that shareholders of publicly held corporations get. As the example of close corporations shows, the common characteristics of publicly held corporations—a combination of freely transferable securities with rights to elect directors, and, ultimately, discharge managers—are hardly universal structures of business organization. Moreover, many investors quite rationally (and profitably) choose the alternative status of debtholder. The differences between shareholders and bondholders, between "owners" and "creditors," between shareholders and employees, between fixed, variable, and residual claimants, are differences in their bundle of rights. In equilibrium in a reasonably efficient market, the selection will be based on the needs and preferences of the participants.

If a policy goal is to identify employees more closely with shareholders, one finds both the achievement and limits of the goal in the close corporation. In the close corporation, the parallel tracks of the employees and the shareholders overlap. But the happy picture of the unity of employees and shareholders has strict limits. The employees as shareholders accept a highly risky return on their now joined human and financial capital. Although they participate in a broad range of governance, they do so in part because no one else has the ability to substitute for them. Similarly, their ability to sell the company is limited because the assets of the close corporation are difficult to value and sell.

When all is said and done, ownership and governance, and the employees' role in it, depend on the four factors that, as industrial organization teaches, are critical to determining the properties of the firm: investments in match, asymmetric information, risk aversion, and transaction costs. When shareholders and employees find themselves in circumstances that are similar along these dimensions, they adopt similar structures, as in the case of the close corporation. When their circumstances differ along these dimensions, they adopt different structures. The classic proposals for involving employees in ownership and "corporate" governance have failed to materialize (except where mandated or subsidized) because they have overlooked the critical industrial organization attributes of the players. In other words, they have misperceived the similarities between shareholders and employees.

References

Azariadis, Costas. 1975. "Implicit Contracts and Underemployment Equilibria." *Journal of Political Economy* 83: 1183–201.

Baily, Martin N. 1974. "Wages and Employment under Uncertain Demand." *Review of Economic Studies* 41: 37–50.

Baker, George P. 1992. "Incentive Contracts and Performance Measurement." *Journal of Political Economy* 100: 598, 608.

Barry, Christopher B., and others. 1990. "The Role of Venture Capital in the Creation of Public Companies: Evidence from the Going-Public Process." *Journal of Financial Economics* 27: 447.

Beer, Michael. 1993. "Comments to Kohn 'Rethinking Rewards.'" *Harvard Business Review* (November/December): 37–49.

Blasi, Joseph R. 1988. "Employee Ownership: Revolution or Ripoff?" Cambridge, Mass.: Ballinger.

Blasi, Joseph, Michael Conte, and Douglas Kruse. 1996. "Employee Stock Ownership and Corporate Performance among Public Companies." *Industrial and Labor Relations Review* 50: 60.

Brown, Charles. 1990. "Firms' Choice of Method of Pay." *Industrial and Labor Relations Review* 43: 165-S.

Bureau of National Affairs. 1992. *Basic Patterns in Union Contracts.* 13th ed. Washington, D.C.

Coase, Ronald. 1937. "The Nature of the Firm." *Economica* 4 (4): 386.

Easterbrook, Frank L., and Daniel R. Fischel. 1983. "Voting in Corporate Law." *Journal of Law and Economics* 26: 395.

———. 1991. *The Economic Structure of Corporate Law.* Harvard University Press.

Ehrenberg, Ronald G., and Robert S. Smith. 1994. *Modern Labor Economics: Theory and Practice.* 5th ed. Glenview, Ill.: Scott, Foresman.

Fenn, George W., Nellie Liang, and Stephen Prowse. 1995. "The Economics of the Private Equity Market." Working Paper 168. Board of Governors of the Federal Reserve (December).

Freeman, Richard. 1982. "Union Wage Policies and Wage Dispersion within Establishments." *Industrial Labor and Relations Review* 39: 3.

Freeman, Richard B., and James L. Medoff. 1984. *What Do Unions Do?* New York: Basic Books.

Gompers, Paul A. 1995. "Optimal Investment, Monitoring, and the Staging of Venture Capital." *Journal of Finance* 50: 1461.

———. 1996. "Grandstanding in the Venture Capital Industry." *Journal of Financial Economics* 42: 133.

Gorman, Michael, and William A. Sahlman. 1989. "What Do Venture Capitalists Do?" *Journal of Business Venturing* 4: 231.

Gould, William B. 1993. *Agenda for Reform: The Future of Employment Relationships and the Law.* Cambridge, Mass.: MIT Press.

Gower, Laurence. 1969. *Principles of Modern Company Law.* 3d ed. London, England: Stevens.

Hansmann, Henry. 1988. "Ownership of the Firm." *Journal of Law Economics and Organization* 4: 291–96.

———. 1990. "When Does Worker Ownership Work? ESOPs, Law Firms, Codetermination, and Economic Democracy." *Yale Law Journal* 99: 1749.

———. 1993. "Worker Participation and Corporate Governance." *University of Toronto Law Journal* 43: 589.

———. 1996. *The Ownership of Enterprise.* Harvard University Press.

Hyde, Alan. 1991. "In Defense of Employee Ownership." *Chicago-Kent Law Review* 67: 159.

Hylton, Keith N. 1994. "An Economic Theory of the Duty to Bargaining Obligations." *Georgetown Law Journal* 19.

Jensen, Michael, and W. H. Meckling. 1969. "Rights and Production Functions: An Application to Labor-Management Firms and Codetermination." *Journal of Business* 52: 469–506.

Kay, Ira T. 1992. *Value at the Top: Solutions to the Executive Compensation Crisis.* New York: Harper Business.

Kling, Jeffrey. 1995. "High Performance Work Systems and Firm Performance." *Monthly Labor Review* 118: 29.

Kohn, Alfie. 1993a. "Why Incentive Plans Cannot Work." *Harvard Business Review* (September/October): 54–63.

———. 1993b. "Rethinking Rewards." *Harvard Business Review* (November/December): 37–49.

Lazear, Edward, and Sherwin Rosen. 1981. "Rank-Order Tournaments as Optimum Labor Contracts." *Journal of Political Economy* 89: 841.

Lerner, Joshua. 1994. "Venture Capitalists and the Decision to Go Public." *Journal of Financial Economics* 35: 293.

———. 1995. "Venture Capitalists and the Oversight of Private Firms." *Journal of Finance* 50: 301.

Lerner, Joshua, and Robert P. Merges. 1996. "The Control of Strategic Alliances: An Empirical Analysis of Biotechnology Collaborations." Working Paper, Harvard Business School (September).

Levin, William R. 1985. "The False Promise of Worker Capitalism: Congress and the Leveraged Employee Stock Ownership Plan." *Yale Law Journal* 95: 148.

Lewin, David, and Daniel Mitchell. 1995. *Human Resource Management: An Economic Approach.* 2d ed. Cincinnati, Ohio: South-Western.

Lorsch, Jay W. 1989. *Pawns or Potentates: The Reality of America's Corporate Boards.* Harvard Business School Press.

Malcomson, James M. 1984. "Work Incentives, Hierarchy, and Internal Labor Markets." *Journal of Political Economy* 92: 487–88.

Mitchell, Daniel J. B., David Lewin, and Edward E. Lawler III. 1990. "Alternative Pay Systems, Firm Performance, and Productivity." In *Paying for Productivity,* edited by Alan S. Blinder, 64. Brookings.

Miyazaki, Hajime. 1984. "On Success and Dissolution of the Labor-Managed Firm in the Capitalist Economy." *Journal of Political Economy* 92: 909.

O'Connor, Marleen A. 1993. "Human Capital Era: Reconceptualizing Corporate Law to Facilitate Labor-Management Cooperation." *Cornell Law Review* 78: 899.

O'Neal, F. Hodge, and Robert Thompson. 1986 (Supp. 1995). *Close Corporations: Law and Practice*. 3d ed. Mundelein, Ill.: Callaghan.

Powers, Michael R. 1988. "Note: The GM-UAW Agreement: A New Approach to Premature Recognition." *Virginia Law Review* 74: 89.

Putterman, Louis. "Ownership and the Nature of the Firm." *Journal of Comparative Economics* 17: 243–63.

Riordan, Michael H., and Michael L. Wachter. 1982. "What Do Implicit Contracts Do?" Unpublished paper, Center for the Study of Organizational Innovation (December).

Rock, Edward B., and Michael L. Wachter. 1996. "The Enforceability of Norms and the Employment Relationship." *University of Pennsylvania Law Review* 144: 1913.

———. 2000. "Waiting for the Omelet to Be Finished: Match-Specific Assets and Minority Oppression in the Close Corporation." In *Concentrated Corporate Ownership*, edited by Randall Morck. University of Chicago Press. Forthcoming.

Sahlman, William A. 1990. "The Structure and Governance of Venture-Capital Organizations." *Journal of Financial Economics* 27: 473, 493.

Summers, Clyde W. 1982. "Codetermination in the United States: A Projection of Problems and Potentials." *Journal of Comparative Corporate Law and Securities Regulation* 4: 155, 170.

———. 1994. "Employee Voice and Employer Choice: A Structured Exception to Section 8(a)(2)." In *The Legal Future of Employee Representation*, edited by Matthew W. Finkin. Ithaca, N.Y.: ILR Press.

Wachter, Michael L. "A Beacon in the Fog: A Unified Rule for Subcontracting and Relocation." Working Paper. University of Pennsylvania Institute for Law and Economics.

Wachter, Michael L., and Randall D. Wright. 1990. "The Economics of Internal Labor Markets." In *The Economics of Human Resource Management*, edited by Daniel J. B. Mitchell and Mahmood A. Zaidi, 89. Cambridge, Mass.: Basil Blackwell.

Williamson, Oliver. 1984. "Corporate Governance." *Yale Law Journal* 93: 1197.

PART Two

German Codetermination

5

Codetermination: A Sociopolitical Model with Governance Externalities

KATHARINA PISTOR

Codetermination and corporate governance have a common purpose: to control economic power associated with large corporate enterprises. The two concepts diverge in other respects, however. Codetermination gives economic power to those who control the means of production and uses employee participation as a tool to counter the interests of capital. The prevailing corporate governance paradigm, by contrast, places major control in the hands of capital owners and uses management as their agents. Employees are treated as stakeholders in a corporation, but usually not as substantial collaborators in the control over management. In essence, the main difference between the two concepts is that codetermination offers social governance, whereas corporate governance provides firm-level governance.

Social governance and firm-level governance have different socioeconomic roots. The concept of codetermination originates

I would like to thank Roberta Romano for commenting extensively on an earlier draft of this chapter and the participants of the Columbia Law School conference on employees and corporate governance for their comments and suggestions.

in the social movements of late nineteenth-century Europe. Active participation of employees in the decisionmaking processes of the company was seen as a way to overcome the contradiction between the classic liberal ideals of self-determination and the rights of the individual, on the one hand, and the reality of industrialization, on the other, which was, as Marx termed it, the alienation of workers from the fruits of their labor. This assessment of the status of workers in large corporations was not limited to leftist circles. Otto v. Gierke, an acclaimed nineteenth-century scholar of German legal tradition and business organization and a social conservative, wrote in 1868 that the "property-less classes have been or are at least threatened to be deprived of their economic personality by the development of the capitalist large enterprise. The old economic organisms . . . have been dispersed into loose atoms. From these atoms have been built extreme powerful entities which are constantly gaining additional power, for which capital is the basis and the master, while labor is only an adjunct tool."[1]

Corporate governance is a younger concept. It first found great acclaim in the United States in the early 1930s, with the publication of a classic work on the modern corporation by Adolf Berle and Gardiner Means.[2] This concept emerged not in response to social conflicts, but rather as a result of developments in the American economy, which seemed to be giving dispersed shareholders less and less control and allowing managers to become ever stronger. In the language of the social advocates of the nineteenth century, one might call this the "alienation of owners from their capital." The corporate governance debate, with its focus on the separation of ownership and control, did not command full attention in Germany until the 1980s. Corporate governance was certainly not a major issue in the debate that preceded the adoption of the 1976 law on codetermination in Germany. The emphasis was on social governance, and the implications of codetermination for corporate governance were of secondary importance.[3] Furthermore, the corporate governance debate is not a homegrown but an imported controversy, as revealed by the widespread use in Germany of the English terms "corporate governance" (sometimes translated as *Unternehmensführungskontrolle*) or "shareholder value." The interest in Ger-

---

1. V. Gierke (1868) as quoted in Kübler, Schmidt, and Simitis (1978, pp. 114).

2. Berle and Means ([1932] 1991). For a recent comprehensive treatment of the relationship between managers and owners in the United States, see Roe (1994).

3. Hopt (1994, p. 211). For an early critical analysis of the possible impact of German codetermination on corporate governance, see Mertens and Schanze (1979).

many in firm-level governance is largely the result of the growing interest among scholars in comparing systems of corporate governance.

Until the 1980s, Germany was preoccupied with the antagonism between labor and capital and hence paid little attention to the fact that the interests of capital may be divided between the interests of shareholders and the interests of management. Since then, there has been a growing sense in Germany that management is operating in a control vacuum, and that as a result firm-level governance has fallen prey to a number of deficiencies, most notably some blatant failures in monitoring company management. Legislative reforms were enacted in 1998 to improve existing control mechanisms.[4] However, the reforms have stopped short of questioning the concept of codetermination and its impact on the functioning of the supervisory board, that is, the board that holds ultimate responsibility in the German corporate structure. The consensus is still that codetermination has succeeded in establishing not only social governance but also social peace (*Sozialfrieden*), and that any attempt to alter the institutional setting currently in place would endanger this achievement. In fact, earlier proposals to reduce the number of supervisory board members mandated by the law have already been dropped from the current reform agenda, because of mounting opposition from labor unions and their political allies, who regard this as an attack on the principles of codetermination.

This chapter attempts to assess the impact of codetermination on firm-level governance. The discussion opens with a brief overview of the historical evolution of codetermination in Germany. It then turns to the concept of governance externalities produced by codetermination within a framework of coalition building among multiple parties, and examines the empirical evidence of the impact of codetermination on the relationship between shareholders, employees, and management in the German governance setting.

The Evolution of German Codetermination

In Germany today, codetermination is practiced on two levels: at the shop-floor level, through workers' councils, which give employees the right to obtain information and to participate in decisions that directly affect their workplace; and at the corporate level, through employee and union repre-

4. Law on Control and Transparency of Enterprises, April 27, 1998, RGBl I, p. 786.

sentation on supervisory boards. Firm-level participation dates back to the last decade of the nineteenth century.[5] A July 1891 amendment to the law on entrepreneurial activities (*Gewerbeordnung*) stipulated that workers' councils could be established within companies on a voluntary basis. During World War I, labor unions and the Social Democratic party seized an opportunity to make these councils mandatory when a "law on support services for the fatherland" (*Gesetz über den vaterländischen Hilfsdienst*) was passed to force the male population not actively involved in warfare to participate in military production. These groups persuaded the government to include provisions that made mandatory the creation of workers' councils and worker's arbitration bodies. Once the law went into effect, the antagonism between employees and labor union representatives intensified, and the union representatives were accused of siding with capital and the war hawks and of compromising the workers' rights and interests.[6] These early signs of a potential conflict of interest between organized labor and employees in the realization of codetermination are interesting to note, for they arise again later. The timing of the introduction of mandatory codetermination also suggests that serious political and economic crises play an important role in shaping a nation's social and legal institutions.[7]

After World War I, Germany's Weimar Constitution gave workers' councils constitutional recognition not only as entities of the firm, but also as political organizations that represented the interests of labor. Hence these councils were called on to play a political role in state administration on the regional and federal level.[8] However, subsequent legislation put this provision into effect only at the firm level. In 1920 Germany passed a law creating workers' councils in firms, then in 1922 passed another law establishing that workers' councils were to send delegates to the supervisory board in joint stock companies, thereby extending workers' participation beyond the shop floor.[9] These laws were rescinded under the fascist regime, as the overriding *Führerprinzip*, the principle of an undisputed central leader, precluded participatory models.

---

5. For an overview of the historical development of codetermination, see Kübler, Schmidt, and Simitis (1978, pp. 113–19); and Decision of the Constitutional Court on Codetermination, in Collection of Constitutional Court Decisions (BVerfGE), vol. 50, pp. 290, 294–97 (Codetermination Decision).

6. Thum (1991, p. 25).

7. Roe (1996).

8. Thum (1991, p. 30).

9. The two laws are the *Betriebsrätegesetz*, enacted February 4, 1920, RGBl, p. 147, and the *Gesetz über die Entsendung von Betriebsratsmitgliedern in den Aufsichtsrat*, enacted February 15, 1922, RGBl, p. 209.

The development of codetermination after World War II was strongly influenced by Germany's experience with fascism. One of the pillars of fascist power had been the alliance between powerful private capital—particularly the coal and steel industries concentrated in the Ruhr valley—with the political regime. Konrad Adenauer, chancellor of Germany and head of the Christian Democratic party, declared in 1947 that "the Ruhrindustry— and by that I mean coal mining and the entire heavy metal industry—has politically exploited the tremendous economic power that was accumulated in the years leading to 1933 to the detriment of the German people."[10] The prevailing view at the time was that political democracy must be combined with social constraints over the use of private capital, a concept that has been termed "economic democracy" (*Wirtschaftsdemokratie*).

The 1949 Constitution explicitly provided in Article 15 for the possibility of nationalizing industries. Moreover, it established a constitutional link between the protection of private property and the social context in which private property rights are realized. Article 14 of the 1949 Constitution guarantees the right to private property and inheritance but stipulates that "the contents and scope of property rights shall be determined by the law." In addition, section 2 of the same article explicitly states that property is not only a right but also an obligation, and that the exercise of private property rights shall also benefit society as a whole.

Political leaders in postwar occupied Germany also wished to prevent a dismantling of the nation's large industries, which were thought to be indispensable for postwar reconstruction. To appease the occupying powers as well as the European neighbors while preserving key industries, a governance structure was designed that combined features of social governance, in the form of codetermination, with multilateral governance through the integration of former war industries into a European organization. The European Coal and Steel Community—known in Germany as the *Montanunion* (where *Montan* refers to coal and steel)—that emerged from this multilateral effort became the centerpiece for further European integration.

The institutional basis for workers' participation was created with the enactment of legislation on corporate codetermination in the coal and steel industries in 1951 and by a 1952 law on the internal organization of the firm (*Betriebsverfassungsgesetz*). The 1952 law revived firm-level employee participation of the sort that had existed in the Weimar Republic. The 1951 law on Montan-Codetermination granted employees equal representation on supervisory boards in the coal and steel industry, while the 1952 law gave

10. Quoted in Kübler, Schmidt, and Simitis (1978, p. 120).

employees in companies in other industries the right to delegate employees to the supervisory board if the companies had more than 500 workers and required the board to reserve one-third of its seats for employees. Later, the 1976 Codetermination Law would extend equal employee representation on the supervisory board to all of the largest companies in Germany irrespective of the industry sector.

Codetermination in the Montan Industries (1951)

The 1951 Law on Montan-Codetermination applies to companies involved in mining and processing coal and steel that have more than 1,000 employees.[11] This law is still in force. Codetermination was realized by granting workers representation on the supervisory board. According to German corporate law, the supervisory board, the members of which are elected by the shareholders, is in charge of appointing and dismissing the executive board of the corporation, supervising the executive board, and providing the management body with advice. The supervisory board is precluded by law from day-to-day management of the corporation, which is done by the executive board. However, because the supervisory board appoints the executive board, it has the ultimate power to exert control over the company's management.

The 1951 law increased the size of supervisory boards to accommodate employee representatives. Companies were mandated to create a supervisory board with eleven members.[12] Under this law, five members are elected by the shareholders, and five members by the employees of the company. The law thus creates two "benches" within the supervisory board: the shareholder bench and the employee bench. Four members of each bench must be rank-and-file shareholders or employees, and the fifth member an outsider. He or she must not be a member of an employers' federation or a labor union, and must not have occupied the position of either a shareholder or an employee in the company in the twelve months preceding the appointment. Additional restrictions apply to the employees' representa-

11. Gesetz über die Mitbestimmung der Arbeitnehmer in den Aufsichtsräten und Vorständen der Unternehmen des Bergbaus und der Eisen und Stahl erzeugenden Industrie (sog. Montan-Mitbestimmungsgesetz) of May 21, 1951, RGBl, I, p. 347, hereinafter quoted as MontanG.

12. This applied irrespective of the legal form of the company. Although only joint stock companies have a supervisory board according to the general provisions of German corporate law, companies organized as limited liability companies with a work force exceeding 2,000 also had to create such a body.

tives. The three employee representatives must include at least one blue-collar and one white-collar worker elected in separate procedures. The members of the employee bench must be approved by the relevant labor union association. The eleventh member, the so-called neutral man who serves as the chairman of the supervisory board, is elected by the shareholder meeting upon recommendation by the five shareholders and the five employee representatives already elected. To be nominated, a candidate has to obtain at least three votes from each bench, and the law provides an elaborate conciliation procedure in case a proposal fails. The Montan-Codetermination Law also affects the composition of the executive board, which is in charge of day-to-day management. It legislates the inclusion of a special workers' director, the *Arbeitsdirektor,* and gives the employee bench additional weight in appointing this director. The appointment of the *Arbeitsdirektor* requires not only a majority of votes of the supervisory board, but also the majority of votes from the employee bench. The *Arbeitsdirektor* has the same rights as other directors, but is expected to specialize on aspects of corporate management that are of particular concern to employees, such as working conditions, wages, and benefits.

The Effects of Montan-Codetermination

From a firm-level governance point of view, the particularly interesting feature of codetermination is that it allocates control functions to agents whose positions are determined by their interests as employees, not as providers of capital or holders of cash flow rights. The interests of these agents may well be at odds with those of shareholders. For employees, the survival of the company, the protection of the workplace, as well as their wage and nonwage benefits are naturally of primary interest.[13] Shareholders, by contrast, are likely to focus on the monetary value of their investment.

The empirical evidence on the functioning of supervisory boards under the 1951 law is rather limited. Most empirical studies on codetermination that were conducted in the 1950s and early 1960s studied the impact of workers' participation on the self-esteem of workers, rather than looking at possible conflicts on the board.[14] This research agenda reflected the per-

13. Hansmann (1990, 1996).
14. For a summary and critique of the major studies conducted in the first ten years after the adoption of the Montan-Codetermination Law, see Dahrendorf (1965). A few exceptions to the rule that research focused on the social aspects and ignored the implications for corporate governance did exist. See, for example, Brinkmann-Herz (1972, 1975).

ceived purpose of codetermination: the integration of workers as active participants in the corporate enterprise. In the late 1960s, however, especially with the ascendance of the Social Democrats to the government in 1969, a debate began about whether to extend codetermination to all large companies. This debate resulted in a more systematic study of the effects of the 1951 law.

The most comprehensive study was sponsored by the government, which established a special commission to study the effects of codetermination (the Commission).[15] The Commission found that the potential antagonism between shareholders and employees had not led to constant conflicts or inertia. This may have been due to the division of labor that evolved between shareholders and employees on the board: the shareholder bench focused on investment decisions and financial returns, while the employee bench concentrated on the working conditions for the company's work force. Parties from both sides found the relationship cooperative and assessed the results of codetermination as positive.[16] In its analysis of the economic effects of codetermination, the Commission did not find that codetermination had a detrimental effect on company performance. In particular, companies that were not subject to codetermination did not seem to have performed better, although such comparisons were always complicated by the fact that, by definition, companies not subject to codetermination were in sectors other than coal and steel and might face different issues.

Although the Commission arrived at an overall positive assessment of codetermination, it also pointed out several negative tendencies. Codetermination, it suggested, was likely to favor strategies that shielded companies from competition, such as high investment or cartelization.[17] Especially when a company comes under stress, the interests of management and employees tend to converge: their joint primary interest is the survival of the firm. As a result, both support high investment strategies to foster employment and give the appearance of a thriving company, and both tend to view exogenous factors that endanger the company strictly from the company's point of view. One of the arguments in support of codetermination had been that it would act as a deterrent against cartelization, because employees would resist mergers to protect their own interests. The Commission in fact confirmed that employees frequently delayed merger decisions to ensure that the interests of the work force were taken into

15. Mitbestimmungskommission (1970), also commonly referred to as Biedenkopf-Bericht.
16. Mitbestimmungskommission (1970, pp. 54).
17. Mitbestimmungskommission (1970, pp. 71, 78, and 158).

consideration. However, employees generally supported cartelization if the increase in the company's market share was expected to yield positive effects for the employees and union representatives.

In addition to the investigation of the Commission, several academic studies analyzed codetermination at this time. From a firm-level governance point of view, the most interesting data are provided in a study by Dorothea Brinkmann-Herz.[18] The study looked at supervisory boards in companies subject to codetermination and those not subject to it. The study confirmed what was already well known about the supervisory board, namely, that with or without codetermination, the supervisory board plays primarily an acclamatory role in the appointment of the executive board. Candidates are selected in an informal procedure, in which a key role is played by the chairman of the executive board, but in which individuals and even outsiders sometimes participate. When the actual election for the executive board takes place, the supervisory board is usually presented a single candidate for each post to be filled. The ability of the supervisory board to exert influence on the executive board after it has approved its members is not very significant, either. In practice, information from the executive board was often found to be insufficient or was provided too late to allow detailed analyses by the supervisory board.

According to the results of Brinkmann-Herz's study, the effect of codetermination under the 1951 Montan legislation was not that it reduced the effectiveness of an otherwise well-functioning governance system. Rather, it introduced new internal dynamics into the supervisory board, and into the relationship between the supervisory board and the executive board, without changing the overall passive role of the supervisory board. The division of the supervisory board into two benches led to the formation of two subgroups with separate decisionmaking processes. Employees met in advance and determined a coherent voting strategy, while this was not necessarily the case for the shareholder bench. The two benches showed relatively little interaction with each other: as noted already, the employee bench specialized in social and employment-related topics, while the shareholder bench remained in charge of financial issues and major business strategies.

These results suggest that a codetermined company gives social and employment-related issues greater weight when determining the strategies for the corporation, but that labor does not conquer the domain of capital. The observed communication patterns show that both benches relate inde-

18. Brinkmann-Herz (1972; 1975, esp. p. 64). See also Edwards and Fischer (1994, pp. 210–14).

pendently to the eleventh member of the supervisory board, the neutral man, and to the executive board. As a result, a four- or even five-party configuration has emerged, consisting of the shareholder bench, the employee bench, the "neutral man," the executive board, and within the executive board, the *Arbeitsdirektor* (special workers' director) versus the chairman or the other members.

The 1976 Model and Its Evolution

When the results of the Brinkmann-Herz study were published in the first half of the 1970s, the discussion about the extension of codetermination to all large companies was already in full swing. Different models for the future of codetermination were developed by the three major political parties: the Christian Democrats (CDU), the Social Democrats (SPD), and the Liberals (FDP), as well as by the National Federation of Labor Unions (DGB). The participation of all major political powers in the formulation of new codetermination concepts suggests a consensus had been reached about the need for and desirability of an expansion of codetermination. The main arguments in favor of codetermination were the same as those used in 1951 to justify Montan-Codetermination: it would empower employees who provide the production factor and thereby enable them to become equal partners with capital in the capitalist production process. Firm-level participation was considered too low to achieve this goal, since employees on workers' councils had little input into decisions that had substantial bearing on policy change. The solution was to have workers participate in decisions that concern key strategies of the company, as these decisions ultimately determine their fate.

One intriguing aspect of the political debate was that all parties devoted considerable attention to minuscule variations in the design of the codetermination models under consideration, while ignoring even the limited evidence available on how the 1951 law had fared in practice. The question of whether the anticipated goal of effective social governance could be met with the chosen prescription was hardly ever posed. As Brinkmann-Herz put it with respect to the labor unions:

> In their long struggle to prepare public opinion and the political arena for an extension of codetermination, [the unions] identified effective codetermination with the model of equal representation on the supervisory board. Any attempt to question this identity therefore would undermine all efforts to expand codetermination together with the successes

that had already been achieved.[19]

The structural issues that were most disputed among the political parties and labor unions were whether there should be a director on the executive board in charge of social and employment affairs (the *Arbeitsdirektor*); whether the board should include a third bench, with representatives of the state, the region, or the municipality; whether the board should include representatives from the labor unions who are not simultaneously employed by the company on the employee bench; how many representatives should be named to the two benches; whether a "neutral man" should be included; and what should be the ratio of white-collar to blue-collar workers on the employee bench.[20] The Social Democrats, the National Federation of Labor Unions, and the various individual labor unions typically favored a stronger role for outsiders on the supervisory board, be it representatives of the state or the labor unions. For example, the Social Democrats recommended that up to half of the representatives on the employee bench should be outsiders proposed for election by labor unions. Alternatively, a third bench with representatives of the public interest was proposed by the white-collar labor union and the Catholic labor movement so as to have representatives that could mediate between the other two benches when necessary. In addition, the Social Democrats sought to strengthen the influence of employees over the company's management by mandating a two-thirds majority for electing members to the executive board.

The Christian Democrats, the conservative party, also came out in support of giving employees and shareholders equal representation on the supervisory board, and of including outside representatives on the employee bench. They suggested that the supervisory board be increased to twenty members—ten on the shareholder bench, and ten on the employee bench—and that it include at least one white-collar worker, five blue-collar workers, and four outsiders elected by the employees, but that these should be proposed by the labor unions.

The Liberal party, the FDP, was opposed to having outsiders on the employee bench and placed greater weight on the role of white-collar workers on the supervisory board. One of the two models advocated by different factions within this party suggested that shareholders and blue-collar workers have equal representation but that two additional white-collar

19. Brinkmann-Herz (1975, p. 107).
20. For a discussion of the details of individual proposals that are touched on here and in the following paragraphs, see Brinkmann-Herz (1975, pp. 28–33).

workers be included. The FDP's proposal regarding white-collar workers met with stiff opposition from the labor unions. The position of their major clientele, said the unions, would be undermined by representatives who were inclined to side not with their constituency, but with the company's management, and thus with capital.

All models that were proposed called for a director in charge of social and employment issues—an *Arbeitsdirektor* along the lines of the coal and steel model—on the executive board of the company. Except for the labor unions, however, none of the proposals made the election of this director subject to approval by the majority of the employee bench, as was the case in the Montan model.

In 1976 Germany finally adopted the Law on Codetermination, after more than seven years of public debate.[21] It applies to all companies with more than 2,000 employees outside the Montan industries, which continue to be regulated by the 1951 law. The 1976 law provides for equal representation of employees and shareholders on the supervisory board. The size of the supervisory board mandated by the law varies from twelve members in companies with up to 10,000 employees, to sixteen members in companies with 10,000 to 20,000 employees, and twenty members in companies with more than 20,000 employees. Shareholder representatives are elected by the corporate body designated by the relevant law. For a joint stock committee, this would be the shareholder meeting; for a limited liability firm, it would be the assembly of partners, and so on. The representatives of the employment bench are elected by delegates who are elected by the two employee subgroups, which are made up of blue- and white-collar workers. White-collar workers receive special notice. Their representation on the employee bench is the result of a delicate compromise between the majority party at that time, the Social Democrats, and its coalition partner, the Liberals. The latter were the major advocate for the interests of white-collar (often management) employees. Instead of reserving a fixed number of seats for white-collar workers, as originally proposed by the Liberal party, the law stipulates that the employee bench shall represent blue- and white-collar workers in proportion to their representation in the company.

The employee bench is not elected directly. Instead, the employees elect delegates, who in turn elect the members of the employee bench. These elections are held at company expense, at a cost that for large companies can

---

21. Gesetz über die Mitbestimmung der Arbeitnehmer (Mitbestimmungsgesetz), May 4, 1976, RGBl, 1153, often referred to as MitbestG.

range from 1 million to 5 million deutsche marks.[22] A set of voting regulations was issued to provide some guidance for companies of different size and structure.[23] White- and blue-collar workers elect their delegates in separate procedures. Representatives of the labor union, who hold a minority position on the employee bench, are elected by the same delegates upon proposal by the labor union. Unlike the Montan-Codetermination Law of 1951, the 1976 law does not require that the elected members of the employee bench receive the approval of the relevant labor union.

Once the two benches are elected, the supervisory board elects its chairman from among the current members of the board. In contrast to the Montan Codetermination Law, the 1976 law does not stipulate that the chairman must be a "neutral man"; rather, the chairman may be recruited from either the shareholder or the employee bench. If the supervisory board is unable to arrive at a majority decision for one candidate—which is a common situation, given that labor and management unite behind their own candidates—then the chairman of the supervisory board shall be elected by the shareholder bench and his deputy by the employee bench. This arrangement typically prevails in practice. The affiliation of the chairman of the supervisory board is important, because in the event of a tie vote, he or she has the right to break the tie. Because of this bias toward the shareholder side, the model has been aptly characterized as "quasi-parity codetermination," as opposed to the "full parity codetermination" under the 1951 Montan Model.[24] Also, the members of the executive board of codetermined companies must be elected by a two-thirds majority, so as to ensure that a director may not be appointed against the vote of the employee bench.

Legal Appeals

The public debate over the 1976 codetermination law did not end with the adoption of the law. During the years preceding the enactment of the law, a strong opposition had formed, made up of employers' associations, corporations that were subject to the law, and shareholder organizations. A

22. Bamberg and others (1987, p. 97).
23. Special voting rules, for example, exist for holding companies. For further references, see Mertens and Schanze (1979, p. 80).
24. Hopt (1994, p. 204).

group of claimants made up of the German Federation for the Protection of Share Ownership, nine companies affected by the new law, and twenty-nine employer associations challenged the constitutionality of the law. Interestingly, the main challengers of the law were not shareholders, but companies and employers' associations made up of company executives as the legal representatives of companies that are members of these associations. It is therefore not surprising that the main issue in the entire proceeding was not whether codetermination would dilute shareholder value, but whether it interfered with the interests of the corporation and the way it was managed. The way in which a company is managed certainly affects shareholder value. However, the "interests of the company" is an ambiguous term that may in some contexts be a simple proxy for the interests of the company's management.

Germany's Constitutional Court upheld the law in 1979. The court stressed that the law was aimed at certain socioeconomic goals, and that the legislature had a right to determine these rules, even if they limit the rights of individuals or entities. These rights have to yield to the "public interest," unless the goals themselves or the means used to implement them are either unconstitutional or evidently not able to reach the goals, and for this reason present an unjustified limitation of the rights of said individuals or entities.[25] These arguments are in line with the generally restrained position of the Constitutional Court in judging the constitutionality of legislative acts. However, the court's terminology and its legal arguments show that it adopted the prevailing view of an enterprise as a joint undertaking of labor and capital and hardly recognized the potential for conflicts of interests between the different representatives of capital, management, and shareholders.[26] Throughout its ruling, the court used the term *Unternehmen,* or "enterprise," rather than "corporation." This is not only a question of semantics, but it reflects a century-old debate about the difference between the legal form of the corporation and the identity and rights of the enterprise for which it provides a shell. Many American legal scholars—after long deliberation—have concluded that the corporation beyond the legal fiction of the corporate entity with certain legal rights is a "nexus of contracts," but German legal scholars, judges, and politicians continue to see the enterprise behind the corporate shell as a unit with its own

25. Codetermination Decision, BVerfGE, vol. 50, pp. 290, 331.
26. Codetermination Decision, BVerfGE, vol. 50, pp. 290, 319, 352.

rights.[27] In this enterprise, the major antagonism is the one between labor and capital, not between owners and agents.

Codetermination and the Dynamics of Corporate Governance with Multiple Players

The debate preceding the adoption of the 1976 codetermination law and the model finally implemented focused on how to ensure social governance through worker participation. The implications of codetermination for firm-level governance were largely ignored. Whatever the underlying concepts that determine the contents of legal rules, once they are enacted they may have effects not anticipated by the legislators. The goal of codetermination was to give social governance the upper hand over private capital by strengthening the role of employees in the governance of firms. Taking this goal as a benchmark, we might expect various outcomes: the law succeeded and codetermination led to greater participation by employees in the firm's governance; the law did not succeed and employees played a negligible role in firm governance; or codetermination affected the dynamics of governance in ways that are hard to categorize as simple failure or success. It is difficult to prove whether the first or second propositions hold. Empirical studies are scarce. Moreover, all such studies face the problem that given the many known deficiencies of the supervisory board before the enactment of codetermination, it would be difficult to attribute the fact that employees do not exert the type of influence that was expected to a failure of codetermination.

The more interesting proposition to consider is whether the dynamics of firm governance changed in response to the introduction of codetermination. From a theoretical point of view, the effect of codetermination on corporate governance can be expected to generate two outcomes. First, it raises the cost of collective decisionmaking by increasing the heterogeneity of interests represented on the supervisory board. Second, it alters the relationship between the supervisory board and the management of the company from one of bilateral control—that is, a relatively unified supervisory board overseeing a relatively unified executive board—to a multiple-party arrangement characterized less by control and more by coalition building.

27. Jenson and Meckling (1976); Fama (1980); Easterbrook and Fischel (1991, p. 12). For a discussion of the debate between advocates of a "nexus of contracts" theory of the firm and advocates of an older view in the law, the "entity" theory of the firm, see chapter 2 in this volume.

The Cost of Collective Governance

Firm-level governance arises whenever a firm is not managed directly by a single owner. This happens when either multiple owners with diverging interests are involved in the management of the firm, or management is delegated to an agent. Where multiple owners are involved in the governance of firms, the cost of decisionmaking increases. The extent of this rise in costs depends on the diversity among the different types of owners, which in turn is determined by their relation to the firm as investors, producers, workers, or consumers.[28] Within each of these different groups, one may find different interests, but the spread of different interests is likely to be more pronounced in some groups than in others. Even though investors may differ by their tax status, interests as creditors, and preferences about risk and liquidity, they typically converge on the common interest of maximizing the value of their investment. The interests of different groups of employees tend to be more diverse, especially in large firms (which helps to explain why employee ownership is concentrated mainly in firms with relatively homogeneous employee profiles). Where multiple owners with diverging interests are involved in the governance of firms, the cost of collective governance will surely increase.

Firm-level governance may also entail agency costs, which arise when firm owners bring in professional managers to act as their agents.[29] Of course, the danger is that managers may pursue interests other than maximizing shareholder value, so that owners must find ways to control management and to align its activities with their interests. A variety of mechanisms may be helpful here. Internal mechanisms include corporate boards, whose task is to monitor management and give shareholders or boards the right to approve major decisions. Such internal mechanisms may be backed by judicial review, although the extent of judicial review varies considerably across different legal systems. Market mechanisms, including pressures through the product, managerial labor, and capital markets, also provide some checks on the management of firms.

Codetermination raises the costs of collective governance and agency costs. Although employees do not become owners of the firm, they are represented on the corporate board, whose task it is to monitor management. This increases the heterogeneity of interests on the board and consequently

---

28. The discussion in this paragraph draws on Hansmann (1996, esp. pp. 20, 89).
29. Jensen and Meckling (1976).

raises the cost of decisionmaking. The diversity of interests goes beyond the conflict between capital and labor; remember that the 1976 law puts not only blue- and white-collar employees on the employee bench, but also labor union representatives. It seems plausible that including employees on the supervisory board will raise agency costs, because it will be more difficult for a supervisory board of diverse and conflicting interests to monitor management. However, one party may gain a great deal from the cumulative effect of the higher cost of collective governance and increased agency costs: that party is management.

Corporate Governance as a Multiplayer Game

Codetermination not only adds to costs of firm-level governance, but it also alters the dynamics in ways that will tend to reduce the company's control over management.[30] An example of the dynamics that may unfold in corporate governance with multiple players is given by recent takeover scenarios in the United States, where not only management, current shareholders, and raiders participated, but labor unions played an active role by supporting different parties. The most important implication of the multiple-party paradigm is that the traditional focus of the corporate governance debate on the dichotomy between owners and managers loses much of its explanatory power, for "the public corporation should be viewed less as a 'series of bargains' than as a 'series of coalitions.'" In takeover scenarios where several labor unions participated, "every coalition that could be formed was formed: management allied with one union against another; the unions allied with each other and with management; and ultimately the unions allied with a powerful shareholder to outflank management." The major outcome of multiple-player governance in takeover situations is that all possible parties form unstable coalitions. As a result "the locus of power and authority within the corporation is less certain."[31]

The fact that labor unions become more active in extraordinary situations, such as takeovers, does not necessarily mean that they also play an active role in day-to-day governance. Still, to the extent that their participation in extraordinary situations is anticipated, this may alter the bargaining power of the other participants in the governance game. If management ceases to be the object of control and instead becomes one of

---

30. The title of this subsection is taken from the subtitle of an article by Coffee (1990).

31. Coffee (1990). The quotations in this paragraph are from pp. 1496, 1525, and 1496, respectively.

the multiple players who engage in building coalitions with changing partners, new possibilities arise for management to escape control.

German codetermination established multiparty governance as the standard model for firm-level governance in large firms. This model differs from the American takeover scenarios in several ways. First, whereas in the United States coalitions are formed in the wake of a hostile takeover, in Germany multiple parties participate in the corporate game in the long term. In the language of game theory, codetermination has provided the basis for repeat games.[32] As a result, coalitions tend to be more stable.

Second, the position of the various players in Germany is protected or even mandated by legal and institutional arrangements. Labor union representatives as well as white- and blue-collar workers are represented on the employee bench of the supervisory board, because this is what the law provides. The relationship between management and employees is determined by additional legal arrangements and does not need to rely on implicit and typically unenforceable contracts. Payments to employees are part of a collective labor contract system (*Tarifvertragssystem*) to which labor unions, on the one hand, and employer associations, on the other hand, are parties.

According to German collective labor law, labor unions and the employers' federation bargain for wages and nonwage benefits for all companies under their jurisdiction on an annual basis. This bilateral agreement is binding until it is replaced by a new collective labor contract and may be extended to all companies in a certain industry sector by decision of the Ministry of Labor. Thus the parties and their relationships are bound by law, their flexibility is limited, and they cannot opt out of these explicit agreements.

Third, with labor union representatives on the supervisory board, the future of the individual company may not be the only objective for the board to bargain about. Strategies for an entire industry sector may also be at stake. This potential spillover effect of company affairs to industry affairs and vice versa is likely to reduce the willingness of all parties concerned to build coalitions with the other parties in the game. For example, management may be reluctant to disclose to union representatives information that might signal the bargaining position of the employers' associations in upcoming collective labor contract negotiations. Ideological constraints also influence the dynamics of coalition building. As long as employee representatives view themselves as advocates of labor opposed to the interests of capital, they are unlikely to bridge this gap and form coalitions with

32. Coffee (1990, p. 1543).

shareholder representatives for the purpose of controlling management. As a result, management gains the upper hand in the process of coalition building, because it is most flexible in selecting from among the opposite parties, and the position of both shareholders and employees as agents of corporate governance is weakened.

Empirical Evidence on the Effects of Codetermination

Empirical analysis of the functioning of codetermined supervisory boards is constrained by the lack of systematic data. Although numerous studies were conducted in the first five years after the law was enacted, no long-term studies have been undertaken.[33] Given the scarcity of data on the functioning of firm-level governance in Germany before the enactment of the 1976 law, there are also no well-controlled "before-and-after" studies. Furthermore, because all large corporations had to implement codetermination, it is difficult to sample firms with and without codetermination. It is true that a number of firms escaped codetermination by reorganizing into legal forms not covered by the law or by splitting into smaller units not subject to the law. But these measures entailed comprehensive restructuring of the companies involved, with the result that these companies are difficult to compare with those that implemented the new law.

The following analysis therefore relies primarily on two sets of behavioral data: a survey of structural changes in the by-laws of companies that had to implement the 1976 law; and court cases that dealt with instances in which the legality of such changes was challenged. Data about formal changes that companies adopted in response to codetermination do not provide information about the actual practices of codetermined boards. However, given the highly institutionalized character of the German corporate governance system, these changes do indicate how those affected by the new law sought to counter it.

Formal changes in the corporate statutes are well documented: a comprehensive study conducted in the early 1980s surveyed all companies that had to adjust their constitutive documents to the law on codetermination and collected data on the composition of the two benches of the supervisory board in these companies. The study included all companies subject to the new law on codetermination irrespective of their legal form: this came to a total of 281 joint stock companies and 174 limited liability com-

---

33. For an overview over the available empirical studies see Kißler (1992, p. 150).

panies. However, since the more detailed data are available for joint stock companies, the following summary of the results of the study focuses on joint stock companies only.[34] Court cases also illustrate, albeit on a case-by-case basis, how companies and shareholders sought to soften the impact of codetermination. In addition, they demonstrate the limits of formal changes that were introduced to circumvent codetermination rules, as German courts upheld the principle of codetermination in the majority of cases.

The Composition of Codetermined Boards

The introduction of quasi-parity codetermination in 1976 extended labor representation in large companies from one-third of the seats—as required by the 1952 law on the internal organization of firms—to one-half. The bargaining power of labor clearly increased when employee representation rose to half and the law mandated that the appointment of the executive board by the supervisory board required a two-thirds majority.

In most companies, the majority of the supervisory board members elected by shareholders were made up of the following three groups: other companies with an equity stake exceeding 50 percent, the state, and foreign companies. This reflects the ownership structure of Germany's large joint stock companies, which is characterized by cross-shareholdings among companies, a significant share of state ownership, and a substantial share of foreign ownership. Somewhat surprisingly, representatives of companies without an equity stake ranked as the fifth largest group, right after those representing companies with an equity stake of less than 50 percent. This seems to suggest that codetermined companies have a substantial number of friendly directors on their supervisory boards.

The composition of the employee bench in the companies studied was largely predetermined by the codetermination law, as the law mandated the inclusion of white-collar workers as well as labor union representatives. The majority of seats on the employee bench are indeed occupied by employees of the company. Typically, they are also concurrently members of the company's workers' councils. The second largest category is made up of outsiders: labor union representatives who are not employees of the company. This outcome is remarkable because, according to the law, labor union representatives may also be chosen from among the employees. However,

34. Gerum, Steinmann, and Fees (1988).

unions argued strongly and apparently successfully that external labor union representatives were needed to represent general social interests and to counter "firm-egoistic" tendencies.[35] The third largest group in most cases—though significantly smaller than the other two—consists of members of the workers' councils of subsidiaries.

The interests of these three largest groups within the employee bench are likely to diverge on many of the issues the supervisory board must face. The interests of employees of the company may not be the same as those of the company's subsidiaries, or those of labor union representatives, who are likely to pursue sector or even economy-wide strategies rather than focus strictly on the interests of the company or its employees. However, employees must ensure that they vote together; if they split their vote, the outcome will often be determined by the shareholder bench. For this purpose, it is typical to have employee bench meetings before the meeting of the board. The additional time and effort put into the organization of separate employee bench meetings is a clear indication that collective governance in heterogeneous groups pushes up governance costs. Separate employee bench meetings also reduce the chance of building coalitions across the two benches; given the inclusion of white-collar workers on the employee bench, the crossing of party lines would otherwise not be an unlikely scenario. It is difficult to predict patterns of coalition building from the composition of the two benches alone. Still, it is fair to say that the shareholder bench is typically management friendly enough not to pose serious threats to the interests of management. The relation of management with the employee bench could be more controversial given the dominance of blue-collar employees and labor union representatives. However, employee representatives may choose the shareholder bench, not necessarily management, as their main target. Moreover, any antimanagerial strategies that might emanate from the employee bench may be mitigated by white-collar representatives who can hold up the process of reaching a consensus among members of the employee bench.

The Powers of Codetermined Supervisory Boards and Their Committees

The introduction of codetermination led to a de facto reallocation of the powers and responsibilities of the supervisory board, the executive board,

---

35. Bamberg and others (1987, p. 147).

and the shareholder meeting. According to the corporate law, which was left unchanged, the executive board is in charge of day-to-day management of the company. The supervisory board appoints and "supervises" management but is prohibited from directly participating in the day-to-day management of the company. However, the by-laws of the corporation or regulations of the executive board may provide that the supervisory board shall approve decisions to be taken by the executive board. Finally, the shareholder meeting elects the members of the shareholder bench on the supervisory board, makes decisions about changes in the corporate by-laws, appoints the auditors, and relieves the members of the executive board as well as the supervisory board at the end of the fiscal year.

Available data show that many companies changed their by-laws or the rules governing the internal affairs of the supervisory board in expectation of the enactment of the 1976 law or shortly thereafter, usually in a way that restricted the powers and responsibilities of the supervisory board.[36] As a result of these changes, the number of transactions that required supervisory board approval was reduced, or the approval right was transferred from the supervisory board to the shareholder meeting. For example, supervisory board approval is not mandated by the law, but it used to be fairly common in major transactions before the enactment of the 1976 law. Of the 281 joint stock companies surveyed after the execution of the law, however, 104 (or 37 percent) lacked rules that required the approval of the supervisory board. Four of the companies surveyed even prohibited any transaction from being subjected to the approval of the supervisory board, which is in clear contradiction to German corporate law.

Without comparable data on companies without codetermination or on companies before the law was passed, it is difficult to assess whether these findings were caused only or primarily by the introduction of the codetermination law. It is intriguing that the coal and steel companies under the 1951 Montan-Codetermination Law, for example, were much more likely to give the supervisory board approval rights for many transactions than companies that introduced codetermination under the 1976 law. A closer analysis reveals that factors other than employee representation may have also affected the elimination of approval rights. The survey data show that companies with a high level of state ownership were more likely to include approval rights for the supervisory board, whereas companies owned by foreign investors were less likely to do so. Still, many of the

---

36. The discussion throughout this paragraph draws on Gerum and others (1988, p. 72).

changes were introduced around the time of the enactment of the Codetermination Law, which suggests at least a partial causal link.[37]

The survey data also revealed a tendency to strengthen the shareholder
bench. One strategy used to achieve this was to enact provisions in the by-
laws mandating that the chairman of the supervisory board had to be
elected from among shareholder representatives, which the 1976 law calls
for only in the case of a stalemate. Another strategy was to elect more than
one deputy chairman of the board. The purpose of the latter was presumably to dilute the influence of the first deputy who, according to the law,
must be an employee representative whenever the chairman is a member
of the shareholder bench. These changes provide evidence that companies,
or possibly a coalition of shareholders and managers, sought to neutralize
the impact of employee participation.

However, the composition of the codetermined supervisory boards, the
composition of board committees and the powers of the supervisory board
were all heavily litigated.[38] The general tendency of the decisions was to
make it more difficult for companies to block the intended effects of
codetermination. In 1982, the Supreme Court—which is distinct from the
Constitutional Court—issued its first ruling in a case that dealt with new
regulations for the supervisory board adopted by the shareholder meeting.[39]
Under the by-laws of the corporation in this case, the supervisory board was
to elect not only the chairman and his deputy, but also a second deputy, and
this second deputy had to be elected from the shareholder bench. The
chairman, the two deputies, and an additional member elected by the
employee bench were to form a presidium whose task was to propose candidates for the executive board to the supervisory board. In case of a stalemate, the chairman was given two votes. The court held that the election of
a second deputy chairman from the shareholder bench was a violation of
the 1976 law, because it undermined the equality of all members of the
supervisory board. The court also voided the provision on the creation of
a "presidium" of the supervisory board. It argued that the creation of subcommittees of the supervisory board was the prerogative of this body, not
of the shareholder meeting.

In a second ruling issued on the same day, the Supreme Court declared
the by-laws of another company void.[40] Under the rules in that case, the

---

37. See Ulmer (1977).
38. For details, see chapter 7 in this volume.
39. Supreme Court of 25.2.1982, in *Der Betrieb*, no. 14 (1982), p. 742.
40. Supreme Court of 25.2.1982, in *Der Betrieb*, no. 14 (1982), p. 747.

supervisory board reached a quorum and was thus able to adopt binding decisions if a minimum of 50 percent of the members of the shareholder bench, including the chairman of the supervisory board, were present. The court regarded this as a violation of the principle of equality, which requires that all members of the supervisory board have equal weight, irrespective of the constituency that elected them.

In both decisions the Supreme Court remained within the framework set by the Constitutional Court for interpreting the codetermination law. In other words, both decisions abided by the precept that shareholders and employees should participate equally in the corporation through representation on the supervisory board, and that it is the duty of the courts to uphold this intention. The fact that the law gives shareholder representatives the right to elect the chairman if the two benches cannot agree on a candidate, and that the chairman—who is typically a shareholder representative—has the decisive vote in deadlock situations does not weaken the underlying principle of equal representation. In all other matters every member of the supervisory board must have strictly equal rights.[41]

In a subsequent decision in 1984, the Supreme Court had to deal with the by-laws of a limited liability company that was subject to codetermination.[42] The by-laws of the defendant in this case stipulated that the supervisory board elects the members of the executive board but also provided that the details of the employment contract between the corporation and the members of the executive board, including salary level and benefits, should be determined not by the supervisory board, but by the shareholder meeting. The court declared that provision to be void. It argued that the rights of the supervisory board to appoint the members of the executive board are seriously curtailed if it cannot take into consideration salary as well as other aspects of the employment contract. In voiding this provision, the court prevented the transfer of important rights of the supervisory board to the shareholder meeting and thus safeguarded its control rights over management.

One of the most disputed and most litigated issues of the 1976 law was the extension of parity or quasi-parity representation to the various committees of the supervisory board. The codetermination law was followed by a noticeable trend toward delegating the preparation of decisions to board committees.[43] The creation of supervisory boards with up to twenty

---

41. See also the commentary by Kallmeyer (1982).
42. Supreme Court of 14.11. 1983, in *Der Betrieb,* no. 2 (1984), p. 104.
43. *Münchener Handbuch* (1988, §29 Rn 3 6).

members that resulted from codetermination would have given grounds to create smaller bodies where actual deliberation and decisionmaking could take place. However, the prospect of reducing the influence of employees on the board's activities by creating committees that favored shareholders created additional incentives for the proliferation of committee activities. Most disputes concerning supervisory board committees focused on the committee in charge of executive affairs. Survey data suggest that shareholder representatives came to dominate these committees. In 79 percent of the 281 joint stock companies, shareholders occupied either the majority of seats or determined the outcome of votes by controlling the chairmanship with two votes in case of a stalemate.

The allocation of positions in favor of shareholder representatives on supervisory board committees was upheld by the courts. The Supreme Court as well as the majority of appellate courts argued that nothing in the 1976 law suggested that equal representation had to be extended to all aspects of the work of the supervisory board.[44] In particular, the courts held that the allocation of two votes to the chairman of such committees did not violate the 1976 law, which after all included a similar provision. Even where the election of committee members resulted in the dominance or exclusive representation of shareholders, this did not necessarily contravene the letter or the spirit of the law. The limit was that shareholder dominance should not go as far as systematically excluding employee representatives from committees. In several companies, shareholder representatives attempted to exclude employee representatives from such committees altogether on the grounds that employee representatives lacked the necessary expertise to become involved in the details of appointment procedures and employment issues, and that employees of the company should not participate in the appointment of those who acted as their employers. The Supreme Court ruled that these arguments were flawed and that regulations

44. Supreme Court of 25.2.1982, *Wirtschaftsmitteilungen* (WM) 1982, 363 (Dynamit Nobel AG); Appellate Court (Hamburg), 6.3. 1992, *Der Betrieb* (DB), 1992, 774 (Hamburg-Mannheimer Versicherungsverein); Supreme Court, 17.5.1993, *Der Betrieb* (DB) 1993, 1609 (Hamburg-Mannheimer Versicherungsverein). See also Appelate Court (Hamburg), 25.4.1984, *Der Betrieb* (DB), 1567 (Beiersdorf AG). The case dealt with changes in the supervisory board's regulation regarding the committee for executive board affairs. The number of committee members was reduced from four to three, and the election procedure foresaw that each of the twelve members of the supervisory board received one vote for each of the total number of candidates nominated. In the actual elections—whose validity was disputed in the case—only one of the four candidates was an employee representative and the three members elected were all shareholder representatives.

that excluded employee representatives from key committees, such as committees for executive board affairs, did contradict the 1976 law.[45] Still, this decision left earlier decisions intact that denied employees equal participation in supervisory board committees.

Thus despite many attempts by shareholders and company management to reduce the influence of employees and labor unions through formal changes of the company law, in most cases the letter of the law prevailed. The only device the courts granted shareholder representatives that could be used to expand their rights in relation to employee representatives was the right to delegate decisions to committees that were not subjected to the same standards of codetermination as the board itself. These results suggest that the 1976 codetermination law was implemented without many compromises.

The Functioning of Codetermination Today

In the absence of empirical data, the following information on the current functioning of codetermination has been gleaned from selected interviews with representatives of labor unions, political parties, and legislators.[46] Because this information is largely anecdotal, it must be treated with caution. As a well-known legal scholar and expert in corporate law once said: "There is no subject that people lie about as much as they do about codetermination!" The social consensus is still that codetermination is a great achievement because it contributed to, if not caused, social peace between labor and capital. However, the responses do suggest certain trends in connection with the general themes of the current debate.

From the comments of representatives of different parties, the government, and labor unions, people still seem to think that the positive aspects of codetermination outweigh its negative aspects. The most important positive aspect, according to all sides, is that it involves employees in a company's decisionmaking process at a relatively early stage. Although this prolongs decisionmaking in matters that affect employees negatively, such as a proposed downsizing or company closing, the consensus is that employee participation significantly reduces the potential for conflict when these measures do take effect. In other words, codetermination may delay such decisions, but it does not prevent them, and it facilitates their implementa-

45. See most recently Supreme Court, 17.5.1993, in *Der Betrieb* (*DB*) 1993, 1609.
46. I am grateful to Dr. Rüdiger von Rosen of the Deutsche Aktieninstitut for providing me with numerous contacts. As many of them wished to preserve confidentiality, I would like to thank all of them here for their cooperation. Interview notes are on file with the author.

tion after they have been adopted. In this setting, employee representatives on the supervisory board are likely to find themselves in a difficult position. They are forced to participate in a process that is likely to have negative effects for the company's employees, yet they must do so and must also pledge the continued support of a constituency whose interests are opposed to such measures. It may be that the involvement of external employee representatives plays an important role in avoiding a pure defense strategy by the workers. Given the more general interests of the labor unions that represent entire industry sectors, there is also potential for antagonism among employee representatives, as the closure of one company may be the price paid for the survival of another. However, differences among representatives are typically solved in the meetings of the employee bench that precede the meeting of the supervisory board and are therefore not disclosed. At the board meeting, employees always vote together.

In light of the sociopolitical objectives of codetermination, the greater involvement of employees does indeed suggest that the concept has met with some success. However, a related goal of codetermination is to give employees an opportunity to participate in long-term strategies. This broader goal has only partly been met. Employee representatives on the board continue to "specialize" in employee matters, such as the workplace, social concerns, wages, and benefits.

They have not made the leap to participating in business strategy connected with, say, production abroad. Representatives of labor unions admit this and see the greater involvement of employees in these decisions as their main task for the future. Apparently employees have had even less influence in product selection and marketing strategies. A major problem, according to labor union representatives, is that employee representatives are unqualified to deal with matters such as accounting and finance. The lack of skills needed to exercise management control in these areas is part of a broader criticism of the current supervisory board structure. Indeed, it is widely recognized that all members of the supervisory board need to be able to approach their control duties with greater "professionalism." To improve the qualifications of employee representatives, the National Federation of Labor Unions has established training programs for board members. Still, a DGB representative suggested to me that the most difficult task is to persuade long-standing labor union functionaries that they need to improve their qualifications and to expand their perception of their role beyond promoting workers' interests in the narrower sense. In view of these ideological obstacles, training programs will not suffice to promote firm-level governance through employee participation.

Even though people across the political spectrum acknowledge that social governance has benefited from codetermination, many interviewees were of the opinion that codetermination also affects firm-level governance in a way that makes it harder to control management. Three concerns were frequently mentioned by interviewees: the fractionalization of the supervisory board, the dilution of the supervisory board's powers and influences, and the coalition building (or collusion) by one of the two benches with company management.

The fractionalization of the supervisory board is most closely associated with "bench meetings." The practice of holding bench meetings before the full board meetings, which first emerged in the coal and steel companies subject to Montan-Codetermination, is common among codetermined companies today. Shareholder and employee benches meet separately and both benches typically invite the chairman of the executive board to brief them about the company's situation. As a result, the chairman often reports to board members three times: to the shareholder bench, to the employee bench, and to the entire board. The actual decisionmaking process takes place in separate bench meetings, and the meetings of the supervisory board serve mainly as a forum for exchanging the different conclusions reached and to vote on them, some would say to rubber-stamp decisions already agreed upon by management with at least one of the benches. Separate meetings are a logical solution to the diversity of interests represented on each bench of the board. However, having the decisionmaking processes take place outside the supervisory board does not alleviate the danger that management may use its monopoly over information to influence the decisionmaking process in its own favor. Moreover, it reinforces the purely acclamatory function of the corporate board. It should be remembered that back in the 1950s the supervisory board was already being criticized for acting as merely an acclamatory body, and so codetermination should not take all the blame for this situation. Still, the practice of separate board meetings has caused things to deteriorate, not improve. Much of the blame for this has been placed on the fact that external labor union delegates have a place on the board, which is said to have fostered a more aggressive tone between the two benches, although open hostility has faded over time. In fact, some evidence suggests that company employees focus primarily on their company, while union representatives frequently pursue sectoral or national union policies and the interests of the unions.[47]

47. Hopt (1994, p. 206).

Although the courts have by and large prevented statutory changes from being used to mitigate employee influence on the supervisory committee, there are other ways to ensure that employees do not interfere with the interests of shareholders or company management. Most important among these are measures to control and limit the information flow to the supervisory board and to marginalize its role by holding meetings infrequently. Before the amendment of the corporate law in 1998, which now mandates quarterly board meetings for publicly traded companies, the supervisory board had to meet at least once every six months, but should have met once a quarter. In practice, supervisory boards rarely met more than once a quarter.[48] Further evidence of the control of the flow of information can be seen in the distribution of the auditor's report before the 1998 legal change. According to a 1965 amendment to the German corporate law, the auditor reported not to the supervisory board but to the executive board, which in turn was supposed to provide this information to the supervisory board.[49] This change has now been revised so that the auditor reports to the supervisory board. Only in a few corporations do all members of the supervisory board actually receive the auditor's report.[50] Frequently, the auditor's report was only handed out during a meeting and immediately collected at the end of it, a practice that has become known as "table presentation" (*Tischvorlage*). The justification for this practice is the fear that employees and labor union representatives, in particular, may misuse the information provided in the report outside the company for their own sectorwide or national strategies. This fear is not just hypothetical; in a number of cases, information about pending merger decisions and the like has indeed been leaked by union representatives.[51]

Conclusion

In the absence of extensive survey data, it is difficult to draw firm conclusions about the impact of codetermination on firm-level governance. However, there is some preliminary evidence to indicate that while codetermination has not caused many of the problems that plague corporate governance in Germany today, it has certainly reinforced them and added to the

---

48. Hopt (1994, p. 206).
49. Before that, the auditor reported directly to the supervisory board. See Götz (1995, p. 341).
50. For further references, see Götz (1995, p. 343).
51. Hopt (1994, p. 206).

lack of control over management that already existed. With two benches of equal size representing capital and labor, codetermination has tended to pit these groups against each other (even if they do not engage in open conflict), rather than unite them in the task of controlling management. Thus it has set the rules for multiple-party corporate governance in such a way that the net beneficiaries are those who ought to be controlled: the company's management.[52]

References

Bamberg, Ulrich, Michael Bürger, Birgit Mahnkopf, Helmut Martens, and Jörg Tiemann. 1987. *Aber ob die Karten voll ausgereizt sind . . . 10 Jahre Mitbestimmungsgesetz 1976 in der Bilanz.* Bonn: Bund Verlag.

Berle, Adolf A., and Gardiner C. Means. [1932] 1991. *The Modern Corporation and Private Property.* New Brunswick, N.J.: Transaction.

Brinkmann-Herz, Dorothea. 1972. *Entscheidungsprozesse in den Aufsichtsräten der Montanindustrie, Beiträge zur Verhaltensforschung.* Berlin: Duncker and Humblot.

———. 1975. *Die Unternehmensmitbestimmung in der BRD, Der lange Weg einer Reformidee.* Cologne: Kiepenheuer and Witsch.

Coffee, John C. Jr. 1990. "Unstable Coalitions: Corporate Governance as a Multi-Player Game." *Georgetown Law Journal* 78 (5): 1495–549.

Dahrendorf, Ralph. 1965. *Das Mitbestimmungsproblem in der deutschen Sozialforschung: Eine Kritik.* 2d ed. Munich: Piper Verlag.

Easterbrook, Frank L., and Daniel R. Fischel. 1990. *The Economic Structure of Corporate Law.* Harvard University Press.

Edwards, Jeremy, and Klaus Fischer. 1994. *Banks, Finance and Investment in Germany.* Cambridge University Press.

Fama, Eugen. 1980. "Agency Problems and the Theory of the Firm." *Journal of Political Economy* 88 (2): 288–307.

Gerum, Elmar, Horst Steinmann, and Werner Fees. 1988. *Der Mitbestimmte Aufsichtsrat, Eine Empirische Untersuchung.* Stuttgart: C. E. Poeschel Verlag.

Götz, Heinrich. 1995. "Die Überwachung der Aktiengesellschaft im Lichte jüngerer Unternehmenskrisen." *Die Aktiengesellschaft* 40 (8): 337–53.

Hansmann, Henry. 1990. "When Does Worker Ownership Work? ESOPs, Law Firms, Co-determination, and Economic Democracy." *Yale Law Journal* 99 (8): 1749–816.

———. 1996. *The Ownership of Enterprise.* Harvard University Press.

Hopt, Klaus J. 1994. "Labor Representation on Corporate Boards: Impacts and Problems for Corporate Governance and Economic Integration in Europe." *International Review of Law and Economics* 114 (2): 203–14.

---

52. This possible outcome was suggested by Mertens and Schanze (1979, p. 83) at the time the 1976 law was enacted.

Jensen, M. C., and W. H. Meckling. 1976. "Theory of the Firm: Managerial Behavior, Agency Costs and Ownership Structure." *Journal of Financial Economics* 3 (October): 305–60.

Kallmeyer, Harald. 1982. "Die Gleichbehandlung der Mitglieder des Aufsichtsrats." *Der Betrieb* 35 (25): 1309.

Kißler, Leo. 1992. *Die Mitbestimmung in der Bundesrepublik Deutschland, Modell und Wirklichkeit.* Marburg: Schüren.

Kübler, Friedrich, Walter Schmidt, and Spiros Simitis. 1978. *Mitbestimmungsproblem als Gesetzgebungspolitische Aufgabe.* Baden-Baden: Nomos Verlagsgesellschaft.

Mertens, Hans Joachim, and Erich Schanze. 1979. "The German Co-determination Act of 1976." *Journal of Comparative Corporate Law and Securities Regulation* 2 (1): 75–88.

Mitbestimmungskommission. 1970. *Mitbestimmung im Unternehmen—Bericht der Sachverständigenkommission zur Auswertug der bisherigen Erfahrungen bei der Mitbestimmung.* Stuttgart: W. Kohlhammer.

Münchener Handbuch des Gesellschaftsrechts. 1988. Bd. 4 *Die Aktiengesellschaft.* Munich: C. H. Beck'sche Verlagsbuchhandlung.

Roe, Mark. 1994. *Strong Managers, Weak Owners: The Political Roots of American Corporate Finance.* Princeton University Press.

———. 1996. "Chaos and Evolution in Law and Economics." *Harvard Law Review* 109 (3): 641–68.

Thum, Horst. 1991. *Wirtschaftsdemokratie und Mitbestimmung, Von den Anfängen 1916 bis zum Mitbestimmungsgesetz 1976.* Cologne: Bund Verlag GmbH.

Ulmer, Peter. 1977. "Die Anpassung von AG-Satzungen an das Mitbestimmungsgesetz— eine Zwischenbilanz." *Zeitschrift für das gesamte Handels-und Wirtschaftsrecht* 141: 490.

6

Codetermination and German Securities Markets

MARK J. ROE

A distinctive feature of Germany's economy is its lack of good securities markets. Initial public offers (IPOs) are infrequent, securities trading is shallow, and even large public firms typically have big blockholders that make such firms resemble "semiprivate" companies. These characteristics are often attributed to poor legal protection of minority stockholders, the lack of an equity-owning culture, the lack of an entrepreneurial culture (one that would create many new businesses and IPOs), and permissive rules that allow big banks and bank blockholding in ways barred in the United States.[1] All these factors tend to undermine diffuse ownership.

Codetermination (by which employees control half the seats on a firm's supervisory board) can also weaken German securities markets, by undermining diffuse ownership for two related reasons. First, diffuse owners may be unable to create a blockholding "balance of power" that stockholders would prefer as a counterweight to the employee block. Second, during the 1980s and

---

1. See La Porta, Lopez-de-Silanes, Schleifer, and Vishny (1997) (minority stockholders); "Launching Deutsche Telekom," *The Economist,* October 26, 1996, p. 73 (culture); Roe (1997, pp. 94–101, 169–97) (banking rules).

1990s managers and stockholders failed to turn the supervisory board into a serious governance institution in the face of global competition and technological change. Board meetings remain infrequent, information flow to the board is poor, and the board is often too big and unwieldy to be effective. Instead, out-of-the-boardroom shareholder caucuses and meetings between managers and large shareholders substitute for effective boardroom action. But diffuse, public stockholders need a plausible board at key points (if the firm faces a succession crisis, a production downfall, or a severe technological challenge). Diffuse ownership would end blockholder governance, because the block would dissipate into a diffuse securities market. But shareholders may be wary of a strong board, because it would further strengthen labor. Public, diffuse stockholders would have to decide whether to charge up the board (and hence further empower the employee half of the governance structure) or live with substandard (by current world criteria) boardroom governance. In the face of such choices, German firms (that is, their managers and blockholders) retain their semiprivate blockholding structure, and German securities markets do not develop. Codetermination fits better with the semiprivate, closely held nature of most German firms than it does with truly public, diffusely held firms.

The German Boardroom

In reaction to German codetermination, players inside the German firm, namely managers and shareholders, seem to want to keep the large firm's supervisory board weak (see chapter 5), despite global business changes that have led to its strengthening elsewhere. German businesspeople, the German business press, and business academics at times complain that Germany lacks vibrant securities markets to take innovative firms public and help stimulate the German economy. Many of them see this as a failing both on the demand side, because Germany lacks an equity-holding culture, and on the supply side, because it lacks an entrepreneurial culture of businesspeople who create new firms. Some, arguing from the regulatory perspective, also blame inappropriate securities laws and opaque accounting, and some, taking the public choice perspective, cite the influence of the banks in business and politics. But even if these problems (which are common in several Western European countries) were overcome, Germany would face an additional hurdle in that the codetermined structure fits poorly with diffuse ownership. This poor fit makes founders less willing to sell off their block into IPOs and distant buyers more wary of owning stock in the German firm than they would otherwise be.

Codetermination and Boardroom Reaction

German codetermination may affect the board's structure and function, particularly information flow, the size of the board, and the frequency of board meetings. In the case of size, the linkage is quite explicit because the codetermination statute mandates that the board's size must be in the range of twelve to twenty members, depending on the company size. Some American studies, however, have found that smaller boards are more effective than big ones; German boards do not have the option of keeping their structure tighter and smaller.[2]

Codetermination may also account in part for some of the nonmandated features of German boards, such as the infrequency of board meetings, the formalized information flow, and the composition of the shareholder side. By law, German boards had to meet at least twice a year, and most have met two to four times. (Recently German law was changed to require four meetings annually.) By comparison, U.S. boards meet about eight times a year. Although the German board is free to meet more frequently, many do not.[3] And some dilute the requirement by having one quick meeting before the annual shareholders' meeting, and then another just after it, thereby knocking off two required meetings in a single day. Those that do meet more often typically do so only four times a year. (True, a few boards meet more often, and perhaps recent governance problems have led to more frequent meetings. The story here is not of uniformity, but of average tendency.) All else being equal, a board that seldom meets will obviously be less informed and less able to monitor management than one that meets frequently.

Moreover, less information flows to the board, as many key documents only reach board members at these meetings (see chapter 5). Directors thus lack the facts and time they need to examine the firm's financial results and to closely question managers. It has also been suggested that as a result of codetermination the board avoids controversial topics.[4]

If there are gains to be made by strengthening governance, but it is not strengthened, then perhaps increasing its strength also brings on costs,

2. As Pistor explains in chapter 5, companies with more than 20,000 employees must have a twenty-person board; those with less than 10,000 must have a twelve-person board; and those with 10,000 to 20,000 must have a sixteen-person board.

3. Edwards and Fischer (1994, p. 213). Recent pressures pushed some supervisory boards up to meeting more often. See Liener (1995), cited in André (1996, n. 21).

4. See Schilling (1994, p. 11), reporting on a survey of business and political leaders who conclude that the supervisory board is weak; the board, as a result of codetermination, avoids controversial topics.

either to the firm or to players inside the firm. And here codetermination might play a role in the internal calculus of the firm's players, and perhaps in the firm's performance as well. True, the German supervisory board was never formally intended to have a hands-on role, but that is not critical to this discussion.[5] The question put here is why the German boardroom did not evolve to be more hands-on. One cannot dismiss the possibility that, for the German supervisory boards to evolve, the players needed a formal legal mandate, and, absent that mandate, the board could not evolve even if business pressures pushed to increase their power (presumably because formalities are more important in determining the authority of the German boardroom than they are for American boards).[6] But this, too, begs our question: even if the lack of formal authority to go beyond nomination of management board personnel blocked evolution, we would still not know why the German corporate system did not turn to the parliamentary granters of formal authority to request that their authority be upgraded. The hypotheses I offer in this chapter help to explain the lack of demand for formal change as well as for substantive change.

The German firm can best be analyzed by abstracting it into three parts: management, labor, and capital. Managers who must face an independent board may perform better than those who do not. But boards will not be able to scrutinize managers unless they meet frequently and get good information about the firm. Capital might want this scrutiny, or managers might from time to time ask for it, or firms with this scrutiny might tend to prosper and those without it to contract. Normally the board would be the vehicle for this scrutiny.

Now suppose that capital does not want labor to be well informed. Their reason might be functional, neutral, or dysfunctional. The functional concern of financiers is that labor might damage the firm, especially if its representatives voice the goals of employees with only a few years left to work at the firm (since those employees might be too "shortsighted"). In such a case, if employees had greater voice in corporate affairs, they could increase that damage. Conflict, even apart from capital-labor disputes, is a serious cause of failure in closely held firms, since owners who fight to divide value can thereby harm the firm by diverting the actors from productive activity; increased information and voice for labor could increase conflict, and increased conflict could fritter away firm value.

5. See, for example, Hopt (1997, p. 6).

6. The supervisory board cannot formally take on management functions. See André (1996, p. 1824, n. 19), citing AktG Section 111, para. 4, Stock Company Act, Aktiengesetz, 1965 BGBl. I 1089.

The financiers' intention could instead be neutral here. Or internal rent seeking between capital and labor could be in play: capital might want to keep labor in the dark so that labor is less effective in internal rent seeking and capital more effective. In some instances, their desire to keep the board weak could be dysfunctional. Labor-management decisions require trust, and well-informed labor that gets good information through the board could enhance that trust in shop-floor activities. But if enhanced firm performance is offset by capital's perception that it would lose value because labor would be able to rent-seek more effectively (or capital's rent seeking would be less effective), or by management's fear that consulting labor would constrict their own autonomy, then capital's (and management's) desire to keep labor in the dark becomes dysfunctional.[7]

It is easy to see why capital (and management) might prefer to keep labor ill-informed. But if the supervisory board is theoretically the best (or a good) conduit for information to capital as well, then capital, by cutting down on (or by failing to increase) the information flow to the board, would be reducing the information flow to itself as well. This cut in information could be rational if the costs to capital from labor being better informed were greater than the gains to capital from better firm performance: that is, capital might prefer to take its chance with unmonitored managers rather than with well-informed labor.

Or capital might decide it can get enough information elsewhere: through informal discussions, control of the "speaker's" seat on the supervisory board (the chair of the supervisory board is from the shareholder side), separate meetings between management and the shareholder "bench" of the board, or bank loan channels. Capital may know that these channels could be enhanced with better boardroom information, but if that means better-informed labor, capital may prefer the codetermined board to be less well-informed than it could be. Bankers believe they get no more information from their seats on the supervisory board than they get as a creditor of the firm.[8]

---

7. One study suggests codetermination brought overall social gains but decreased firm-level productivity and profitability (without affecting wage rates). See FitzRoy and Kraft (1993). These results suggest that internal rent seeking by labor and shareholder governance counters is plausible.

8. Mülbert (1996). Labor could similarly seek alternative information channels, through the works councils or straightforward union negotiation. Board seats may also become a patronage item, one that compensates employee-side players who enter the boardroom and become less likely to confront the firm and its managers in other arenas. Hence capital and managers may have other reasons to maintain the current system of few meetings and limited work, for example, as a means of coopting some players who could disrupt the firm elsewhere.

Shareholders and managers may look at meeting frequency in much the same way as they look at information flow to the board. They may expect more monitoring to improve operations somewhat, at least at critical junctures, and they may believe that more meetings will improve monitoring. But more meetings would also enhance labor's voice in the codetermined boardroom, making management and capital shy away from greater frequency.

The available evidence suggests that some players sought to weaken labor's voice in the supervisory board after the 1976 expansion of German codetermination. More than half of the German boards adopted one or more of the following "equity-enhancing" characteristics: additional stockholder vice-chairs of the board (under German corporate law, the vice-chair is to come from the labor side, the chair from the equity side); equity-controlled subcommittees; enhanced power of the chair (who is from the shareholder side) to control the agenda; quorum rules that favored equity; additional authority of the chair to postpone a substantive action if the chairperson could not be present; the requirement that the chair cast the tie-breaking vote where such a vote is necessary; and requiring board members to refrain from making statements out of the boardroom.[9]

Securities Markets and Public Choice

As I mentioned at the outset, Germany lacks good securities markets. In the United States, incumbent players sometimes block the passage or the enforcement of laws that might undermine their position, and it would not be surprising if incumbent German industrial giants did not want competition from upstart, IPO-financed new firms.[10] Nor would it be surprising if incumbent German bankers did not want competition from upstart investment bankers or if they did not want to be forced to learn a new set of investment banking skills. These hypotheses seem plausible, though they have not yet been explored in detail in the literature.

A related public choice hypothesis is that corporate governance and securities markets are linked and that German codetermination may have lowered the demand for good securities laws and for good securities distri-

9. Gerum, Steinmann, and Fees (1988). Their study, however, dealt with data from 1979 and so is now somewhat stale.

10. On bankers calling for laws that regulate stock and bond issuances, see, for example, Macey and Miller (1991). On ideology, policy, and small-town bankers and farmers versus city bankers, see Langevoort (1987). And on commercial versus investment bankers, see Macey (1983).

bution institutions. In the United States, securities markets and diffuse ownership are said to induce special governance features, such as the Berle-Means corporation, takeovers, and enhanced agency costs. The standard American thinking is that firms went public either to finance the firm itself or to finance the owners' diversification out of the firm they founded, and as the purchasers diversified into small lots, corporate power shifted from dispersed shareholders with poor information to concentrated inside managers who had good information about the corporation.

In Germany's case, the codetermined supervisory board might suppress corporate issuers' demand for securities markets and their supporting apparatus, such as good securities laws and transparent accounting. Although family founders, like their American counterparts, may wish to cash out, diversify, and retire, if the securities buyers are unwilling to pay "full" price for the stock because the buyers would have to deal either with a weak board or strong labor inside a strong board, then the founders may find it worthwhile to retain the block and induce the next generation in the family to enter and run the firm. When they do sell, they might sell a block to new blockholders who can monitor the firm and its managers. Indeed, the evidence suggests this is so, with many sales of shares being sales of controlling blocks.[11]

This possibility may explain why few entrepreneurs are willing to set up new firms. If sales have to be made to other blockholders in order for the successful entrepreneur to diversify, potential entrepreneurs may be unable to find many bidders for their firms. In contrast, blockholder bidders in the United States must compete with underwriters who can sell the blockholders' stock into the securities markets. This competition from the securities markets in pricing an entrepreneur's sellout may be critical. In Germany, the seller may often be unable to get "full" price because the number of blockholder buyers is small and they do not need to compete with public securities market underwriters. Purported cultural attitudes, such as the supposed lack of entrepreneurial spirit or a stock-owning culture may accordingly be economically motivated. The weak securities market may partly depend on the mandated codetermined structure of the boardroom.

We can illustrate this by imagining the constraints on a family that built a successful business and now wants to sell it in an IPO. The heirs do not want to run the business but would prefer to sell out in public markets and bring in professional managers. The firm is worth, say, $500 million to the heirs if they run it themselves.

11. See Franks and Mayers (1997).

They consider selling out in an IPO, expecting that they will eventually sell most of their stock to the public. But a public offering would decrease the power of equity to counterbalance labor in the boardroom, and if a balance of power in a powerful boardroom were to become important in preserving shareholder value, this lack of balance could be costly to the stockholders.

Alternatively, the founders' heirs could make (or keep) the boardroom unimportant, thereby decreasing labor's influence (and thereby reducing potential shareholders' desire to have a balance of power inside the boardroom). But if the boardroom does not become important, then agency costs from poorly monitored managers would decrease the value of the firm. The firm might face a crisis and react badly. Either way—with a powerful board that lacks balance or with a weak but balanced board—stockholders would lose. If the firm would then be worth not $500 million, but only $250 million to public stockholders who determined that this lower amount is the value to them of having little control in a codetermined firm, then it "costs" $250 million to the heirs to sell out their stock instead of managing the firm.[12] They thus have a low "demand" for good securities markets.

This low demand could manifest itself both in fewer IPOs and a lower demand for good, well-enforced securities and corporate laws that would make such stock sales more effective. Family ownership through several generations may well be a feature of German culture, as it is said to be. But culture may have an economic base, and family-oriented ownership may also result from an institutional structure that disfavors the fully public, diffusely owned firm. German families thus have economic and not just cultural reasons to induce the next generation to take over the family firm.[13]

A pattern of maintaining a firm within a family generation after generation may in time be unstable: heirs may be unable to run the firm well or have a high demand to sell out. This might press the system to change; in particular, the demand for secondary sales should increase. Thus far the demand from families to sell has been met by sales to new blockholders.[14]

---

12. The close owners would have a codetermined board of some sort, but with their stock concentrated, they would counterbalance labor. And even if the family were not involved in the corporation from day to day, their block would enable them to keep informed and to influence the firm outside of the boardroom. If the stock were dispersed, these advantages to stockholders would be lost, and presumably the total value of equity would go down.

13. A continuing strength of family ownership is based here on a poor securities market and poor monitoring structures. If we observe continuing family ownership, however, we do not know whether the poor securities market is due to poor legal protections or to shareholders' fears of diffuse ownership in a codetermined firm.

14. See Franks and Mayer (1997).

While it is true that stockholders in the closely held, codetermined firm will bear some of these costs of internal rent seeking, the net costs to stockholders should be lower than the costs to stockholders of rent seeking in the public firm, because the blockholding counterbalances labor's voice.[15] But if the block were dissipated in a public offering, the value of the shares would, all other things being equal, decline, because the "countervailing power" of the large block would be lost to shareholders.

Potentially diffuse shareholders would in all likelihood anticipate this loss in value and accordingly would pay less for the stock than it would be worth to capital owners if the owners held it in block form.[16] In turn, the blockholders, anticipating the diffuse owner's discount, would sell only reluctantly. This analysis is consistent with evidence that blockholders in Germany sell frequently but almost always keep the block intact by selling it to a new blockholder.[17]

Thus, until now, one key source of demand for better securities markets that may be missing from the German system is the selling founders.[18] On the average, German businesses may thus tend to stay longer in one family's hands for more generations that American businesses do.

Substitutes

The point here is not that boardroom monitoring is the sine qua non of securities markets, nor that American boardroom monitoring is superior to Germany's. Rather, securities markets require that managers be monitored from time to time. The principal monitoring mechanisms are market competition (in capital and product markets), takeovers, good boards of directors, and concentrated ownership. The United States is strong in the first control mechanism (competition) and passable in the next two. Germany has historically been weak on competition, lacks takeovers, and is weaker in boardroom governance. All that is left for large German firms at this time is the fourth, blockholding. Were German firms to dismantle blockhold-

15. Moreover, the closely held firm, the GmbH, will have lower costs to shareholders from codetermination because, as Fritz Kübler has pointed out to me, the owners of the GmbH can address their instructions directly to managers, thereby bypassing the codetermined supervisory board.

16. Again, it is possible that the loss is not a social loss, but a transfer from stockholders to labor.

17. See Franks and Mayer (1997).

18. More generally, German analysts bemoan the lack of good securities markets in Germany. But the connection between securities markets and labor presence does not seem to be well analyzed. Codetermination may arise from the "balance" of power between the German banks and other equity holders, but once it is in place, dispersal of equity interests could debilitate the firm.

ing, via a diffusion in ownership of their largest firms, they would leave themselves with no significant control device, either internal or external. Evidence of this may be the fact that more than 85 percent of Germany's largest firms persist in having a stockholder owning more than 25 percent of the firm's stock.[19] Large blockholders' representatives meet informally with managers, outside the formal meetings, and this seems to be Germany's significant monitoring mechanism, one for which the United States has substitutes (or improvements) and one for which German firms, lacking substitutes, would pay a price if the blocks were dissipated.[20] If the other substitutes for monitoring improved enough, because of, say, enhanced European product market competition after implementation of Maastricht or a European Monetary Union, then perhaps the German governance trade-off would also change.

Conclusion

Much remains to be understood about the German supervisory board, codetermination, and the historical weakness of German securities markets. But by linking these salient institutions, we can pose fundamental questions. The weakness of the supervisory board might be structurally linked to codetermination. If so, prevailing reform proposals (such as limiting the number of boards an individual can serve on) may fail to improve the board much because they fail to address a fundamental structural dilemma for Germany.

Moreover, the weakness of German securities markets may be largely, or at least partly, due to the weakness of the German supervisory board. Diffuse stockholders would face either a labor-dominated board or a weak board. Neither choice may appeal to distant stockholders, so potential buyers may not pay up to buy from blockholders, and blockholders may be unwilling to take the loss. Stock remains in big blocks, and fluidity comes not from IPOs but from blocks changing hands. The demand for good securities market institutions may not be strong and hence these institutions may not arise.

To be sure here, I do not mean to assert that German codetermination initially *caused* Germany's weak securities market, tight family ownership,

19. See Franks and Mayer (1997).

20. See Kaplan and Minton (1994); Kaplan (1994). They show roughly similar corporate governance executive and director turnover results in Germany, Japan, and the United States in recent times.

and bank influence. Indeed, the historical evidence suggests the *opposite*, as I have stated elsewhere.[21] Possibly the historical sequence, and Germany's prior history of repressing labor,[22] has obscured today's functional interdependence from analysts. The point is that when *both* sets of complementary institutions are in place (codetermination and block ownership), it is hard for one to exit without the other also exiting. The two institutions are reciprocally complementary, each calling forth the other.

Nor do I wish to paint a picture of German uniqueness here on all levels of abstraction. One might argue that no nation allows unbridled shareholder control of the firm. In Japan, lifetime employment, inside boards, and ownership by major creditors all brake unbridled shareholder control. French and Italian state ownership and state regulation check unbridled shareholder control. And even in the United States managerial control may be viewed as a means of preventing unbridled shareholder control of the firm.

The German institutions of block, family ownership, and codetermination can be linked in other ways. If Germany has deficient securities and corporate laws (and enforcement), then one must ask how this came about, because the task of writing a passable law and getting a plausible enforcement agency in place is not insurmountable, and Germany is not incapable of good government administration. Public choice forces could help explain the perceived deficiency. Incumbent firms, which did not want to compete with securities-financed entrants, or incumbent bank lenders, which preferred to avoid a new competitive arena, may both have been in play. Moreover, firms' founders may only weakly want to sell out in secondary sales; if the firm would be worth much less to scattered outside owners because of a "balance-of-power" problem inside the firm, then the firm's founders and their heirs would seek to preserve concentrated ownership. Hence the players' demand to sell, and their political demand for good securities market institutions and laws, would be low.

References

André, Thomas J. Jr. 1996. "Some Reflections on German Corporate Governance: A Glimpse at German Supervisory Boards." *Tulane Law Review* 70: 1819–49.
Edwards, Jeremy, and Klaus Fischer. 1994. *Banks, Finance and Investment in Germany.* Cambridge University Press.

21. See Roe (1994, pp. 213–14).
22. See Roe (1998) and the sources cited therein.

FitzRoy, Felix R., and Kornelius Kraft. 1993. "Economic Effects of Codetermination." *Scandinavian Journal of Economics* 95: 365–73 .

Franks, Julian, and Colin Mayer. 1997. "Ownership, Control and the Performance of German Corporations." Paper presented at the Columbia Law School Sloan Project Conference, April 1997.

Gerum, Elmar, Horst Steinmann, and Werner Fees. 1988. *Der Mitbestimmte Aufsichtsrat— Eine Empirische Untersuchung.* Stuttgart: C. E. Poeschel.

Hopt, Klaus. 1997. "The German Two-Tier Board (Aufsichtsrat): A German View on Corporate Governance." In *Comparative Corporate Governance: Essays and Materials,* edited by Klaus Hopt and Eddy Wymeersch, 3–20. Berlin: Walter de Gruyter.

Kaplan, Steven N. 1994. "Top Executives, Turnover, and Firm Performance in Germany." *Journal of Law, Economics and Organization* 10: 142–59.

Kaplan, Steven N., and Bernadette A. Minton. 1994. "Appointments of Outsiders of Japanese Boards: Determinants and Implications for Managers." *Journal of Financial Economics* 36: 225–58.

Langevoort, Donald. 1987. "Statutory Obsolescence and the Judicial Process: The Revisionist Role of the Courts in Federal Banking Regulation." *Michigan Law Review* 85: 672– 733.

La Porta, Rafael, Florencio Lopez-de-Silanes, Andrei Schleifer, and Robert Vishny. 1997. "Legal Determinants of External Finance." *Journal of Finance* 52: 1131.

Liener, Gerhard. 1995. "The Future of German Governance." *Corp. Board* 1.

Macey, Jonathan. 1983. "Special Interest Group Legislation and the Judicial Function: The Dilemma of Glass-Steagall." *Emory Law Journal* 33: 1–40.

Macey, Jonathan R., and Geoffrey P. Miller. 1991. "Origin of the Blue Sky Laws." *Texas Law Review* 70: 347–97.

Mülbert, Peter O. 1996. "Empfehlen sich gesetzliche Regelungen zur Einschränkung des Einflusses der Kreditinstitute auf Aktiengesellschaften?" Gutachten E, zum 61. *Deutschen Juristentag* 49.

Roe, Mark J. 1994. *Strong Managers, Weak Owners: The Political Roots of American Corporate Finance.* Princeton University Press.

———. 1998. "Backlash." *Columbia Law Review* 98: 217–40.

Schilling, Florian. 1994. "Die Aufsichtsrat ist für die Katz." *Frankfurter Allgemeine Zeitung,* August 27.

7

The Market Value of the Codetermined Firm

THEODOR BAUMS AND
BERND FRICK

A s noted in chapter 6, the term "codetermination" describes labor representation on corporate boards, that is, the participation of employees or union representatives in the decision-making of the board. Two broad arguments have been directed against laws that mandate such cooperation between employees and employers: one argument rests on political economy considerations, the other on the logic of profit maximization. The political economy case for rejecting legal intervention to encourage cooperation has been summarized in this way:

> Efforts by government to . . . reshape the firm have not led to particularly desirable results. The approach taken has emphasized the "political" aspect of the firm and the importance of corporate governance while failing to give much attention to broader economic issues and to the relation between the firm's total property-rights structure and its performance. By granting workers major control rights without regard to their actual investment position in the firm, state programs have violated an important rule for ensuring rational allocation—namely, the rule that those making decisions should bear the full costs

of the decisions they make. This defect, together with the costly system used to apportion the firm's quasi rents between workers and stockholders, means that the orthodox co-determined firm does not possess a truly efficient organizational structure.[1]

The market-oriented case against legally mandated codetermination was given nearly twenty years ago:

If co-determination is beneficial to both stockholders and labor, why do we need laws which force firms to engage in it? Surely, they would do so voluntarily. The fact that stockholders must be forced by law to accept co-determination is the best evidence we have that they are adversely affected by it.[2]

There are also plausible arguments that even though codetermination may be able to provide gains to both workers and firms, it could still be underprovided by the market. For example, if workers invest in firm-specific skills—or "durable reliance investments"—the firm's profits may well rise and help boost wages.[3] In a world of informational asymmetries, however, the firm may be unable to check on the extent to which employees are making firm-specific investments. Moreover, workers may be reluctant to invest in firm-specific skills because it makes them vulnerable; after all, such an investment will only pay off if they can be assured of being at the same firm for some time into the future, and they risk serious economic loss in the case of dismissal. In this context, cooperation may be advantageous to both parties; if workers are protected by institutional or contractual safeguards, then they become willing to invest in firm-specific skills, and all parties can benefit.[4] Codetermination is a type of governance structure that is capable of dealing with maximizing agents having conflicting interests.

This perspective can also be viewed in terms of a prisoner's dilemma. All firms would benefit if they introduced worker participation, but codetermined firms require—among other things—a compressed wage structure to encourage "group cohesiveness" and dismissal protection to lengthen the time horizon of workers. Traditional firms, on the other hand, motivate their employees through the fear of dismissal and a sharply differentiated wage structure. It is highly unlikely that under such circumstances a participative equilibrium will emerge, because any single codetermined firm will

---

1. Furubotn (1988, p. 178).
2. Jensen and Meckling (1979, p. 474).
3. Furubotn (1985, p. 167).
4. See Alchian (1984); Furubotn (1985, 1988).

be threatened by adverse selection: it will attract the less motivated job seek-ers, and its best workers will be poached by traditional firms that can pay them more. Hence a competitive market will be systematically biased against the codetermined workplace, and the economy will be locked in a socially suboptimal position. Mandated codetermination would overcome this dilemma by requiring all firms to introduce the machinery of participation.[5]

Given these incompatible positions, theory offers no definitive guidance as to the likely effects of mandated codetermination. The beneficial and detrimental effects of codetermination must therefore be demonstrated empirically. This chapter offers evidence from Germany. After discussing German laws mandating codetermination and reviewing the existing evi-dence on its previously described effects, we offer some new evidence drawn from an event study, the objective of which was to determine how court decisions that extend or limit employees' codetermination affect the stock prices of the firms concerned.

The Legal Environment for Codetermination in Germany

Larger German firms typically have two tiers of boards—the supervisory board and the management board—as opposed to the Anglo-American one-tier system. "Codetermination" refers to the representation of employ-ees on the supervisory board (*Unternehmensmitbestimmung*) but does not encompass labor participation at the plant level, which is provided by sep-arate works councils (*betriebliche Mitbestimmung*). The supervisory board appoints the members of the managing board, generally for five years, and may dismiss them, though only for cause. The supervisory board is respon-sible for monitoring management, although in practical terms it acts as an advisory committee rather than as a monitoring panel, except in times of financial difficulty. To accomplish its duties, the supervisory board has the right to receive comprehensive information. Management must report to it periodically on all important questions, and the supervisory board

5. The scenario in this paragraph was suggested by Levine and Tyson (1990). In a similar model, Freeman and Lazear (1995) analyze the efficiency properties of works councils. They argue that although the works council is likely to increase the joint surplus of the enterprise as a result of infor-mation exchange, consultation, and participation, the firm's profits are nonetheless expected to be lower in the presence of a works council. Therefore, management will either oppose the installation of a works council or vest it with too little power. For this reason, the institution has to be mandated by government to reach a (potential) Pareto optimum.

reviews the financial reports and balance sheets of the firm. The board may require management to obtain its prior approval before entering into certain important transactions.

Germany has three systems of labor participation on corporate boards: one-third participation for corporations with more than 500 employees, full parity for coal and steel companies, and quasi-parity codetermination for corporations with more than 2,000 workers. Some institutional background on these forms is useful in understanding the evidence that follows.

In the case of one-third participation, the Industrial Constitution Act (*Betriebsverfassungsgesetz*) of 1952 mandated that one-third of the supervisory board of stock corporations and limited liability companies with more than 500 employees must be appointed by the employees and two-thirds by the shareholders. The clear majority of voting power is hence held by the shareholders' representatives, while the employees' representatives are in a counseling position.

The second approach, full parity for coal and steel companies, was set up by the Coal, Iron, and Steel Industries Codetermination Act of 1951. Corporations and limited liability companies in the mining and steel industries with more than 1,000 employees must have a supervisory board consisting of at least eleven members and up to a maximum of twenty-one, depending on the size of the firm. On boards with eleven members, five are appointed by the employees (three by the union directly), five are elected by the shareholders, and a further "neutral" member (with a casting vote) is appointed by the majority of both sides of the supervisory board.

The third model, quasi-parity codetermination, is based on the Codetermination Act of 1976. In corporations and limited liability companies outside the iron and coal industries with more than 2,000 employees, shareholders elect half the members, and the employees and trade unions elect the other half. Again, the size of the board will depend on the number of employees. For instance, in a firm with not more than 10,000 employees, shareholders will elect six, the employees (blue- and white-collar, as well as lower-ranking management) four, and the trade unions two members. The maximum size for the biggest firms is twenty members. If there is a stalemate in a vote by the board (a rare event), the chairman who is elected by the shareholders, rather than by the employees, has a (tie-breaking) vote. The term "quasi-parity codetermination" is used to describe this system because of this slight superiority of the shareholders.

When challenged in court, the Codetermination Act of 1976 was pronounced constitutional on March 1, 1979, by the Federal Constitutional Court. Apart from this basic decision, a number of others in the area of codetermination have been reached by courts of all levels (state and federal). Parties to those disputes comprised the employees' representatives or unions, on one side, and the respective firms, shareholders' associations, or employers' associations, on the other. These court rulings may be understood and categorized as either extending or restricting the reach of codetermination.

Previous Studies of Germany's Codetermination Acts

To date, a limited number of studies have investigated the influence of the codetermination acts on the economic performance of German firms (see table 7-1 on page 212). The overall conclusion one would draw from these studies, though they use rather different data and test designs, would be that the acts of 1951 and 1976 had a rather modest—if any—influence on the sectors and firms affected.

A small but increasing number of studies have also examined the influence of supplementary forms of workers' representation, such as unionism and works councils, on the economic performance of sectors and firms. These studies have used a variety of measures to this end, including productivity levels and growth, financial performance and profitability, investment in human and physical capital as well as in research and development, and job generation. Most studies on the influence of trade unions report negative but statistically insignificant coefficients of union density on some measure of productivity.[6] A comparative analysis of the impact of works councils on productivity has produced no clear conclusions, either.[7] All in all, it seems difficult to say that there is an effect, much less specify its direction or magnitude.[8]

Thus the empirical studies would seem to imply that codetermination does not have pronounced economic consequences one way or another.[9] The results are inconclusive for several reasons. For one thing, many of the

---

6. Studies on the productivity effects of German trade unions include Addison, Genosko, and Schnabel (1989); Kraft (1992); Lorenz and Wagner (1991); Schnabel (1989); Schnabel and Wagner (1992); and Mainusch (1992).

7. For an overall evaluation of these studies, see Frick (1995). Individual studies include Addison, Kraft, and Wagner (1993); Addison and Wagner (1995); Addison, Schnabel, and Wagner (1996); FitzRoy and Kraft (1985a, 1985b, 1987a, 1987b, 1990); Frick (1996a, 1996b); Frick and Sadowski (1995); and Kraft (1986).

8. Belman (1992, p. 58).

9. Hodgson and Jones (1989).

samples examined have been rather small. For another, the studies have concentrated on single events—the introduction of the Codetermination Act of 1976, in particular—without considering that this act had been anticipated by firms (and potential investors) since the late 1960s and early 1970s. Furthermore, they have had great difficulty adjusting for all the appropriate factors, since in most cases no detailed longitudinal data are available to indicate all the relevant differences between firms. In addition, some methodological problems have not yet been solved. (For example, a typical assumption is that firms with and without unionized work forces, or works councils, have identical production functions.) It is not even clear that workers' representation should be treated as a totally exogenous variable, given that the degree and extent of that representation probably have endogenous components.

New Evidence from an Event Study

Between January 1, 1954, and December 31, 1995, German courts at various levels decided forty-six cases concerning the application of the Codetermination Act of 1951, the Industrial Constitution Act of 1952, and the Codetermination Act of 1976. Six of these cases are omitted from the present analysis because they were decided before January 1, 1974, which is the date when daily stock return data became available. Moreover, sixteen of the forty-six decisions affected stock corporations that either had never been traded or were not yet being traded at the time of the decision. Since one case involved a shareholders' association instead of a single enterprise, that leaves us with twenty-three court decisions. These decisions affected twenty-eight companies, however, because in one case six enterprises (together with twenty-nine employers' associations) lodged a joint appeal to the Federal Constitutional Court.

Table 7-2 records the outcome of these cases and the number of companies involved. The first entry shows that for fourteen of the twenty-eight companies involved in these cases, the court "extended" codetermination, whereas for ten companies the decision resulted in a "restriction." Ten companies were on the winning side of the lawsuit, ten on the losing side. And in eight cases both parties had to give up their initial positions to more or less the same extent. The cases in which firms lost and the cases in which codetermination was extended are not identical, since it is possible for a company to "lose" the court case, while the general wording of the decision has the effect of reducing codetermination, or vice versa. Three-quarters of

Table 7-1. *Productivity Effects of Codetermination*

Author(s)	Sample	Productivity measure(s)	Indicator(s) of codetermination	Effect of codetermination
Benelli, Lederer, and Lys (1987)	8 two-digit manufacturing industries, 1954–76	Annual stock return variances	Introduction of Codetermination Act of 1951	Although not statistically significant, the return variances are lower in industries subject to parity codetermination than in other industries. This pattern is not observed in other European countries.
	40 codetermined and 18 noncodetermined firms, 1973–83	Three monthly portfolio return variances, January 1973–December 1977 vs. January 1978–April 1983	Introduction of Codetermination Act of 1976	The return variance of the portfolio of codetermined firms declines significantly following the imposition of codetermination. Since the same phenomenon occurs in firms not subject to codetermination, the imposition of the law had apparently no discernible impact on the stock return variance.

40 codetermined and 18 noncodetermined firms, 1973–83	Average monthly stock return, January 1973–June 1976	Introduction of Codetermination Act of 1976	In the case of firms directly affected by codetermination, average monthly stock returns decreased by 0.008 percent during the period immediately preceding its imposition; in the case of noncodetermined firms, the respective decline was even larger (0.013 percent). This difference was not statistically significant.
Benelli, Lederer, and Lys (1987)	42 matched pairs of firms (codetermined and non-codetermined), 1970–76 vs. 1977–82	Earnings before interest and taxes/total assets Net income/total equity Dividends/net income Total debt/total assets Long-term debt/total assets Current assets/total assets (Current assets − inventories)/short-term debt Net investment in fixed assets/total assets Labor costs/total sales	Introduction of Codetermination Act of 1976	There is no evidence that codetermination affects firm policies. Using parametric and nonparametric test procedures, the authors find that none of the mean comparison tests produce statistically significant results.

(*continued*)

Table 7-1. (continued)

Author(s)	Sample	Productivity measure(s)	Indicator(s) of codetermination	Effect of codetermination
FitzRoy and Kraft (1993)	68 large and codetermined vs. 44 smaller and non-codetermined firms, 1975 and 1983, publicly traded, metal industry only	Value added per employee	Introduction of Codetermination Act of 1976	Significantly higher in codetermined firms in 1975, but not in 1983.
		Total labor costs per employee		Significantly higher in codetermined firms in both years.
		Return on equity (pre-tax accounting profits/equity capital)		Difference between codetermined and noncodetermined firms insignificant in both years.
		Total factor productivity growth, 1975–83		Significantly lower in codetermined firms.
Gurdon and Rai (1990)	63 large enterprises (37 affected and 26 unaffected by 1976 Codetermination Act), 1970–85	Stock value of plant and equipment/number of employees	Introduction of Codetermination Act of 1976	The capital-labor ratio increased significantly more in firms that were not affected by the 1976 legislation. The introduction of legislation led to a significantly lower productivity and a significantly higher profitability in codetermined firms.
		Change in revenue per unit of labor		
		Change in profits per unit of capital		

| Svejnar (1981) | 3 two-digit manufacturing industries, 1935–38 and 1949–76 | Relative hourly earnings in iron/steel and coal mining compared with textiles | Introduction of Codetermination Act of 1951 | Following the introduction of the Codetermination Act, hourly earnings are significantly higher in the iron and steel industry compared with textile industry, but not in coal mining, although both industries are heavily unionized compared with the reference industry, where the Act was not introduced. |
| Svejnar (1982) | 14 two-digit manufacturing industries, 1950–76 | Value added per hour worked by production workers | Introduction of Codetermination Act of 1951 and of Works Constitution Acts of 1952 and 1972 | In general, the establishment of codetermination through the 1951, 1952, and 1972 laws had no perceptible effect on productivity. In mining, 1972 legislation had a significantly negative productivity effect; in iron and steel, none of the three laws had a significant impact. |

Table 7-2. *Outcome of Court Decisions under Consideration*

Decisions and Courts	Number
Decision	
Extends codetermination	14
Partly extends/partly restricts	4
Restricts codetermination	10
Company wins/union loses	10
Both parties win/lose equally	8
Company loses/union wins	10
Relating to single enterprise	7
Industry wide importance	21
Court	
Court of first instance	9
Appellate court	10
Federal civil court	3
Federal constitutional court	6[a]

a. One decision affecting six companies.

the companies in the lawsuits were in cases of industry- or even economy-wide importance, while only 25 percent of the firms were in cases that affected just a single enterprise. For nine companies the lawsuit was decided by a court of first instance; for ten companies by an appellate court; for three companies by the Federal Civil Court; and for six companies, in a single case, by the Federal Constitutional Court. For the twenty-three cases in our sample, table 7-3 lists the company involved, the statute, the court involved, the case number and date, and the publication date for the decision.

The new evidence presented here is drawn from event studies.[10] It consists of daily stock return data from twenty-eight firms that were subject to court decisions concerning the application of the Codetermination Act during the period January 1, 1974, to December 31, 1995. These data reflect the impact of codetermination on the stock price of the respective firms. Despite the potentially problematic characteristics of such data for other purposes—such as high autocorrelation in the daily price movements—daily data generally present few difficulties in the context of event study methodologies.[11]

10. See Thompson (1995); and Brown and Warner (1980).
11. Brown and Warner (1985).

Research strategies based on an ordinary least-squares regression model and using standard parametric tests are usually well specified under a variety of conditions. To preview one of our results, the stock market, rather surprisingly, did not react in a significant way to these court decisions.

In the second step of our analysis, we investigate another context to determine whether the degree of codetermination is not a signal of considerable importance to investors. It could be, for example, that compared with the overall importance of the Codetermination Act of 1976 and the long discussion preceding its introduction, single court decisions may be of minor importance only. Thus we ask whether the introduction of the Codetermination Act or the ruling of the Federal Constitutional Court that the act is compatible with the constitution of the Federal Republic of Germany had any influence on the performance of those sectors most heavily affected by the decision.

Empirical Results

We begin by looking at the abnormal stock returns on the day the respective judicial decision was issued and the short-run development of cumulated abnormal returns in the ten days before and after the single events. The abnormal return is calculated as the return of the firm at a given time, minus the return of the whole stock market at that time. The cumulated abnormal return is the sum of all abnormal returns during the period under investigation.

The overall stock market indices we use have been compiled in the "German Finance Data Base."[12] The calculation of the global index, the so-called DAFOX, is based on all those stocks that have been traded in the official market on the Frankfurt Stock Exchange since January 1974. The daily index values are computed using daily spot prices from the official price fixing at 12:30 p.m., which are weighted by the number of shares outstanding. Moreover, it includes an adjustment factor for cash distributions, representing cash dividends and capital changes. Apart from the overall index, two market indices (for "blue chips" and "small caps") and twelve industry indices are calculated by the same method and will be used later in the analysis.[13]

---

12. Bühler, Göppl, and Möller (1993).

13. For an overall discussion of the index, see Göppl and Schütz (1993, 1994). Göppl and Schütz (1994, pp. 20–35) compare the suitability of the DAFOX with the efficiency of other stock market indices that are available for Germany on a daily basis and find that the efficiency hypothesis has to be rejected for all but one of the other indices, but not for the DAFOX.

Table 7-3. *Codetermination Cases and Their Outcomes, 1953–95*[a]

Subject	Decision date[b]	Court[c]	Publication date	Company name
Constitutionality of the Codetermination Act of 1976.	3/8/78 (I, e, l)	OLG Düsseldorf	WM 1978, 381 (4/15/78); DB 978, 697 (4/7/78); BB 1978, 466 (4/10/78)	Girmes
Constitutionality of the Codetermination Act of 1976, § 7 (1) and (2).	4/10/78 (I, r, w)	LG Hamburg	DB 1978, 990 (5/19/78); WM 1978, 528 (5/20/78); BB 1978, 760 (5/30/78)	Beiersdorf
The extended codetermination of the employees according to the Codetermination Act of 1976 is compatible with the constitutional rights of the corporations affected, the stockholders, and the employers' coalitions.	3/1/79 (I, e, l)	BVG	WM 1979, 389 (4/7/79); DB 1978, 593 (3/23/79)	Beiersdorf Bayer Braun Daimler-Benz Hoechst Varta
Permissibility of a provision of the articles concerning the supervisory board's quorum by which the shareholders' predominance is secured.	7/23/79 (I, r, w)	LG Mannheim	DB 1979, 1899 (9/28/79)	Bilfinger & Berger Bau
Regulations concerning the election of several vice chairmen of the supervisory board and the composition of the supervisory board's committees.	1/16/80 (I, e, l)	LG München	WM 1980, 689 (6/14/80); DB 1980, 678 (4/4/80)	Siemens

Quorum of the supervisory board.	6/20/80 (I, e, l)	OLG Karlsruhe	WM 1980, 1182 (10/11/80); DB1981, 362 (2/13/81); BB 1980, 1232 (8/30/80)	Bilfinger & Berger Bau
At par composition of supervisory board's committees.	11/4/80 (I, r, w)	LG Hamburg	WM 1980, 1399 (12/6/80); DB 1981, 359 (2/13/81); BB 1980, 1711 (11/30/81)	Beiersdorf
Supervisory board; election of two vice chairmen; composition of committees; supervisory board chairman's right of a second vote; staff committee.	4/29/81 (I, r, w)	OLG München	WM 1981, 530 (5/16/81); DB 1981, 1077 (5/22/81); BB 1981, 809 (5/20/81)	Siemens
Limits to the provisions of the articles of a public limited company; several vice chairmen of the supervisory board; composition of supervisory board's committees.	2/25/82 (I, partly r/ partly e, l)	BGH	WM 1982, 359 (3/27/82); DB 1982, 742 (4/9/82); Ankündigung in DB 1982, 534 (3/12/82)	Siemens
Provision of the articles concerning the supervisory board's quorum.	2/25/82 (I, e, l)	BGH	WM 1982, 365 (3/27/82); DB 1982, 747 (4/9/82); Ankündigung in DB 1982, 534 (3/12/82)	Bilfinger & Berger Bau
Supervisory board's committee; regulation of composition in the supervisory board's rules of procedure; additional vice chairmen of the supervisory board.	7/23/82 (I, partly r/ partly e, l)	OLG Hamburg	WM 1982, 1090 (7/23/82); DB 1982, 1765 (8/27/82); BB 1982, 1686 (10/10/82)	Beiersdorf
Composition of a supervisory board.	2/28/83 (E, e, l)	BGH	WM 1983, 446 (4/23/83)	Beiersdorf

(continued)

Table 7-3. (continued)

Subject	Decision date[b]	Court[c]	Publication date	Company name
Supervisory board; pyramid structure of group of companies.	11/10/83 (I, r, w)	LG Nürnberg-Fürth	WM 1984, 263 (2/25/84); DB 1983, 2675 (12/16/83)	Energieversorgung Oberfranken
Election to a supervisory board and its composition of employee representatives.	5/25/84 (I, partly r/ partly e, w)	OLG Hamburg	WM 1984, 965 (7/21/84); DB 1984, 1567 (7/27/84)	Beiersdorf
Applicability of Codetermination Act of 1976, § 5, on groups of companies.	12/19/85 (E, r, w)	LG Frankfurt/M.	WM 1986, 885 (7/19/86)	VDM
Applicability of Codetermination Act of 1976, § 5, on groups of companies.	11/10/86 (E, r, w)	OLG Frankfurt/M.	BB 1986, 2288 (12/10/86); WM 1987, 237 (2/21/87)	VDM
Unconstitutionality of the Codetermination in the Mining Industry and the Iron and Steel Production Industry Act of 1952.	1/8/91 (I, e, w)	OLG Düsseldorf	DB 1991, 445 (2/22/91)	Mannesmann
Phasing out of codetermination through transfer of enterprise to a new holding company (Codetermination in the Mining Industry and the Iron and Steel Production Industry Act of 1952).	9/30/92 (E, r, w)	LG Hannover	WM 1993, 63 (1/16/93)	Preussag

Description	Citation	Court	Decision date (type)	Company
Phasing out of codetermination through transfer of enterprise to a new holding company.	BB 1993, 957 (5/20/93)	OLG Celle	3/22/93 (E, r, w)	Preussag
"Elimination" of German codetermination through foreign holding company and a German intermediate holding company.	DB 1993, 1711 (8/27/93) BB 1993, 1541 (8/10/93)	LG Stuttgart	5/11/93 (E, r, w)	Charles Vögele Holding
Codetermination when setting up supervisory board's committees.	AG 1994, 428 (9/1/94)	LG Passau	5/31/94 (I, e, l)	Vogt Electronic
Codetermination when setting up supervisory board's committees.	WM 1995, 978 (6/3/95)	OLG München	2/27/95 (I, partly r/ partly e, l)	Vogt Electronic
Composition of the supervisory board; admission of previous members of supervisory boards as guests (Industrial Constitution Act of 1952).	WM 1996, 65 (1/13/96)	OLG Düsseldorf	10/10/95 (E, e, l)	Deutsche Babcock

a. Decisions relate to interpretation of the Codetermination Act of 1976 except as indicated.

b. E = firm specific; I = industrywide; r = restricting codetermination; e = extending codetermination; w = won by company; l = lost by company.

c. LG = court of first instance; OLG = appellate court; BGH = federal civil court; BAG = federal labor court; BVG = federal constitutional court.

Figure 7-1. *Short-Term Development of the Average Abnormal and Cumulated Abnormal Return*

Percent

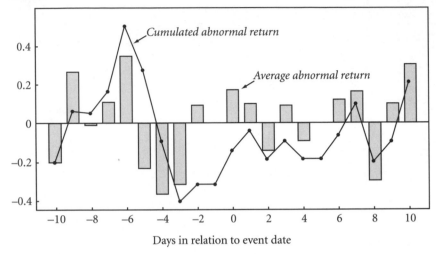

Days in relation to event date

In figures 7-1 to 7-3, the abnormal daily return is shown with bar graphs, while the cumulative return over the ten days before and after the judicial announcement is shown by the line. Figure 7-1 shows that the average abnormal return on the event day is slightly positive, which is rather surprising, given the fact that the number of cases in which codetermination rights were extended by the courts is larger than the number of cases in which these rights were restricted (fourteen versus ten).

Figure 7-2 is based only on the fourteen cases in which codetermination was extended; figure 7-3 is based only on the ten cases in which it was restricted. It appears that an extension of codetermination rights went together with a slight, statistically insignificant *increase* in abnormal returns on the day that they occurred, whereas a restriction went hand in hand with a daily *decrease* that also proved to be insignificant. The development of the abnormal returns is erratic and shows no discernible pattern; thus the cumulative abnormal returns are rather low and not systematically related to the type of decision.

Figures 7-4 and 7-5 divide the cases differently. Figure 7-4 is based on the experience of the ten companies that won their case, while figure 7-5 is based on the ten companies that lost. But a company's success in the respective lawsuit did not lead to a significant increase in the abnormal return on either the event day or one of the following days, nor does a company loss

Figure 7-2. *Short-Term Development of the Average and Cumulated Abnormal Returns if Codetermination Is Extended*

Percent

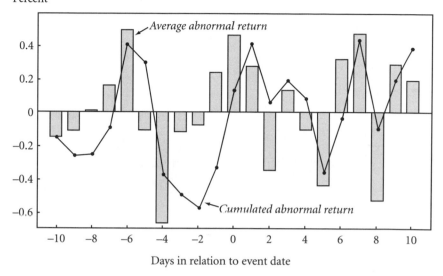

Days in relation to event date

Figure 7-3. *Short-Term Development of the Average and Cumulated Abnormal Returns If Codetermination Is Restricted*

Percent

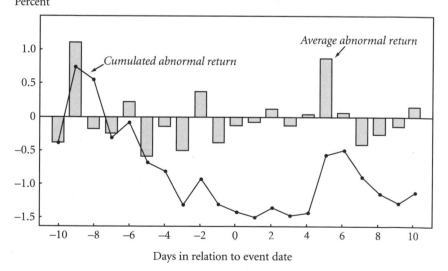

Days in relation to event date

Figure 7-4. *Short-Term Development of the Average and Cumulated Abnormal Returns in the Case of a Firm Win*

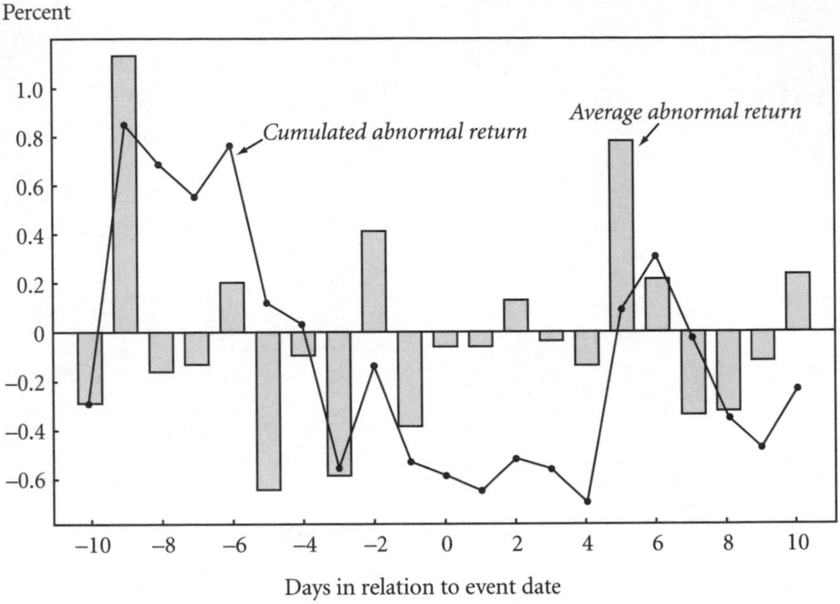

Percent

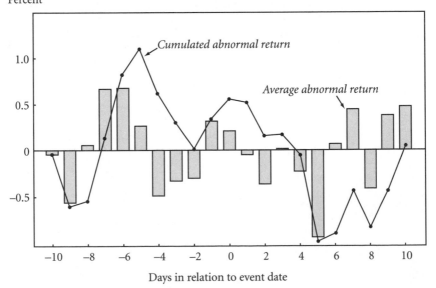

Days in relation to event date

Figure 7-5. *Short-Term Development of the Average and Cumulated Abnormal Returns in the Case of a Firm Loss*

Percent

Days in relation to event date

have the opposite impact on the development of the relative capital market performance of the companies affected.

We investigated these results more thoroughly with several ordinary least-squares regressions. We used the (cumulated) abnormal return as a dependent variable and then used as explanatory variables the divisions already presented in table 7-2: the outcome of the respective court's deliberations (the firm wins, the employees' representatives win, or no party wins), the basic character of the decision (restriction or extension of codetermination), the type of court involved (court of first instance, appellate court, Federal Civil Court, or Federal Constitutional Court), and the relevance of the decision (affecting a single enterprise only or economy-wide importance) serving as independent variables. In only one case did one of the independent variables have a statistically significant impact on the capital market's reactions: cases tried in an appellate court had a positive effect on cumulative returns, significant at the 10 percent level. Although the findings are not statistically significant—and should not be relied upon too heavily—it is worth noting that some of the variables even had effects going in the unexpected direction. For example, an extension of codetermination led to an *increase* in the cumulated abnormal return; a company win led to a *decrease* in the abnormal return; a company loss led to an *increase* in the abnormal return; and a restriction of codetermination rights led to a decrease in the cumulated abnormal return. Again, none of these results were significant.

We tested these results using a variety of specifications, and they were quite robust. For example, since twenty-three cases and twenty-eight firms constitute a rather small sample, one or a few outliers could in theory have a strong influence on the results. Therefore we recoded our dependent variables as dummy variables—that is, negative versus positive (cumulated) abnormal return—and estimated logistic regressions with the same explanatory variables as above. This left our findings virtually unchanged. We also experimented with a number of different sizes of the event window, which did not change the findings. We reestimated the regressions with and without adjusting for firm characteristics—such as size, sector affiliation, value added per employee, capital stock, and so on—without affecting the regression coefficients by much. When we pooled the data for all twenty-eight enterprises over a period of twenty-one days (ten days before the event plus the event day plus a period of ten days following the event) to reduce the standard errors of our coefficients, the empirical analysis still did not produce statistically significant results. For the sake of brevity, we do not report the results of the various regression estimates, but they can be obtained from the authors on request.

New Evidence from an Event Test
Using Industrial Sectors

One can offer various explanations for our not finding a connection
between the court decisions on codetermination and the stock price of individual firms. For example, perhaps information about the legal disputes or
lawsuits was disseminated through the press before publication of the judicial opinion, in which case the stock market may already have incorporated that information. One could presumably test this hypothesis using the
dates of news stories in major business publications, although we have not
compiled the necessary data on this point. Another argument might be
that the stock market does not react because the Codetermination Act itself
does not influence the performance of the firms concerned, or because the
judicial decisions on codetermination are too limited in their effect to have
an important impact.

If this last interpretation were correct, then even if many of the court
decisions were too small to have much effect on the stock price of firms, one
might be able to find effects on overall sectors of the economy from more
substantial events. Thus in this section we use sectoral stock market data to
analyze the influence of two substantial events: the enactment of the
Codetermination Act on July 1, 1976; and the final ruling of the Federal
Constitutional Court on March 1, 1979, in which it considered the act to
be constitutional.

The sectors to be analyzed are based on the parties to the appeal lodged
with the Federal Constitutional Court against the main provisions of the
Codetermination Act. This appeal was supported by ten single firms (of
which only six are traded on the stock market) and twenty-nine employers' associations from four sectors: banks and insurance companies,
chemical industry, engineering industry, and steel production and manufacturing. Only the first three of these sectors were chosen for the empirical analysis, because the last one has already been covered by the 1951 act.
It seems reasonable to assume that firms from these sectors were also more
in opposition to the enactment of the 1976 legislation itself, as shown by
their willingness to contest the legislation in court.

It also seems reasonable to assume that in our specific context the aggregated indices are likely to measure the "pure" effect of codetermination,
because data on individual firms are—owing to enterprise-specific factors—
much "noisier." In other words, sectoral performance measures are probably
more suitable for longitudinal analyses such as the following one because
firm-specific factors disappear.

Figure 7-6. *Capital Market Performance of the Banking and Insurance Sector, 1976*

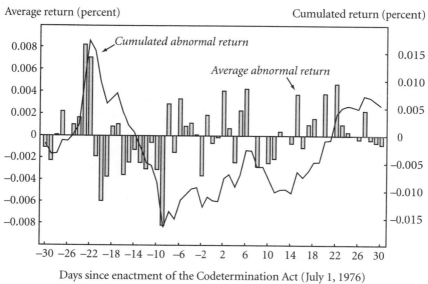

Days since enactment of the Codetermination Act (July 1, 1976)

Figures 7-6 to 7-11 display the results of this analysis. The daily abnormal returns for the sector, compared with the market as a whole, are again shown by the bar graphs, while the cumulative abnormal returns are shown by the line. The sectoral indices are calculated using the stock market performance of twenty to fifty publicly traded firms from each sector. This is problematic insofar as not all publicly traded firms are subject to codetermination, and not all codetermined firms are publicly traded. At the risk of increasing the noise in the data, we increased the number of days in the event window to a considerable extent, because otherwise we would have been unable to detect long- or medium-term changes in investment behavior. Figures 7-6 to 7-8 show the window for each sector around the 1976 enactment of the Codetermination Act, while figures 7-9 to 7-11 show the window around each sector for the 1979 decision of the Federal Constitutional Court.

Looking at the development of the cumulative abnormal returns, one again finds no common pattern. As for the 1976 event, although the abnormal returns are by and large positive in the five days following the enactment of the Codetermination Act, they are also rather erratic, and none of the changes proved to be statistically significant. In the banking and insur-

Figure 7-7. *Capital Market Performance of the Engineering Industry, 1976*

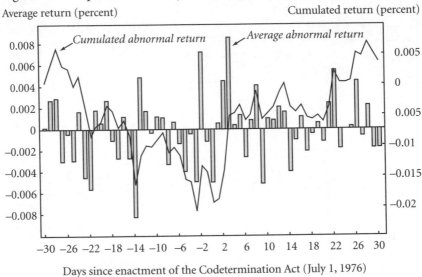

Average return (percent)   Cumulated return (percent)

Days since enactment of the Codetermination Act (July 1, 1976)

ance sector and in the engineering industry, the cumulative abnormal returns were slightly higher at the end of the period under investigation than they were in the beginning. In the chemical industry, they were slightly lower. In all three sectors, however, the margins in which the cumulative abnormal returns varied were rather small.

Similarly, in the first few days after the Federal Constitutional Court's decision in 1979, there was no sign in any of the three sectors under consideration that the sector-specific rate of return differed in a statistically meaningful way from the market return. In the chemical industry the majority of the abnormal rates of return within the "critical" five-day period following the event was slightly positive; in the remaining two sectors (banking and insurance, engineering) they were negative. The cumulative abnormal rate of return showed a constant upward trend in the chemical industry, whereas in the remaining two sectors it showed a clear (engineering industry) and a less clear downward trend (banking and insurance). In neither case, however, did the cumulative abnormal rate of return exceed a margin of +2 percent or –1 percent, respectively. Further tests reveal that neither the enactment of the Codetermination Act nor its general acceptance by the Federal Constitutional Court caused any significant volatility of

Figure 7-8. *Capital Market Performance of the Chemical Industry, 1976*

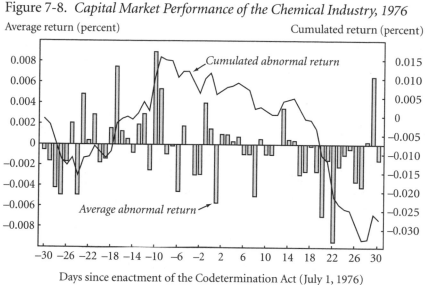

Average return (percent)   Cumulated return (percent)

Days since enactment of the Codetermination Act (July 1, 1976)

the stocks or in the extent to which they varied along with other stocks in the market.[14]

We also carried out formal statistical tests comparing the three sectors that should have been more heavily affected by codetermination (banking and insurance, chemicals, and engineering) with three sectors that were much less affected by the new legislation as reference industries (construction; retail trade; and food, beverages, and leisure services). In the banking and insurance sector and also in the chemical industry, the percentage of employees working in codetermined and publicly traded firms is relatively high, at 70 to 80 percent, whereas in the engineering industry it is about 50 percent.[15] In the three "reference industries," the figure is less than 25 percent. In this case, we looked at the abnormal returns for these sectors in the two and a half years before the day of the event and compared it with the abnormal returns for ten days after the event. With only one exception, neither the enactment of the Codetermination Act nor the fact that it was

14. With regard to the enactment of the law in 1976, the volatility measures are close to zero in every case and do not differ significantly. The beta factors are 1.84 (before the event) and 2.20 (afterward) in the chemical industry, 0.81 and 0.41 in the engineering industry, and 1.89 and 0.42 in the banking and insurance sector. None of these differences is statistically significant.

15. Author's calculations based on unpublished data provided by the Federal Labor Office and on data from Müller-Jentsch (1989, pp. 194–95).

Figure 7-9. *Capital Market Performance of the Banking and Insurance Sector, 1979*

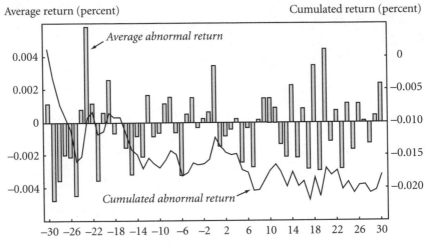

Average return (percent)   Cumulated return (percent)

Days since the Federal Constitutional Court's final decision (March 1, 1979)

later declared constitutional by the Federal Constitutional Court resulted in a significant change in the average abnormal rates of return in any of the six sectors under consideration. The statistically insignificant results went in mixed directions. The one exception was that the return for the chemical industry *rose* significantly (at the 10 percent level) after the 1979 court decision that found the Codetermination Act to be constitutional. We conducted a similar analysis with the date of the oral presentation at the Federal Constitutional Court as the event date. Here, too, the capital market's reactions were statistically insignificant. Similar results were also obtained using several alternative reference indices.[16]

Again, one likely explanation for our inability to obtain statistically significant results from this event study is that changes in stock prices (if there were any at all) occurred long before the enactment of the law or the court

16. Although most reasonable indices will be very highly correlated, this does not mean that the exact composition is unimportant. Göppl and Schütz (1994, p. 26), for example, show that the correlation of the overall DAFOX with the DAFOX for blue chips is +.995 for the period January 1974–December 1991. The respective coefficient for the overall DAFOX and the DAFOX for small caps is +.892 only, and for the DAFOX for blue chips and the DAFOX for small caps it is +.846. However, when we replicated our analysis using the DAFOX for small caps instead of the overall DAFOX, the results did not change dramatically. Although in most cases the post-event performance was slightly lower than the pre-event performance, the difference proved to be insignificant in every single case. The full results of the tests are available from the authors on request.

Figure 7-10. *Capital Market Performance of the Engineering Industry, 1979*

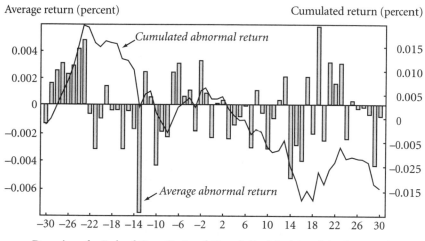

Days since the Federal Constitutional Court's final decision (March 1, 1979)

decision, because potential investors anticipate possibly detrimental consequences of codetermination and thus redirect their investment behavior. Thus the thirty-day window preceding the events in figures 7-6 to 7-11 may well be too short. It is also possible that even an event window of two and a half years before the event might be too short in this case, because the political discussion about codetermination can be traced back to the late

Figure 7-11. *Capital Market Performance of the Chemical Industry, 1979*

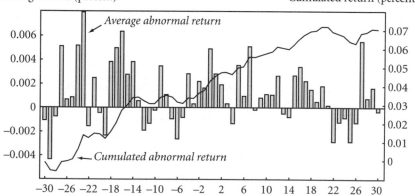

Days since the Federal Constitutional Court's final decision (March 1, 1979)

1960s. It is possible that shareholders who had already invested in the sectors and firms most heavily affected by the new legislation later on experienced a reduction in their abnormal returns long before the law came into force. However, it is not possible to test this hypothesis with our methodology, because the stock market data are only available from January 2, 1974, onward and because the second event occurred less than three years after the first.

Summary and Implications

In tracking a sample of judicial decisions concerning the application of Germany's Codetermination Act of 1976, we did not find that stockholders experienced financial losses due to judicial decisions extending codetermination rights of workers. Moreover, neither the enactment of the Codetermination Act of 1976 nor its legal examination by the Federal Constitutional Court in 1979 led to significant reductions in the (cumulated) abnormal returns in those sectors of the German economy in which most of the firms must obey the respective legislation.

One can offer various explanations for our findings. As is always true with event studies, a possible criticism is that the events we looked at were anticipated by the market; after all, the court decisions and the passage of the 1976 Codetermination Act were all discussed in the press before the judicial decisions were actually announced or the law was actually passed.

The findings here are also consistent with the hypothesis that codetermination does not influence the performance of firms either negatively or positively. It may be that while some investors dislike codetermination, others may favor it, say, employees of the respective firms who are shareholders at the same time. In that case, changes in the amount of codetermination may lead to trading where a different group holds the stock, but without a change in price. To investigate this claim, one could test for an increase in the number of securities traded around the events given here. But so far, at least, none of the positions on the impact of codetermination on firm value receives much empirical support.

References

Addison, John T., Joachim Genosko, and Claus Schnabel. 1989. "Gewerkschaften, Produktivität und Rent-Seeking." *Jahrbücher für Nationalökonomie und Statistik* 206 (2): 102–16.

Addison, John T., Kornelius Kraft, and Joachim Wagner. 1993. "German Works Councils and Firm Performance." In *Employee Representation: Alternatives and Future Directions*, edited by Bruce E. Kaufman and Maurice M. Kleiner, 305–38. Madison, Wisc.: Industrial Relations Research Association.

Addison, John T., Claus Schnabel, and Joachim Wagner. 1996. "German Works Councils, Profits, and Innovation: Evidence from the First Wave of the Hannover Firm Panel." Report 156, University of Lüneburg, Department of Economics and Social Sciences (January).

Addison, John T., and Joachim Wagner. 1995. "On the Impact of German Works Councils: Some Conjectures and Evidence from Establishment-Level Data." Report 142, University of Lüneburg, Department of Economics and Social Sciences (January).

Alchian, Armen. 1984. "Specificity, Specialization, and Coalitions." *Journal of Institutional and Theoretical Economics* 140 (1): 34–49.

Belman, Dale. 1992. "Unions, the Quality of Labor Relations, and Firm Performance." In *Unions and Economic Competitiveness*, edited by Lawrence Mishel and Paula B. Voos, 41–107. Armonk: M. E. Sharpe.

Benelli, Giuseppe, Claudio Loderer, and Thomas Lys. 1987. "Labor Participation in Corporate Policy-Making Decisions: West Germany's Experience with Co-determination." *Journal of Business* 60 (4): 553–75.

Brown, Stephen J., and Jerold B. Warner. 1980. "Measuring Security Price Performance." *Journal of Financial Economics* 8 (3): 205–58.

———. 1985. "Using Daily Stock Returns: The Case of Event Studies." *Journal of Financial Economics* 14 (1): 3–31.

Bühler, Wolfgang, Hermann Göppl, and Peter Möller. 1993. "Die Deutsche Finanzdatenbank (DFDB)." In *Empirische Kapitalmarktforschung*, edited by Wolfgang Bühler, 287–331. Düsseldorf: Handelsblatt.

FitzRoy, Felix R., and Kornelius Kraft. 1985a. "Mitarbeiterbeteiligung und Produktivität: Eine ökonometrische Untersuchung." *Zeitschrift für Betriebswirtschaft* 55 (1): 21–36.

———. 1985b. "Unionization, Wages and Efficiency: Theories and Evidence from the U.S. and West Germany." *Kyklos* 38 (4): 537–54.

———. 1987a. "Efficiency and Internal Organization: Works Councils in West German Firms." *Economica* 54 (216): 493–504.

———. 1987b. "Formen der Arbeitnehmer-Arbeitgeber-Kooperation und ihre Auswirkungen auf die Unternehmensleistung und Entlohnung." In *Mitarbeiter-Beteiligung und Mitbestimmung im Unternehmen*, edited by Felix R. FitzRoy and Kornelius Kraft, 173–96. Berlin: de Gruyter.

———. 1990. "Innovation, Rent-Sharing and the Organisation of Labour in the Federal Republic of Germany." *Small Business Economics* 2 (2): 95–103.

———. 1993. "Economic Effects of Co-determination." *Scandinavian Journal of Economics* 95 (3): 365–75.

Freeman, Richard B., and Edward P. Lazear. 1995. "An Economic Analysis of Works Councils." In *Works Councils: Consultation, Representation and Cooperation in Industrial Relations*, edited by Joel Rogers and Wolfgang Streeck, 27–52. University of Chicago Press.

Frick, Bernd. 1995. "Produktivitätsfolgen (über-)betrieblicher Interessenvertretungen." In *Managementforschung*, vol. 5: *Empirische Studien*, edited by Georg Schreyögg and Jörg Sydow, 215–57. Berlin: de Gruyter.

————. 1996a. "Co-determination and Personnel Turnover: The German Experience." *Labour* 10: 407–30.

————. 1996b. "Mitbestimmung und Personalfluktuation: Zur Wirtschaftlichkeit der bundesdeutschen Betriebsverfassung im internationalen Vergleich." In *Regulierung und Unternehmenspolitik: Methoden und Ergebnisse der betriebswirtschaftlichen Rechtsanalyse,* edited by Dieter Sadowski, Hans Czap, and Hartmut Wächter, 233–56. Wiesbaden: Gabler.

Frick, Bernd, and Dieter Sadowski. 1995. "Works Councils, Unions, and Firm Performance: The Impact of Workers' Participation in Germany." In *Institutional Frameworks and Labor Market Performance,* edited by Friedrich Buttler, Wolfgang Franz, Ronald Schettkat, and David Soskice, 46–81. London: Routledge.

Furubotn, Eirik G. 1985. "Co-determination, Productivity Gains, and the Economics of the Firm." *Oxford Economic Papers* 37 (1): 22–39.

————. 1988. "Co-determination and the Modern Theory of the Firm: A Property-Rights Analysis." *Journal of Business,* 61 (2): 463–74.

Göppl, Hermann, and H. Schütz. 1993. "The Design and Implementation of a German Stock Price Research Index (Deutscher Aktien-Forschungsindex DAFOX)." In *Mathematical Modeling in Economics,* edited by W. E. Diewert, K. Spreman, and F. Stehling, 506–19. Berlin: Springer.

————. 1994. "Die Konzeption eines Deutschen Aktienindex für Forschungszwecke." Universität Karlsruhe, Institut für Entscheidungstheorie und Unternehmensforschung, Diskussionspapier 162. Karlsruhe.

Gurdon, Michael A., and Aloop Rai. 1990. "Co-determination and Enterprise Performance: Empirical Evidence from West Germany." *Journal of Economics and Business* 42 (4): 289–302.

Hodgson, Geoffrey M., and Derek C. Jones. 1989. "Co-determination: A Partial Review of Theory and Evidence." *Annals of Public and Cooperative Economics* 60 (3): 329–40.

Jensen, Michael C., and William H. Meckling. 1979. "Rights and Production Functions: An Application to Labor-Managed Firms and Co-determination." *Journal of Business* 52 (4): 469–506.

Kraft, Kornelius. 1986. "Exit and Voice in the Labor Market: An Empirical Study of Quits." *Zeitschrift für die gesamte Staatswissenschaft* 142 (4): 697–715.

————. 1992. "Produktivitätswachstum und gewerkschaftliche Organisation." *Jahrbücher für Nationalökonomie und Statistik* 209 (5–6): 419–30.

Levine, David I., and Laura D. Tyson. 1990. "Participation, Productivity and the Firm's Environment." In *Paying for Productivity: A Look at the Evidence,* edited by Alan S. Blinder, 183–237. Brookings.

Lorenz, Wilhelm, and Joachim Wagner. 1991. "Bestimmungsgründe von Gewerkschaftsmitgliedschaft und Organisationsgrad." *Zeitschrift für Wirtschafts-und Sozialwissenschaften* 111 (1): 65–82.

Mainusch, Stefan. 1992. *Die Gewerkschaft als Determinante von Produktivität und Profitabilität.* Regensburg: Transfer.

Müller-Jentsch, Walter. 1989. *Basisdaten der industriellen Beziehungen.* Frankfurt/M: Campus.

Schnabel, Claus. 1989. *Zur ökonomischen Analyse der Gewerkschaften in der Bundesrepublik Deutschland.* Frankfurt/M: Peter Lang.

Schnabel, Claus, and Joachim Wagner. 1992. "Unions and Innovative Activity in Germany." *Journal of Labor Research* 13 (4):393–406.

Svejnar, Jan. 1981. "Relative Wage Effects of Unions, Dictatorship and Co-determination: Econometric Evidence from Germany." *Review of Economics and Statistics* 63 (2): 188–97.

———. 1982. "Co-determination and Productivity: Empirical Evidence from the Federal Republic of Germany." In *Participation and Self-Managed Firms,* edited by Derek C. Jones and Jan Svejnar, 199–212. Lexington, Mass.: D. C. Heath.

Thompson, Rex. 1995. "Empirical Models of Event Studies in Corporate Finance." In *Handbooks in Operational Research and Management Science,* vol. 9, *Finance,* edited by Robert Jarrow, Vojislav Maksimovic, and William T. Ziemba, 963–92. Amsterdam: Elsevier.

PART Three

Japanese Corporate Governance

8

The Political Economy of
Japanese Lifetime Employment

RONALD J. GILSON AND
MARK J. ROE

L arge firms in Japan have a strikingly different relationship
with their employees than do firms in the United States. In
Japan large firms guarantee many employees lifetime employment, whereas at-will employment is more typical in the United
States, although actual tenure is often long-lasting. This difference
is said to be of great importance in the Japanese system. Lifetime
employment for core workers is said to be at the center of Japanese corporate governance and labor relations, is said to provide
an incentive for firms to invest in workers' human capital, and is
said to be supported by other Japanese governance institutions,
such as cross-shareholdings, inside boards of directors, and the
main bank system.[1] U.S. firms, in contrast, offer workers neither

We thank Mark Barenberg, Harold Baum, Margaret Blair, Takeo Hoshi, Curtis
Milhaupt, Kenichi Osuji, Katherine Stone, and participants in the Columbia Law
School conference on employees and corporate governance for comments on an earlier draft; Columbia Law School's Sloan Project for research support; Alex Gould for
research assistance; and Saori Horikawa, Junko Oikowa, and Shinobu Yamaguchi for
research assistance and translation. For a related article, see Roe (1998b).

1. See, for example, Gordon (1982); Mincer and Higuchi (1988); Kanemoto and
MacLeod (1991); Garvey and Swan (1992); Aoki (1994); Milgrom and Roberts (1994).

explicit nor implicit guarantees of permanent employment, and the corporate governance system rarely involves labor.

We explore these differences through three hypotheses about the origins and functioning of lifetime employment. First, lifetime employment as conventionally understood in the United States is unlikely to have had the purported human capital advantages claimed for it by admiring American analysts. Second, its origins lie more in politics and the struggle for labor peace in a disrupted postwar Japan than in the economics of developing human capital. Third, after it arose for political purposes, other governance institutions evolved to support efficient production. In our analysis, the firm's promise of lifetime employment (the "bright" side of Japanese labor practices) is tied to the lack of an external labor market in which employees could easily move from firm to firm (the "dark" side of Japanese labor practices). This dark side probably does more of the "work" in encouraging employee productivity and commitment to the firm than does lifetime employment.

Lifetime Employment's Purported Incentives

The conventional view is that Japanese firms promised lifetime employment to give workers the proper incentive to invest in human capital, or at least their promises had that as a primary effect. Allen Blinder states: "After all, because of the lifetime employment system, it is the core employees who ... make extensive, immobile investments [in human capital]."[2] Similarly, others say that "the lifetime employment system, combined with a ranking hierarchy, has served to encourage skill acquisition on the part of workers and to maintain a high level of effort,"[3] and they wonder whether the United States could import lifetime employment and its benefits.[4] That may not

2. Blinder (1992, pp. 51, 54); see also Garvey and Swan (1992, pp. 247–48): "One of the most prominently cited reasons for the success of postwar Japanese firms is their ability to maintain valuable implicit agreements with their employees[, agreements] ... providing relatively stable employment [in a] system [that] seems to encourage both high levels of individual effort and cooperation between employees." Mincer and Higuchi (1988, p. 97) note: "The starting point ... is the proposition that intensive formation of human capital on the job is the basic proximate reason for the strong degree of worker attachment to the firm in Japan." And Gordon (1985, p. 35) asserts that "the lifetime employment system ... [arose in spurts after World War II because] the new production processes required workers with narrow skills on particular machines rather than broad, easily transferable skills. ... [F]irms moved to the lifetime employment system in order to amortize their specific training investment." Gordon portrays the interwar efforts as unsuccessful. See also the discussion on lifetime employment later in the chapter.

3. Kanemoto and MacLeod (1991, p. 167).

4. Kanemoto and MacLeod (1991, p. 167); see also Blinder (1992, p. 62).

be so easy in the open external labor market of the United States.[5] Indeed, it is not the firm's promise of lifetime employment alone, but its complement—a closed external labor market, limiting employees' ability to move to other firms—that helped develop human capital investment incentives in Japan. Japanese firms may well invest in their employees' human capital, but they do so *not* because they have promised the employees lifetime jobs, but because their employees cannot readily move elsewhere.[6] Importing lifetime employment into the United States with many American firms promising not to fire employees would not itself directly encourage human capital investment; to work at all in encouraging human capital investment, it would need its complement, the absence of an external labor market, which does the heavy lifting in Japan, but which most Americans would find unacceptable.

The Basic Argument: Generic and Industry-Specific Skills

Human capital is conventionally divided into two categories: general, which is valuable to many employers; and firm-specific, which is valuable to only a single employer.[7] General skills are said to be a central attribute of Japanese workers, particularly their ability to move readily from one task to another.[8] In the next section we look at firm-specific skills. For neither type of skills does the firm's promise to the employee of a lifetime job directly induce the employee or the employer to pay to develop the employee's human capital.

MISALIGNED INCENTIVES IN DEVELOPING HUMAN CAPITAL. Imagine an economy in which deep general skills are important: workers need to work in teams, to develop new skills as markets change, and to run different machines as technologies and customer tastes evolve. Who will pay for employees to develop these skills? When external labor markets are fluid, firms underinvest in their employees' human capital because other firms

---

5. In internal labor markets, employees move inside the firm from job to job; in external labor markets, employees move from firm to firm.

6. Lifetime employment is sometimes understood by Japanese analysts as a two-way street: employers promise a lifetime job and employees promise not to leave. The latter half of the bargain seems only dimly reflected in the American literature, and it is this half—or its institutional cousin, a closed external labor market—that we believe best explains the pattern of human capital investment and that would be anathema to most Americans.

7. See Becker (1993, pp. 30–51).

8. See Aoki (1990, pp. 3–14).

can poach the employees after they have been trained. The poaching firms can pay the workers more, because the poachers have no training costs. True, if their employees received outside offers, the training firm could keep the employees it had trained by matching the competing firms' wage offers. But if the training firms matched the higher external wages after having already paid for the training, then they would earn nothing on their investments in training. The poaching firms and the employees would split the returns on the prior investments in training (minus the costs of relocation) for which the training firms paid; thus the training firms would pay but would get no return. Firms will anticipate these free-rider problems, or learn from their mistakes, and stop paying to train other firms' future employees. Accordingly, employers lack the incentives to invest heavily in general human capital when their external labor markets are fluid.[9]

Alternatively, employees could pay for their general skills themselves, as basic human capital theory suggests, either directly, by paying the tuition for training programs and education, or indirectly, by accepting a lower wage while they are being trained.[10] (This is partly the "American" solution.) When employees pay for all of their own training, employers have less reason to fear opportunism from poaching competitors or migrating employees. Employers may underinvest, but employees pay for their own general skills; or, for some, public investment in vocational education may offset underinvestment by employers.

Although employees might in general have incentives to develop their own human capital, any idea that employees at Japanese firms pay for most of their general human capital confronts two problems, one empirical and one theoretical. The empirical problem is that Japanese firms pay *more* of the costs of training in general skills than do American firms.[11] Why do they pay more? And does the firm's promise of lifetime employment facilitate its investment? These are the principal questions addressed in this chapter.

The theoretical problem is that employees are often ineffective buyers of human capital, because they are less informed than the employer about the skills needed for the future. Even if the employer offers guidance, employees may mistrust the employer's advice regarding either what skills should be developed or, if the employee is to accept a lower wage now, whether the

9. Japanese labor markets are not fluid, but we start our analysis with fluid labor to help lead to our conclusion, which is that the constricted labor market, not the firms' promises of lifetime employment, is what induces the players to invest in human capital.

10. See Becker (1975, p. 34).

11. See Tilly and Tilly (1994, p. 300), citing Dertouzos and others (1989, pp. 81–93). See also Acemoglu and Pischke (1998), who argue that the willingness of firms to finance training in employees' general skills is a factor of informational asymmetry.

employer will compensate the employee later. And, even if employees could determine the right skills in which to invest, they might be unable to afford to invest or be unwilling to invest. Credit markets for employees are imperfect, particularly for those at the beginning of their careers.

Thus neither the employer nor the employee has the right incentives to invest in general human capital: the employer fears losing its investment if the external labor market is fluid; the employee fears losing his or her investment if the employer reneges on the promised return and often neither knows what human capital fits with the market nor has the funds to pay for that human capital. Firms and employees therefore underinvest in human capital. An economy that could invest more in the right kinds of human capital would perform better over time.

IRRELEVANCE OF LIFETIME EMPLOYMENT TO EMPLOYEES' INCENTIVES. Could lifetime employment solve these problems? Would firms in a fluid external labor market offer lifetime employment to align the firm's and the employee's incentives to invest in this general human capital? We believe they would not.

Suppose that the lifetime employee pays for the general skills by taking a lower wage earlier in his or her career. Although lifetime employment protects the employee's *job*, the employer who offers lifetime employment is not guaranteeing that future *wages* will be high enough to pay the employee back for his or her investment. Lifetime employment does not reduce employee mistrust much if wages remain flexible, and Japanese wages are said to be even *more* flexible than American wages. True, the labor market protects employees here (albeit imperfectly), but the theoretical problem with lifetime employment in a perfectly fluid labor market is that the labor market *always* protects the employee. Employees do not need a promise of lifetime employment in the first place because they can take their skills onto the labor market. Of course, labor markets are not perfect and one must take into account firms' and employees' incentives in realistic but imperfect markets, as we do later in the discussion. But when skills are general and labor markets frictionless, lifetime employees will pay to get those skills as long as they can sell those skills to others, even if the firm where the employees happen to be working can reduce their pay. The firm's promise of lifetime employment adds little, or nothing, to the employees' willingness to pay to acquire general skills in a fluid labor market.

Similar weaknesses afflict the familiar claim that lifetime employment encourages Japanese employees to train their own successors because with lifetime employment the training employee does not risk that he is training his own replacement. Lifetime employment only means that one's job is safe, not that future wage increases are ensured. Once a trainer trains a successor, the firm can lower the trainer's variable wages (or fail to raise them enough). Again, lifetime employment alone does not solve the labor contracting problem.

IRRELEVANCE OF LIFETIME EMPLOYMENT TO EMPLOYERS' INCENTIVES. The interesting issue in Japan is why *employers* pay for their employees' general human capital. Lifetime employment is said to facilitate the firm's investment, but we disagree with that view.

If the firm guarantees employees their jobs, then, if the external labor market were fluid, it would be heads the employees win, tails the firm loses. If an employee developed good skills at the firm's expense, the employee could jump to another firm, which could pay more because it had paid no training costs. If employees could signal to potential new employers when they have acquired high skills, the result would be perverse: the employer who paid for training would tend to lose its best employees (heads) and be stuck with its worst ones (tails). In this "reverse lemons market," a firm promising lifetime employment would be committing itself to keeping its *least* skilled employees. The firm, anticipating this unfavorable result, would invest *less* in its employees' general skills with lifetime employment than without it.

So why do Japanese employers invest heavily in general and industry-specific skills? In our view, it is not because of the friendly Japanese institution of firms' promising their employees lifetime employment, an institution often viewed admiringly in the American literature. Rather, a dark and gloomy closing of the external labor market played a key role: employees cannot change jobs because the Japanese external labor market is weak, and deliberately weak. If they could change jobs easily, they could take along their general skills. It is the closed external labor market, not their promises to employees of lifetime jobs, that assures employers that they can earn a return if they invest in their employees' general human capital.

With the "dark" side of a weak external labor market in place, the firm can comfortably invest in its employees' general and industry-specific skills, knowing that other firms will not raid its employees: the dark side makes the employees' general human capital an asset of the training firm. Even if lifetime employment played a role here, if it also needed a closed external labor market to work well, the package would be unattractive to an American culture that values mobility.

Firm-Specific Skills

Lifetime employment is also conventionally said to facilitate Japanese firms' investment in their employees' *firm-specific* human capital. This, too, seems doubtful to us.

WAGE FLEXIBILITY AND FIRM-SPECIFIC HUMAN CAPITAL. Suppose that employees paid for their own firm-specific capital. If so, the firm could act opportunistically and later on "expropriate" the returns on those employees' investments.

Firm-specific human capital is worth more to the employer than to its competitors, because the firm-specific skills are those that could help make *this* firm, not others, more productive. The employee's firm-specific skills include knowledge of the firm's proprietary processes or the quirks of its work groups. Were the employee to invest in developing firm-specific skills, the employer could opportunistically pay the employee at the lower compensation level of the employee's next best job, a job at another firm that would not pay the employee for skills that the other firm could not use. Hence the employer could reap the return from the employee's investment in himself or herself.

Because the employee would at that time have no higher-paying alternative, the employee would have to accept the lower wage. But the employee could anticipate this unfavorable scenario when deciding whether to pay for his or her own firm-specific human capital in the first place, and, fearing the firm's potential opportunism, would underinvest in those skills.[12]

Firms and employees can reduce the employing firm's potential for opportunism here by developing a good reputation for paying up later, as we explain shortly. The fact is, lifetime employment could not credibly reduce employer opportunism because the employer gives up very little of its power to be opportunistic by promising not to *fire* its employees. Once employees have invested in firm-specific human capital, it is *not* in the opportunistic firm's interest to *fire* them, but to exploit their wage vulner-

---

12. See Furubotn (1989, pp. 46–48), who argues that if workers must bear the costs of developing their own skills, they may choose instead those jobs that require only general skills. The same result follows if the employer pays for the employee's firm-specific human capital, although more weakly. Because the employee must spend time to absorb the firm-specific training, the employee invests time that could have been used to develop *general and more marketable* human capital. If the employer pays the employee up-front for this forgone investment, then the employer cannot treat the employee opportunistically as to this investment, but if the employer promises to pay up later, then the employee's time investment is firm-specific and at risk of employer opportunism.

ability by lowering the employees' salaries down to the employees' value on the labor market (rather than keep the employees' wages near their value to the firm). Conventional analysis seems to miss this point.

True, the firm's potential opportunism is not unlimited. If it tried to exploit too much, some disgruntled employees would become less productive or quit. Firms would find that they could exploit their employees only once; thereafter the employees would not pay for new or deeper skills. Even if employees invested in one large chunk at the beginning of their careers, firms that lost a reputation for fairness would find future employees uncooperative and unwilling to invest in their own firm-specific human capital. The point is not that these risks of firm opportunism are without cure, but that the firm's promise of lifetime employment is neither sufficient nor necessary to the cure.

THE FIRM'S INVESTMENT IN ITS EMPLOYEES' FIRM-SPECIFIC HUMAN CAPITAL. We do not dispute that Japanese firms invest in their employees' human capital, but we do dispute whether the firm's promise of lifetime employment explains why. If the firm pays for the investment, it risks that an employee may quit. The firm's unwillingness to pay for the skills is induced by the employee's potential to quit, a potential that the firm's promise of lifetime employment does not directly affect.

Once again, other institutions may make firms willing to invest in human capital. For example, firms may invest in a way that allows them to pay the employees something above their opportunity wage, thereby reducing the level of quits. The back-loaded wage scale over employees' careers fits this pattern. We have no quarrel with such models (and contribute to them below), but we again emphasize that lifetime employment is not critical to these models; the closed labor market in Japan might be, but this is not the Japanese institution attractive to Americans.

INDUSTRY-SPECIFIC HUMAN CAPITAL. Much purportedly firm-specific human capital is actually industry-specific human capital.[13] A worker who can use a lathe or a software system at a firm, or who has the flexibility skills associated with just-in-time automobile production, can use much the same skills at any firm in the industry. An employee with recourse to an external labor market has the incentive to acquire industry-specific skills,

13. The literature focuses on the firm-specific human capital of the Japanese employee. See, for example, Mincer and Higuchi (1988); Abe (1994). Like Sabel (1998), we view many of the skills as principally industry specific. The basic skills of employees at one large firm in an industry may resemble the skills of employees at another large firm in the same industry. See Itoh (1994, pp. 233, 249).

because even if the firm reneges, the employee "owns" the skills and can "sell" them elsewhere in the industry.[14] But when employment is certain, but mobility impossible, employees will spend less time and money acquiring skills because of the already discussed risk of employer opportunism. The employer's incentive to pay for specific skills increases, but only because a closed external labor market bars *employee* opportunism. The employer comes to "own" the human capital. In a U.S.-style external labor market, the uncertainty of the firm's employment commitment may *increase* the employees' motivation to keep their *industry*-specific skills high.

Lifetime employment—in the sense of the employer's promise to the employee of a lifetime job—thus seems unlikely to directly induce either the employer or the employee to invest in industry-specific skills. If the employee can sell those skills to others in the industry, it is *that* capacity that motivates the employee to buy the industry-specific skills himself or herself, and lifetime employment adds little or nothing. And if the employee can sell those skills in a robust external labor market—something the employee cannot do in Japan—then the firm would be deterred from paying for those industry-specific skills. (And, to be clear again here, *it is the closed external labor market* that yields the human capital benefits, *not* the firms' promises of lifetime employment.) The hard question now is this: if the employer's promises of lifetime employment do so little to promote investment in labor market skills, why did the Japanese firms promise it?

Why Lifetime Employment?

Lifetime employment resulted more from political forces than from human capital–based economic forces. Once the institution was in place, complementary institutions developed to support human capital.

Structure of a Historical Account

Seeking the historical roots of lifetime employment risks seeing causation when it is not there. Hindsight can give the illusion of causation because events earlier in time were followed by later events. Without more, however, random sequencing and tight causation are equally compelling. Similarly, the conventional claim that lifetime employment is rooted in Japanese culture (and needs no more explanation) is not enough.[15] Indeed, it would

14. But see note 73 and accompanying text for impeding frictions.
15. See, for example, Abegglen (1958).

be remarkable if a key economic institution were antithetical to a country's culture; either the institution would change or the culture would change. At times in the early twentieth century many midcareer Japanese employees moved to other companies, and at other times employers fired many midcareer employees. Culture and practice can diverge or converge. If culture and practice are now consistent (if we assume that lifetime employment really fits better with Japanese culture than does a fluid labor market, which is doubtful), then one must wonder what made the two finally converge after decades of divergence.

An historical inquiry runs another risk: complex facts allow for alternative accounts. How much labor turnover contradicts a statement that lifetime employment is present? Suppose half the work force turns over. But then half the work force is permanent. Is this lifetime or at-will employment? Finding that firms fired workers in Japan before World War II, as we do, presents the same problem. Would those who were fired have been lifetime employees under the post–World War II pattern? We will not debate these issues here; we will only note that lifetime work has been a marked feature of large Japanese firms in the postwar period, and we accept this as fact.

We also do not aim to authoritatively account for lifetime employment's historical origins. Instead we sketch a path-dependent account that the literature supports, with hypotheses that others will have to test.

History and politics shape some initial conditions from which the economy evolves. Some institutions are fixed, and their existence induces complementary institutions to arise, pushing the system to efficiently combine institutions. We see Japanese labor history through a lens that highlights a need for political peace at a key moment. In examining this history, some of which is well-known to labor scholars, some not, we observe path-dependent adaptation from political starting points.

This history did not happen "all at once," of course. It did not simply spring up during a single moment and then develop along a particular path without interruption. Further political circumstances came into play. Economic evolution is closely intertwined with political events, which constantly shape and reshape the course of that evolution. But enough happened more or less "at once" in postwar Japan that we can abstract a plausible starting point.

Japanese Employment Structure before the End of World War II

Stable employment is *not* a continuous Japanese cultural tradition. Indeed, just after the First World War, when Japanese labor markets were tight, skilled workers often changed jobs. Employment was impermanent because employees had an external labor market: early turnover rates of around 75 percent were the norm in most industries during World War I.[16] While firms tried to reduce turnover with wage and seniority policies that would become familiar in post–World War II Japan, such as year-end bonuses, seniority bonuses, and regular pay raises, these experiments failed to stymie labor turnover:

> So long as economic conditions made job-switching easy, and experienced workers saw movement as the best way to advance in skill, wages penalizing skilled job switchers would be self-defeating: they would not attract the best workers. Skill rather than seniority, therefore, had to remain a fundamental determinant of a worker's income in this era, despite varied efforts to change matters. This, in turn, encouraged or allowed mobile workers to continue moving.[17]

An economic downturn in the 1920s led to a surplus of labor, which eroded companies' enthusiasm for seniority incentives; many firms retreated from their prior commitments to seniority bonuses, regular pay raises, or retirement funds. Firms then began to recruit inexperienced workers directly out of school and gave them on-the-job training: "A newly attractive pattern of long-term or career employment began to take shape . . . in the 1920s, but we must not exaggerate the extent of the change. Insecurity and short-term commitment (on both sides) continue[d] to dominate."[18] Although voluntary mobility decreased, the job shortage that resulted from the economic downturn best explains the employees' decreased mobility.[19]

16. See Gordon (1985, p. 87). Gordon says the surveys show voluntary separations ranging from 20 to 70 percent of total turnover, and concludes "that the traveling worker, polishing his skills through movement from job to job, remained dominant" as the 1920s began (p. 94). Gordon emphasizes Japanese cultural features that differ from the employer paternalism that is sometimes said to explain lifetime employment. He stresses a craft pattern wherein skilled journeymen, licensed by a guild following apprenticeship, move from master to master to sharpen their skills. "The footloose traveler . . . of the Meiji period, who moved with alacrity between factories and shipyards . . . [was] following time-honored customs" (p. 22).

17. On efforts to use seniority promotions during this period, see Gordon (1985, pp. 96, 98–101).

18. Gordon (1985, p. 133). Aoki (1994, p. 30) accepts this assessment of the period.

19. See Gordon (1985, p. 139). Taira (1970, p. 154) reaches a similar conclusion: "Behind this [labor] stability in the 1920s was the generally stagnant state of employment, which culminated in the depression of 1929–1931." Taira also notes the difference between the reality of work force conditions and the ideal type contemplated by the tentative structural reforms of the 1920s. He stresses the problem of investing in training when "there was no guarantee that the internally trained workers would not change jobs before the investment in their training was recouped" (pp. 158–59). Mosk (1995, pp. 76–78), however, places more emphasis on these interwar structural changes.

Lifetime employment did not take root during this period, because employers neither promised to refrain from, nor did they actually refrain from, laying off employees during economic downturns. When jobs became scarce and an oversupply of workers ensued, "employers were ready to fire when business was slow, and seniority was no guarantee of exemption. To the contrary, they more often fired the older worker with seniority, but very likely declining skills as well. Throughout the decade, management fired workers and reduced work-force size."[20] Even when elements of lifetime employment from time to time appeared, temporary labor market conditions, not a long-term commitment to lifetime employment, induced them. Quitting was common when labor was in short supply, and firings began when labor was in surplus.

Employment instability continued in the 1930s and the war years, even as better economic conditions tightened the external labor market.[21] As in the tight World War I market, firms offered pay and training to induce employee loyalty, but to little avail. Skilled workers again moved between large companies. "The reemergence in the late 1930s of such mobility *between* large factories is a signal that policies to retain workers, some dating back to World War I or the 1920s, were of limited impact."[22]

During World War II the Japanese government tried to shape the external labor market. In April 1939, it restricted employers from pirating other firms' workers. To hire a new employee, a firm needed government approval; and to hire a skilled worker, the firm needed permission from the employee's former employer as well. By 1941, firms needed the government to approve all hiring, firing, and voluntary termination; in effect, the government tried to freeze all workers in their existing jobs.[23] Although turnover dropped, even government directives failed to end it entirely: "Skilled workers . . . remained ready to shift jobs, even illegally, throughout World War II."[24]

From World War I through the end of World War II, worker mobility in external labor markets eroded labor stability when labor was tight, and employers' willingness to fire even senior workers eroded labor stability when labor markets were not tight. Employers tried but failed to build wage and seniority structures to induce workers to stay during labor shortages.

---

20. Gordon (1985, pp. 139–40).

21. See Gordon (1985, p. 156).

22. Gordon (1985, p. 158). See also Nomura and Koyoo (1994, pp. 187–90); long-term employment was tried in 1920s, but did not stick.

23. See Gordon (1985, pp. 267, 272); Garon (1987, p. 255).

24. Gordon (1985, p. 274).

Government intervention reduced but failed to stop turnover. Workers were mobile and employers poached, even when mobility and poaching were illegal.

Post–World War II Labor Markets

At the end of World War II, as in the early 1930s, labor was in surplus, but the size of the surplus and its consequences were far larger and especially hard for workers to bear in a devastated economy:[25] "Companies quickly turned to mass dismissals. Millions lost their jobs."[26] The import of job loss was of the highest order: "Fear of starvation [was common]. . . . Japan lacked an effective public-welfare system, and, in 1945 or 1946, the threat of unemployment was literally a threat to survival."[27]

During earlier economic setbacks, Japanese firms fired workers. The immediate post–World War II period was *less* favorable to lifetime employment than the prewar period: labor was abundant, people without jobs starved, and firms could hire at low wages and fire at will. Yet lifetime employment emerged *during this period of labor surplus*. That labor surplus *and* lifetime employment occurred simultaneously presents a puzzle, one that standard economic motivations fail to explain, but that politics can.

LABOR STRIFE. Organized labor in Japan gained power in the two years following World War II's end. Labor strife was common, some of it induced by the American occupation authorities. The Trade Union Law of 1945, enacted at the urging of the occupation administration, SCAP—Supreme Commander, Allied Powers—to bring democracy to Japan, guaranteed workers the right to form unions and to strike. Workers, fearing and experiencing mass layoffs, used both rights: they formed unions and they struck. Union membership jumped from 381,000 when the Trade Union Law was enacted to more than 3 million a year later, and nearly 5 million by the end of 1946.[28]

These strikes threatened managers in ways beyond just halting production; workers sometimes actually took over and ran the factories without

---

25. See Garon (1987, p. 180).

26. Gordon (1985, p. 362).

27. Gordon (1985, p. 363). Price (1997, pp. 38–39) notes: "Actual production for 1946 was down 70 percent from 1934–36 levels. Tokyo and Osaka ... [saw] 60 percent of all buildings destroyed.... Rice production was seriously deteriorating. For city dwellers, starvation was not only possible but imminent."

28. See Gordon (1985, pp. 331–32); Garon (1987, p. 238); Mosk (1995, pp. 95–96).

the managers. The workers paid themselves, paid the factory's other costs, and then deposited any residual in a company bank account. The first such "takeover" occurred in the fall of 1945. Within the first six months of 1946, Japanese managers faced 255 such "takeover strikes." After a fifty-day strike at Toshiba in 1946, for example, labor won for themselves basic elements of managerial control of the factories.[29]

By 1947 SCAP had changed its mind about Japanese unions, coming to see then-prevailing union activity as threatening America's new anticommunist cold war strategy. Japan's new role, in SCAP's plan, was to be a capitalist bulwark against communism. Worker control of production threatened that plan, so SCAP abandoned its pro-union policy of 1945 and prodded Japanese managers to reassert control. In 1947 Japanese unions planned a general strike, but SCAP barred them from striking and then encouraged the Japanese Parliament to ban all public sector employees from striking.[30] American tanks directly supported Japanese police at least once in ousting workers.[31]

Toshiba's managers, encouraged by American authorities and Japanese officials who wanted an example, began an antilabor offensive in 1948, shutting down labor-controlled Toshiba factories by physically regaining control and removing key machines, dismissing workers, buying other workers' voluntary resignations, and ending labor union authority over basic management of Toshiba factories.[32] SCAP's concern over communist influence within the labor movement culminated in 1950 with the Red Purge; 12,000 employees said to be Communist party members were fired from their jobs and barred from union activity. Existing, often communist-influenced, unions were replaced with more cooperative enterprise unions.[33] At the same time, socialists threatened to win legislative victories, which leads to our first political hypothesis.

PEACE AS A PREDICATE TO PRODUCTION. A plausible political strategy for managers or conservative politicians would have been to split a labor coalition by privileging one influential segment of labor through lifetime employment, in return for reducing the size of the labor force and increasing management control over the rest of production. The impetus could

---

29. See Yamamoto (1983); Gordon (1985, p. 332); Mosk (1995, p. 96); Price (1997, p. 54). See also chapter 9 by Hiwatari in this volume. But Moore (1983, pp. 214–15) argues that the violent Toshiba strike yielded the union mixed results but its ferocity deterred other firms from taking on the unions.

30. See Gordon (1985, pp. 332–33); Mosk (1995, pp. 96–97).

31. See Price (1997, p. 66).

32. See Yamamoto (1983).

33. See Gordon (1985, p. 333); Mosk (1995, p. 96); Price (1997, pp. 83–97).

have come from the top down: conservative political and business leaders could have decided on lifetime employment for favored sectors to diminish the chance of socialist electoral success in response to economically induced industrial restructurings. "Macro" politics could have led to a "deal" that allowed restructuring while bringing social peace, suppressing radical labor, and reducing the chance of a socialist electoral victory by privileging one sector of labor.[34]

The impetus also could have been "local" and "micro," which is where our second political hypothesis begins: when managers sought to rationalize production in a restructured firm, they might have privileged the surviving employees with lifetime employment to reduce labor unrest after the restructuring.[35] If many firms faced the same need to downsize, their senior managers may have decided on the same solutions, which would have gathered momentum as each firm acted. Then, in this bottom-up story, government institutions may have confirmed the norm that many individual managers (and the surviving employees) had chosen in a deal to bring about labor peace.[36] (We do not mean that there was a single, one-time, economy-wide transaction. This "deal" seems to have come out of multiple disputes and was perhaps cemented by an emergent norm or "macro" political understanding.) This explanation is "political" in that the firms used lifetime employment not for the contractual goals of inducing skills development, but for the "political" goal of downsizing without energizing radical labor organizations.[37]

34. Price (1997, p. 253) notes: "In exchange for union acceptance of the performance-based wage system and limited union input in regulation of the workplace, workers received some job security. . . . This 'deal' had evolved at the workplace level in the 1950s after the large layoffs that occurred in the late 1940s." Price reports 400,000 layoffs in the private sector during only part of 1949 (p. 76, table 5).

35. "[Many] employees were dismissed, as well as radical unionists, [leading] management and union leaders . . . to incorporate remaining workers into the firm by promising employment security" (Hiwatari, meeting draft of chapter 9 in this volume).

36. For example, the "deal"—employment security in return for labor peace and cooperation— is reflected in the principles associated with the government-sponsored 1955 founding of the Japan Productivity Center. See Price (1997, pp. 152–54).

37. Raff (1988) argues that when Henry Ford announced his famous five-dollar day for workers whose next best job opportunities paid half as well, he quite plausibly was buying them away from the Wobblies, because he feared his new assembly line method was conducive to organizational appeals from the Wobblies. Support for a Japanese parallel can be found in Nishiguchi (1994) (suggesting a political component to the lifetime employment bargain, although acknowledging efforts along these lines in the interwar period). Eisenstadt and Ben-Ari (1990, p. 71) state: "[During the] offensive against labour during 1949, . . . state policies (mass lay-offs and the rescinding of union rights in the public sector . . .) [induced] major private players . . . to reassert their authority. Management [won] . . . showdowns with militant enterprise unions. At the same time, the big firms accepted union demands for job security and linking wages to worker [age]."

We paint a grim picture: workers struggle to survive, workers and managers struggle to control the factories, the American occupation authorities first foster and then seek to crush strong unions, and in the end a deal is cut. Although grim, this picture is realistic. A more positive spin on the same basic facts would see employees as seeking security, community, and dignity, and managers as resisting and then acceding to some workers' demands for security, a security that makes the favored workers more willing to cede control to management.[38] Whatever spin one prefers, human capital considerations do not motivate the adoption of lifetime employment.[39]

By the mid-1950s, the central features of lifetime employment were in place: fixed employment for part of the work force, and temporary employment for the rest, whose numbers could be shrunk or expanded as economic conditions demanded. The favored portion of the work force and the company were protected from changes in the external labor market by the capacity of temporary workers, many of them women, to absorb economic shock.[40]

Encouraging workers to invest in firm-specific human capital need not have been the goal either of the American occupation authorities intent on building a capitalistic Japan or of Japanese managers intent on regaining control of their factories and breaking militant unions. Japan reached a political solution to an explicitly political confrontation: control over production and management authority.

We do not dismiss economic efficiency as a selection mechanism, but at times politics "trumps" private economic goals. Afterward conditions settle and then economic selection and evolution act on these newly "initial" conditions. Once politics defined for Japan the political "given" of lifetime employment for some workers, Japan's economic problem was to craft associated institutions that could function effectively in the framework of the

---

38. In return for supporting employment stability, managers got functional control over the workplace: the freedom to adjust working conditions, including employee transfer. See Araki (1994, pp. 269–71).

39. The "grim" narrative resembles that of Japanese labor scholars here, whereas the happy view is more common among American analysts of labor history. See Gordon (1983, pp. 373, 374).

40. See Gordon (1985, p. 400): "The prominence of temporary workers in the Japanese settlement of the 1950s suggests that the group of full members made gains only at the expense of people on the margins." We have not tracked the history of an additional core component of Japanese labor structure: enterprise unionism, in which a company-bounded union promotes a cooperative relationship between lifetime employees and management. See, for example, Sugeno and Suwa (1996). Hiwatari says enterprise unionism arose from the same forces that gave rise to, and were part of the same package as, the lifetime employment bargain (see chapter 9 in this volume).

politically imposed lifetime employment. Lifetime employment was more a part of the peace predicate than of the productivity supplement.[41]

The Strength of the Political Deal

But why did the political deal—lifetime employment and a closed external labor market—persist when the labor surplus disappeared during the economically strong 1960s?[42] Why did employers not poach employees from competitors again? Why did employees not become mobile again? We offer four noncompeting hypotheses. Two see employers forbearing from laying off employees; two see employers forbearing from poaching.

First, individual managers may have remembered the postwar labor strife and feared losing any such conflict if they ended lifetime employment in their firm.[43] Labor disputes in declining industries surely heightened their worries, especially after the Miike coal strike, the most famous example in Japan. By 1959 the Japanese coal industry had become unprofitable, and Mitsui planned large layoffs at its mines. When the union at the Miike mine, one of the most radical in Japan, resisted, management locked labor out, and in July 1960, 20,000 strikers and labor activists violently confronted 10,000 policemen.[44]

Second, Japanese courts buttressed lifetime employment.[45] Although the basic Japanese employment rule was "employment at will" with notice, Japanese courts responded to the "scarcity of employment opportunities

41. Peace is a prerequisite to production, so deals that keep peace are not without efficiency properties. Roe (1998a) discusses how political backlash can disrupt systems otherwise thought to be efficient or lead to others designed to avoid more serious backlash. The question posed then is whether the firms' promises of lifetime employment were the "peace" predicate, as we argue seems plausible, or part of the productivity "supplement."

42. See Hanami (1979).

43. Although this concern would be less significant during the economic expansion starting in the late 1950s and ending with the oil shock in 1973, it would be significant in the period of restructuring that followed. It would also account for the provisions of the 1974 Employment Insurance Law, which granted "employment adjustment benefits"—subsidies—to firms trying to maintain employment levels in the face of economic adversity. See Sugeno (1992). (Sugeno is frequently viewed as the leading Japanese labor law academic.) One could see this managerial action as an economic agency cost to shareholders of management being separated from ownership, if the risk consisted more of psychological pain to the manager than of labor strife that would damage the firm's stockholders.

44. See Garon and Mochizuki (1993, pp. 145, 159–60); Price (1997, pp. 191–218). As ultimately resolved with extensive government mediation, layoffs were allowed, but with managers both trying harder to find alternative employment for those to be terminated and increasing compensation on dismissal (Price, 1997, p. 216).

45. See Sugeno (1992, pp. 395–412); Araki (1994, pp. 251–56); Foote (1996, pp. 639–65). Although these commentators see the courts as supporting the lifetime employment commitment, they do not see the courts as buttressing the no-poaching commitment.

in the chaotic post-War economy," with an "abuse of rights" doctrine that required that employers not dismiss employees "abusively."[46] The open-ended doctrine, eventually endorsed by the Japanese Supreme Court, declared any "dismissal which is not 'objectively reasonable and socially appropriate' . . . an abuse of the right to dismiss."[47]

In the expanding economy of the 1960s, the doctrine was seldom tested, so it was unclear how strongly firms were committed to lifetime employment and whether courts would rebuke defectors. After the 1973 oil shock the potential bite of the judicial doctrine could be felt, however.[48] Most employers kept to the implied rules of lifetime employment. When economic reversals pushed firms to downsize, firms first restricted new hiring, then farmed out excess workers to affiliates, then terminated temporary workers, and then solicited early retirement. Firms laid excess workers off *only* after using the other downsizing tools.[49] The courts adopted these tools into their notion of abusive dismissal, ruling that the employer must show economic need to downsize;[50] must exhaust alternatives to layoffs, one of which might be to transfer excess employees to affiliates; and must treat workers fairly and consult with them.[51]

Thus courts were not enforcing a long-standing cultural norm, but the postwar practice that had recently developed. A deal was made to end the postwar labor strife, and then the courts made sure that one element of the deal was kept.[52] Had the need for labor peace not led to the deal, the Japanese courts might well have defined abusive dismissal differently.[53] Thus courts buttressed the postwar lifetime employment norm by raising the costs to any firm that wanted to change the deal.

These two hypotheses could help explain why firms did not retract their promises of lifetime employment, but they do not explain why firms did not start to poach on one another and thereby open up the closed labor market. Our third hypothesis is that managers may have considered such poaching

---

46. Sugeno and Suwa (1995).

47. Araki (1994, p. 251).

48. See Sugeno (1992, pp. 407–08).

49. See Sugeno (1992, p. 409).

50. Sugeno and Suwa (1995, p. 29) note that "although in the vast majority of cases the court eventually upholds the management decision to implement the necessary personnel reduction measures, it still examines the enterprise's business circumstances in detail and renders its own judgment on the reasonableness of the decision."

51. See Sugeno (1992, pp. 408–10).

52. See Sugeno and Suwa (1995, pp. 27, 29).

53. The judicial rule may operate here simply to slow down change. If a future consensus in Japan is reached that employers must, say, downsize to be competitive, judicial doctrine may flexibly adjust. See Sugeno (1992).

a threat to the morale of the firm's existing employees and thus to the effectiveness of the internal labor market. Once promises of lifetime employment became widespread in Japan, and internal promotions became the normal way for employees to advance, a firm that brought in outsiders would risk demoralizing its own lifetime employees.

Moreover, managers may have feared that their poaching would induce other firms to retaliate and end labor understandings, leading to renewed local or national labor strife. If a vibrant external labor market reemerged, it would have threatened their firm's internal labor market. True, although firms collectively wanted a weak external labor market, free-rider effects might have undermined managers' resolve and prompted firms to poach anyway, since no firm acting alone could reopen the labor market entirely. (Hence managers would worry mainly about how much they would demoralize current employees by bringing in someone over their heads, and not worry as much about a vibrant labor market reemerging.) Although Japanese history is hazy here, collective institutions, such as the *keiretsu*, the president's council, or government action, could have reduced this collective action problem.[54]

One collective institution provides the basis for our fourth hypothesis here. The Japanese government may have helped destroy the external labor market. It may have discouraged lateral hiring and thereby helped keep the external labor market weak, a weakness that we earlier argued is critical to Japanese human capital investment. Recent accounts of Japanese corporate governance stress the government's role in designing governance institutions,[55] and commentators stress the importance of joint labor-management consultations at the industrial and national levels, through industry-wide councils and study groups.[56] Although we know of no explicit government efforts to shape the antipoaching principle, we do see some tantalizing evidence.[57]

---

54. In Japan, many major firms are in *keiretsu* groups, in which the firms and an affiliated bank own one another's stock. The presidents of the affiliated firms meet regularly in "presidents' council" meetings to discuss common problems. See Anderson (1984, pp. 30, 32); Aoki (1984, p. 12); Gerlach (1992, pp. 80–81).

55. See, for example, Aoki (1995b).

56. Sugeno (1992, pp. 475–77).

57. Hiwatari credits the Ministry of International Trade and Industry with a role in establishing oligopolistic structures in export industries and with inadvertently creating circumstances in which cartel-like behavior to suppress the external labor market could be maintained (see chapter 9 in this volume). More recently, the Japanese Ministry of Labor stated; "The consequences of such a policy [of allowing layoffs] would be unacceptable in Japan: *Employment is the essential condition of social stability* and the success of an enterprise cannot be at the expense of its employees. It's necessary to find a middle road between the traditional system [of lifetime employment], which remains at the heart of employment policy, and the new demands of the economic environment." Philippe Pons, "Le gouvernement refuse d'autoriser les licenciements sec," *Le Monde*, March 4, 1999, p. 2, col. 4 (emphasis added).

First, the Japanese government and the occupation authorities helped design the trade-off that ultimately settled the postwar labor strife: left-wing unions were crushed and the Left curtailed politically, employment levels were reduced, management regained control over the workplace that had been lost in the late 1940s, and part of the labor force obtained job security. Because labor retained potential political influence despite the fact that managers recovered workplace authority in the early 1950s, the government wanted that bargain to remain stable. Second, observers recount such informal government enforcement elsewhere, an example being the informal understanding that delegated main bank monitors would bail out weak affiliated industrial firms.[58] Third, head-hunting activities, a standard feature of vibrant external labor markets, were long illegal in Japan.[59] Government suppression of the external labor market certainly warrants further investigation.[60]

A Complementary, Evolutionary Labor Market Model

We argued earlier that the human capital benefits of Japan's lifetime employment cannot be understood apart from its complement—a closed labor market that shields a firm's investments in its employees' human capital from market mobility. We now fill a gap in prevailing labor and institutional theory, building on two major recent theoretical contributions: one from Masahiko Aoki, who stresses the need to see an entire governance system rather than one attribute; and the other from Paul Milgrom and John Roberts, who stress how complementary institutions in a system can reinforce one another. Prevailing theory does not yet specify how the complementary institutions arise. We seek here to provide that analysis.

---

58. See Aoki (1994, pp. 32–33).

59. See "Japan to OK Job Placement Services," *Jiji Press Ticker Service*, November 14, 1996; Rieko Saito, "Calls Mounting for Job Placement Liberalization," *Japan Economic Newswire*, November 29, 1995.

60. Each of these four hypotheses, particularly the last concerning implicit government support for an antipoaching cartel, is hard to prove. We know of no formal bureaucratic artifacts that definitively demonstrate a governmental role in enforcing an antipoaching principle. A beginning might be the 1955 founding of the Japan Productivity Center under the guidance of the Ministry of International Trade and Industry, to enlist the support of labor in the productivity movement and to promote job security. See Blinder (1992, p. 57); Sugeno (1992, p. 302). But even the absence of such definitive artifacts (beyond our not having located references) fails to disprove the hypothesis. These are not understandings that the parties would want to document. And pervasive interaction between Japanese companies and government bureaucracies allows for informal sanctions that are quite subtle.

A Theory of Complementary Institutions

Masahiko Aoki counsels not to analyze an economic institution apart from related institutions. Complementary institutions function together and may work well only when *all* are in the same national economy. One can not readily cherry-pick.

Paul Milgrom and John Roberts have formulated a theory of complementary institutions, institutions whose strength arises not just directly from their own productivity, but also from making *other* institutions more productive. Greater training enhances productivity, *and* the value of that training is enhanced if the machinery is designed to be especially more productive when operated precisely. Precise machines and well-trained labor are complementary. Complementary institutions shape a development path by favoring new institutions that increase the preexisting institutions' output.[61]

Complementary Institutions: Selection after Lifetime Employment Becomes Fixed

These theories can show how labor institutions fit and interrelate with the Japanese corporate governance institutions. Aoki asserts that in Japan, the only shareholders who can readily influence managers are the shareholders who are also the firm's bankers. (That is, the firm's main bank typically owns stock in the firm, nonbank shareholders cannot easily influence the firm, and the bank—with an eye on its loans—does not seek pure shareholder wealth maximization.) This subdues pure shareholder influence, thereby protecting workers from the opportunism of shareholders who might want to end implicit contracts midstream.[62] (Since we believe the Japanese firm makes the bulk of the human capital investment, we may not agree with Aoki on this element of the model.) But in this model, managers are not free from all accountability in that main bank contingent governance prevents managers from wandering too far from profitability.[63] (That is, banks in this model do

61. See Milgrom and Roberts (1990, pp. 518–27; 1994, pp. 34–42; 1995, pp. 179–206). Their analysis of Japan is deliberately static; they do not try to find the path that explains how the system took its current form, but see the Japanese economy "as emerging from coherent practices in an environment rife with complementarities. That . . . allow[s] us to avoid issues of how the diverse decision-makers are led to pursue coherent policies and focuses instead on why the policies are coherent" (1994, p. 19).

62. The incentives of a banker-shareholder who is a lender differ from those of a pure shareholder; the former's aversion to risk more nearly matches the preferences of employees than those of pure shareholders.

63. Garvey and Swan (1992, p. 266); see Aoki (1994, p. 18); Milgrom and Roberts (1994, pp. 22–23).

not tightly control managers, but if sustained bad results arise, the main bank intervenes inside the firm, often taking board seats and direct influence.) Although the firm is not subject to monitoring from a pure shareholder, the bank will interfere when the company performs poorly, as Aoki points out, but usually not otherwise. This forbearance-unless-performance-is-poor motivates both managers and workers to perform, to maintain their autonomy from banker-shareholders.[64]

Similarly, labor institutions fit with one another. Although lifetime employment might dilute employees' incentives to perform, this job security is offset by the large size of workers' bonuses in relation to their fixed wages and by an internal tournament in which better-performing employees are promoted and the others are not.[65] Security in one area; insecurity in another. And these attributes help support teamwork and horizontal information sharing. Existing institutions attract their complements, because adding a complement increases the productivity of preexisting parts of the system, and the increasing returns thereby create path dependency.[66]

Two other features—the early retirement age and the closure of the external labor market—also are complements. Early retirement at fifty-five is odd in isolation, because older Japanese employees, in whom the firm has invested so much, should be *especially* valuable. But if the firm cannot easily remove subpar employees earlier, then the low retirement age *caps* lifetime employment, making it *less* lifetime than it first appears; the cap allows the firm to select a few stars for senior positions from its white-collar managers and for leadership positions among blue-collar employees; the other fifty-five-year-old employees leave to make room for new entrants. The best employees stay, some from the managerial ranks becoming directors of the company; the others leave.

Moreover, we believe it is the closure of the external labor market that does the work: "Japanese firms, particularly large and established ones, have bound themselves to an implicit code of not hiring former employees of other firms, particularly skilled ones."[67] With lifetime employment in place,

---

64. See Aoki, Sheard, and Patrick (1994, pp. 24–26). Japanese bank shareholding may partly depend on lifetime employment. True, the main bank system also has its own historical roots, which are not directly connected with lifetime employment. Hoshi (1993, p. 307) shows that postwar main bank relations grew directly out of the authoritative wartime allocation of defense companies to particular banks. A question worth future investigation is whether main bank stock ownership arose independently of labor turmoil, arose as a complement to lifetime employment, or arose contemporaneously with lifetime employment.

65. See Kandel and Pearson (1995).

66. See Aoki (1994, pp. 14–18; 1995, pp. 350–52); Milgrom and Roberts (1994).

67. Aoki (1988, p. 83).

it became socially plausible for business to cartelize the labor market, an action that would have been explosive in Japan in the late 1940s, and explosive in the United States at any time.

But where does a system's evolution begin? Any starting point is potentially arbitrary, but Japan's history helps to specify a plausible one. Lifetime employment arose as part of a politically influenced bargain, then it attracted its complements, such as the destruction of the external labor market, performance bonuses and internal tournaments with steep seniority wages, main bank contingent monitoring, promotion at the top to the inside board, and retirement at fifty-five. Japan reached a labor market equilibrium, one that it failed to reach during the interwar years, and one whose initial baseline features came about to reduce social turmoil.[68] A nation that began from a different starting point, say, one that valued autonomy and mobility, as does the United States, might evolve quite differently.

How Do Labor Markets Reach Equilibrium?

How could Japan attain an equilibrium with firms investing in industry-specific human capital? Firms in a fluid external labor market would poach from other firms that train, thereby breaking down a training equilibrium. Either employees pay for training themselves or no one pays. Because a socially worthwhile investment is not made, a nation is poorer overall unless it can break the cycle of poaching and job hopping.

Our political story helps explain how Japan did it. A *direct* government order to bar job hopping would have been politically explosive. But for purposes extrinsic to the economic deal, a nation and its leading firms may agree with sectors of labor that their employment will be lifetime. In that setting, it would have been easier for employers to close the external labor market in ways that could not have worked previously. With the external

68. Stable employment in the United States came from back-loaded wages based on seniority and from reputation effects that tended to bind firms in fluid labor markets. Yet, even if the American and Japanese results were identical (they are not), one would want to know how each nation reached its labor equilibrium. In the United States, rapid growth tended to make firms pay market wages (to recruit new workers) and made reputation important. In Japan, firms tried to get to that combination but failed during the interwar years; after World War II, Japan stabilized employment to promote labor peace. From there (subsequently or simultaneously), features were added in Japan that made the equilibrium work. This difference of historical background between the United States and Japan is reflected in the different assessments of the development of the internal labor market. While the internal labor market in Japan is generally seen as supporting comity between workers and managers, some commentators see it as having developed even in the United States "to maximize the power of employers over workers." Stone (1975, p. 28). See also Price (1997, pp. 259–61), who appears to share Stone's view with respect to Japan.

market closed, firms more willingly invested in their employees' human capital. Once the employees were well trained, the firms had no reason to fire them, because the employees' newly developed human capital made them valuable to the firms. As long as the economy did not systematically degrade the value of the decades of human capital investment, the lifetime employment deal became self-enforcing: firms did not want to fire their high-value employees, and they willingly kept the promises they made of lifetime employment.

Secondary Economic Characteristics of Lifetime Employment

For the sake of completeness, we must also note some potential indirect, secondary effects (or causes) of lifetime employment. None are critical to the main argument we have made.

Lifetime Employment as a Simple Contract Term

Lifetime employment might simply be an employee benefit with no economic function other than compensation. Or, lifetime employment could be part of mutual gift giving: the firm promises lifetime employment and the affected employees work harder at all their tasks.[69] Note though that this gift-giving role is tied to effort rather than skills acquisition. It fosters employee skills only as part of an across-the-board increase in employee effort.

Lifetime Employment as Indirectly Supporting Employees' Investment in Their Own Human Capital

To encourage investment in firm-specific human capital, a firm might develop a reputation for not reneging on paying employees a return on the employees' own investment. (This is secondary because the interesting characteristic of the Japanese system is that *firms*, not employees, pay for human capital.) If a firm reneged on its promised return to employees, some employees might accept the result, but others would complain and become unproductive. A firm not committed to lifetime employment could fire the grousers and keep the pliable employees. Lifetime employment makes the

---

69. See Akerlof (1982, pp. 548–55); O'Connor (1993, p. 1533).

firm live with the grousers and therefore makes the firm less likely to renege on its promise to pay for the employees' investment in human capital.[70]

Second, consider the possibility that employees invest in their own human capital. They do not know which product markets will be valuable in the future. The firm will usually have a better estimate of their product market's future, but if employees make the investment (presumably via lower wages), they may be wary that if they invest and the market turns sour, the firm will lay them off. But a firm that promises the employee a lifetime job, it might be argued, could thereby make more credible its statement that the market for its product is likely to be a good market over the long run; hence employees would arguably be more willing to invest their time (and forgo wages) while developing skills for that market.[71] In insuring the employees' investment, by promising the employees a lifetime job even if the product market collapses, the firm signals to employees that, with better information about the product market's future, it expects the skills to be valuable for a generation.

But we doubt that information signaling is a primary function of lifetime employment, because the firm's insurance is only partial, since Japanese wages are variable, with a large profit-based bonus.[72] The firm might insure product-specific skills, but employees "pay" the "deductible" of potentially lower wages. And it is yet to be seen how lifetime employment will fare when product markets (and the need for the underlying technical skills) become more volatile. Once again, the core issue to explain here is whether lifetime employment supports the *firm's* investment in its employees' human capital, which we believe it would not.[73]

---

70. If this were lifetime employment's *principal* function, however, one would expect its incidence to vary from firm to firm, rather than follow a consistent pattern throughout a nation's economy for privileged labor sectors. The variance would be due to some firms having other means to achieve a reputation for nonexploitation, and to the fact that not all firms need high levels of firm-specific human capital.

71. Employers usually are better informed about product markets than employees. See Williamson (1975, p. 66); Willman (1982, p. 86). So, if lifetime employment reduced employees' mistrust of the firm's request to "pay" for specified skills, the benefits might not be trivial.

72. See Hashimoto (1979).

73. Another information asymmetry is relevant, especially to fluid labor markets. Information asymmetries between firms and employees render real-world labor markets imperfect and hence employees cannot depend on a perfectly fluid labor market. When the employing firm is better informed about the employees' actual skill development than others in the labor market, mobility will not be perfectly smooth. While the skills involved may be general, a competitor considering hiring the training firm's employee may be unable to observe the quality of the potential employee's skills. As such, a potential poacher will reduce its wage offer to account for this information asymmetry: the employer will offer a wage based on the average skill level of those employees willing

Lifetime Employment as Induced by Other Goals

Lifetime employment might be a *consequence* of other labor practices. A firm may make workers multiskilled, and hence the workers may be unafraid of eliminating their own jobs by making technical suggestions. Multiskilled workers then move internally from job to job and appear to have lifetime employment, but the appearance of lifetime employment only derives from their multiple skills.[74] Of course, the firm that has made lifetime promises for political purposes—our view of the situation—may train its workers in multiple skills to keep them valuable over their lifetimes. Finding multiskilled employees and lifetime employment in the same economy does not reveal the direction in which the causality runs.

Or, implicit deals may have wages low early in a career, and high later in a career. The higher-wage employees are immobile because they cannot do better elsewhere, and if the firm does not renege, employment appears to be a long-term, maybe lifetime, commitment. In the United States this pattern gave stability to employment for several decades even without Japanese-style semiformal "lifetime" employment.

Two Brief Comparisons: Germany and the United States

A similar evolutionary story of a political decision giving rise to an institution that then evoked economic reaction and evolution can be seen in German labor and corporate history. American institutions evolved differently, probably because the need for political peace (or the manner of achieving it) was not the same in the United States.

---

to leave, reflecting a mixture of higher and lower skilled workers. To that extent, even *general* human capital is operationally *specific*, and the same problems of opportunism reappear. Acemoglu and Pischke (1996, pp. 79–82) stress information asymmetries as debilitating the external labor market to explain why employers might pay for general training. To the extent that the market wage is lower than a skilled worker's marginal product because of information asymmetries, the employer earns a return on investing in general human capital even when paying the market wage. Greenwald (1986) also considers the connection between an employer's information advantage and the incentive to invest in general human capital. Gilson and Mnookin (1989, pp. 577–78), however, rely on information asymmetry to explain general training of law firm associates. Information asymmetries create a winner's curse: the poaching employer may not recruit an employee with average skill level, but only low-skilled employees whom the previous employer, with better information concerning the extent of the employee's general skills, chose not to retain. See Gibbons and Katz (1991, pp. 352–53).

74. See Carmichael and MacLeod (1993, p. 144).

German Parallels?

Like Japanese lifetime employment, German codetermination, by which German employees select half of the board of directors in large German firms, has a political component, arising from socialist ideologies and revolutionary conflict. Its first pale features appeared during Germany's post–World War I turmoil, when Berlin was briefly run by revolutionaries, as one piece of a grand compromise in 1919 between the Right and the Left that brought Germany temporary political stability. At the same time, a German ideology apart from interest group deals preferred a "middle way" between socialism and capitalism.

After World War II, the occupying powers expanded codetermination in the steel and coal industries, partly at the behest of France and Britain. In 1976, after a series of strikes and seven years of public debate about conflicting models proposed by different political parties, the German Bundestag expanded codetermination, presumably to foster industrial peace. Like Japanese lifetime employment, codetermination originated not in the economics of production, or even the economics of firm-level corporate governance. Rather, its purpose was to bridge the gap between capital and labor in society, or to provide social governance over capital.[75]

Because of codetermination, managers and stockholders probably reduced the flow of information into the German firm's supervisory board, had it meet less often, and minimized its functions.[76] Supervisory board committees were set up, with labor less well represented on the committees than it was on the full boards, or the office of the chair (who comes from the shareholder side) was enhanced. Big stockholder blocks might have persisted in Germany as a key complementary governance institution because the boards were, owing to codetermination, left weak by managers and stockholders.[77]

American Contrasts

The Japanese setting in which lifetime employment arose—during the postwar suffering and starvation—contrasts with the American economic

75. See chapter 5 in this volume; also Hyde (1990, pp. 411–12).

76. Or, despite competitive pressures from a common market and a globalizing economy to energize board performance—pressures readily seen in the United States—German managers and shareholders may have kept an already low-key supervisory board weak, while boards in the United States were becoming more aggressive.

77. See chapter 6 by Roe in this volume.

setting following World War II, when the release of pent-up demand created a labor shortage. Job security in the United States was not a political issue because the external labor market and unemployment compensation protected workers. In the postwar United States, wages eventually became rigid downward. Japan, in contrast, had fixed employment for some but left wages variable.

Rather than inducing human capital investment by fixing employment and varying wages, U.S. employers are said to fix wages by forgoing downward adjustments and to vary employment by laying off employees in less profitable periods. An employer who claims bad times to justify a wage cut may be falsely portraying that its business has worsened. However, a firm that lays off employees because of bad times reduces not just its wage bill, but also its output. If the firm's business is not really bad, then layoffs also would hurt the firm, and thus the firm's representation is made credible. Although ex post the pain may be borne disproportionately by those laid off, the ex ante implicit bargain—wage rigidity with layoffs possible—makes the firm's reaction more credible in the U.S. context than wage flexibility.[78]

Thus we see multiple institutional packages: in Japan, human capital requires fixed employment in a closed labor market, but wages are variable; in the United States, human capital requires fixed wages, but jobs are mobile. These institutional packages differ because each began from different starting positions. Japanese postwar politics fixed one piece—stable employment—and induced complementary adjustments in other parts of the labor package. For the United States, a cultural preference for mobility fixed one piece, and institutions evolved that provided economic incentives for more stability and less mobility.

---

78. Rock and Wachter (see chapter 4 in this volume) state that American firms tend to reduce employment rather than wage rates. Information about product market conditions, they note, is known to the employer but not to the employee. The employer informs its employees about product market conditions indirectly through changes in output and thus employment levels: "If a firm could lower wages in response to a decline in its product market, it would have an incentive to misstate the condition of its product market in order to lower wage rates." The incentive-compatible rule is for the firm to lay off workers. Because the layoffs reduce output, and hence reduce the firm's revenues and profits, they argue, such a rule eliminates the firm's incentives to misstate information. On the positive effects of layoffs on workers' productivity, see Ehrenberg and Smith (1997); Azariadis (1983). On using economic models to show that asymmetric information increases unemployment, relative to situations where marginal product information is public, see Grossman and Hart (1981). The Japanese response to cyclical changes in output is quite different. As Hiwatari notes in chapter 9, during the economic hardships after the oil crisis, the unions at large corporations not only insisted on wage moderation but were willing to flatten seniority wages significantly in order to maintain employment security.

Today's Stress Points

A system with complementary institutions can grow quickly because increasing one input makes the complements more productive. But complementarity has an ominous downside. When external changes devalue an attribute's contribution to the system, productivity may dramatically decline, because the other attributes of the system were built to use the now less important attribute. Stress points arise, and in Japan, one stress point is the firm's relation to its employees.

Internal Labor Markets and Growth

We have outlined a political and economic account of the Japanese labor market. First, to stabilize politics in postwar Japan and to defeat leftist unions, firms agreed to lifetime employment for a key labor sector. Second, lifetime employment, however, reduced employee incentives, and lifetime employment with an *active* external labor market could have reduced the *firm's* incentives to invest in employee human capital because, once trained, employees could have expropriated the employer's investment by taking another higher-paying job. Third, firms reacted to lifetime employment's negative incentives by, we hypothesized, forming an implicit labor cartel, perhaps with government enforcement, to constrict the external labor market. The end of the external labor market motivated firms to pay to develop their employees' skills. Fourth, firms made the bonus a big part of compensation, with the bonus keyed to firm profitability. Firms also built internal tournaments that promoted the most motivated and skilled employees, and firms developed transfer policies to put good but redundant employees into affiliated companies and to place underperforming and redundant employees in dead-end "window" seats that punished the underperforming lifetime employees.

This model works best in expanding firms that can run promotional tournaments more successfully. Growth ensures enough winners that employees will want to play. Growth also allows the firm to bring in many entry-level workers, some of whom will have the talent to become the senior managers and senior employees of the firm's future.

This last point warrants elaboration. A firm's future success depends on selecting skilled workers and managers for promotion. When first hiring, the firm can only crudely identify skill levels from the résumé. Internal tournaments identify the managers who will run the firm in the next generation.

The firm must recruit many to uncover the few who have the talent for the senior managerial and labor positions of tomorrow.

Consider the crunch when growth ends for a firm with many permanent employees. The firm cannot expand; it cuts new hiring, because incumbent lifetime employees can handle the static workload. But by cutting hiring, it constricts the stream of junior employees from whom it would select its future leaders. Lifetime employees clog the promotional filters and reduce their effectiveness.[79] The result: firms lack skilled managers and employees in the right leadership positions because the tournaments become less meaningful (when no one is going upward anyway); and the firm is also less able to insure the value of workers' human capital with permanent employment at historic wage levels. The system is tense.

Our model thus gives structure to the view that the Japanese labor model is unstable. The model may also give texture to the view in Japan that it has a bicycle economy, which at high speeds moves with grace but at slow speeds cannot maintain its balance. If promotional tournaments make lifetime employment work and if promotional tournaments function poorly when many large firms are not expanding, then many Japanese firms and the Japanese economy face problems.

Flexibility

Technological change causes stress. The American and the foreign systems are both flexible, but at different levels. American governance has more "macro"-flexibility, because the external capital market presses for change and, lacking large shareholdings that facilitate credible commitments to their employees, American firms have fewer commitments. Because the United States has a strong external labor market, workers pay for more of their general and industry-specific human capital, and workers lose when their skills become obsolete.

The Japanese system lacks "macro"-flexibility; its commitment to lifetime employment slows down big, rapid adjustments. But it has stronger "micro"-flexibility, in that it can induce greater commitments to human capital, which some American firms cannot induce, and Japanese employees can move and adapt well to modest technological change. Although

---

79. We realize that the timing of blue-collar and white-collar lifetime employment in Japan may have differed, as might the range of causes.

today American macro-flexibility looks fine, it is not obvious which set of costs and benefits produces higher returns over time.[80]

Industrial Districts and Local Employment

Industrial districts can relieve some stress of human capital investments even where employment mobility is high. The districts can decrease the costs to the employee of moving to another firm, thereby reducing the risk of employer opportunism with respect to industry-specific human capital, and, by limiting mobility to the district, they can also reduce the risk of employee opportunism. Similarly, lifetime employment with a weak external labor market may encourage skills investment at times but be undesirable in cultures that value mobility and autonomy, as is the case in the United States. When skills development becomes critical in a system with a significant external labor market, the "demand" for industrial districts such as Silicon Valley is likely to rise.

When would employees invest in industry-specific skills without obtaining either soft assurances of a secure job from their employer or governance rights inside the firm? An employee who can move to another firm without giving up his or her family and local social structure and without having to change residences would worry less about employer opportunism: the lower the transaction costs of changing jobs, the smaller the firm-specific component of otherwise general or industry-specific human capital. Low-cost job change works most easily when similar firms cluster.

> If you left Texas Instruments [which is not in Silicon Valley] for another job, it was a major psychological move, all the way to one coast or the other, or at least as far as Phoenix. Out here [in the Valley], it wasn't that big a catastrophe to quit your job on Friday and have another job on Monday. . . . You just drove off in another direction on Monday morning. You didn't have to sell your house, and your kids didn't have to change schools.[81]

Thus industrial districts fit industries with high industry-specific human capital needs better than they fit other industries. They reduce human capital dilemmas in a way that is exactly *contrary* to the way prevailing in Japan:

---

80. The trade-off is less flexibility versus commitment, than it is a trade-off between micro-flexibility, at the level of the worker, versus macro-flexibility, at the level of the firm. The former effectively responds to moderate change; the latter responds to radical change. See Aoki (1994); Gilson (1998).

81. Saxanian (1994, p. 35), quoting a Silicon Valley engineer.

enhancing the external labor market enhances employees' incentives to invest in their human capital, and employment is made even more impermanent by the easy switching inside the district.

In contrast, where labor is geographically *immobile*—as it is by choice, culture, or language in many other nations—industry-specific skills turn into firm-specific skills (because an industry-specific skill cannot be used elsewhere, since the employee cannot, or will not, move), thereby increasing the firm's potential for opportunism. If the local steel mill is the only one in town and the workers are averse to moving to another town with another steel mill, then the firm "owns" the employees' skills. If this immobility characterizes Japanese (and German) economic history—a cultural aversion to mobility greater than that in the United States and fewer "industrial districts"—then we have a more refined explanation for greater employee governance rights there than here.[82]

Conclusion

To many in the United States, Japanese firms' promises of lifetime employment seem an attractive institution, one that appears to encourage Japanese firms to invest heavily in their employees' skills and that motivates employees to contribute to productivity. But both theoretical analysis and raw political history tell us that the story is too good to be true.

Lifetime employment in Japan originated more in postwar conservative political efforts to stymie a broad-scale labor coalition and in management's efforts to stymie factory-level unions than in the economics of human capital development. This political origin then shaped how related labor and corporate governance institutions developed in Japan, attracting complements such as a closed labor market.

A firm's promise to employees of lifetime employment does not directly motivate either the firm or the employees to invest in firm-specific, industry-specific, or generic skills, because it fails to eliminate employees' rational fears of firm opportunism in lowering wages or in promoting fewer people later. Japanese firms seem well suited to be opportunistic, because Japanese

---

82. The politics of codetermination in Germany fits our production model: geographic immobility rendered industry-specific human capital firm-specific and thereby heightened the demand for employee involvement in corporate governance. This heightened demand could have expressed itself in contract negotiations and in political demands as well. We could then change our model—with politics independent of production—to make production affect politics.

wages are variable. True, a firm's opportunism could be muted by having the *firm* pay for the employees' skills, and payment by the firm in Japan is the human capital feature to be explained. But payment by the firm risks *employee* opportunism in that it could lead the employee to take away from the firm skills that could be used elsewhere: hence it is the crippling of the external labor market that explains why firms in Japan were less wary than otherwise of paying to develop high skills in their employees. Where the external labor market is weak, firms face less employee and competitor opportunism because neither employees nor competitors can appropriate the returns on the firm's investments. Thus optimistic accounts of Japanese labor relations—which suggest that the sunny side of lifetime employment induces employees and firms to invest better in generic and firm-specific skills—are exaggerated. More plausibly, if any factor was in play in this investment besides an expanding economy for most of the postwar period, it was the "dark side" of a limited labor market.

References

Abe, Yukiko. 1994. "Specific Capital, Adverse Selection and Turnover: A Comparison of the United States and Japan." *Journal of the Japanese and International Economies* 8: 272–92.

Abegglen, J. C. 1958. *The Japanese Factory: Aspects of its Social Organization.* Glencoe, Ill.: Free Press.

Acemoglu, Daron, and Jorn-Steffen Pischke. 1996. "Why Do Firms Train? Theory and Evidence." Discussion Paper 1460. Center for Economic Policy Research, London (September).

Akerlof, George. 1982. "Labor Contracts as Partial Gift Exchange." *Quarterly Journal of Economics* 97: 543–69.

Anderson, Charles A. 1984. "Corporate Directors in Japan." *Harvard Business Review* (May-June).

Aoki, Masahiko. 1984. "Aspects of the Japanese Firm." In *The Economic Analysis of the Japanese Firm,* edited by Masahiko Aoki. Amsterdam: North-Holland.

————. 1988. *Information Incentives and Bargaining in the Japanese Economy.* Cambridge University Press.

————. 1990. "Toward an Economic Model of the Japanese Firm." *Journal of Economic Literature* 28: 1–27.

————. 1994. "The Japanese Firm as a System of Attributes: A Survey and Research Agenda." In *The Japanese Firm: The Sources of Competitive Strength,* edited by Masahiko Aoki and Ronald Dore, 11–40. Oxford University Press.

————. 1995a. "An Evolving Diversity of Organizational Mode and Its Implications for Transitional Economies." *Journal of the Japanese and International Economies* 9: 330–53.

———. 1995b. "Unintended Fit: Organizational Evolution and Government Design of Institutions in Japan." Working Paper 434. Stanford University, Center for Economic Policy Research (February).

Aoki, Masahiko, Paul Sheard, and Hugh Patrick. 1994. "The Japanese Main Bank System: An Introductory Overview." In *The Japanese Main Bank System*, edited by Masahiko Aoki and Hugh Patrick, 1–50. Oxford University Press.

Araki, Takashi. 1994. "Flexibility in Japanese Employment Relations and the Role of the Judiciary." In *Japanese Commercial Law in an Era of Internationalization*, edited by Hiroshi Oda. Boston: Graham and Trotman/M. Nijoff.

Azariadis, Costas. 1983. "Employment with Asymmetric Information." *Quarterly Journal of Economics* 98 (Suppl.): 157–72.

Becker, Gary. 1975. *Human Capital*. 2d ed. New York: National Bureau of Economic Research.

Blinder, Alan. 1992. "More Like Them?" *American Prospect* (Winter): 51–62.

Carmichael, H. Lorne, and W. Bentley MacLeod. 1993. "Multiskilling, Technical Change and the Japanese Firm." *Economic Journal* 103: 142–60.

Dertouzos, Michael, Richard Lester, Robert Solow, and MIT Commission on Industrial Productivity. 1989. *Made in America*. MIT Press.

Ehrenberg, Ronald, and Robert Smith. 1997. *Modern Labor Economics*. 6th ed. Reading, Mass.: Addison-Wesley.

Eisenstadt, S. N., and Eyal Ben-Ari, eds. 1990. *Japanese Models of Conflict Resolution*. London: Kegan Paul International.

Foote, Daniel. 1996. "Judicial Creation of Norms in Japanese Labor Law: Activism in the Service of Stability?" *UCLA Law Review* 43: 635–709.

Furubotn, Eirik G. 1989. "A General Model of Co-determination." In *Co-determination: A Discussion of Different Approaches*, edited by Hans G. Nutzinger and Jürgen Backhaus, 41–72. Berlin: Springer.

Garon, Sheldon. 1987. *The State and Labor in Modern Japan*. University of California Press.

Garon, Sheldon, and Mike Mochizuki. 1993. "Negotiating Social Contracts." In *Postwar Japan as History*, edited by Andrew Gordon, 145–66. University of California Press.

Garvey, Gerald, and Peter Swan. 1992. "The Interaction between Financial and Employment Contracts: A Formal Model of Japanese Corporate Governance." *Journal of the Japanese and International Economies* 6: 247–74.

Gerlach, Michael L. 1992. "Twilight of the Keiretsu? A Critical Assessment." *Journal of Japanese Studies* 18 (Winter): 79.

Gibbons, Robert, and Laurence Katz. 1991. "Layoffs and Lemons." *Rand Journal of Economics* 9: 351–80.

Gilson, Ronald. 1998. "Reflections in a Distant Mirror: Japanese Corporate Governance through American Eyes." *Columbia Business Law Review* 98: 203–21.

Gilson, Ronald, and Robert Mnookin. "Coming of Age in a Corporate Law Firm: The Economics of Associate Career Patterns." *Stanford Law Review* 41: 567–95.

Gordon, Andrew. 1983. "Contests for the Workplace." In *Postwar Japan as History*, edited by Andrew Gordon. University of California Press.

———. 1985. *The Evolution of Labor Relations in Japan: Heavy Industry*, 1853–1955. Council on East Asian Studies. Harvard University Press.

Gordon, Robert J. 1982. "Why U.S. Wage and Employment Behavior Differs from That in Britain and Japan." *Economic Journal* 92: 13–44.

Greenwald, Bruce. 1986. "Adverse Selection in the Labor Market." *Review of Economic Studies* 53: 325–47.

Grossman, Sanford, and Oliver Hart. 1981. "Implicit Contracts, Moral Hazard and Unemployment." *American Economic Review* 71: 301–07.

Hanami, Tadashi. 1979. *Labor Relations in Japan Today*. Tokyo: Kodansha International.

Hashimoto, Masanori. 1979. "Bonus Payments, On-the-Job Training, and Lifetime Employment in Japan." *Journal of Political Economy* 87: 1086–1104.

Hoshi, Takeo. 1993. "Evolution of the Main Bank System in Japan." Working Paper, Research Report 93-04. Graduate School of International Relations, University of California, San Diego (September).

Hyde, Alan. 1990. "A Theory of Labor Legislation." *Buffalo Law Review* 38: 383–464.

Itoh, Hideshi. 1994. "Japanese Human Resource Management from the Viewpoint of Incentive Theory." In *The Japanese Firm: The Sources of Competitive Strength*, edited by Masahiko Aoki and Ronald Dore, 233–64. Oxford University Press.

Kandel, Eugene, and Neil Pearson. 1995. "The Value of Labor Market Flexibility." Bradley Policy Research Center Working Paper FR 95-04. University of Rochester.

Kanemoto, Yoshitsugu, and Bentley MacLeod. 1991. "The Theory of Contracts and Labor Practices in Japan and the United States." *Managerial and Decision Economics* 12: 159–70.

Milgrom, Paul, and John Roberts. 1990. "The Economics of Modern Manufacturing: Technology, Strategy and Organization." *American Economic Review* 80: 511–28.

———. 1994. "Complementarities and Systems: Understanding Japanese Economic Organization." *Estudios Económicos* 9: 3–42.

———. 1995. "Complementarities and Fit: Strategy, Structure, and Organizational Change in Manufacturing." *Journal of Accounting and Economics* 19: 179–208.

Mincer, Jacob, and Yoshio Higuchi. 1988. "Wage Structures and Labor Turnover in the United States and Japan." *Journal of the Japanese and International Economies* 2: 97–133.

Moore, Joe. 1983. *Japanese Workers and the Struggle for Power: 1945–1947*. University of Wisconsin Press.

Mosk, Carl. 1995. *Competition and Cooperation in Japanese Labour Markets*. New York: St. Martin's Press.

Nishiguchi, Toshihiro. 1994. *Strategic Industrial Sourcing: The Japanese Advantage*. Oxford University Press.

Nomura, Masami. 1994. *Shushin Koyo* [Lifetime employment]. Tokyo: Iwanami Shoten.

O'Connor, Marleen A. 1993. "A Socio-Economic Approach to the Japanese Corporate Governance Structure." *Washington and Lee Law Review* 30: 1529–64.

Price, John. 1997. *Japan Works: Power and Paradox in Postwar Industrial Relations*. Ithaca, N.Y.: ILR Press.

Raff, Daniel. 1988. "Wage Determination Theory and the Five-Dollar Day at Ford." *Journal of Economic History* 48: 387–99.

Roe, Mark. 1996. "Chaos and Evolution in Law and Economics." *Harvard Law Review* 109: 641–68.

———. 1998a. "Backlash." *Columbia Law Review* 98: 217–41.

————. 1998b. "Lifetime Employment: Labor Peace and the Evolution of Japanese Corporate Governance." *Columbia Law Review* 98: 508.

Sabel, Charles. 1998. "Ungoverned Production: An American View of the Novel Universalism of Japanese Production Methods." Working Paper, Columbia Law School (February).

Saxanian, Anna Lee. 1994. *Regional Advantage: Culture and Competition in Silicon Valley and Route 128*. Harvard University Press.

Stone, Katherine. 1975. "The Origins of Job Structures in the Steel Industry." In *Labor Market Segmentation*, edited by D. M. Reich and R. Edwards, 27–84. Lexington, Mass.: D. C. Heath.

Sugeno, Kazuo. 1992. *Japanese Labor Law*. University of Washington Press.

Sugeno, Kazuo, and Yasuo Suwa. 1995. "The Japanese Internal Labour Market and Its Legal Adjustments." Paper 426-7. Japan International Labour Law Forum (March).

————. 1996. "Labor Law toward the 21st Century: Supporting Individual Workers in the Labour Market." Paper 7. Japan International Labor Law Forum (March).

Taira, Koji. 1970. *Economic Development and the Labor Market in Japan*. Columbia University Press.

Tilly, Chris, and Charles Tilly. 1994. "Capitalist Work and Labor Markets." In *The Handbook of Economic Sociology*, edited by Neil J. Smelse and Richard Swedberg, 283–312. Princeton University Press.

Williamson, Oliver. 1975. *Markets and Hierarchies*. New York: Free Press.

Willman, Paul. 1982. "Opportunism in Labour Contracting." *Journal of Economic Behavior and Organization* 3: 83–98.

Yamamoto, Kiyoshi. 1983. *Toshiba Sogi* [Toshiba Dispute 1949]. Tokyo: Ochanomizu Shobo.

9

Employment Practices and Enterprise Unionism in Japan

NOBUHIRO HIWATARI

Japanese management is said to have "three sacred treasures": lifetime employment, the seniority wage system, and enterprise unions.[1] However, such institutions are limited to a small segment of the labor market, and even there they do not take the exact form popularly ascribed to them. So-called lifetime security exists only at the largest corporations, which also have the earliest mandatory retirement, so what is meant by lifetime employment is actually a guarantee of the need for postretirement employment. Wages at these large firms do rise with seniority, but they flatten at the age of about fifty. And enterprise unions, the sole form of unionization in Japan, exist only in relatively large firms. In the high-growth years of the 1960s, the unionization level in Japan was at about one-third of all workers, gradually dropping after the oil crisis. Why, then, has the myth developed that these corporate governance practices are ubiquitous "sacred treasures"? That question is explored in this chapter, with particular emphasis on enterprise unionism, its historical development, and comparative uniqueness.

---

1. See for example, Johnson (1982, p. 11).

Enterprise unions are noted for the following characteristics: membership is limited to permanent employees, blue- and white-collar workers join a single union, membership is automatic upon joining the firm, union dues are collected automatically, union officers retain their employee status during their tenure, and union sovereignty is retained at the enterprise level.[2] The only unions in Japan that cross firm boundaries are the industrial union of seamen and the general union of day-workers and construction workers. Enterprise unions operate by cooperating with firm policies as long as the firm is committed to employment security and provides wages and fringe benefits comparable to those offered at other large corporations in the same industry.

The system of governance at firms with enterprise unions has become a subject of renewed attention in recent decades because Japan is one of the few countries to have maintained low unemployment despite a series of economic crises since the early 1970s: the first oil shock of 1973–74, the rapid yen appreciation of 1977–79, the second oil crisis of 1979, another rapid yen appreciation in 1985–87, and the recession of the early 1990s.[3] It seems plausible that Japan's enterprise unionism has played a role in coordinating moderate wage demands, keeping unemployment rates low during economic fluctuations, and letting the firm achieve the investment levels and production reorganization necessary to remain competitive. The real challenge is to explain how enterprise unionism at a limited number of firms had nationwide effects. Japan's nationwide wage coordination and low unemployment rates can be attributed to three factors: institutionalized coordination among oligopolistic export-oriented industries with enterprise unions, market-led adjustment at fragmented industries, and policy regimes based on the dualism of industry-centered and market-led adjustment. Thus Japan's record of low unemployment was achieved not solely or even primarily by cooperative enterprise unions, but rather because of the surrounding labor market institutions.

Japan's enterprise unionism emerged in the years after World War II, largely as an unintended outgrowth of revolutionary unionism, which was committed to socialist revolution and subordinated to political mobilization. Political and economic constraints of the 1940s and early 1950s set it on a different path, for the structures created by industrial policy in the early 1950s provided a critical intermediary between firm-level cooperation and nationwide wage coordination. That cooperation continued during the

2. See Kawada (1974, pp. 235–38); Shirai (1979); Shirai (1983, p. 119); Kikuchi (1984).
3. See especially the survey by Cameron (1982).

1970s, when the unions of oligopolistic export-oriented industries responded to stagflation and other recurring predicaments after the first oil crisis by calling for wage restraint and collaboration with industry and the state, a strategy that in turn led to the legitimization of enterprise unionism and the total reorganization of the national unions. In this way, enterprise unionism and industry-centered adjustment, once institutionally locked in at critical historical junctures, defined Japan's future adjustment pattern to economic fluctuations. As this chapter shows, the Japanese form of unionism is quite different from the revolutionary unionism of France and Italy, the decentralized unionism of the liberal Anglo-American labor markets, and the neocorporatism of Sweden.

The Consolidation of Enterprise Unionism

Japan's labor situation in the first three years after the Second World War can be viewed as a battle between the revolutionary ideal of seizing power and the moderate idea of neocorporatist collaboration. Paradoxically, enterprise unionism at large corporations somehow emerged from a revolutionary ideal that was extremely hostile to firm-level collaboration. The question is, how did this transformation occur?

The Initial Dominance of Revolutionary Unionism

With the end of the war, Japanese workers were emancipated from repressive wartime state-corporatist labor arrangements. Revolutionary unionism, led by communists liberated by the occupation, soon had the upper hand. In part, this was because the prewar leaders of the moderate unions were discredited after the war.[4] Managerial authority had also broken down. A few attempts were made to preserve the old state-corporatist organizations at the firm level (as at Nippon Steel, the national railways, and in the maritime industry), but for the most part these attempts were short-lived, since the occupation authorities made it clear they would not tolerate anything short of free independent unions.[5]

---

4. At Yawata Steel, for example, the workers were "surprisingly hostile to the pre-war union leaders," "suspecting that they would only use the union as a step for further promotion," or, as "[a base] to run for the National Assembly." Cited in Yamamoto (1977, p. 224). See also Fujita (1974, p. 353).

5. See Yamamoto (1977, pp. 197–256); Naitō (1958a).

The revolutionary union movement shared certain features. It was led by college-educated white-collar employees, and it concentrated on advanced heavy and chemical industries, which had a large reservoir of such educated employees. The banner of the movement was "democratization" of the firm, which meant the abolishment of the distinction between blue- and white-collar employees and the demand for increased employee power over managerial decisions. Within a year after the war, the unionization rate in Japan jumped from less than 5 percent to more than 40 percent. The unions were militant enough that "production controls" became fairly common; that is to say, revolutionary unions took over management functions when managers resisted changes and fled or were expelled. Production controls peaked in the first few months after the war, while the militant labor offensives continued well into the late 1940s.[6]

The struggle at Yomiuri Newspaper in September and October 1945 merits detailed examination both for its own sake and because it provided a well-known national model of labor disputes, which was propagated by the newspaper itself.[7] Yomiuri, a successful newspaper known for its wartime collaboration, rapidly hired a large number of university graduates as reporters, despite the popularity of communism at the best universities. The struggle started when reporters—left-wing intellectuals harshly critical of the newspaper's wartime stand—demanded the "democratization" of the company, by which they meant prosecution of its top managers, the establishment of a union, and employee participation in managerial decisions.[8] These demands were rejected by the newspaper's owner-president, but the occupation authorities subsequently indicted him as a war criminal and allowed the revolutionary leaders to run the paper. Under production control, management and union were fused, as blue-collar workers, such as typesetters, type pickers, and printers, joined the white-collar workers. Similar movements were seen at two other major newspapers, Asahi and Mainichi, although the struggles in these cases did not go as far as production control because management there yielded to union demands and resigned.

Moderate prewar union leaders did try to assert their power, but with little success. One of their movement's strongest footholds in the prewar years had been in the cotton-spinning industry, staffed by unskilled workers. Because moderate union leaders sought help from management to organize, however, they were widely suspected of making clandestine deals. A scandal erupted when a textile company manager disclosed that firm lead-

6. On production control, see Moore (1983).

7. Rōdō Sōgi Chōsakai (1956, p. 20).

8. Yamamoto (1977, pp. 257–65; 1978, pp. 20–62).

ers had made political contributions to several prominent union leaders to set up collaborative unions and soon afterward the union leaders were selected for top government posts in the Socialist-led government.[9] The view that moderate union leaders were tainted was shared by the occupation authorities even in the early 1950s. In May 1950, for example, Tokuda Chieko was invited to the United States as a member of a labor mission. However, her union refused to appoint her as a union representative, accusing her of being a communist sympathizer, which confirmed the suspicion of the Occupation Labor Division that moderate unions were not protecting the rights of their members. Although not all moderate unions were creatures of collaboration, as long as they were created from above they usually could not withstand the challenges by revolutionary leaders, and there were a large number of instances of revolutionary unionism overturning moderate leadership.[10]

The ascendance of revolutionary unionism became apparent when the revolutionary and moderate unions created separate national organizations one year after the war. The communist-affiliated Sanbetsu Kaigi, or All-Japan Congress of Industrial Unions, with approximately 1.57 million workers, was twice the size of the moderate Sōdōmei, the Japan General Federation of Trade Unions, with approximately 860,000 members.[11] Revolutionary unionism gathered further momentum in the second half of 1946 when Sanbetsu Kaigi orchestrated the so-called October offensive. At this time, the national railway had planned to discharge 127,000 employees and the Shipping Operation Association 46,000. Then, in the seamen's union and the national railway union, rank-and-file employees sided with the communists against the moderate union leaders and succeeded in forcing the employers to withdraw their plans.[12] In this period, many white- and blue-collar workers amalgamated their unions under radical leaders against the management and moderate union leaders, as seen at the major steel companies of Yawata Steel and Kawasaki Steel, and an advanced chemical firm, Asahi Kasei.[13] At firms already under revolutionary leadership, such as Toshiba Electronics and Tōhō Movies, the unions were able to defeat

9. This is known as the "Shirihage incident." Shirihage was the labor relations director of a major textile firm. Shiota (1954, pp. 289–20).

10. For example, several unions emerged immediately after the war at the national railways but became united under Communist leadership (Yamamoto, 1977, pp. 232–45; Rōdō Sōgi Chōsakai (1954, p. 33). Other cases of revolutionary leadership taking over were the Shoden incident and the shack boat dispute of February 1946 (Yamamoto, 1977, pp. 242, 251–52).

11. Sanbetsu Kaigi Shi'ryō Seiri I'inkai, (1958); Masumi (1983, p. 19).

12. Sengo Rōdō Sōgi Chōsakai (1957, pp. 160–64); Takemae Eiji (1982, p. 160).

13. For details of the struggle at Yawata, see Naitō (1958a, pp. 113–17, 123–30; 1958b, p. 142).

plans to cut the work force, reinforce their power over managerial decisions, and encourage other firms in the same industry to follow their lead; for instance, Hitachi followed Toshiba's lead, and major film companies looked upon Tōhō as their model.[14] However, revolutionary unionism was unable to install an even more radical and much-desired wage system that would have set wages according to living costs, as a function of necessary calories per person, food prices, age, and family composition, in a way completely unrelated to firm productivity or profits, employee status, or worker performance.[15]

Toshiba and Tōhō provide a glimpse of revolutionary unionism at the time. Toshiba, an advanced electronics firm, was the spearhead for revolutionary unionism. During production control immediately after the war, the employees had won union recognition, labor rights, and partnership in joint determination of personnel policies, all in addition to wage increases. The Toshiba factory unions also reorganized themselves into three regional federations and established the Electronic Workers Industry Union. The Toshiba unions defeated company plans to close local factories and lay off workers, first in May 1946 and again during the October 1946 "offensive." During the latter push, fifty-three of the sixty-three Toshiba factory unions carried out a two-month strike against the dismissal plan, defended their power over personnel matters, and won substantial wage increases. During the October offensive, unions of the two major movie companies, Daiei and Shōchiku, established rights similar to those of the Tōhō Union—which had won a voice in management and production plans as a result of production control in early 1946—and the three unions went on to win improved working conditions, install a closed shop, and form a united movie industry union affiliated with Sanbetsu Kaigi.[16] Thus revolutionary militancy breathed life into the Japanese unions after World War II by uniting white- and blue-collar workers and affirming union rights and participation.

Emergence of Enterprise Unionism

With social unrest growing following the October 1946 offensive, the unions scheduled a general strike for February 1, 1947, but then it was canceled at the last minute by the occupation authorities. To placate the public, they called an election. At this juncture, the efforts of the leaders of

14. Hosoya (1985, p. 13).
15. Fujita (1974, p. 327).
16. Rōdō Sōgi Chōsakai (1956, pp. 35–53); Hasegawa (1976, pp. 23–30, 151–61).

the moderate Sōdōmei to construct local organizations paid off handsomely, despite the difficulty they had experienced in mobilizing workers within individual firms. Many Sōdōmei leaders were elected on the Socialist tickets in the 1947 general election, which returned the Socialists as the largest party to lead a center-left coalition government.

The new center-left government had a clear mandate: to reconstruct the economy by planning, and to pacify labor unrest by institutionalizing its participation in decisionmaking. Thus, with the full sanction and support of the occupation authorities, wartime controls and rationing were reinstated; a state bank to provide industrial credit became fully operational; a superagency, which stood above all government ministries, was established to be the "general headquarters" for planning; and plans to nationalize major industries were approved. Priority industries for economic recovery, such as coal, steel, and fertilizers, were provided with generous government subsidies and loans from the state bank.[17] To incorporate both industry and unions into the planning apparatus, the so-called reconstruction councils—tripartite bodies composed of industry, union, and government officials—were set up at the national and industry levels, and were to be linked up with joint management-labor councils at each firm. On the business side, progressive leaders launched the Committee for Economic Development (Keizai Dōyukai) to collaborate with the moderate union leaders of Sōdōmei.[18]

Despite this flurry of activity, economic planning proved a failure. It achieved neither economic stability nor labor incorporation, and instead exacerbated hyperinflation, radicalized labor and business, and polarized politicians. The underlying problem with economic planning as practiced at this time was that government subsidies were too generous and state-controlled banks provided loans to encourage increased output, all of which was financed by the Bank of Japan, which in turn meant simply printing more money. This produced runaway inflation and wage increases, which in turn fueled labor and industrial militancy.

At the same time, the revolutionary unions became divided over the issue of political mobilization. Communist radical leaders advocated strikes and other forms of protest to destabilize the government, whereas noncommunist radical leaders insisted that political and industrial action be kept separate. A similar split within communist-led unions occurred in France and Italy in 1947–48, when the unions called for greater political

17. Nihon Ginkō Hyakunenshi Hensan I'inkai (1985, p. 182).
18. Keizai Dōyū-kai (1956, pp. 49–70); Sōdōmei Gojyū-nen-shi Kankō I'inkai (1968, pp. 179–86); Ōtake (1987, pp. 353–56, 359–60).

mobilization in the face of an intensifying cold war. However, only in Japan did the communists lose their grip on the union movement entirely. The critical difference in Japan was an abrupt change in economic policy, ordered by the occupation authorities.

By the end of 1948 it seemed clear that economic planning was failing, and the Yoshida Liberal party (which should be viewed as a conservative party) won an absolute majority over the center-left coalition in the 1949 general election. At this point, the occupation authorities abruptly switched to supporting economic policies of fiscal austerity, deflation, and market competition. The new policy mix was supervised by General Douglas MacArthur's special economic adviser Joseph Dodge, and was commonly known as the "Dodge Line." The centerpiece of the Dodge Line was extreme austerity to wipe out hyperinflation by balancing the budget, eliminating all government deficits and liabilities, abolishing the state central bank, and dismantling the planning apparatus. Indeed, none of the national budgets between 1949 and 1951 were formulated without Dodge's approval; Japanese legislators were only allowed to rubber-stamp the decisions. The Dodge Line cut major firms off from state assistance and threw them into market competition. To survive, such firms had to resort to drastic rationalization of production, which usually meant the dismissal of one-quarter to one-third of their work force. Confrontation with militant unions was inevitable, and protracted and bloody disputes occurred at many major firms.

Interestingly, when the survival of the firm was at stake, the protracted strikes and industrial conflict led to surprisingly uniform results. The union would split, as cooperative white-collar employees (especially in sales) who accepted the need for drastic rationalization for the firm to survive would leave its ranks. This caused the revolutionary white- and blue-collar alliance to collapse. Management then carried out massive layoffs and purged the unions of their radical leaders, moves that the weakened unions were unable to block. In the aftermath of these protracted struggles, management accepted the revival of unions as representatives of employees, as long as their interests accorded with the survival of the firm. New cooperative union leaders shepherded the remaining employees into enterprise unions. Then to reunite the employees, management and the new unions placed emphasis on employment security, managerial participation, and improved worker benefits, all linked to the growth of the firm. The defeat of the revolutionary white- and blue-collar alliance and its replacement by a new one marked the solidification of enterprise unionism both in form and in substance.

Note, however, that it was not political intervention or a cultural shift toward cooperation that led to the consolidation and spread of enterprise unionism, but rather the pressures created by the abrupt return to market competition.[19] The degree of political intervention that would have been needed to suppress revolutionary unionism and bring about enterprise unionism was too extreme to be applied to a large number of firms. This can be illustrated by two cases—Yomiuri and Tōhō Movies—where such force *was* applied. Indeed, the occupation authorities had decided to suppress the forces of revolutionary unionism at Yomiuri and Tōhō because of the importance of the media industry. The trouble began when the occupation news director accused the paper of violating the occupation army's press code and threatened to shut it down for being an organ of the Communist party. A protracted struggle ensued that took several twists and turns, ending only when a sit-in strike by the blue-collar workers was broken up by force, at which point the company expelled radical union leaders, and the original union was absorbed into the second union set up by management and cooperative employees. The new union reunited the white- and blue-collar workers.[20] This intervention was carefully planned by the top echelons of the government and occupation authorities.[21] Similarly, the struggle at Tōhō started when management decided to expel the Reds and to abolish the closed union shop. A four-month struggle resulted, which ended only when the unionists were evacuated by police and American forces. The studio was surrounded by armed police officers, accompanied by U.S. troops, tanks, and air-fighters.[22] It would have been impossible to take such extreme action at a large number of other firms without social chaos.

The disputes at Toshiba and Hitachi also merit attention, for they illustrate how union consolidation at one firm triggered similar actions at others. As already mentioned, in 1947–48 Toshiba was the bastion of revolutionary unionism: firm and union representatives were equally represented at both the factory and the company, and since union consent was necessary on personnel policies, the company could not dismiss workers. The union also freely held rallies, which frequently turned into mock trials of managers. Nevertheless, worker morale was low. Production stag-

---

19. For a cultural explanation, see Gordon (1993).

20. Yamamoto (1977, pp. 158, 180–85, 252–54); Hasegawa (1976, p. 18).

21. The labor section of the occupation authorities intervened in favor of the radical faction when the police arrested strikers, because police intervention in labor disputes was a taboo for the labor section. Yamamoto (1978, pp. 203, 228–48, 286–300).

22. See Hasegawa (1984, pp. 195–233) and the chapter on the Tōhō dispute in Rōdō Sōgi Chōsakai (1956).

nated as workers skipped work to go to the black market, where they sometimes sold goods and equipment that had been stolen from the factory. Toshiba was heavily in debt, and wages accounted for 60 percent of its operation costs.[23] With the implementation of the Dodge Line, Toshiba's breakup under the 1947 Elimination of Excessive Concentration Law was finally decided. As the deadline under a 1946 law for corporate reorganization approached, Toshiba's management launched an offensive against the unions.[24] Of the 28,400 Toshiba employees at that time, 96.5 percent were unionized, and 86.3 percent of the unionized members were affiliated with the Toshiba Union. The union was composed of forty-one factory unions, twenty-three of which (with 67.6 percent of the work force) were affiliated with Sanbetsu Kaigi. The unions prepared for a major showdown by integrating factory union federations into a unified enterprise union.[25] In facing the union, the company first proclaimed that each factory must be financially autarkic and refused central bargaining. Next, it declared the existing labor contract—with its assurances of codetermination—void when negotiations for a new contract reached a deadlock. Finally, Toshiba announced a rationalization plan to dispose of twenty-eight of its fifty-four factories, release approximately one-fourth of its employees, and place a moratorium on wage increases.[26]

The dispute at Toshiba occurred along two fronts. At remote local factories destined to be abolished, workers took over the facilities—as they had at the Kamo (Nigata prefecture) and the Kawagishi (Nagano prefecture) factories—only to be removed by law enforcement officials after violent clashes and scores of arrests.[27] At advanced facilities, management locked out workers to preempt production controls or strikes, thus triggering the split of the union and the launch of a secondary union by more cooperative leaders. However, the final outcome was determined not by the tepid success of the new union, but by an exodus of workers who voluntarily settled for severance pay after becoming disillusioned with the protracted struggles. Faced with low worker morale, the outgoing union leaders ignored the directives of the Communist party, which regarded Toshiba's struggle as part of a broader struggle against the government, and concentrated on winning specific material benefits. This strategy revived the union

---

23. Yamamoto (1983, pp. 5–6, 45–56, 95–98); Hasegawa (1984, vol. 1, pp. 91, 159, 253–63).

24. See Yamamoto (1983, pp. 121–26); and the chapter on the Toshiba dispute in Fujita and Shiota (1963).

25. Hasegawa (1984, vol. 1, pp. 261–66; vol. 2, p. 25). Also Yamamoto (1983, p. 22).

26. Fujita and Shiota (1963, pp. 27–28); Yamamoto, (1983, pp. 74–77, 163–68).

27. Hasegawa (1984, vol. 2, pp. 25–28).

movement at Toshiba, as strikes carried out during much of mid-1949 delayed the company's reconstruction plans.[28] Toshiba agreed to negotiate wages and other benefits and allowed the union to have a say in the company's reconstruction plans. Management had to assure the remaining employees that there would be no further dismissals. This move to encourage employees to identify their interests with those of the company in exchange for employment and to institutionalize union participation in the discussion of such matters marked the birth of enterprise unionism at Toshiba.

The case of Hitachi, Toshiba's major rival, shows how market competition encouraged the spread of enterprise unionism. Like Toshiba, Hitachi had to take severe measures to reconstruct the firm in the wake of the Dodge Line. In 1950, the company responded to union demands for wage increases by deciding to dismiss 5,555 employees. Local factory sit-in strikes (to protest the lock-out of dismissed workers), workshop meetings, and kangaroo courts erupted at Hitachi factories, supported by nearby private railway and automobile workers. Two months into the dispute, the company's production dropped to 50 percent, its revenue to 40 percent, and its new orders to 60 percent of their earlier levels.[29] When the company seemed about to collapse, unions at sales offices decided to accept the management's proposals and withdraw from the central union, for fear of further dismissals.[30] As an increasing number of branch unions signed contracts with the company, the union leadership was forced to accept the company's rationalization proposal and wage freeze.[31] The point is that Hitachi's dispute occurred a year after the one at Toshiba. To compete with Toshiba, Hitachi had little choice but to confront revolutionary unionism, while the sales-office unions, being sensitive to the forces of competition, agreed to align themselves with company management. Market competition induced managers and white-collar employees at one firm after another to move in a similar direction.[32]

Why Enterprise Unionism at Large Corporations?

At first glance it may seem odd that enterprise unions emerged in the large advanced firms, which had been the bastions of revolutionary unionism,

28. Yamamoto (1983, pp. 227–35); Hasegawa (1984, vol. 2, pp. 29–37).
29. Hasegawa (1984, vol. 2, p. 256).
30. Cited in Hasegawa (1984, vol. 2, p. 263).
31. Rōdō Sōgi Chōsakai (1956, p. 83); Hasegawa, (1984, vol. 2, p. 265).
32. Shin-Sanbetsu Nijyū-nen-shi Hensan I'inkai (1969, p. 38).

rather than in smaller firms or in the public sector. The alignment of white- and blue-collar workers and the abrupt return to market competition after 1949 were critical factors here, as becomes clearer when one looks at the experience outside the large corporations.

As might be expected, management-union relations in fragmented industries consisting of small firms appear to have been more adversarial, as is common in the United States and United Kingdom. Small firms did not experience revolutionary unionism and did not have to make concessions to employees in confronting radical union leaders. Moreover, smaller firms were more vulnerable to market fluctuations and unable to institutionalize job security, so they had less to offer an enterprise union. Thus corporate governance in fragmented industries evolved from paternalistic to adversarial relations.[33]

Although systematic data on labor relations at Japan's smaller firms are scarce, developments in the coal industry suggest that enterprise unionism did not fully emerge there because unionist forces were never radical enough to unify blue- and white-collar employees and establish participation in managerial matters. In the late 1940s, Japan's coal industry was divided between the modern large-scale mines of Hokkaidō, which were a center of revolutionary unionism and production control, and the small mines of Kyūshū, a bastion of labor collaboration. However, it was at Kyūshū, not Hokkaidō, that the rationalization of Japan's coal industry in the late 1950s and early 1960s saw the bloodiest battles, characterized by some as a showdown between capital and labor. By contrast, mine closures at Hokkaidō were achieved peacefully because of enterprise unionism.[34]

The situation in public sector unions was again different. Political radicalism there persisted well into the 1980s, despite attempts at repression, until public corporations faced privatization. Furthermore, no one in the sector was quite like the white-collar workers at large firms, who equated the well-being of a firm's employees with the competitive survival of the firm.

The repression in the public sector began with an order from General MacArthur to Prime Minister Hitoshi Ashida in July 1948 restricting the labor rights of public sector workers (Potsdam Ordinance 201). More specifically, public workers were divided into government employees and

33. Data are available on textiles, chemical industries (ammonium sulphate, oil and fat, rubber, and others) and independent small firms. On the chemical industry, where moderate unions were powerful in small firms, see Hirata and Ando (1958, pp. 121–36). On cotton spinning as the stronghold of the moderate Sodomei, see Rōdō Sōgi Chōsakai (1954, pp. 67, 109–16).

34. On the coal mines, see Nakamura (1957); Hasegawa (1984, vol. 1, pp. 27–31). Documentation of the famous Mitsui-Miike struggle is available in any book on Japanese labor history.

public corporation workers: the former were stripped of their rights to strike and to collective bargaining, leaving them the right to unite, whereas the latter were only prohibited from striking.[35] MacArthur's action was taken in response to militant strikes led by the national railway and postal workers against the center-left government and its wage guidelines. The communist-led public sector unions had also undermined the occupation authorities' prohibition of general strikes (after the cancellation of the February 1, 1947, strike) by carefully coordinating regional strikes that paralyzed public services. Although the occupation authorities distrusted prewar moderate union leaders, they could not tolerate social unrest caused by revolutionary unionism. The immediate result of Ordinance 201, however, was an intensified struggle between the communist and socialist factions in each union. The socialist faction accused the communists of provoking an extreme response from the occupation forces, while the communists denounced the rule as illegal, only to become the target of arrests and prosecution.[36]

Massive dismissals in the public sector, in association with the fiscal austerity of the Dodge Line, exacerbated these factional struggles, as socialists used the occasion to expel their communist rivals. The government planned to cut 187,000 employees: some 120,400 from the national railways and most of the remainder from the postal service. The resistance to these proposals originally strengthened the communists, but then three mysterious incidents surrounding the dismissal plan led to the expulsion of communist union leaders by the socialists. Two days after 37,000 national railway employees were sent their pink slips, the body of the national railways president was found on a railway track in the suburbs of Tokyo. Not long after this, a crewless train plunged into some houses near Mitaka station in Tokyo, killing several people. Then a train derailed in Matsukawa, north of Tokyo, causing heavy casualties. Believing that these incidents were the result of subversive activities by the communists, socialist union officers launched a coup against the majority communist faction. Three days after the Mitaka incident, communist members of the national railway union's central committee were expelled.[37] The postal workers union experienced similar factional bickering.[38] Without an issue such as the survival of the firm to reunite the employees, their union and others in the public sector remained ideologically divided. They were also fiercely antiemployer and antigovernment.

35. See Takemae (1982, pp. 209–51).
36. Hasegawa (1984, vol. 1, pp. 246–49).
37. Hasegawa (1984, vol. 1, pp. 241–46; vol. 2, pp. 65–70, 106–10); Rōdō Sōgi Chōsakai (1957).
38. Hasegawa (1984, vol. 2, pp. 112–34).

This comparison of fragmented industries and the public sector supports the conclusion that revolutionary unionism and the sudden advent of market competition formed the basis of enterprise unionism. Enterprise unionism failed to develop at small firms in fragmented industries because they did not experience the initial surge of revolutionary unionism that united employees in favor of managerial participation, and it failed to develop in the public sector unions because they did not go through market-led incorporation of employees, as did private firms. In the next section, I explain how enterprise unionism at the large firms led to overall macroeconomic coordination on wage policies as a result of mediation by industrial structures.

Enterprise Unionism and Industry-Centered Adjustment

Once the enterprise unions were consolidated, they became isolated from one another and withdrew from the national scene. None of the private sector unions of the early 1950s showed any desire to create a new national labor center. However, two factors linked enterprise unions with institutionalized wage coordination in Japan: a national union strategy of luring enterprise unions back into national struggles by staging annual wage-bargaining sessions, known as *Shuntō*; and the creation of oligopolies at export industries that facilitated mutual wage coordination by employers.

The Birth of Industry-Centered Wage Coordination

In the early 1950s it became apparent that the new enterprise unions were contributing little to broader political arguments, and, as a result, the national labor movement was being led by public sector unions and was focusing on political struggles. Also at this time, public sector workers were particularly hard hit by the austerity budgets of the Dodge Line. The government refused to pay even the wage increases recommended by the National Personnel Authority, which had been created to determine wages for government employees who had lost their rights to strike and bargain collectively. In protest, the public sector unions formed a liaison organization, the Kankōrō (Council of Japanese Government and Public Workers Unions), to carry out joint struggles. They were joined by utility workers, transportation workers, and miners, since government regulation of public utility rates and fees constrained the wage increases offered by these industries. The participants in these struggles became the Sōhyō (General

Council of Japanese Trade Unions). The Sōhyō's initial convention in 1950 was attended by representatives of the postal union, the national railway union, the private railway union, the coal miners' union, the miners' union, the teachers' union, and the electric power union.[39] Not surprisingly, considering its genealogy, Sōhyō was fiercely political and antigovernment. Under the stewardship of Minoru Takano, it not only resisted the strong pressure from the occupation authorities to join the International Confederation of Free Trade Unions (ICFTU) but also led mass political protests on issues such as the peace treaty, the U.S.-Japan Security Treaty, the "anti-bomb" movement, and the anti-U.S. base movement. Economic "bread-and-butter" issues had lower priority than political issues, such as the subordination of Japan under the "U.S.-Japan security regime."

As enterprise unionism in the private sector became consolidated, a new breed of postwar union leaders, led by Kaoru Ōta and Akira Iwai, began stirring things up in the early 1950s. It accused the leadership of adopting pro-communist policies and of deviating from the principle separating union activities from politics. They invented *Shuntō* in 1955 with a view to attracting private sector unions, which had been indifferent to Sōhyō's political struggles, by leading the fight for higher wages. The major labor disputes at the time were at Nissan Automobiles (1953), NKK Muroran Factory (1954), and Amagasaki Iron (1954). All of these cases showed the typical pattern of labor being incorporated in enterprise unions, radical union leaders being purged by management, and white-collar employees being concerned about losing competitiveness. More and more, labor's struggles became isolated because market competition prohibited cooperation among the unions.[40] The new Sōhyō leaders took enterprise unions as given but wanted to overcome their isolation and weakness by concentrating wage negotiations within a short period. They hoped that a militant "leading hitter" union would win a large wage increase, and that the increase would spread nationally as other unions struck until they won similar increases.[41] The first *Shuntō*, led by unions at medium-sized firms in chemical and metal industries, was more of a political than an economic success, since it

39. Nihon Rōdō Kumiai Sohyogikai (1964, pp. 161–64, 182–85); Shin-Sanbetsu Nijyū-nen-shi Hensan I'inkai (1969, pp. 139–45, 156–69); Murakami and others (1980, pp. 133–35).

40. For details of the Nissan case see Rōdō Sōgi Chōsakai (1956, chap. 6); Nishimura (1963); Tsunoda (1963); Murakami and others (1980, p. 167). For details on Takano's tenure, see Nihon Rōdō Kumai Sōhyōgikai (1964, pp. 247–73, 297–98); Shin-Sanbetsu Nijyū-nen-shi Hensan I'inkai (1969, pp. 407–12); Murakami and others (1980, pp. 138–41, 178–80, 198–201, 218).

41. On the spring offensive, see Funahashi (1967); Kojima (1975); Kamizuma (1976); Takagi (1976); Ujihara and others (1977).

led to the downfall of Takano and the rise of Iwai and Ōta. As soon as it was launched, however, *Shuntō* was compromised by the constraints imposed on it. The most militant unions could not continue winning large wage increases, since they were either in fragmented industries that were vulnerable to economic fluctuations or in the public sector, where their leaders would suffer massive dismissals if they carried out illegal strikes to increase wages. Thus by the late 1950s *Shuntō* had fizzled out.[42]

Oligopoly and Embedded Enterprise Unionism

While the public sector labor unions were attempting to mobilize and tap into the private enterprise unions, the advanced firms, the core of enterprise unionism, were going through reconstruction. The Dodge policies returning to free market competition were so drastic that the government had no choice but to step in to save many firms. Thus economic planning and the planning agency were replaced by an industrial policy designed to assist in the development of future industries, under the aegis of the Ministry of International Trade and Industry (MITI). Government industrial policy that in effect created oligopolies in export industries can be viewed as an unintended result of the approach to market liberalization taken by the Dodge Line. MITI nurtured industries in two ways: it provided incentives and controlled market entry. The former is well understood, thanks to a pioneering study by Chalmers Johnson, while the latter is less discussed and thus deserves some exploration here.

Industrial policy in its fully elaborated form of the late 1950s consisted of the following measures:

> First, an investigation was made and a basic policy statement was drafted within the ministry on the need for the industry and on its prospects. . . . Second, foreign currency allocations were authorized by MITI and funding was provided by the Development Bank. Third, licenses were granted for the import of foreign technology. . . . Fourth, the nascent industry was designated as "strategic" in order to give it special and accelerated depreciation on its investments. Fifth, it was provided with improved land on which to build its installations. . . . Sixth, the industry was given tax breaks. . . . Seventh, MITI created an "administrative guidance cartel" to regulate competition and coordinate investment among the firms in the industry.[43]

42. Kojima (1975, pp. 31–38, 61–66, 85–97, 102–03); Kamizuma (1976, pp. 26, 38–41).
43. Johnson (1982, pp. 236–37).

Table 9-1 shows the trend in production capacity of major companies in ethylene, the basic material of the petrochemical industry. Notice in particular the orderly expansion of an oligopolistic structure: the number of firms increased gradually, but the early entrants retained their relative advantage in production capacity.

The reason for this pattern is that MITI inadvertently created oligopolies by trying to limit the number of entrants, while at the same time providing strong incentives for firms to enter a promoted industry. Given Japan's technological lag and the wartime destruction of industrial facilities, a considerable number of firms wanted to enter new markets by using imported technology. In these cases, MITI controlled market entry by requiring firms to employ the most advanced (imported) technology and efficient (large-scale) facilities as a condition for receiving nurturing policies. As production took off, however, MITI had to use its market-entry control to accommodate conflicting interests between early entrants and latecomers aspiring to enter the expanding market. Such cross-pressure led the ministry to admit new entrants gradually, while letting early entrants maintain a relative advantage in production capacities. By coordinating this compromise, MITI was able to maintain both its control over the industry and its political autonomy.

In 1955–56 MITI decided to nurture the petrochemical industry and designated former military facility sites as production centers. It then became involved in the companies' plans to procure imported technology, set a minimum requirement of ethylene production per plant (5,500 tons per year), and mediated business ties between petrochemical firms and upstream oil-refining firms and downstream chemical manufacturers.[44] For instance, MITI forced one chemical company (Shōwa Denkō) to revise its plans to make ammonia and polyethylene from naphtha independently and forced it to use the naphtha center at Kawasaki. After the completion of this first round of investment in 1959, MITI announced guidelines for the second round, which gave preferential treatment to firms already in operation and limited new entrants to corporations with advanced (preferably domestic) technology. Since 1957 firms with plans to enter the market had applied for MITI's approval, in what was called the "petrochemical rush." In selecting entrants, MITI maintained the industrial boundary between oil refining and petrochemicals, on the one hand, and between petrochemicals and intermediate chemicals, on the other, by rejecting applications from firms that planned to operate across more than two industries. The agency

---

44. Sekiyu Kagaku Kōgyō Kyōkai (1971, pp. 63–68).

Table 9-1. *Production Capacity Trends of Petrochemical Firms, 1958–69*

Percent per year

Firm	1958	1960	1963	1964	1966	1969
Mitsui Petrochemicals	62.5	24.8	26.1	22.4	13.3	14.7
Sumitomo Petrochemicals	37.5	16.8	17.9	12.1	9.3	11.1
Mitsubishi Oil and Chemicals		27.3	26.7	11.5	15.1	17.9
Nihon Petrochemicals		31.1	16.3	14.0	16.6	10.5
Tōnen Petrochemicals			13.0	11.6	17.0	10.8
Daikyōwa Petrochemicals				5.8	3.4	2.2
Maruzen Petrochemicals				6.1	12.0	7.9
Kasei Mizushima				6.3	5.0	6.3
Idemitsu Petrochemicals				10.2	8.3	8.4
Ōsaka Petrochemicals						5.3
Shōwa Denkō						5.2

Source: Sekiyu Kagaku Kōgyō Kyōkai (1971, p. 198).

set the minimum capacity for each site at 40,000 tons per year and intervened in numerous instances to coordinate domestic competition and to transfer foreign technology effectively. Similar conditions for new entrants were set during successive investment rounds: 100,000 tons in 1963 and 300,000 tons in 1967. The figures represented a compromise between operating firms and new entrants. For example, although the production requirement in 1967 was 300,000 tons, MITI had rejected as premature earlier plans by Sumitomo to build a 300,000-ton facility, because it felt the earlier plan was aimed at deterring new entrants. During the third round, MITI also arbitrated the merger of separate plants to build a new naphtha center, fearing a saturated market.[45]

This mode of oligopolistic expansion is prevalent among other industries nurtured by MITI, such as the synthetic fiber industry, one of the downstream users of petrochemical products.[46] Moreover, this sort of competition among five to ten large oligopolistic firms is not common in other industrial nations. Japan's automobile industry provides one example, with its five major companies: Toyota, Nissan, Mazda, Mitsubishi, and Honda. Their domestic market shares as of 1980 were 29.8, 23.9, 10.1, 10.0, and 8.7 percent, respectively. In crude steel, Japan has had five major companies:

45. Sekiyu Kagaku Kōgyō Kyōkai (1971, pp. 102, 133, 184–89). For testimonies on MITI's activities, see Hasegawa (1977, pp. 112, 122–23); Iwanaga (1977, p. 100).

46. For similar tables showing the expansion of the synthetic fiber industry, see Uekusa and Nambu (1977, p. 169).

Nippon Steel, NKK, Sumitomo, Kawasaki, and Kōbe. In computers, Japan has six major computer firms: Fujitsu, Hitachi, Toshiba, NEC, Mitsubishi, and Oki. In European nations such as Germany, France, or the United Kingdom, it is much more common to see one or two dominant firms in these industries, perhaps followed by some smaller competitors.[47]

Once created, oligopolies in the new markets established vertical linkages, known as *keiretsu*, with small producers and distributors. The method used by oligopolies to create vertical alliances was similar to that of MITI in shaping industrial structures. Major firms established affiliates by providing incentives such as managerial, technical, and financial assistance but also forced affiliates to compete with each other, and thus avoided being captured by the affiliates.[48] The creation of vertical linkages was reciprocal, since it allowed parent firms to expand upstream or downstream effectively by converting existing firms, while it provided small firms with stable markets and various kinds of assistance, albeit under the control of the parent firm. Two groups of employees were generally deployed from parent firms to their affiliates: young employees, who provided technological assistance, and retired employees, who assumed managerial positions and served as ties to the parent firm. Dispatching personnel to affiliated firms was also critical for oligopolistic firms, where the mandatory retirement age was young, in guaranteeing postretirement employment.

Instances of *keiretsu*-building were seen in the 1960s, when synthetic fiber companies incorporated cotton-spinning companies that had failed to enter the synthetic fiber market to produce mixed polyester-cotton goods and utilize downstream firms already affiliated with cotton spinners, such as weavers, dyers, wholesalers, retailers, and other secondary and tertiary processors.[49] By incorporating cotton spinners in the 1960s, synthetic fiber companies could efficiently extend their control over related production and distribution processes. Similarly, in the automobile industry, parts producers, machinery firms, and metal-processing firms became affiliated with the assemblers, as assemblers provided technology, used equipment, engineers, and technicians to help the small firms modernize and adopt new management techniques, while forcing affiliates to compete with each other to obtain stable orders. Toyota, for example, offered numerous forms of assistance to ancillary firms, especially in their early stages of development, such as loaning or selling secondhand production facilities (machine tools

47. See Jéquier (1974); Wells (1974); Iwami (1983, pp. 172–78).
48. Auto assemblers usually gave the same order to multiple firms and at times threatened in-house production to encourage competition among affiliates. See Asanuma (1989); Miwa (1990).
49. Fuji'i (1967, pp. 114, 230–43, 26).

and others) at nominal prices, sending a group of experienced workers headed by a qualified officer, providing special programs for the training of production workers, and supplying other nonpecuniary and financial help.[50] Labor productivity at automobile parts firms grew rapidly in the 1970s in response to the growth of the major assemblers.

Industry-Centered Wage Coordination

Although the *Shuntō* spring wage offensive was launched by Sōhyō leaders to mobilize private unions in 1955, it did not fully develop as a nationwide mechanism for coordinating wages until the oligopolistic export-industry unions began participating in it in the mid-1960s, at which point it had turned into something quite different from the original concept. The steel and shipbuilding unions participated in *Shuntō* for the first time in 1959, when unions of oligopolistic firms indicated they were unwilling to strike and preferred to settle with wage increases that did not hurt investment plans, the competitiveness of the firm, or the prospects of employment. Moreover, the typical wage increases management offered were high enough to satisfy labor and maintain rank-and-file support for cooperative union leaders. Enterprise unions began showing their true nature when the steel industry was designated to spearhead the 1962 *Shuntō*. Instead of showing militancy, the steel unions called off the scheduled strikes at the last minute, when strike ballots were defeated at NKK and Kobe Steel. This marked the radical transformation of *Shuntō*, for the steel industry has emerged as the wage-setter ever since.[51]

In the mid-1960s, *Shuntō* became a mechanism for making the wage increases of the oligopolistic sector the nationwide standard. In its fully developed form, *Shuntō* occurred in several stages. First, militant unions of small firms submitted their demands for high wage increases. Second, the steel industry responded with a "one-call" settlement, so dubbed because the steel unions always accepted the management's offer without a strike. Surveys within the steel industry show that the wage-setter Nippon Steel kept total wage increases in line with increases in sales or added value, and that the other four steel firms pegged their wages to Nippon Steel either by cutting personnel costs (by restricting new recruitment and relying on nor-

---

50. See Odaka and others (1988, pp. 58–59, 71–72, 78–82, 254–58). See also Ueno and Muto (1976); Amagaya (1982); and Ōshima (1987).
51. Kojima (1975, pp. 156–60); Kamizuma, (1976, pp. 91–101).

mal attrition through retirement) if their business was sluggish, or by increasing bonuses when business was good.[52] Third, major export industries—automobiles, electronics, shipbuilding, and heavy machinery— pegged their wage increases to those of the steel industry. In addition, wage settlements of parent firms affected affiliated firms and related industries. For instance, wages at large comprehensive chemical and ammonium sulfate firms were followed by related manufacturers such as pharmaceuticals, paint, glass, explosives, oils and fats, organic chemicals, and film. Finally, the public and private railway unions, a typical domestic nontradable sector, spread the wage increase standards nationwide through local wage standards: small businesses had to offer wage increases comparable to those of large firms or railways because they faced acute labor shortages.[53]

Thus nationwide wage standards were set by two separate mechanisms: interfirm and interindustry coordination among oligopolistic industries, and labor market conditions for fragmented industries. In the oligopolistic industries, coordinated wage setting avoided wage competition and allowed firms to invest aggressively, which in turn helped guarantee employment security. Although wage increases at oligopolistic firms fell within the range of productivity increases, small firms also had to offer wage increases comparable to those of major companies to attract new graduates and skilled workers. By the mid-1960s, oligopolistic firms had tightened the labor market for new graduates, since new graduates preferred to work at large corporations that offered employment stability, fringe benefits, and social status.

The influence of steel wage settlement is confirmed by numerous data: one survey has shown that more than half of all firms with over 1,000 employees in the mid-1970s listed steel as their primary referent in determining wage increases. According to 1975 data, even 32.8 percent of medium-sized firms (with 100 to 499 employees) listed steel as their primary referent.[54] Since steel was the spearhead union, its wages constituted the floor. Mechanisms unique to the steel industry were designed to compensate for this: separate allocation of fringe benefits, whereas in most industries they were included in the wage settlement; allowances not seen in other industries; and an autumn wage revision.[55]

Japan's wage differentials narrowed and stabilized with the institutionalization of *Shuntō* after the late 1960s. Figure 9-1 shows the wage conver-

---

52. See especially Takagi (1976, chap. 1).
53. Ishida (1976 pp. 227–36).
54. See Ono (1968, 1979); Ishida (1976, pp. 177–82, 234–42).
55. Ishida (1976, pp. 156-57); Takagi (1982, pp. 304–07).

Figure 9-1. *Wage Increases in Major Industries, 1960–75*

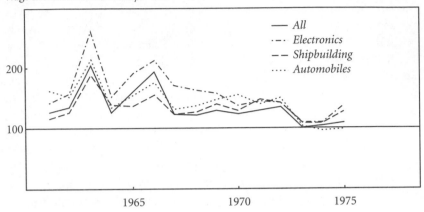

Wage increase: steel industry = 100

— All
·—· Electronics
— — Shipbuilding
···· Automobiles

200

100

1965   1970   1975

Source: Rōdō-shō Rōdō Daijin Kanbō Rōdō Tōkei Chōsa-bu, *Rōdō Kumiai Kihon Chōsa Hōkoku,* Annual.

gence across major industries, while table 9-2 shows the *Shuntō* wage increase in relation to the tightening of the labor market, and table 9-3 the rapid expansion of both formal and informal *Shuntō* participants.

Another important result of *Shuntō* was the alignment of unions in the same industry. Since enterprise unions weakened ties with outside unions when they emerged, their national affiliations were untidy and weak. Even within the same industry, it was not uncommon to find some enterprise unions affiliating with Sōhyō or other minor national centers, others leaving them, and still others joining the newly created moderate Dōmei (the Japanese Confederation of Labor), which amalgamated the moderate wing of Sōdōmei unions with Sōhyō defectors dissatisfied with its Marxism. The institutionalization of *Shuntō* strengthened lateral ties among enterprise unions in the same industry across ideological and national affiliations. In 1964, for instance, the unions of five major metal industries—steel, electronics, shipbuilding, automobiles, and metal processing—not only increased interindustry ties but launched their own liaison organization, the International Metalworkers Federation—Japan Council (IMF-JC). At the same time, the two major public workers' unions, the national railway union and the postal workers' union, started to drift apart, as each strengthened ties with private firms in the same industry.[56] Such private-public

56. Kamizuma (1976, pp. 78–81); Kojima (1976, pp. 116–32).

Table 9-2. Shuntō *Wage Increase, Wage Variance, Labor Demand, 1956–75*
Percent

Year	Wage increase	Wage variation[a]	Labor demand[b]
1956	6.3	0.57	n.a.
1957	8.6	0.39	n.a.
1958	5.6	0.58	n.a.
1959	6.5	0.39	n.a.
1960	8.7	0.34	0.6
1961	13.8	0.27	0.7
1962	10.7	0.26	0.7
1963	9.1	0.31	0.7
1964	12.4	0.20	0.8
1965	10.6	0.31	0.6
1966	10.6	0.24	0.7
1967	12.5	0.13	1.0
1968	13.6	0.14	1.1
1969	15.8	0.13	1.3
1970	18.5	0.12	1.4
1971	16.9	0.14	1.1
1972	15.3	0.15	1.2
1973	20.1	0.11	1.8
1974	32.9	0.13	1.2
1975	13.1	0.32	0.6

Source: *Kōza Gendai no Chingin*; Ishida (1976, p. 181).
n.a. Not available.
a. Standard deviation.
b. Labor demand = positions listed/employment seekers (except new graduates).

cooperation was facilitated after a 1964 agreement between the prime minister and Sōhyō leaders to peg public sector wages to the private sector, which had the effect of incorporating the public sector into the *Shuntō* process.

It should be obvious by now that wage agreements at private sector enterprise unions can have a powerful effect on wages throughout the Japanese economy. The *Shuntō*, the industrial policy by the government to nurture advanced industries by creating oligopolies, the vertical intercorporate (*keiretsu*) ties between the oligopolies and existing small firms in traditional fragmented industries, and ongoing economic pressures all combine to magnify the power of enterprise unions to set wages for Japan's economy as a whole.

Table 9-3. *Participants of the Spring Wage Offensive, 1955–75*
Thousands

Year	Formal participants (A)	Riders[a] (B)	A + B	A + B/Org[b]	A+ B/Total[c]
1955	734	. . .	734	11.7	4.20
1956	2,993	. . .	2,993	46.3	15.5
1957	3,226	. . .	3,226	47.7	16.0
1958	3,686	. . .	3,686	52.8	17.3
1959	3,964	. . .	3,964	55.0	17.6
1960	4,094	183	4,227	55.8	18.0
1961	4,385	553	4,938	59.1	20.4
1962	4,838	554	5,392	60.1	20.9
1963	5,229	803	6,032	64.5	22.4
1964	5,192	700	5,892	60.1	19.2
1965	5,567	780	6,347	62.6	21.8
1966	5,678	1,108	6,786	65.2	22.3
1967	5,782	1,087	6,869	65.0	22.2
1968	5,817	1,213	7,030	64.7	22.3
1969	5,925	1,311	7,256	64.5	22.6
1970	5,965	2,048	8,013	69.0	24.5
1971	6,034	3,136	8,169	69.2	24.1
1972	5,995	2,288	8,283	69.7	24.0
1973	6,109	2,326	8,435	69.7	23.2
1974	6,216	2,354	8,570	68.8	23.5
1975	6,506	2,388	8,894	70.8	24.5

Source: Ishida (1976, p. 179); Takanashi (1977).
   a. Non-Sōhyō national center (such as Dōmei and Shin-sanbetsu): affiliated union members who synchronized their wage bargaining with *Shuntō*.
   b. Organized workers.
   c. Total employees.

Enterprise Unionism and Macroeconomic Adjustment

After the oil crises of the 1970s, the ability of Japan's economy to adjust while keeping unemployment low became widely appreciated. The pattern from the beginning of the oil crisis and continuing up to Japan's economic slowdown in the 1990s can be summarized as follows: explicit endorsement of wage moderation by export-industry enterprise unions in exchange for firm commitment to employment security; enactment of public policy to assist such industry-centered adjustment; and the widespread legitimization of enterprise unionism as a result of the ascendance of export-industry unions within the national union movement. The key point here is that the combination of enterprise unions, *Shuntō*, oligopolies, *keiretsu*, and market orientation has made it possible to achieve a coordinated moderation of wage demands throughout Japan since the mid-1960s.[57] Coordinated wage setting remains in practice to this day, although when steel became a structurally depressed industry, electronics and automobiles took over the leadership of wage setting. As a result, Sōhyō was stripped of its nominal leadership of *Shuntō*.[58]

In exchange for wage moderation, large corporations maintained their commitment to employment. Wage costs were cut by reducing overtime, reducing the number of new recruits, conducting transfers within the firm, laying off temporary workers, transferring some to other firms, and, finally, providing special severance schemes for voluntary departure or early retirement. Firms resorted to early retirement or postretirement transfer only when other options were exhausted, and usually only with older employees.[59] The steel and shipbuilding industries faced the hardest test of the employment commitment, since both experienced rapid restructuring and downsizing in the 1970s and 1980s. The shipbuilding industry as a whole had to eliminate more than 35 percent of its facilities and 40 percent of its work force between 1974 and 1979. During the slump of 1987–88, all major shipbuilders announced multiyear plans to cut capacity by another 40 to 60 percent. Similarly, the rapid appreciation of the yen in 1985–87 forced the steel industry to close seven of its thirty-two furnaces, and to draft plans to cut at least 37,000 and up to 43,000 employees.

Despite such pressures, large firms almost never laid off workers. In the late 1970s, for instance, Nippon Steel sent workers to nearby automobile and electronic plants of firms with which it had business ties.[60] Mitsubishi Heavy Industries, a shipbuilding and heavy machinery giant, transferred 52.6 percent of the 8,923 workers who left the firm to another firm during the shipbuilding slump of 1976–77; the remaining workers retired (16.5 percent) or left voluntarily (30.9 percent). Major corporations also avoided

---

57. Ikuo Kume (1988) argues that union-business-government relations in Japan changed after the first oil crisis, and the changes—the advent of wage moderation and union participation in politics—were the result of increased export dependency and the political vulnerability of the ruling Liberal Democratic party. Kume's data contradict his argument. Wage moderation had been in effect a decade before the oil crisis. Japanese export dependency reached a plateau around the first oil crisis and the steel industry had the lowest export dependency rate among the industries he cites.

58. Tsujinaka (1986a, 1986b).

59. Ogata (1980, pp. 227–39); Akita (1993, pp. 87–91).

60. Ishida (1986, pp. 145–50).

dismissing workers by depending on affiliated firms and creating new subsidiaries; although most new subsidiaries created by oligopolies in shipbuilding and steel, for instance, were spin-offs in new industries intended to
diversify business, some were set up solely to absorb redundant workers. In
1981 Hitachi Shipbuilding created more than 23 local subsidiaries and dis-
patched redundant workers to affiliated firms when it merged its facilities in
the Osaka-Hiroshima area. Similarly, the five major steel firms created a
total of 215 new subsidiaries between 1985 and 1989 to absorb redundant
employees. Among such firms, 86 were in new materials, electronics, and
information technology; 59 in chemicals, engineering, and metals; 13 in
finance and insurance; and the remaining 55 in service. It is estimated that
more than half of the actual 27,000 workers who left the steel firms in
1987–89 were relocated to such subsidiaries.[61]

In general, surveys show manager-union consultation over business
plans increased after the mid-1970s, in terms of both meeting frequency
and amount of information exchanged. In such sessions, management presented information on the current firm conditions and asked for union
cooperation in formulating plans for production reorganization or relocation. The same surveys showed that unions became more assertive in negotiating compensation for workers directly affected by these changes.[62] When
Nippon Steel announced plans in 1975–77 to cut and eventually stop production at obsolete plants, the union persuaded unions at affected plants
to accept the company's plans for relocating or transferring its workers,
while at the same time maintaining a united front of plant unions—which
included unions at advanced plants that were not affected by reorganization—against management to win more concessions. These came in the
form of assurances that the firm would disclose future plans and guarantee
compensation for relocated workers and reemployment for departing
workers in other firms. The unions also pressed firms to compensate workers for differences in wages, bonus payments, or fringe benefits between
their old jobs and new ones.[63]

Typically, unions negotiated for modifications of company plans, not
for their repeal. When shop supervisors and foremen felt measures were
needed to keep the firm competitive, they sided with the company over the
union leaders. This preference was seen at the Nissan union in 1986, when

61. Yuasa (1982, pp. 202–08); Aida (1983, pp. 51–53); Serizawa (1987a, 171–93; 1987b, pp.
100–08); Yamamoto (1989, pp. 231–33, 244–67); Kawabe (1991, pp. 34–41); Mizota (1991, pp.
183–84, 202–03); Ōba (1991, pp. 31–38); Uriu (1996, pp. 186–90, 195–201, 202–11, 213–20, 230–36).
62. Sato and Umetsu (1983, pp. 407–16).
63. Ishida (1986, pp. 145–50, 163–72); Nitta (1988, pp. 241–48, 253–74).

shop supervisors launched a coup against the powerful union leader because he began to veto company plans to increase productivity, cut bonus payments, and dispatch workers at a time when Nissan was lagging more and more behind its rival Toyota.[64] The 1986 Nissan labor contract concluded by the new union leaders was modeled after that of Toyota, allowing the firm to introduce flexible production, quality control circles, and small group activities.[65]

For depressed industries and small firms in depressed regions, government policy assisted industry-centered employment adjustment. Japan's 1974 Employment Stabilization Law marked a modest step from reactive unemployment insurance toward preemptive employment policy, when it created a special fund to subsidize employers for retaining workers. The expansion of this law in 1977 and the enactment of related laws in 1977–78 completed the creation of Japan's adjustment policy regime for depressed industries and regions. It consisted of employment policies to subsidize firms for retaining, retraining, redeploying, and reemploying redundant workers; and industrial policy to help firms dispose of excessive capacity, rationalize production, and, if necessary, diversify or convert business into new markets. Industrial and employment policies were linked together. Firms applying for government assistance to adjust production had to submit employment plans to the government—with the consent of the unions—and to apply for employment subsidies. The adjustment regime of 1977–78 was revised and reinforced in 1983, 1987–88, and most recently in 1992. During the revisions, the emphasis shifted from facilitating collaboration among firms in scrapping redundant capacity, as in the 1978 Industrial Stabilization Law, to promoting diversification into new markets.

The reinforcement of enterprise unionism and industry-centered adjustment after the mid-1970s, amid recurring unfavorable economic conditions, also led the unions themselves to legitimize enterprise unionism. Initially, the call by export-industry union leaders for wage moderation and government lobbying were met with harsh criticism by the leaders of the then dominant Sōhyō, who instead emphasized the need to defend real wages and force the government to prohibit layoffs and wage cuts. However, export-industry unions won the struggle within the union movement by continuing wage coordination and creating organizations to coordinate government lobbying. As a result, organizations for wage coordination and lobbying became the core of a newly founded national center, Rengō, which

64. Totsuka and Hyōdō (1991, pp. 81–85); Hata (1992, pp. 138–46).
65. Saruta (1991, pp. 46–48); Totsuka and Hyōdō (1991, pp. 213–35).

replaced Sōhyō and unified the Japanese labor movement in the 1980s.[66] Rengō endorsed the principles of enterprise unionism. As the leaders of Sōhyō changed their policies and allowed its member unions to join the moderate Rengō, the founding fathers of Sōhyō—among them Kaoru Ōta and Akira Iwai, whose role in creating the *Shuntō* was mentioned earlier— left Sōhyō to launch a new organization in order to preserve the class-based labor movement based on antimonopoly capitalism, which had been the core tenet of Sōhyō prior to the mid-1970s.

Thus economic adjustment since the oil crisis did not change enterprise unionism or industry-centered adjustment but instead made them the tenets of Japanese labor. The legitimization of enterprise unionism brought with it a total reorganization of the national union, a phenomenon unparalleled in other countries.

Japan's Enterprise Unions in Comparative Perspective

Japan's unique enterprise unionism is the result of particular historical contingencies and institutional settings, notably the managerial offensive against revolutionary unionism, the embedding of the initial *Shuntō* into the Japanese industrial structure, the creation of oligopolistic export industries, and the evolution of events since then. The nature of Japan's labor relations becomes even clearer when compared with the situations in France and Italy, which also experienced revolutionary unionism but not the same managerial offensive that generated enterprise unionism; the United States and the United Kingdom, which did not have the industrial structures to promote firm-level cooperation nationwide; and Sweden and Germany, which did experience such cooperation through mechanisms different from Japan's industry-centered adjustment.

In the immediate years after World War II, the strength of revolutionary unionism in France and Italy closely resembled that in Japan. The difference was that in Japan the movement was the offspring of firm-level mobilization, whereas in France and Italy, it was the product of political concerns at the national level. The French and Italian unions were initially used to muffle worker discontent when the Communist party was in United Front governments, and later, after 1947–48, to rally political protests against the government after the Communist party was ejected. Political mobilization

---

66. Murakami and others (1980, pp. 383–416); Shinkawa (1984, pp. 191–232); Tsujinaka (1986a, pp. 285–88).

exacerbated ideological splits at both firm and national unions and drastically weakened union participation in the workplace.

In France, the Confédération générale des travailles (CGT) dominated the labor scene, with a tremendous increase in new members after the Liberation. By 1946, the Communist party (PCF) controlled more than twenty-one key CGT federations, including almost all of the federations in the mass-production industry and four-fifths of the CGT's departmental unions. However, because the Communists were in power until 1947, the CGT cooperated in "the battle of production" to prove that it could discipline the entire working class, despite a decline in the standard of living and the spread of wildcat strikes. Thus the communist-led union movement in France did not bolster firm-level mobilization of blue- and white-collar employees, as in Japan. Furthermore, it was not the CGT, but the Christian Democrats who, during Charles DeGaulle's provisional government, proposed worker participation and profit sharing. They set up plant committees with responsibility for social matters within the firm and a system of workers' representatives who had the right to discuss working conditions with management. However, these mechanisms did little to expand labor participation because the political parties had different conceptions of the role of the plant committees. The Socialists saw them as a means of training workers for larger responsibilities in the economy, the communists as a base for plant-level mobilization, and the Catholics as a means of encouraging business-labor cooperation. When the CGT mobilized the plant committees as strike committees starting in the strike waves of 1947–48 and denounced any group willing to bargain with management, any chance of employer acceptance of the committees evaporated.[67]

In Italy, the national union, the Confederazione generale italiana del lavoro (CGIL), was launched in 1944 by the anti-Fascist forces: the Communists, the Socialists, and the Christian Democrats. By the 1947 union congress, the Communists had become dominant, winning 57.8 percent of the vote. In accordance with the Communist strategy of avoiding isolation and strengthening its mass base, the CGIL sacrificed the short-term interests of the working class and accepted the repeal of a ban on dismissals and a seven-month wage truce, despite the noticeable deterioration of workers' living standards. As in France, organizations for worker participation such as the work councils and the workshop committee were set up by the anti-Fascist parties. While the Communist party was in power, the work councils

---

67. Lorwin (1966, pp. 104, 131–32, 258–73); Ivring (1973, pp. 120–22); Tiersky (1974, pp. 122–34); McCormick (1981, p. 349); Ross (1982, pp. 24–27).

acted as mediators to stimulate worker morale, discipline, and production, but later they became organs for criticizing factory policy and rapidly disappeared. Workshop committees, the sole remaining representative bodies for workers at the plant, became ideologically divided and were gradually stripped of their powers as management regained control in the workplace. Furthermore, since the CGIL maintained that only political change could resolve Italy's economic crisis and opposed company-level contract negotiations, the number of CGIL members and percentage of voters at workshop committees declined after 1948.[68]

Thus in France and Italy, ideological rivalry and weak firm-level participation reinforced each other. After being evicted from government, the French and Italian Communist parties mobilized the unions for anti-U.S. and anticapitalism protests. As a result, in France the Force ouvrière (FO) split from the CGT in pursuit of social democracy, which was influential among white-collar unions in the civil service and the public sector, and the Catholic Confédération française des travailleurs chrétiens (CFTC) consolidated its strongholds. Similarly, in Italy, mass mobilization by the CGIL against NATO, the Marshall Plan, the Korean War, and the atomic bomb prompted Christian Democratic union leaders to launch a union (CSIL) emphasizing collective bargaining instead of political strikes. In both countries, this ideological rivalry led to a splintered and weak union in the workplace. This, in turn, led to recurring cycles of protests in both countries, because rank-and-file discontent could only be expressed by general strikes and mass protests. Revolutionary unionism in France and Italy remained focused on national political power rather than on firm-level issues. As a result, a Japanese-style movement from revolutionary unionism to well-established enterprise unions did not occur, and the labor movement as a whole has been continually fragmented. Instead, the national union movements in France and Italy look similar to Japanese public sector unions. These patterns of labor in France and Italy explain their high industrial dispute rates and their inability to institutionalize labor participation, collective bargaining, or wage coordination.[69]

The United States and the United Kingdom were different again, in that industrial structures played a role in institutionalizing wage coordination. With the liberal, decentralized markets common in the United States and United Kingdom, collaborative arrangements were limited to particular

68. Catalano (1972, p. 77); Salvati (1972, pp. 193–201); Blackmer (1975, pp. 31–32); Weitz (1975, p. 545); Lange and Vannicelli (1982, pp. 102–03, 112–113); Barkan (1984, pp. 21–25, 40–41).
69. Lorwin (1966, pp. 187–89); Salvati (1972, pp. 201–02); Tiersky (1974, pp. 160–67); Blackmer (1975, pp. 45–47); Ross (1982, pp. 39–58); Barkan (1984, p. 22); Rioux (1987, pp. 126–30).

firms and industries. The decentralized union structure and the unwillingness of management to ensure employment made the unions in both countries similar to small-firm unions in Japan.

In the United States, the end of World War II saw dramatic growth in the number of unionized workers and in labor militancy. Clashes over compensation for the wartime wage freeze, control of employee benefits, and workplace conditions threatened to spill over into areas of corporate pricing, investment, and plant location. However, an attempt at labor incorporation similar to the Japanese reconstruction councils of 1947–48 also failed in the United States. Instead, labor militancy, frequent strikes, and pay boosts led to the passage of the 1947 Taft-Hartley Law, which restrained the legal boundaries of unionization and industrial action. In particular, the law banned wildcat strikes; allowed the courts to fine unions for damages in such strikes; made secondary boycotts, sitdown strikes, and job slowdown illegal; made certification of a union more difficult; gave employers a variety of tools ("free speech" rights) to interfere in the organizing process; and made it legal for states to pass laws banning the union shop ("right to work" laws). In response to this law, unions began concentrating their struggles on securing firm- or industry-specific benefits such as automatic cost-of-living adjustments, wage increases designed to reflect productivity increases, and fringe benefits. However, this climate of adversarial labor relations also meant that anti-union consultants and nonunion firms increased, especially as industries moved to the Sun Belt.[70] Thus the U.S. case shows that the presence of unions that focus on economic issues is not sufficient to explain coordinated wages in Japan.

The situation in the United Kingdom shows further that wage coordination is difficult to achieve under liberal markets and decentralized collective bargaining, even if it is desired by the government. During the Labour governments immediately after World War II, the unions strongly rejected compulsory incomes policies or government interference in the "voluntarist" industrial relations system, despite their endorsement of economic planning, nationalization, and participation in economic policymaking. The unions also refused to assume any responsibility in the management of companies. Thus the government strengthened union positions in collective bargaining but dismantled any institutional bases for economic planning. In this setting, Britain's wage coordination in the early 1950s was based on gentlemen's agreements, in which the employers' orga-

70. Stein (1969, pp. 197–204); Goldfield (1987); Goodwin (1989, 90–104); Griffith (1989, 68–70); Liechtenstein (1989, pp. 148–50, 131–42, 152).

nization persuaded its members to restrain dividends in exchange for wage moderation by the unions. Successive voluntary agreements in the 1960s and 1970s broke down during economic hardships. A statutory incomes policy was not possible, either, since it was requested at a time during the 1970s when the government had to control inflation and impose fiscal austerity, which meant the government could not provide compensation to the unions in exchange for wage restraint. Thus prolonged calls for wage restraint ignited rank-and-file revolts and waves of strikes, forcing wages to rise above the regulated standards.[71] The experience of the United States and United Kingdom resemble the small-firm sector in Japan and indicate that institutions that mediate between the firm and the economy are necessary to coordinate a social arrangement in which employment security is provided in compensation for wage moderation.

The neocorporatist states of Sweden and Germany did develop institutions to coordinate wages in exchange for full employment, but the institutions and their dependence on union-based parties differ from each other, and from Japan. Wage coordination emerged in Sweden in the 1930s and was consolidated in the 1950s. Initially, wage moderation was realized when the export-oriented metal industry and its union aligned to oppose wage demands by the highly paid domestic construction industry. This intervention not only enabled the government to pass the Social Democratic party's crisis package but also permitted the metal industry and its union to gain power within the business and labor associations. The class compromise of the late 1930s based on this cross-class alliance of export industries formed the basis of the Rehn model of the early 1950s. The model proposed "solidaristic" wages, which meant equal pay for equal work regardless of the employer's ability to pay, and active labor market policy, which guaranteed income, training, and transfer of redundant workers released from inefficient firms because of squeezed profits due to solidaristic wages. In practice, however, the wages were set by export industries, as in Japan, while the unions depended on the Social Democrats to install the active labor market policy and other policies to facilitate wage-earner solidarity, such as income-related pensions, public housing, and wage earner funds.[72] Similarly, in post–World War II Germany unions were set up as industry unions that included blue- and white-collar employees. The com-

71. Leruez (1975, pp. 37–54, 61–62, 67–69); Panitch (1976, pp. 12–13, 27–29); Warde (1982, p. 48); Bornstein and Gourevitch (1984, pp. 19–26); Morgan (1984, pp. 98–99, 125–27).

72. Elvander (1974, pp. 427–28); Martin (1984, pp. 204–05, 241–46); Sharpf (1987, p. 266); Esping-Andersen (1985, p. 229); Lewin (1988, pp. 204–25, 274–304); Schmidt (1988); Swenson (1989, pp. 42–49); Swenson (1991).

petitive metal-industry union aligned wages to the less competitive industries to maintain union solidarity so that it could press the Social Democrats to enact compensation polices such as vocational training, a shortened workweek, and expanded codetermination.[73]

Thus the neocorporatist regimes of Sweden and Germany shared with Japan the leadership of export-oriented metal industries in coordinating wages and in uniting white- and blue-collar interests. However, wage coordination in Sweden was based on the peak negotiations between industry and labor associations, whereas in Germany it was achieved by lateral coordination among industries. Moreover, because unions depended on labor-based parties to realize full employment and other compensation policies, these neocorporatist regimes differed greatly from the unions in Japan in their emphasis on union solidarity. In Sweden and Germany, nationwide wage coordination was accepted by the unions of competitive industries to maintain the coherence of the national union, which in turn was necessary to make the Social Democratic parties enact policies that compensated for wage coordination. Thus in Sweden and Germany, reinforcement of wage coordination strengthened the national unions, whereas in Japan, it weakened the national unions and emphasized the industry and enterprise-level labor negotiations instead.

In Japan, employee mobilization and economic incorporation at the firm level were clearly instrumental in the rise of enterprise unionism there, while industry-centered coordination spread its effects nationwide through mechanisms permitting the exchange between wages and employment. It is also clear that the countries just discussed took different paths in corporate governance as a result of different political responses at critical junctures in their history (immediately after a major war), and as a result of the different market and political structures in which the dominant unions were nested. Thus cross-national diversity may be institutionalized at key points in history, but after that, countries follow different trajectories because of the reinforcing effect of different surrounding structures, even when common problems, such as the global stagflation of the 1970s, would appear likely to compel them to converge.

References

Aida, Tosho. 1983. "Nohon Zōsengyo no Dōkō to Koyo Mondai." *Shakaiseisaku Gakkai Hōkokushū*, vol. 27.

73. See Markovits and Allen (1984); Markovits (1986, chaps. 1 and 2); Thelen (1991).

Akita, Nariaki. 1993. "Koyō Kankō to Haichi Tenkan, Shukkō." In *Nihon no Koyo Kanko no Henka to Hō,* edited by Nariaki Akita. Tokyo: Hōsei Daigaku Shippan-bu.

Amagai, Shyōgo. 1982. *Nihon Jidōsha Kōgyō no Shiteki Tenkai.* Tokyo: Aki Shobō.

Asanuma, Banri. 1989. "Nihon ni Okeru Maker to Supplier to no Kankei." In *Nihon no Chūshō Kigyō,* edited by Moriaki Tsuchiya and Yoshirō Miwa. Tokyo: Tokyo Daigaku Shuppan-kai.

Barkan, Joanne. 1984. *Visions of Emancipation: The Italian Workers' Movement since 1945.* New York: Praeger.

Blackmer, Donald L. M. 1975. "Continuity and Change in Postwar Italian Communism." In *Communism in Italy and France,* edited by Donald L. M. Blackmer and Sidney Tarrow. Princeton University Press.

Bornstein, Stephen and Peter Gourevitch. 1984. "Unions in a Declining Economy: The Case of the British TUC." In *Unions and Economic Crisis: Britain, West Germany, and Sweden,* edited by Peter Gourevitch and others. London: George Allen and Unwin.

Cameron, David. 1982. "Social Democracy, Corporatism, Labor Quiescence and the Representation of Economic Interest in Advanced Capitalist Society." In *Order and Conflict in Contemporary Capitalism,* edited by J. H. Goldthorpe. Oxford: Clarendon Press.

Catalano, F. 1972. "The Rebirth of the Party System." In *The Rebirth of Italy 1943–1950,* S. J. Woolf. London: Longman.

Elvander, Nils. 1974. "Collective Bargaining and Incomes Policy in the Nordic Countries." *British Journal of Industrial Relations* 12 (3): 417–37.

Esping-Andersen, Gøsta. 1985. *Politics against Markets: The Social Democratic Road to Power.* Princeton University Press.

Fuji'i, Mitsuo. 1967. *Nihon Seni Sangyō Shi: Sengo Bōseki kara Gōsen Made.* Tokyo: Mirai-sha.

Fujita, Wakao. 1974. "Labor Disputes." In *Workers and Employers in Japan: The Japanese Employment Relations System,* edited by K. Ōkouchi, B. Karsh, and S. B. Lavine. University of Tokyo Press.

Fujita, Wakao, and Shobei Shiota, eds. 1963. *Sengo Nihon no Rōdō Sogi,* vol. 1. Tokyo: Ochanomizu Shobo.

Funahashi, Naomichi, ed. 1967. *Kōza Rōdōkeizai,* vol. 2: *Nihon no Chingin.* Tokyo: Nihon Hyōron-sha.

Goldfield, Michael. 1984. *The Decline of Organized Labor in the United States.* University of Chicago Press.

Goodwin, Craufurd D. 1989. "Attitudes toward Industry in the Truman Administration: The Macroeconomic Origins of Microeconomic Policy." In *The Truman Presidency,* edited by Michael J. Lacey. Cambridge University Press.

Gordon, Andrew. 1993. "Contests for the Workplace." In *Postwar Japan as History,* edited by Andrew Gordon. University of California Press.

Griffith, Robert. 1989. "Forging America's Postwar Order: Domestic Politics and Political Economy in the Age of Truman." In *The Truman Presidency,* edited by Michael J. Lacey. Cambridge University Press.

Hasegawa, Akishige. 1977. "Senpatsu Gaisha no Keiei Senyaku." In *Sengo Sangyō-shi he no Shōgen,* vol. 2: *Kyodaika no Jidai,* edited by Ekonomisto Henshu-bu. Tokyo: Mainichi Shinbun-sha.

Hasegawa, Hiroshi. 1976. 2.1 *Suto Zengo to Nihon Kyosanto.* Tokyo: San'ichi Shobō.
————. 1984. *Senryōki no Rōdō Undō.* 2 vols. Tokyo: Aki Shobō.
Hata, Takashi. 1992. "1980-nen-dai no Jidōsha no 'Rōshi-Kankei': 84-nen Ichijikinn Kōsho ni okeru Rōshi Tairitu no Yōsō." *Yamaguchi Keizai-gaku Zasshi* 37 (5–6): 127–54.
Hirata, Tomitaro, and Tetsukichi Ando. 1958. "Sengo Rōdō Undo no Sui'i (1): Shusen kara Go'ka Rōren ma'de." In *Sengo Rōdō Sōgi Jittai Chōsa VIII: Kagaku Kogyo no Sō'gi to Kumiai Undō,* edited by Rōdō Sōgi Chōsakai. Tokyo: Chūō Kōron-sha.
Hosoya, Matsuta. 1985. "Sengo Minshu-shugi to Rōdō Kumiai no Seiritsu." In *Shyōgen: Sengo Rōdō Kumiai Undō-shi,* edited by Akira Takanashi. Tokyo: Tōyō Keizai Shinpō-sha.
Ishida, Hideo. 1976. *Nihon no Chingin Kettei to Rōshi Kankei.* Tokyo: Toyo Keizai Shinpo-sha.
Ishida, Mitsuo. 1986. "Nihon Tekkō-gyō no Rōshi Kankei: B Seitetsu-jo no Jirei Chōsa." *Shakai Kagaku Kenkyū* 38 (2): 135–78.
Ivring, R. E. M. 1973. *Christian Democracy in France.* London: George Allen and Unwin.
Iwami, Tōru. 1983. "EC Shokoku-to no Hikaku." In *Nihon Sangyō no Seido-teki Tokuchō to Boeki Masatsu,* edited by Uekusa Masu. Tokyo: Gaimu-shō Keizai-kyoku.
Iwanaga, Iwao. 1977. "Ethylene 30-Man Ton Taisei." In *Sengo Sangyō-shi he no Shōgen,* vol. 2: *Kyodaika no Jidai,* edited by Ekonomisto Henshū-bu. Tokyo: Mainichi Shinbun-sha.
Jéquier, Nicolas. 1974. "Computers." In *Big Business and the State: Changing Relations in Western Europe,* edited by Raymond Vernon. Harvard University Press.
Johnson, Chalmers. 1982. *MITI and the Japanese Miracle: The Growth of Industrial Policy, 1925–1975.* Stanford University Press.
Kamizuma, Yoshiaki. 1976. *Shuntō: Sōhyō-shi no Danmen.* Tokyo: Rōdō Kyōiku Sentā.
Kawabe, Heihachirō. 1991. "Tekkō Sangyō." In *Nihon-teki Rōshi -Kankei no Henbō,* edited by Makino Tomio. Tokyo: Ōtsuki Shoten.
Kawada, Hisashi. 1974. "Workers and Their Organizations." In *Workers and Employers in Japan: The Japanese Employment Relations System,* edited by K. Ōkōchi, B. Karsh, and S. B. Lavine. Tokyo: University of Tokyo Press.
Keizai, Dōyū-Kai. 1956. *Keizai Dōyū-kai Jyū-nen-shi.* Tokyo: Keizai Dōyū-kai.
Kikuchi, Kōzō. 1984. "The Japanese Enterprise Union and Its Function." In *Industrial Relations in Transition: The Cases of Japan the Federal Republic of Germany,* edited by S. Tokunaga and J. Bergemann. University of Tokyo Press.
Kojima, Kenji. 1975. *Shuntō no Rekishi.* Tokyo: Aoki Shoten.
Kume, Ikuo. 1988. "Changing Relations among the Government, Labor, and Business in Japan after the Oil Crisis." *International Organization* 42 (4): 659–87.
Lange, Peter, and Maurizio Vannicelli. 1982. "Strategy under Stress: The Italian Union Movement and the Italian Crisis in Developmental Perspective." In *Unions, Change and Crisis: French and Italian Union Strategy and the Political Economy, 1945–1980,* edited by Peter Lange and others. London: George Allen and Unwin.
Leruez, Jacques. 1975. *Economic Planning and Politics in Britain.* London: Martin Robertson.
Lewin, Leif. 1988. *Ideology and Strategy: A Century of Swedish Politics.* Cambridge University Press.

Liechtenstein, Nelson. 1989. "Labor in the Truman Era: Origins of the Private Welfare State." In *The Truman Presidency,* edited by Michael J. Lacey. Cambridge University Press.

Lorwin, Val R. 1966. *The French Labor Movement.* Cambridge: Harvard University Press.

Markovits, A. S. 1986. *The Politics of the West German Trade Unions.* Cambridge University Press.

Markovits, A. S., and C. S. Allen. 1984. "Trade Unions and the Economic Crisis: The West German Case." In *Unions and Economic Crisis: Britain, West Germany, and Sweden,* edited by Peter Gourevitch and others. London: George Allen and Unwin.

Martin, Andrew. 1984. "Trade Unions in Sweden: Strategic Responses to Change and Crisis." In *Unions and Economic Crisis: Britain, West Germany, and Sweden,* edited by Peter Gourevitch and others. London: George Allen and Unwin.

Masumi, Jun'nosuke. 1983. *Sengo Seiji,* 1945–1955, vol. 1. Tokyo: Daigaku Shuppan-kai.

McCormick, Janice. 1981. "Gaullism and Collective Bargaining: The Effect of the Fifth Republic on French Industrial Relations." In *The Fifth Republic and Twenty,* edited by William G. Andrews and Stanley Hoffman. State University of New York Press.

Miwa, Yoshiō. 1990. *Nihon no Kigyō to Sangyō Soshiki.* Tokyo: Tokyo Daigaku Shuppan-kai.

Mizota, Seigro. 1991. "Tekko-gyō no Kōzō-Kaikaiku." In *Gendai Nihon no Sangyō-Kōzō,* edited by Miwa Yoshirō. Tokyo: Nihon Hyoron-sha.

Moore, Joe. 1983. *Japanese Workers and the Struggle for Power, 1945–47.* University of Wisconsin Press.

Morgan, Kenneth O. 1984. *Labour in Power 1945–1951.* Oxford University Press.

Murakami, Hiroharu, and others. 1980. *Sōhyō Rōdō Undō 30-nen no Kiseki.* Tokyo: Rōdō Kenkyu Center.

Naitō, Masaru. 1958a. "Nittetsu Yawata no Sōgi, Shōwa 20-25-nen." In *Sengo Rōdō Sōgi Jittai Chōsa VII: Tekkō Sō'gi,* edited by Rōdō Sōgi Jittai Chōsa. Tokyo: Chūō Kōron-sha.

———. 1958b. "Kawasaki Seiban no Sōgi, Shōwa 22-23-nen." In *Sengo Rōdō Sōgi Jittai Chōsa VII: Tekkō Sōgi,* edited by Rōdō Sōgi Jittai Chōsakai. Tokyo: Chūō Kōron-sha.

Nakamura, Hide'ichirō, and others. 1966. *Nihon Sangyō to Kasen Taisei.* Tokyo: Shinpyō-sha.

Nakamura, Takafusa. 1957. "Kumiai no Seisei to Zentan no Tō'sō: Showa 20-21-nen." In *Sengo Rōdō Sōgi Jittai Chōsa I: Sekitan Sōgi,* edited by Rōdō Sōgi Chōsakai. Tokyo: Chūō Kōron-sha.

Nihon Ginkō Hyakunenshi Hensan I'inkai. 1985. *Nihon Ginkō Hyakunen-shi.* Tokyo: Nihon Ginkō.

Nihon Rōdō Kumai Sōhyōgikai. 1964. *Sōhyō Jyū-nen Shi. Tokyo:* Rōdō Jyunpō-sha.

Nishimura, Hiromichi. 1963. "Ama-Kō So'gi." In *Sengo Nihon no Rōdō Sōgi,* vol. 1, edited by Wakao Fujita and Shyōbei Shiota. Tokyo: Ochanomizu Shobō.

Nitta, Michio. 1988. *Nihon no Rōdōsha Sanka.* Tokyo: Tokyo Daigaku Shuppankai.

Ōba, Yō'ji. 1991. "Tekkō Dokusen no Saihen to 90-nen dai Shijō Shihai Senryaku (1)." *Keizai* 326: 130–50.

Odaka, Kōnosuke, and others. 1988. *The Automobile Industry in Japan: A Study of Ancillary Firm Development.* Tokyo: Kinokuniya.

Ogata, Taka'aki. 1980. "Koyō Seisaku no Genjitsu." In *Nihon-teki Keiei no Tenki,* edited by Kikuo Ando and others. Tokyo: Yūhikaku.

Ono, Tsuneo. 1968. "Dantai Kōshō no Kōka to Genkai." In *Kōza Rōdō Keizai 3, Nihon no Rōdō Kumiai,* edited by Taishiro Shirai. Tokyo: Nihon Hyōron-sha.

————. 1979. "Chingin Hakyū no Mekanisumu: Sangyō Soshiki-ron teki Apurō'chi." In *Gendai Nihon Rōdō Mondai,* edited by Mikio Sumiya. Tokyo: Tokyo Daigaku Shyuppan-kai.

Ōshima, Taku, ed. 1987. *Gendai Nihon no Jidōsha Buhin Kōgyō.* Tokyo: Nihon Keizai Hyōron-sha.

Ōtake, Hideo. 1987. "The *Zaikai* under the Occupation." In *Democratizing Japan,* edited by Robert E. Ward and Yoshikazu Sakamode. University of Hawaii Press.

Panitch, Leo. 1976. *Social Democracy and Industrial Militancy: The Labour Party, The Trade Unions and Income Policy, 1945–1974.* Cambridge University Press.

Rioux, Jean-Pierre. 1987. *The Fourth Republic 1944–1958.* Cambridge University Press.

Rōdō Sōgi Chōsakai, ed. 1954. *Sengo Rōdō Sōgi Jittai Chōsa IV: Sen'i Rōdō Sōgi to Kumiai Undō.* Tokyo: Chūō Kōron-sha.

————. ed. 1956. *Sengo Rōdō Sōgi Jittai Chōsa VI: Rōdō Sōgi ni okeru Tokushyu Keisu,* Tokyo: Chūō Kōron-sha.

————. ed. 1957. *Rōdō Sōgi Jittai Chōsa III: Kōtsu Bumon ni Okeru Sōgi.* Tokyo: Chūō Kōron-sha.

Ross, George. 1982. *Workers and Communists in France: From Popular Front to Eurocommunism.* University of California Press.

Saga, Ichiro, and Toku'ichi Kumagai. 1983. *Nissan Sōgi, 1953: Tenkan-ki no Syōgen.* Tokyo: Satsuki-sha.

Salvati, B. 1972. "The Rebirth of Italian Trade Unionism, 1943–54," In *The Rebirth of Italy 1943–1950,* edited by S. J. Woolf. London: Longman.

Sanbetsu Kaigi Shiryō Seiri I'inkai. 1958. *Sanbetsu Kaigi Syōshi.* Reprinted in *Sanbetsu Kaigi: Sono Seiritsu to Undō no Tenkai,* edited by Rōdō Undō-shi Kenkyū-kai. Tokyo: Rōdō Junpō-sha, 1970.

Saruta, Masaki. 1991. "Jidōsha Sangyō." In *Nihon-teki Rōshi -Kankei no Hanbō,* edited by Makino Tomio. Tokyo: Ōtsuki Shoten.

Satō, Hiroki, and Takashi Umetsu. 1983. "Rōdōkumiai no 'Hatsugen' to Kumai Ruikei." In *80-nen-dai no Rōshi Kankei,* edited by Nihon Rōdō Kyōkai. Tokyo: Nihon Rōdō Kyōkai.

Schmidt, Manfred G. 1988. "The Politics of Labour Market Policy: Structural and Political Determents of Rates of Unemployment in Industrial Nations." In *Managing Mixed Economies,* edited by Frank Castles. Berlin: Walter de Gruyter.

Sekiyu Kagaku Kōgyō Kyōkai, ed. 1971. *Sekiyu Kagaku 10-nen Shi.* Tokyo: Sekiyu Kagaku Kōgyō Kyōkai.

Serizawa, Hisayoshi. 1987a. "Tekkō-gyō ni okeru Rōshi-Kankei no Shin-kyokumen: Sengo Saidai no 'Gōrika' Mondai to Rōdōkumiai Undō (1)." *Kochi Daigaku, Shakai Kagaku Ronshū* 54: 167–203.

————. 1987b. "Tekkō-gyō ni okeru Rōshi-Kankei no Shin-kyokumen (2)." *Kōchi Daigaku, Shakai Kagaku Ronshū* 55: 93–136.

Sharpf, Fritz W. 1987. *Crisis and Choice in European Social Democracy.* Cornell University Press.

Shinkawa, Toshimitsu. 1984. "1975-nen Shuntō to Keizai Kikikanri." In *Nihon Seiji no Sōten,* edited by Hideo Ōtake. Tokyo: San-ichi Shobō.

Shin-Sanbetsu Nijyū-Nen-Shi Hensan I'inkai. 1969. *Shin-sanbetsu no Nijyū-nen,* vol. 2. Tokyo: Shin-sanbetsu.

Shiota, Shyōbei. 1954. "Zen-koku Sen'i Rōdō Kumiai Domei." In *Nihon Rōdō Kumiai Ron: Tan'i Sanbetsu Kumiai no Seikaku to Kinō,* edited by Kazuo Ōkouchi. Tokyo: Yūhikaku.

Shirai, Taishirō. 1979. *Kigyō-betsu Kumiai, Zōtei-ban.* Tokyo: Chūkō Sinsho.

———. 1983. "A Theory of Enterprise Unionism." In *Contemporary Industrial Relations in Japan,* edited by Shirai Taishirō. University of Wisconsin Press.

Sōdōmei Gojyū-Nen-Shi Kankō I'inkai. 1968. *Sōdōmei Gojyū-nen-shi,* vol. 5. Tokyo: Sōdōmei.

Stein, Herbert. 1969. *The Fiscal Revolution in America.* University of Chicago Press.

Swenson, Peter. 1989. *Fair Shares: Unions, Pay, and Politics in Sweden and West Germany.* Cornell University Press.

———. 1991. "Bringing Capital Back In, or Social Democracy Reconsidered: Employer Power, Cross-Class Alliances, and Centralization of Industrial Relations in Denmark and Sweden." *World Politics* 43 (4): 513–44.

Takagi, Ikuro. 1976. *Shuntō-ron; Sono Bunseki, Tenkai, to Kadai.* Tokyo: Rōdō Jyunpō-sha.

———. 1982. "Rōdō Undō-shi ni okeru Kigyō-betsu Kumiai; Rōdō no Jiritsuka Kinō Tenkai no Kanō'sei." In *Sengo Rōdō Kumiai Undō Shi Ron; Kigyō Syakai Chōkoku no Shiza,* edited by Shinzō Shimizu. Tokyo: Nihon Hyōron-sha.

Takanashi, Masaru. 1977. "Shuntō Taisei-ka no Chingin Tōsō no Tenkan." In *Kōza: Gendai no Chingin,* vol. 1, edited by Shōjirō Ujinara and others, 57–86. Tokyo: Shakai Shisō-sha.

Takaragi, Fumihiko. 1985. "Sōhyō Tanjyō Zengo." In *Syōgen: Sengo Rōdō Kumiai Undō-shi,* edited by Akira Takanashi. Tokyo: Tōyō Keizai Shinpō-sha.

Takemae, Eiji. 1982. *Sengo Rōdō Kaikaku: GHQ no Rōdō Seisaku.* Tokyo: Tokyo Daigaku Shuppan-kai.

Thelen, K. A. 1991. *Union of Parts: Labor Politics in Postwar Germany.* Cornell University Press.

Tiersky, Ronald. 1974. *French Communism, 1920–1972.* Columbia University Press.

Totskuka, Hideo, and Tsutomu Hyōdō, eds. 1991. *Rōshi-kankei no Tenkan to Sentaku: Nihon no Jidōsha Sangyō.* Tokyo: Nihon Hyōronsha.

Tsujinaka, Yutaka. 1986a. "Rōdō Daitai: Kyūchi ni Tatsu 'Rōdō' no Seisaku Kettei." In *Nihon-gata Seisaku Kettei no Henyo,* edited by Minoru Nakano. Tokyo: Toyo Keizai Shinpō-sha.

———. 1986b. "Gendai Nihon Seiji no Coporatism-ka." In *Kōza Seijigaku,* vol. 3: *Seiji Katei,* edited by Mitsuru Uchida. Tokyo: Sanrei Shobō.

Tsunoda, Yutaka. 1963. "Nikkō Muroran Sogi." In *Sengo Nihon no Rōdō Sogi,* vol. 1, edited by Wakao Fukita and Syōbei Shiota. Tokyo: Ochanomizu Shobō.

Ueno, Hiroya, and Hiromichi Mutō. 1976. "Jidō'sha." In *Nihon no Sangyō Soshiki,* vol. 1, edited by Hisao Kumagai. Tokyo: Chūō Kōron-sha.

Uekusa, Masu, and Tsuruhiko Nanbu. 1977. "Gōsei Seni." In *Nihon no Sangyo Soshiki,* vol. 2, edited by Hisao Kumagai. Tokyo: Chūō Kōron-sha.

Ujihara, Shō'jirō and others, eds. 1977. *Koza, Gendai no Chingin, Vol. 4; Chingin Mondai no Kadai.* Tokyo: Shakai Shisō-sha.

Uriu, Robert M. 1996. *Troubled Industries: Confronting Economic Change in Japan.* Cornell University Press.

Warde, Alan. 1982. *Consensus and Beyond: The Development of Labour Party Strategy since the Second World War.* Manchester University Press.

Weitz, Peter. 1975. "The CGIL and the PCI: From Subordination to Independent Political Force." In *Communism in Italy and France,* edited by Donald L. M. Blackmer and Sidney Tarrow. Princeton University Press.

Wells, Louis T. Jr. 1974. "Automobiles." In *Big Business and the State: Changing Relations in Western Europe,* edited by R. Vernon. Harvard University Press.

Yamamoto, Kiyoshi. 1977. *Sengo Kiki ni okeru Rōdō Undō: Sengo Nihon Undo-shi ron Dai 1-kan.* Tokyo: Ochanomizu Shobō.

———. 1978. Yomiuri Sō'gi (1945–46): *Sengo Nihon Undō-shi ron Dai 2-kan.* Tokyo: Ochanomizu Shobo.

———. 1983. Toshiba Sōgi (1949): *Sengo Rōdō Undō-shiron Dai 3-kan.* Tokyo: Ochanomizu Shobō.

———. 1989. "Zōsengyō ni okeru Shigugyosha no Kisuu (1 and 2)." *Shakaikagaku Kenkyu.* 41 (3–4): 219–57 (vol. 3); 227–71 (vol. 4).

Yuasa, Yoshio. 1982. "Kōzō Fukyō Chi'iki ni okeru Rishokusha no Dōkō to Koyō Mondai." *Ritsumeikan Keizaigaku* 30 (6): 189–240.

PART Four

Employee Share Ownership

10

Employee Stock Ownership in Economic Transitions: The Case of United and the Airline Industry

JEFFREY N. GORDON

Arguments in favor of employee ownership start with two sorts of normative appeals. First, in the current economic order, equity participation may be a more reliable way for employees to share in the firm's prosperity than wage increases. Real wages for all but the top quintile of wage earners have been essentially stagnant for nearly two decades, while real stock prices have increased almost threefold. Second, ownership carries with it governance rights, which means the opportunity to participate in the organization and management of the workplace. As in any large-scale political regime, direct participation may be constrained, but even so, employee ownership brings the dignity of self-control and accountability to one's fellow employees. Despite these attractive features, employee ownership of controlling stakes is uncommon in large corporations, and such ownership as exists typically uses a tax-favored retirement trust called an

For helpful discussion and comments on earlier drafts, I am grateful to Mark Barenberg, Margaret Blair, Bernie Black, David Charny, Sam Estreicher, Ron Gilson, Henry Hansmann, Eric Orts, Andrzej Rapaczynski, Mark Roe, and Chuck Sabel. For research help I am grateful to Ian Haft. For financial support, I am grateful to the Sloan Foundation and the Columbia/Sloan Corporate Governance Project that it has supported.

employee stock ownership plan, or ESOP, that ordinarily severely limits employee exercise of ownership prerogatives.[1]

Central to my approach, however, are the propositions that employee ownership can take many forms and that the particular institutions of economic participation and governance participation fashioned for a particular firm may matter crucially to the firm's success. I want to suggest that "employee ownership" should not be thought of as a single rigid organizational form, but rather as a reference to a universe of potential organizational forms. Imagine governance participation and profit participation as variables on the axes of a two-dimensional organizational space. "Employee ownership" refers to a set of points in which the resulting organization is sufficiently different from the traditional firm that the new designation seems apt. Lest this definition seem too broad, it should be remembered that we find it useful to use a term like "public corporation" to cover situations as different as a firm with a controlling shareholder, a manager-dominated firm with dispersed shareholders, and a firm dominated by institutional shareholders. Employee ownership may also come in many different forms.

Like many other organizational forms, employee ownership may have special value in specific economic environments. In particular, employee ownership may have decisive advantages in addressing the transition problems associated with significant economic change. Indeed, many recent examples of employee ownership in the large corporation may be found in two industries facing sharply changed economic circumstances: the airline industry following deregulation in 1978, and the steel industry following the rise of low-cost foreign competition. An interesting question to consider is whether employee stock ownership transactions produce a transitional organizational form, which, in the ordinary course of events, reverts back to public shareholder ownership, or whether they produce a durable organizational form especially well suited for ongoing transitions. That question is at the heart of this discussion.[2]

To focus the inquiry, the chapter will turn to an important recent example of an employee stock transaction, the 1994 employee acquisition of majority equity in United Air Lines (UAL). The parties in UAL contemplated employee ownership as more than a transitional device, since the deal is structured to lock up employee stock in an ESOP and to provide strong

---

1. Very useful discussions of employee ownership (and references to further discussion) are found in chapter 1 in this volume, as well as in Blasi and Kruse (1991); Hansmann (1990, 1996); Hyde (1991); Earle and Estrin (1996).

2. For empirical evidence on this same question, see Blair, Kruse, and Blasi (2000).

employee governance rights for the next twenty years. One of the objectives of the transaction was to catalyze a cultural change in UAL's operations so that at least part of the airline could become a low-cost carrier, not just through wage reductions but through operational efficiencies that would require a higher level of employee cooperation. The evidence thus far is that UAL is capable of highly profitable performance, but that governance pressure from the employees is potentially destabilizing. The UAL case also shows that adjustment to prosperity can raise problems almost as difficult as adjustment to economic adversity.

Transition Problems and Employee Ownership

Employee stock ownership transactions can address four sorts of transitional problems: the just allocation of transition costs as between shareholders and employees; efficient bargaining over the allocation of one-time transition costs; efficient bargaining over ongoing transition costs; and the creation of superior structures for transitional environments.

Just Allocation of Transition Costs

"Just allocation" problems arise from changed economic circumstances that reduce the profitability of the firm. In theory, the reduction in cash flow could be allocated against shareholder returns, in the form of reduced dividends or profits, or against employee returns, in the form of reduced wages or layoffs. If some cost sharing is desired as a matter of justice or fairness, then employee stock ownership transactions, in which employees exchange wage concessions and other labor cost-reducing measures for equity in the firm, may serve this purpose.

Two significant problems arise in conceiving of employee stock ownership transactions as addressing the just allocation of transition losses between shareholders and employees. The first is a practical issue: absent a legally enforceable wage and labor amenity claim, usually accomplished through a process of collective bargaining, employees ordinarily have no basis to negotiate an equity-for-concessions swap. This becomes apparent when one compares the case of UAL (and other airlines that have undertaken an employee stock ownership transaction) with that of Delta, which, unlike the other major carriers, is not unionized, except for the pilots. In 1994 Delta announced a program to reduce operating expenditures by 20 percent. Delta's plan sought to eliminate 12,000 to 15,000 jobs out of a work force of approximately 71,000 and called for other concessions. The one Delta employee group that received stock as part of this plan was the pilots, who received approximately 2 percent of the company's equity in exchange for concessions under a collective bargaining agreement. The contrast is stark: explicit contractual rights, but not less enforceable claims, trigger an employee stock ownership transaction.[3]

The existence or not of prior contract rights as a basis for an equity-for-concessions swap does not necessarily resolve the matter, however, since it would be possible to construct a legal regime that mandated special bargaining endowments for employees in appropriately defined cases of economic transition. The problem is the difficulty in identifying the normative basis for such an endowment. Even if, as a matter of social justice or policy, society decides that it is wrong that specific employee groups should bear the costs of economic transitions, it is not obvious why the solution should be located at the level of the individual firm. After all, particular firms will differ in their capacity to provide for transition measures. The bargaining position of different employee groups within firms will differ. Thus the actual benefits will be somewhat randomly distributed, which does not fit well with the posited goal of social justice. Moreover, it is not obvious why the appropriate method of assisting employees should be to encourage them to hold stock in an economically threatened enterprise. "Justice" is a feature of a society overall, not of locally just decisions by every economic institution.[4]

---

3. The UAL case provides a partial counterexample. Among the employee groups that participated in the buyout were the salaried and management employees, who in exchange for a proportionate share of concessions, received approximately 9 percent of the stock—despite the absence of a collective bargaining agreement covering them. There are two theories as to why they were permitted to participate in the employee stock ownership plan on equivalent terms: perhaps senior management self-identified with this employee group and gave an unnecessary benefit at shareholder expense; or perhaps excluding the salaried and management employees from the employee stock ownership transaction would have demoralized them and injured the future prospects of the company.

4. I do feel some conflict about this point in the following way. Assume that society decides to provide protection against transition losses. It would then follow that reducing the amount of such losses is a meaningful goal. Mechanisms that force firms and employees to internalize such transition costs, at least in part, may reduce the costs. In the case of workplace safety, for example, the workers' compensation premiums that are charged to businesses are experience-rated; that is, they rise for firms according to the costs that occur because of accidents at that firm, rather than being spread equally across all firms. The reason behind this, of course, is to give firms an incentive to reduce the level of workplace harm or to monitor medical and income maintenance costs. In the same way, mechanisms that force individual firms to address transition costs may reduce the level of such costs. This is the subject of an ongoing project. See Gordon (1997).

A related problem is how to specify the employee claim at the firm level, particularly in the absence of a collective bargaining agreement or other explicit form of contractual protection. Where no such contract exists, many have argued that the basis for the employee claim is an "implicit" contract with the firm, which should be entitled to judicial or other protection.[5] Such implicit contracts protect two sorts of interests: deferred compensation claims, and rents and quasi rents deriving from firm-specific human capital investment. "Deferred compensation" refers to wages higher than an employee's current marginal productivity that reflect catch-up for periods when wages were below marginal productivity. For example, after training the worker, the firm may suppress wages to shorten the time it will take to recover its investment in training so as to protect against the possibility that the employee will be recruited by another firm. Similarly, an employer may at first pay average marginal productivity to a group of employees until it is clear who are the high performers.

"Rents" and "quasi rents" refer to the returns on the employee's firm-specific human capital investment. Suppose that a worker invests time and energy in learning how to operate a customized machine that makes products that earn economic rents for the owner. The worker will want to be paid according to marginal product, taking into account a return on the employee's investment in learning to operate the customized machine, but the firm will be tempted to pay only as much as the employee's opportunity wage at the next best job, which will be lower because the firm-specific skills are of no use to the employee in that alternate job.

Two distinct concerns are behind implicit contract agreements: first, that the firm will opportunistically expropriate these employee claims; second, that these employee claims should be prior to shareholder claims over a significant range of economic circumstances. I think expropriation is an overstated concern. In fact, a firm cannot systematically expropriate the rent and quasi-rent interests. As long as the firm is earning rents, there will be jockeying over how to divide them. But any employer who is tempted to reduce wages below marginal product—on the view that any payment above the employee's opportunity wage is sufficient to retain the employee—will face considerable risks. The experimental economics litera-

5. See, for example, Schleifer and Summers (1988); Singer (1988); Mitchell (1992); O'Connor (1993); Blair (1995). It is important to distinguish between an "implied" contract as a lawyer would understand the term and an "implicit" contract as used in the economics literature. An implied contract represents a binding contract between the parties that may not have been reduced to definitive form, and that is enforceable in court if proved; an implicit contract in the economists' customary sense depends on market forces for its enforcement.

ture shows that people are often willing to reject even "rational" economic bargains if they are perceived as unfair. Moreover, insofar as the firm would like current or new employees to make investments in firm-specific human capital in the future, any cheating on current implicit contracts would be self-defeating. Of course, changes in market conditions may cause the rents to disappear and lead the firm to impose layoffs or lower salaries, but this merely reflects the fact that the owner's investment and the worker's investment have both depreciated in value and that the conditions under which high wages were paid have disappeared. This is not an expropriation. An implied term of the implicit contract is the continuance of the economic circumstances on which the payout was predicated.

Similar problems would arise for any firm thinking about expropriating implicit deferred compensation. If the employee is part of a work force that the company wants to replenish and employ on the same basis, then the firm will protect accrued deferred compensation claims; otherwise, the firm's promise to protect future deferred compensation would not be credible. The firm's desire to preserve its reputation is what sustains its past implicit promises. Of course, a major economic dislocation may lead a firm to believe that it must make changes out of economic necessity regardless of the impact on its reputation, or even to believe that as a result of the shift in background economic conditions, any changes that affect deferred compensation claims will be broadly recognized as reasonable and thus will not affect its reputation. The nonoccurrence of a major shift is an implied term of the implicit contract. Deferred compensation claims will be honored only in circumstances in which the parties could have reasonably expected the implicit promise to pay them to be credible: where it serves the present interest of the firm.

These insights have some implications for past arguments. One of the major concerns about takeovers and leveraged buyouts since the 1980s has been that the gains were financed out of opportunistic conversion of the employees' deferred compensation claims. The argument was that new owners could treat current employees opportunistically without damaging their continuing reputation.[6] But this claim seems implausible: having decided once to disregard prior claims of deferred compensation, how could new owners credibly commit themselves to protecting new deferred compensation claims? More generally, the debate in the 1980s was over whether takeover entrepreneurs were acting opportunistically or in response to real economic change. The subsequent restructuring, down-

6. Knoeber (1986).

sizing, and reengineering by large firms that were not under the raiders' gun is strong evidence that a change in real economic variables rather than speculative opportunism played the more important role.[7]

This analysis also sheds light on the ongoing question of why shareholders, not employees, ordinarily elect directors. The answer, according to Oliver Williamson, lies in the different claims that shareholders and employees make on the firm's cash flows: shareholders have a residual claim that cannot be described by a complete contingent claims contract and is thus expropriable, whereas employee compensation can be covered by an explicit contract. Margaret Blair and others point out that employees also have residual claims in Williamson's sense, that is, noncontractible interests that can be expropriated, deriving from firm-specific human capital investments.[8] The argument here readily admits that both employees and shareholders have implicit contracts with the firm. However, it emphasizes that the implicit contracts of employees are more likely to be self-enforcing, because employees are making continuous firm-specific investments, and the firm wishes them to keep doing so. By contrast, after an initial period of capital raising, shareholder investments in the firm are made infrequently. Most of the firm's capital needs are supplied through retained earnings or debt. This means the implicit contract with shareholders is not self-enforcing, thus calling for a governance structure that would give shareholders dominance on the corporate board to provide credible protection against expropriation.

The second broad question concerning just allocation is whether employee claims should come ahead of shareholder claims, at least over some range of economic circumstances. Most defenders of the implicit contract claim seem to think that shareholders are better situated to bear the losses of economic transition than workers, since shareholders can diversify their claims in financial markets more easily than workers can diversify their portfolio of labor skills. This is similar to explanations as to why workers usually receive fixed wages and salaries, rather than compensation that varies dramatically with profits, despite the possible incentive effects of profit sharing.[9]

As a matter of justice, this argument is less persuasive than it might at first appear. In times of economic transition, shareholders have usually already borne part of the loss, since the economic changes that threaten

7. Gordon (1991).

8. See Williamson (1985); Blair (1995).

9. For a discussion of these issues, see Charny (1990).

deferred compensation claims have presumably also reduced the firm's cash flows and thus the stock price. Of course, these changes may not spread the transition losses between shareholders and employees in what seems like a fair way, but that is different from claiming that the shareholders do not suffer at all. The airline industry presents an especially challenging case for the employee-preference argument. Many of the employee rents are the legacy of a regulated market structure, not the result of firm-specific human capital investment. Although employees engage in some on-the-job training, many of the skills are acquired elsewhere; for example, many pilots learn to fly in the U.S. military. Moreover, many of the skills are readily transferrable across firms in the industry. Thus airlines offer a case in which employees have received rents owing to government regulation and are quite well paid, whereas most shareholders are earning only a competitive rate of return. In such circumstances, the case for protecting employee rents in preference to shareholder returns on grounds of justice is not the strongest.

One especially difficult aspect of establishing employee priority is to determine how much is enough. A collective bargaining agreement or other explicit contractual undertaking sets out a very clear basis (and limit) for employee priority, whereas implicit contract claims by nature resist quantification. However, without some clear notion of how much should be received, employees cannot know how secure they should be feeling, or whether their claim has been appropriately satisfied.

Another way to pose the question of fairness is to consider the differences between the treatment of UAL employees, who received stock in exchange for reduced wages and labor amenities, and Delta employees, who did not have their wages reduced but had to face a cut in the work force of 15 to 20 percent. Arguably the laid-off Delta employees were deprived of implicit deferred compensation, rents, and quasi rents. On the other hand, the layoffs came following four years in which Delta lost $2.5 billion and faced a strong competitive attack from low-cost start-ups, so the expected rents may not have been very large. Insofar as United's employees received a better deal by trading concessions for stock—not a straightforward conclusion ex ante—it was because of their investment in collective organization and dues, and their willingness to bargain collectively. It is difficult to say which allocation of costs was more just.

Efficient Bargaining over the Allocation of Transition Costs

Although employee stock ownership transactions may be hard to defend on grounds of justice, there are several efficiency rationales for their implementation. "Efficient bargaining" problems arise because of information disparities and other bargaining impediments that may interfere with the renegotiation of fixed claims in a firm facing financial distress. The starting point is a stakeholder group that has made a firm-specific investment that is protected contractually against expropriation, but that loses substantial value in bankruptcy. One example is unsecured bondholders; another is employees covered by a collective bargaining agreement that provides for wages and amenities above the employees' opportunity wage. A successful renegotiation that leads workers to take equity in exchange for lower labor costs (or bondholders to take equity for lower debt repayment) may well preserve economic value for both the workers (bondholders) and the shareholders, as opposed to having the firm end up in bankruptcy. Bargaining failure is, however, a real possibility. In this case, the argument for an employee stock ownership transaction is not a "justice" claim about fair sharing of the costs of transition. Instead, the claim is that equity-for-concessions transactions may conserve value in firms facing economic transitions by providing a mechanism that promotes agreement rather than deadlock in the renegotiation of the employee share of firm cash flows.

The pattern in the airline industry can serve as an example here. Employee compensation at given airlines (as at firms in many other industries) is a function primarily of three factors: compensation levels in the industry, expected revenues of the firm, and employee bargaining power at the firm. Before the airlines were deregulated these factors were relatively stable, so that changes in the cost (or value) of employee services were incremental and were accommodated in the traditional collective bargaining relationship. But deregulation and the newly arising competition in the industry dramatically affected how airlines operated, and thus changed the assumptions on which prior compensation levels had been negotiated. To survive, firms had to compete against carriers that charged much lower prices in part because they hired employees at lower wages and, unconstrained by costly work rules, could make more efficient use of their work force. Both the shareholders' financial capital and the employees' human capital diminished in value. The new environment created a dilemma: shareholders and employees have a common interest in the survival of the firm, but conflicting interests in the allocation of transition costs.

In the airline industry, the relative bargaining positions mean that neither shareholders nor employees can impose all of these costs on the other party. Most costs are fixed, so earnings are sensitive to even a small labor disruption, let alone a full-fledged strike. This gives organized employees substantial bargaining endowments. Yet the airline cannot survive with labor

cost structures set in a regulated era. Quite apart from any particular conception of justice, this situation calls for some sharing of the transition
costs.

However, the uncertainty associated with the new market environment
makes it difficult to set a fixed wage level that respects both the firm's survival and the employees' expectations. In particular, the economic turmoil
resulting from deregulation brings with it an increase in the information
gap between employees and managers at precisely the moment that managers claim unprecedented negative financial outcomes. An employee stock
ownership transaction can help resolve these problems by providing a form
of consideration with a contingent payout that is credibly linked to performance of the firm. Stock can help to overcome the bargaining problems in
a transition negotiation in several ways: by addressing information problems, offering a hedge against misvaluation, ensuring the credibility of payouts, and overcoming some of the heuristic barriers to cost sharing in
economic transitions.[10]

INFORMATION PROBLEMS. The offer of common stock credibly signals to
employees that the firm is facing genuine financial distress, as opposed to
seeking wage reductions for competitive or opportunistic reasons. A firm's
managers typically believe that the market undervalues the firm's stock, and
accordingly will issue new stock to raise funds only where retained earnings and borrowing capability are insufficient. Moreover, an employee stock
ownership transaction brings no external funds into the enterprise. Thus a
firm's willingness to issue stock on this basis should be a credible signal of
financial hardship. Moreover, the greater risk-bearing capacities of diversified public shareholders in comparison with employees means that common stock is ordinarily more valuable in public sale than in sale to
employees. An employee stock ownership transaction makes sense for
shareholders only when that valuation relationship is reversed, a credible
sign of financial distress. In addition, shareholders are likely to dislike and

10. Of course, employee stock ownership transactions in the airline industry are diverse in ways
not fully captured by the generic story told here. There are really three separate cases: first, the
base case of a transaction that arises out of an urgent need to transform the firm's cost structure
because of changing competitive conditions, such as the transactions at Eastern and Pan Am; second, the case that arises because of a perturbation in the market that may correct itself, such as temporary overcapacity or an unexpected falloff in demand, especially if the firm is vulnerable because
of a highly leveraged financial structure, as in the transactions at Northwest and TWA; third, the
case that is employee-initiated and seeks far-reaching goals of structural and cultural change, as in
the case of the United employee buyout. See Gordon (1995). Somewhat different cases will call for
somewhat different employee stock ownership transactions.

distrust employee participation in governance, fearing that it will lead to lower profits and stock prices, so employees know that they would not be offered such participation lightly.

Common stock also helps overcome the information gap by eliciting a credible valuation of the firm from management. If managers are tempted to overstate how negative the firm's prospects have become, then workers will insist on receiving more stock in exchange for a given level of wage concessions. Conversely, if management claims a high value for the stock, then workers will accept correspondingly smaller wage cuts. Because managers wish neither to dilute unnecessarily the interest of public shareholders nor to pay out higher wages than necessary, the use of common stock will produce a more credibly candid revelation of management's assessment of the firm's prospects.

Finally, an employee stock transaction may also provide a justification for giving employees board representation, which enhances the credibility of management's valuation by providing a mechanism for later review of management's candor. As board members, employee representatives obtain access to the detailed financial information that formed the basis for management's negotiating position. A discovery that management had lacked candor in prior negotiations might damage ongoing relations with employees generally, in a way that could hurt the firm's prospects and jeopardize management itself.

A HEDGE AGAINST MISVALUATION. During a time of economic turmoil the future level of firm revenues is highly uncertain. If revenues end up higher than expected, employees who made wage concessions may feel cheated, yet shareholders may insist that wage levels be based on conservative revenue estimates. The use of stock reduces the incentives to hold out because of this uncertainty. Whether the firm does well or poorly, the outcome will be shared between public and employee shareholders. Moreover, employees know that if it turns out that they gave away too much in wages, the stock price will rise and they will share in the gains. Conversely, if the employees gave away too little (wages were too high), the value of their stock will decrease. The use of stock mitigates the effects of uncertainty on distributional outcomes and thus makes it easier to reach agreement.

Another potential source of valuation uncertainty is the impact of the employee stock ownership transaction itself on the firm's revenues. Employees often contend that the change in culture associated with a successful employee transaction will also produce greater productivity from higher morale. Insofar as employees are correct, the stock price will rise, thus increasing the value of both the public stake and the employee stake. But disputes over the likelihood of productivity increases can be resolved with conditions that capture the gains for the employees. In the United Airlines transaction, for example, a dispute over the value of employee ownership was resolved by an agreement stipulating that if the average stock market price of the common stock over the year following the transaction exceeded a certain threshold, the employees would receive additional stock, up to an additional 8 percent of the company. This increased their potential ownership stake from 55 percent to 63 percent. Common stock provides a way to mitigate the effects of this uncertainty and makes agreement easier.

CREDIBLE PAYOUTS. In theory, these various features of wage-concessions-for-equity swaps can be replicated through contractually described contingent compensation that does not involve equity. For example, arrangements for profit sharing might plausibly substitute for common stock ownership and offer some attractive features. Profit sharing can be tailored to performance at a profit center rather than the firm as a whole, which more closely ties compensation to performance; profit sharing can also protect employees against the risk of a falling stock price that results from a general market downturn. The weakness of profit sharing as a substitute for stock is in the many possible definitions of profits and the many chances for manipulation in the reporting of operating results that feed into a profit calculation. Funds may also be diverted for restructurings or refinancings. The risk of opportunistic manipulation will be great—and the fear of it greater—in an environment in which ordinary reputational constraints are undermined by the changing competitive environment that has led to the transition negotiation in the first place. What makes common stock uniquely valuable is that it offers employees a more credible assurance of a payout linked to the performance of the firm than alternative contingent compensation schemes. The share price is a publicly available measure of the firm's profitability that is hard to manipulate. Common stock has the reassuring attribute that it is the same claim held by the public shareholders, so employees know that there are internal monitors (the board) and external monitors (analysts) with an interest in the integrity of this profitability measure.

An additional benefit of a contingent payout in the form of stock is that it is self-financing. In theory, there is no difference between funding a level of contingent compensation with cash or with stock; the stock could be sold on the market with the proceeds going to employees as easily as giving the employees stock directly. In practice, the outcomes are quite different. The market is likely to take the sale of stock as a negative signal, leading the firm to think of ways to finance the contingent payment out of cash flow or additional borrowings, which may divert the firm from its otherwise preferable business plan and add to the risk of bankruptcy. Moreover, if the employee stock goes into a retirement plan such as an ESOP, there is no subsequent employee sale of stock into the market and thus less chance of the new stock pushing down market prices.

HEURISTICS. Equity may also help overcome some of the barriers to selling a concessions agreement to an electorate of workers that is often relatively uninformed and unsophisticated. In the 1994 Northwest Airlines employee stock transaction, for example, the employees received convertible preferred stock that the company guaranteed to repurchase for the face amount of the concessions. However, the guaranteed repurchase could happen only after ten years, and there was no provision for the time value of money, so the discounted present value of this repurchase guarantee was actually no more than a third of the concession amount. Moreover, it would be economically rational to exercise the repurchase guarantee only if the airline was performing poorly, circumstances in which it might be financially unable to perform. But the point was to create an appearance that, after all, the employees were protected against losses on their transaction. Similarly, in the 1983 Eastern transaction, the employees made concessions greater than the market capitalization of the company. The gap between the deemed value of the common stock they received and the concession amount—the extent of possible employee loss—was nominally covered by a class of preferred stock with a high liquidation preference whose value in the deal was stated to be equal to the extent of any possible employee losses. But in an actual liquidation, the value of the preferred shareholders' claim would have been closer to 0 than 100¢ on the dollar.

In sum, an employee stock ownership transaction may add value in ways different from the familiar account of incentive effects flowing from employee ownership. Its particular value in a transition (and perhaps more generally) is that it addresses information disparities and uncertainty. A transition shock upsets conventional assumptions about wage levels and the value of the firm. In such cases employee stock ownership can facilitate renegotiation by providing a structure for the sharing of losses and possible gains in the new, uncertain state of the world.

Efficient Allocation of Ongoing Transition Costs

A typical restructuring is commonly imagined as a one-time event. But in a dynamic economic environment, transition adjustments rarely consist of a one-time restructuring, in which the labor input is simply repriced and the firm moves forward with a new cost structure. Sometimes, especially in collective bargaining situations, labor concessions are made only on a temporary basis, after which the baseline "snaps back" to the preexisting wage level, or even to the industry average at the time of the new negotiation. But even more commonly, the implications of a major transition are not immediately apparent, so that additional adjustments are required over time. In circumstances of sharp economic change, it is easy to foresee a continuing need to renegotiate wage levels, the size of the work force, and the organization of work, including work rules that affect productivity. An employee stock ownership transaction can put in place economic incentives and a governance structure that reduces the likelihood of bargaining failure in the course of successive renegotiations over ongoing transition costs and promotes the efficient allocation of these continuing transition costs.

The airline industry after deregulation provides a remarkable example of ongoing restructuring. The industry technology is largely unchanged over the period; the regulatory structure has been stable since the early 1980s; input prices and the demand for air travel have also been relatively stable (except for perturbations associated with the Gulf War in 1990–91). Nevertheless, the intensity of competitive pressures has made much of the period a turbulent one for almost all of the carriers. A number of well-known incumbents such as Braniff, Pan Am, and Eastern have been forced out of the business, while others such as Continental and TWA have made trips through Chapter 11. Consider the example of TWA, in which employees initially received a 35 percent equity interest in exchange for concessions that were part of TWA's emergence from bankruptcy in 1994. However, the financial restructuring proved inadequate, and as part of another transition negotiation the employees accepted dilution to a 25 percent equity stake. The airline barely survived the decline in passenger loads following the 1996 crash of Flight 800 and the ensuing boardroom disagreements among groups representing bondholders, managers, and employees. TWA is currently riding the airline industry's boom but still is barely profitable.[11] In

11. Barnaby J. Feder, "The St. Louis Phoenix: From Its Heartland Hub, T.W.A. Is Rising, but Wall St. Has Some Doubts," *New York Times,* February 10, 1998, p. D1.

general, the recent prosperity of the airlines is unusual, and, according to many industry observers, not destined to last.

In circumstances of ongoing transition, there are three distinct barriers to striking a bargain: asymmetric information, strategic miscalculation about the possible settlement range, and concern about opportunistic behavior after the agreement is reached. Stock ownership entails two distinct features that have the potential to reduce these three barriers: governance participation and economic participation.

GOVERNANCE PARTICIPATION: INFORMATION. The most important form of governance participation comes through representation on the board of directors.[12] In the typical public firm, whose directors are elected by a majority vote of shares, a minority stake will not ensure even minimal board representation. In the case of employee stock ownership transactions that address transition problems, however, it has been common to establish special classes of stock with the right to elect directors, thus assuring employees some representation on the board. (By contrast, the establishment of an ordinary ESOP—although it may occasionally hold as much stock as found in an employee stock ownership transaction—has not usually led to employee board representation.)

From the perspective of allocating ongoing transition costs, the major advantage of employee board representation is that employees have credible information about the firm's business and financial condition. Employee board representatives receive the same information as other directors. Corporate directors will insist on a certain level of information disclosure and on the reliability of such information, both for the sake of preserving their personal reputations and because they can be personally sued for failing to take due care in investigating suspicious or worrisome facts about the firm. Especially close attention is paid to such information in the case of a firm that is visibly experiencing economic distress. The access to such high-quality information through employee directors means that employees and management will bargain on the basis of common, credible information. This will reduce the risk that parties will negotiate from radically different premises about the firm's financial condition and reduce the potential for the fact or appearance of bad faith bargaining.

---

12. One potential loophole here is worth mentioning. Conceivably, some of the work of the board could be delegated to committees that exclude employee directors. Explicit provisions about the role of committees and the involvement of employee directors in committees may be necessary to address credibility problems.

One may wonder, if employee board representation helps to solve these information problems, why are employee directors not more common on the board? There are two obvious answers. First, in normal times, the information asymmetries may not be so critical, because the situation of the firm is fairly well understood by all parties. Second, board membership would give employee directors governance power as well as information, and management and other shareholders typically prefer not to give such power to employees unless forced to do so in a situation of financial distress.

GOVERNANCE PARTICIPATION: NARROWING THE SETTLEMENT RANGE. Board representation can also facilitate subsequent transition adjustments by reducing the risk of miscalculating the settlement range. Employee directors will come to a better understanding of the market environment in which the firm operates and the economically feasible level of wages and other labor amenities. This means that bargaining should not be derailed by clearly mistaken beliefs about contracting possibilities. This is particularly important where an industrial sector is in transition and the customary economic relationships are in flux. However, it should also be admitted that governance participation can sometimes increase the intensity of disagreements, depending on the personalities involved. In the case of Eastern Airlines, it is widely believed that the board membership of a union director who was certainly strong-willed, if not willful, contributed to the bargaining failure that led to sale of the firm to the unions' least favorite airline operator, Frank Lorenzo, at a bargain price.

GOVERNANCE PARTICIPATION: OPPORTUNISM AFTER AN AGREEMENT IS REACHED. Stock ownership brings the right to vote in matters that are submitted to shareholder vote. Although this right is ordinarily not regarded as the most important feature of corporate governance, it can protect an employee shareholder group from management opportunism after an agreement has been reached. For example, employees might worry that wage and productivity concessions that enhance the firm's economic viability merely set the stage for a sale of the firm (in whole or in part) or a merger, in which an acquirer might try to extract additional concessions from the employees. It is common for an employee stock ownership transaction to be drafted in such a way as to give employees an effective veto power over such deals, even if the employees do not have majority ownership of the firm. Such governance participation rights help address the employee concern that management will subsequently enter into an opportunistic transaction.

ECONOMIC PARTICIPATION: INFORMATION. Employee stock ownership offers a distinct way of addressing information problems. Transforming employees into shareholders makes the stock price a credible and common reference point for the business prospects of the firm. Publicly reported financial information is often hard to interpret, and notwithstanding the antifraud protection of the federal securities laws, not always credible in part, because, as even a casual reader of financial statements can see, the adjustments, assumptions, and footnotes are a barrier to straightforward interpretation. The stock price distills this information, shakes it loose of management's efforts to spin the facts, and communicates whether the firm is doing relatively well or poorly. A negative stock price movement may provide a signal of the need for a transition adjustment that is mostly protected from the possibility of managerial misrepresentation or manipulation. An employee stock ownership transaction dramatically changes the employees' relation to the stock price. The stock price becomes a focal point of discussion at work, and owning the stock may be the occasion for discussion of the financial reports received in the mail. Thus, even apart from governance participation, the economic element of employee stock ownership may also reduce information barriers to successful adjustment negotiations.[13]

ECONOMIC PARTICIPATION: NARROWING THE SETTLEMENT RANGE. After an employee stock ownership transaction, employees will have two economic interests to protect: the ongoing cash flow from their jobs and the value of their stock. The presence of this additional economic interest will facilitate agreement on subsequent transition matters. Employees know that at least some of their concessions will come back to them in the form of a stock price increase that protects the value of stock they already own. Without the prior stock ownership transaction, their interest in a subsequent adjustment is solely the return on their human capital. Thus stock ownership reduces the redistributive element of contracting, as discussed above, and narrows the settlement range. This is not to say, of course, that employees will readily accept wage cuts in the expectation of a compensating stock price increase. Many factors affect the stock price, not only wage levels; moreover, the stock might be locked up in retirement plans, meaning that

13. The stock price as a commonly accepted signal of the firm's condition and prospects also may be valuable in addressing a problem that has not yet entered the analysis: the fact that employee stock ownership transactions are typically negotiated with multiple employee groups that will be competing among themselves to minimize concessions and maximize claims on the firm's cash flows. A common point of valuation can limit certain kinds of strategic bargaining among the employee groups.

the consumption value of a stock price increase is much less than the comparable wage increase. Nonetheless, a prior employee stock transaction should lead to greater employee willingness to make future concessions if competitively necessary, because they will see some positive impact on the stock they already own. Thus such transactions should reduce the possibility of bargaining failure in ongoing negotiations.

ECONOMIC PARTICIPATION: OPPORTUNISM AFTER AN AGREEMENT IS REACHED. Economic participation can also reduce the risk to employees of a subsequent opportunistic transaction by management. If management were to seek a concessionary labor agreement with the idea of selling the firm, employee stock ownership in its economic dimension ensures that employees will also capture some of the gain from the transaction. This assurance may facilitate a transition adjustment, both in the initial transaction and afterward.

Superior Structures

There may be ways of restructuring workplace relations and culture that will enable a firm to adapt more quickly than its competitors and so minimize the transition costs that must be allocated. Two particular points of interest arise here: first, the possibility that the particular governance structure and gain-sharing structure of an employee stock ownership transaction can help promote a more productive, competitively superior environment within the firm; and second, that in such an environment employees are less likely to experience the wipeout of human capital investments that gives rise to the most severe transition costs issues.

The greatest potential upside of employee stock ownership is its ability to promote organizational innovations in workplace relations and culture that will make the firm a superior competitor. This may be particularly important in an environment of sharp economic change, because once-successful models may not point the way to future success. This places a premium on a pragmatic style of learning by monitoring in which collaboration among and between employees and managers may give the firm a comparative advantage in a competitive market and thus increase its chances for survival and prosperity.[14] The goal is not simply to persuade employees that competitive conditions require lower wages and more flexible work rules, in effect, a repricing of their labor. Rather, the goal is to induce employees to

14. Sabel (1994).

generate cost-savings and other productivity enhancements for a more competitive firm and further, to create a commitment to continuous improvements. In most firms, this requires a change in what might loosely be called "corporate culture." An employee stock ownership transaction may serve such objectives through both the governance participation and the economic participation features of equity.[15]

GOVERNANCE: BOARD MEMBERSHIP. Employee governance participation, especially through board membership, can obviously entail more than the absorption of credible information for the next transition negotiation. The board can be structured in a way to make use of information about the firm provided by employees, to provide a credible signal that such information is regarded as valuable, and to signal that employee interests will be given significant and sometimes decisive weight in matters of apparent conflict with public shareholder interests. It may be especially helpful to have employee directors assigned to board committees where much of the actual work, and much of the informal discussion, takes place. Employees are often in a good position—much better than public shareholders—to evaluate the exercise of managerial authority within the firm: whether managers appear to be capable and well motivated, whether production moves smoothly, whether resources of labor and capital are efficiently used. Thus they are especially well suited for assignments such as the compensation committee, where senior management is evaluated, and the executive committee, where important policies may be formulated. In these ways, board structure can help sustain the creation of a more collaborative corporate culture.

The tough governance question is how much power to give to employee directors. Even if most boards act by consensus rather than divided vote, the allocation of directorships and formal voting rules on majority versus supermajority requirements for particular board actions will often shape the consensus outcome. Because of the concerns of public shareholders and financial intermediaries, employees will rarely elect a majority of the board even where they hold a majority of the shares. In the UAL transaction, for example, only three of the twelve board members are designated by the

15. On this conception, an employee stock ownership transaction can serve both to govern better the shifts of economic transitions and also to create a stronger firm. However, it is important to note that employee stock ownership transactions will differ quite significantly, depending on the goals. If the purpose is merely to allocate transition costs, then the level of ownership may be rather modest and the governance rights nonexistent. If the purpose is a cultural shift, then one would expect a high level of ownership and extensive governance rights.

unions, despite majority employee ownership. However, it is possible
through by-law or charter provisions to give certain groups of directors
blocking power over all or some decisions. Some by-laws, for example,
provide that a group of employee directors plus some number of outside
directors—but less than a majority of the whole board—can block certain
large-scale business decisions, such as the capital budget for the firm.

At first glance, these provisions (and other potential governance innovations) may seem to elevate employee interests over shareholder interests
in crucial decisions. The risk here is that the firm may act inefficiently to satisfy a rent-seeking constituency—a strategy that may be unwise, or even
fatal, for the firm in the long run. On the other hand, such provisions are a
credible signal about the importance that the firm now places on employee
interests. In reality, there may be few occasions in which important decisions will come out differently because of pressure from employee directors (and the employees' equity stake may partly constrain rent seeking),
so the efficiency loss may well be small. If the goal is to change corporate
culture, the signal of giving employee representatives real power on the
board may add more value than any resulting suboptimal decisions may
subtract.

GOVERNANCE: VOTING. Shareholder voting is an additional element of
governance participation that can be expanded beyond its legally required
role to cover transactions that would change the firm in some substantial
way, such as asset sales or other forms of disinvestment. Depending on the
voting rules, employees can be given a veto or merely a significant voice.
Employee voting power may make more difficult a disinvestment or any
other transaction that threatens layoffs, because of the equality norms that
employee ownership fosters. Nevertheless such provisions credibly signal
that employees will not be opportunistically treated in a subsequent business restructuring and may be seen as opening the way to bargaining over
the sharing of gains and losses in such transactions.

ECONOMIC PARTICIPATION. Perhaps the most salient feature of employee
stock ownership is employee participation in the firm's economic residual,
through stock appreciation and increased dividends. Such participation
should advance the effort to instill a corporate culture of continuous
improvement. Economic participation provides incentives for employees to
worker harder and smarter, to cross-monitor one another and to monitor
managers, and to undertake discretionary efforts to improve the operations of the firm.

If the goal is a culture change, employee stock ownership also offers advantages over other vehicles for economic participation. For example, employee stock ownership is a way for a firm to commit itself to share the gains of competitive success that does not depend on subsequent renegotiation of wages. Gain sharing through stock ownership can avoid some risk of manipulation of profit-sharing benchmarks.[16] Stock ownership more powerfully transmits the consequences of improvement (or failure), in that it amplifies changes in profitability through a multiplier effect. For example, assume a $1 per share increase in profits for a firm trading at price earnings that are a multiple of 10. All else equal, this will lead to a $10 per share stock price increase, a much more vivid addition to employee wealth than a corresponding distribution of cash. Stock ownership also automatically locks in prior gains in a way that increases the employees' investment in the firm, which in turn enhances the incentive effects for subsequent periods. If profit sharing is used, then employees do not build up any stake in the firm over time. But in the case of stock ownership, unless the employee sells off stock, the value of the residual claim will increase over time. Most employee stock ownership transactions place significant limitations on employee stock sales, partly to foster this effect of giving the employee an economically more valuable ownership stake and the incentive to protect and enhance its value.

Stock ownership serves symbolic purposes as well. All employees have a common mode of economic participation. Unlike a profit figure, which is announced only quarterly, the stock price is a constant reminder of the common endeavor and the potential gains of success. Of course, this particular symbol will also sometimes lead to discouragement, as employees may experience the frustration associated with a stagnant or declining stock price, despite what they know to be their personal diligence and innovative work and a similar performance by the work force generally.

In summary, although employee stock ownership transactions could usefully serve as a vehicle for the "just allocation" of transition costs, the case for such allocation is not convincing. With regard to other transition issues, in particular the bargaining dilemmas that arise when sharp economic change requires new expectations, employee stock ownership transactions can help to conserve or enhance the value of the firm. Employee stock ownership

16. A firm with substantial employee governance participation has risks of opportunism with regard to the definition and accrual of profits that go in both directions. There is, of course, the usual concern that a focus on stock prices will lead to "short-termism." But gain sharing based on stock ownership may also insulate management from pressure to pursue short-term profits to fatten current employee payouts at the expense of long-term value.

transactions also have a role to play in environments in which a high degree of employee cooperation may produce a competitive advantage.

The Employee Stock Ownership Transaction at United Air Lines

The potential value of employee stock ownership led to a number of transactions in the airline industry following deregulation, including those at Eastern, Northwest, Republic, TWA, UAL, and, as an initial ownership form, at Southwest and Kiwi.[17] The UAL transaction, in which the employees acquired majority equity ownership, is especially important because its aim was to create a new organizational form, a public corporation with large employee blockholders. Unlike many employee stock ownership transactions, it did not arise under the pressure of imminent financial distress. The parties clearly perceived the UAL buyout not as a one-time rationalization of transition costs, but as a vehicle for making UAL a superior competitor in the industry. The parties also thought that the governance and economic participation arrangements were crucial. The institutions they devised were somewhat novel, probably as much the result of compromise as a disinterested search for the "best" system, but the success of this particular example of employee stock ownership may turn on their handiwork.

The UAL employee transaction took place in July 1994 and consisted of acquisition of 55 percent of the company's equity in exchange for wage reductions and work rule changes valued at approximately $4.9 billion. On the employee side, the transaction had its impetus from the pilots, who decided that employee ownership offered the greatest degree of economic security against the buffeting course of the airline industry. On the management/public shareholder side, the decisive factor seemed to be the necessity for employee cooperation in cost reduction and in the establishment of a low-cost short-haul carrier, later known as Shuttle by United, to compete with Southwest Airlines in west coast markets that fed UAL's longer flights. The bargaining endowments of the employees, particularly the pilots, meant that management could not impose its desired wage and work rule changes unilaterally, and, of course, management could not unilaterally impose a new culture of cooperation, either. These bargaining positions led toward an employee stock ownership transaction.

17. I have explored some of the transactions in related work, bearing out the theme that transaction-specific structures matter critically to outcomes. See Gordon (1995).

What is extraordinary about the United case is that the employees obtained a majority equity interest in the firm, an unprecedented outcome in a large public corporation not at insolvency's door. The results of the transaction can show not only whether employee ownership is desirable in a transition environment, but also whether a mixed ownership structure, in which employees own a majority of the equity but share control with public shareholders, can survive. The UAL acquisition was financed with a minimal amount of employee capital, and yet UAL has maintained its customary relationships with external capital suppliers to finance the transaction, airline purchases, working capital, and long-term capital needs. Thus in the broadest view, the long-term success of the United transaction may suggest that the dominant pattern of public share ownership and control is more the product of path dependence than of inherent efficiencies. The public shareholder form gave rise to a set of complementary institutions for management, governance, and monitoring; the transformation of ownership requires a new set of organizational complements. In this view, the United transaction may help establish a template for a new organizational form, a public corporation in which the large blockholders are employee groups.[18]

Transactional Background

The United pilots, the employee group that first pushed for the transaction, seemed to understand that they received substantial rents and quasi rents that were at risk in the increasingly competitive air travel market following deregulation in 1978.[19] The competition from new entrants (and from incumbents seeking to increase market share) was so fierce as to make prior labor cost structures unsustainable. The question was how to divide the costs of transition between shareholders and employees, and how to allocate any remaining rents between the two groups.

The employees were facing risks on several fronts. First, the company might use economic pressure in contract negotiations to lower labor costs. Indeed, the United pilots took a twenty-nine-day strike in 1985 in resisting such pressures. Second, the company might use airline cash flows for alter-

---

18. Blair, Kruse, and Blasi (2000) find that an increasing number of publicly traded firms have large blocks of shares held by, or on behalf of, their employees.

19. In parallel work, I am trying to quantify the rents and quasi rents of the various airline worker groups, by airline, over the period 1978–94. At the time of the UAL buyout, the present value of average pilot rents and quasi rents was in the vicinity of $900,000.

native business investment, in effect disinvesting from the airline business, which would lead to layoffs and lower wages. United did in fact diversify into the non–airline travel business in the mid-1980s, through acquisition of the Hertz rental car company and two hotel chains. Third, the company might be taken over in a leveraged buyout that would serve as a mechanism to force down employee wages. In fact, takeover entrepreneur Marvin Davis proposed a leveraged takeover of the airline in 1989 that led to a management and pilots' buyout proposal that collapsed under the weight of its flawed projections.

What precipitated the 1994 employee buyout was a company restructuring proposal that was a peculiar combination of all three of these strategies. Over the period 1990–93, UAL lost more than $1 billion, partly because of the industry-wide falloff in air traffic associated with the Gulf War, but more seriously because of the competitive encroachment of low-cost carriers like Southwest. The company's restructuring proposal would have produced widespread layoffs, subcontracting of certain services, and a spinoff of part of the airline's operations into its own low-cost short-haul carrier.

Financial Terms

It took a year of bargaining to arrive at the final terms. "Old" United shareholders received a total of $2.1 billion in cash and 45 percent of the common equity equivalents in the recapitalized airline, for total consideration valued at $3.2 billion. The participating employee groups (all participated except the flight attendants) received 55 percent of common equity equivalent, implicitly valued at $1.9 billion.[20] In exchange, the employee groups agreed to wage cuts of approximately 15 percent for at least three years and to changes in work rules, locked in for twelve years, that would permit the higher pilot utilization, quick turnarounds, and streamlined service necessary for the low-cost operation of a United short-haul carrier. The wage changes were valued at $3.3 billion and the work rule changes were assigned a value of $1.6 billion, for a total employee contribution valued at $4.9 billion.

20. The value for the employees' 55 percent of the equity is more than proportionately greater than the value of the public's 45 percent share. This is because the employees received convertible preferred stock, which carried an 8 percent dividend and a liquidation preference and was deemed to be worth 138 percent of the value of a common share. Until the share was allocated to an employee account, the dividend was available to pay down the debt of the employee stock option plan—a leveraged ESOP was used to obtain tax advantages—and higher value associated with the preferred stock increased the tax advantage.

In addition to the 55 percent equity stake, the union employees successfully bargained for additional job security provisions. For example, the new collective bargaining agreements provide layoff protection for all present employees, require labor to be protected in the case of significant asset sales, and perhaps most important, restrict the scope of the Shuttle by United operation both as a percentage of the entire system and the route structure.

Overall, it appears that the employees were well compensated for their concessions. In return for cash labor savings on the order of $3.3 billion they received stock with an implied value of $1.9 billion, a significant element of control for which no value was assigned, and highly prized job security provisions. The UAL buyout illustrates the capacity of organized employees to use an employee stock transaction to share transition losses and gains with stockholders on favorable terms.

Governance Arrangements

The key to protecting employee stock and increasing its value is to devise a governance regime that successfully addresses the many potential conflicts of employee ownership. In a sense, the critical parties in the devising of governance arrangements are not the public shareholders, whose investment in the firm is in effect sunk at the time that negotiations begin, but rather the third parties who have strong exit (or no-show) options, such as lenders, lessors, suppliers, and customers. These parties need to be shown that the employees cannot readily expropriate cash flow in a way that will threaten the firm's solvency. This problem was especially salient in the UAL transaction, since the $2 billion cash payout to shareholders was to be financed through the sale of UAL senior securities. Thus the UAL governance arrangements struggled to include employees and professional management, and to insulate employees somewhat from labor matters. These matters were addressed both in the structure of the board and in shareholder voting.

Three aspects of the board structure are particularly notable: the board's composition, the committee structure, and the voting rules. The board consists of twelve members: five public directors, three employee directors, and the main innovation, four independent directors.

Of the five public directors, three must be outsiders with no prior affiliation with the company, while the other two will be insiders, the chief executive officer and the chief operating officer. The outside public directors are nominated by a committee of the incumbent outside public directors.

As it turns out, only the three outside public directors are accountable solely to the public shareholders.

Of the four independent directors, at least two must be either a senior executive of a major company (with revenues in excess of $1 billion) or a board member of a major public company (with market capitalization in excess of $1 billion). The four independent directors are in one sense a self-perpetuating group, in that they will be elected by vote of a special class of preferred stock that they will hold. However, the nominees for these slots are presented by a nominating committee that adds two employee directors to the independent directors and requires the consent of at least one union director to any particular independent director nominee.

The three employee directors are divided into two union directors and one salaried and management director. The employee directors are not elected by the relevant employees voting as shareholders. Rather, each employee director will be elected by a special class of preferred stock that in the case of the pilots and the machinists is held by the union and presumably voted by the union leadership. In the case of the salaried and management employees, a representative body makes a binding nomination.

The fact that employee board representation will come through the union leadership rather than direct election may well lead to at least two significant problems. First, the union leaders who control the nomination of directors may be tempted to pursue personal agendas, such as to retain office, rather than the best interests of the employee shareholders. The second problem, more subtle, arises from the discontinuity between employment and stock ownership that will grow over time. The buyout is structured so that new hires will receive proportionately less stock; and those hired more than six years in the future will receive no stock at all. As employee shareholders retire, their preferred stock converts into common stock, which they can sell. Over time the employee groups will be divided on the basis of shareholder status, and employee leaders will face an inevitable conflict of interests. (Of course, the anticipation of this conflict may lead to the negotiation of a further employee stock ownership transaction that would include new employees.)

Overall, employee groups will select three of the twelve board members, will have a say in the nomination of the four independent directors, and will exert some influence over who is chosen chief executive officer (CEO) and chief operating officer (COO), even if the three employee directors could not, acting alone, force their dismissal. The initial CEO, for example, was selected by the employee coalition at an early stage in the negotiations, and his successor, a longtime company veteran, was chosen after an alternative candidate was vetoed by the employees. The scope of employee influence over the selection of directors is a potential weakness in the board structure. In a crunch, the employee groups could substantially change board composition, although such an act would undoubtedly be taken as bad faith by outside capital suppliers as well as public shareholders.

Many corporate functions will be under the charge of specially designated committees of the board. For example, a Competitive Action Plan Committee is responsible for overseeing the rollout and operation of Shuttle by United. This committee consists of eight directors: the CEO, three outside public directors, two independent directors, and the two union directors. It has "exclusive authority" to modify the very elaborate arrangements relating to the Shuttle, although the union directors cannot vote on labor issues and any amendment to the collective bargaining agreements must be referred to another committee, the Labor Committee.

The Labor Committee will consist of three or more directors, including at least one outside public director, one independent director, and at least one other director, but no union director, and will have "exclusive authority" with regard to the company's collective bargaining agreements. Six years out, the entire labor agreement can be renegotiated, but all subsequent labor negotiations will be conducted against the background of job security agreements, seniority protection, and similar protective provisions in the initial agreement. The company will also have to bargain separately with the flight attendants, who did not participate in the buyout and who therefore have made no wage or work rule concessions.

The sensitive matter of compensation of senior management is addressed by a complicated committee structure. In general, managerial compensation will be established by a seven-member Compensation Committee, consisting of the CEO, one public outside director, two independent directors, and all three employee directors. This obviously gives the employee directors an important voice in setting managerial salaries, and this structure has led to significant changes in managerial compensation. It had previously been the practice to give all managers above a certain level a fixed number of stock options. The employee directors challenged this and hired well-known compensation consultants; as a result, the compensation system has been revamped, with a lower level of options overall and explicit performance targets for the grant of options. The Compensation Committee may delegate to the Compensation Administration Committee "specific responsibilities" with respect to compensation of the CEO. That committee consists of two independent directors and one outside public director. In other words, it contains no employee directors.

This committee structure represents an effort to reduce the risk of certain conflicts. The Labor Committee, for example, is expected to avoid the nightmare scenario in which anger from difficult contract negotiations spills out into the boardroom, poisoning relationships and skewing decisionmaking. The objective of having a separate committee with all board power in these matters is to contain these conflicts outside the boardroom. Of course, such a committee could minimize conflict and avoid tough bargaining by sending all collective bargaining agreements to arbitration, which would probably mean a less favorable outcome for public shareholders.

The Competitive Action Plan (CAP) committee, which deals with the United Shuttle, is an attempt to create a more focused group to push for a new corporate culture. But the Shuttle's operations have been so critical to the company that matters concerning it are routinely taken up by the entire board, and the CAP Committee has rarely met. Except for the matters in which the CAP Committee and the Labor Committee act for the entire board, most other board actions are taken by a majority vote of a quorum (although "quorum" is defined in a way to limit strategic nonattendance decisions). Certain "extraordinary matters" require a 75 percent board vote, including approval by one union director, or 75 percent approval at a shareholders' meeting. These matters include mergers or acquisitions as target or acquirer, entry into new lines of business, asset sales, and the sale of equity-equivalent securities that would dilute the employees' ownership interest. The practical consequence is to give the three employee directors veto power over such a transaction, since it seems extremely unlikely that their concerted opposition would not carry at least half the employee voters, and half of the 55 percent employee stake would be sufficient under the 75 percent approval rule to block shareholder approval. Indeed, the two union directors alone have an effective veto over such a transaction, since their members hold 45 percent of the shares.

Shareholder voting is a subsidiary governance mechanism. As mentioned earlier, employee shareholders do not directly elect the employee directors; instead, those directors are selected by a special class of stock controlled by the union or other employee group leadership. However, in the case of "extraordinary matters," the shareholders have the rights provided under Delaware law (simple majority voting for charter amendments and a limited class of transactions) and, as noted earlier, voting rights in cases where the board splits. The employees' voting stock is held by the employee stock ownership plan, subject to directions to the trustee of the ESOP to "pass through" votes in the way that employees choose.[21] These shareholder voting rights, although limited, can serve useful purposes. They can restrain the enthusiasm of employee directors who might become co-opted by management's vision of corporate expansion. Or they can take the heat off employee directors who, for the sake of boardroom comity, may not want to oppose management's expansion plans directly and can lay the matter on employees. Both factors may have been at work in UAL's unsuccessful investigation of a possible merger with USAir in 1995.

One final concern is that the structure of the deal, as it evolves over time, could lead to a mismatch between the economic stake of current employees and their governance power. As has been noted previously, stock accrues over a six-year concessions period, meaning that newer employees will not necessarily own any stock (or very much). Moreover, the voting structure of the deal provides that the employees as a group will continue to have a majority vote (55 percent) and will retain an influence over the election of nine of the twelve directors (as explained earlier) until the level of beneficial employee ownership falls, through retirement-related sales, below 20 percent. The "sunset" date is not expected until 2016 and could easily extend beyond. Any change in these arrangements would require concurrence by the employee voters and their representatives.

These two factors reinforce one another. As the employees' collective economic interest from stock ownership diminishes, full governance power will be exercised by union leaders accountable to a membership that, in the

---

21. The parties have established these voting rules through an elaborate classification of stock. The employee stock held by the ESOP is in two classes: one class is a convertible preferred stock that has dividend rights but no voting rights; another class has voting rights but no dividend rights. As concessions accrue, the ESOP allocates stock (of both classes) into employee accounts, but holds onto the stock until the employee retires or leaves the company, at which point the employee receives the common share equivalents of the convertible preferred, and the separate voting share is extinguished. Why the division of employee stock into two classes? First, this gives the employees an immediate 55 percent voting interest even though the economic interest, the convertible preferred stock, will be acquired by the ESOP over the six-year concession accrual period, not immediately. The ESOP stock acquisition was stretched out over the period to maximize expected tax advantages (the company deducts the value of the stock at the time acquired and the parties believed the stock price would increase over time; convertible preferred stock was the favored instrument because its dividend right and conversion privilege are a basis for asserting a valuation higher than the publicly traded common). Second, the ESOP trustee is supposed to vote nonallocated shares via "mirrored voting," but recent Department of Labor rulings may require the trustee to exercise independent judgment as to nonallocated shares. This could have significant consequences in the event of a hostile takeover bid. So the parties have provided that if the trustees ignore the employee instructions, the ESOP voting stock loses its vote, another shareholder vote is required, and the employee voting interest shifts to the director voting stock.

main, owns no stock at all. This could be a prescription for disaster, since the employees' economic interest as shareholders is an important check on the use of governance power for distributive purposes. On the other hand, it is a problem that will not materialize for some time. The very point may be to force the parties to ensure a succession of employee owners. That is, one of the limits to employee ownership as a stable form has been the desire of some employee stockholders to cash out quickly, and the eventual sale by retirees. UAL stock is held by the employee stock ownership plan on behalf of individual employees, closing off the quick-sale avenue of employee exit (since employees can sell the stock only if they leave the firm or retire). But retirements and turnover will inevitably come. What is needed is an ongoing program of employee stock ownership, perhaps financed with new concessions or as part of a company-sponsored retirement plan. The potential mismatch may spur the necessary action.

How Is Employee Ownership of United Doing?

Has the UAL employee stock ownership transaction produced a structure that has conserved or enhanced value? UAL's current status in this regard can be evaluated on several fronts: financial performance, stock price, cost data, the success of the United Shuttle, and the effect on employee morale and performance. Perhaps the most straightforward performance measure is stock price data. As table 10-1 demonstrates, UAL was an industry laggard in the pre-buyout period and a star after the buyout. UAL's stock price performance in the pre-buyout period, January 1990 to July 1994, was a negative 5.4 percent, somewhere in the middle of industry performance, between industry standout Southwest (+48.5 percent) and industry laggard USAir (−27.7 percent), and, in a narrower range, between Delta (−9.3 percent) and American (−0.2 percent). UAL's post-buyout performance has been splendid: 46.5 percent annualized returns over the three-year period beginning July 1994. But the entire industry has enjoyed sparkling returns, especially Northwest (with +36.4 percent annualized returns), a case of a leveraged buyout saved from bankruptcy by an employee stock ownership transaction; Continental (+66.1 percent), a firm coming out of bankruptcy; and USAir (+77.1 percent), aided by the grounding of low-cost competitor ValueJet. Putting aside those turn-around situations, UAL's returns significantly dominated all others, including those of rivals American and Delta.

Another related reflection of the buyout's success is the increase in UAL's public market capitalization, from $1.1 billion to approximately $5.5 billion

Table 10-1. *Annualized Stock Returns (including Reinvested Dividends) of United Airlines and Other Major Publicly Traded Airlines, January 1, 1990, to July 13, 1997*[a]

Percent

Airline	1990–94	1994–97
United (UAL)	−5.4	46.5
American	−0.2	14.4
Continental	n.a.	66.1
Delta	−9.3	20.5
Northwest	n.a.	36.4
Southwest	48.5	−1.0
USAir	−27.7	77.1
Non-UAL average	−2.9	39.6

n.a. Not available.

a. July 14–July 13 of each fiscal year, except 1990, which begins on January 1.

by the end of 1997. Similarly, the employee equity appreciated in its shadow value from $1.9 billion to approximately $8 billion, an increase that nearly doubles the deemed amount of employee investment. These figures strongly support the efficiency properties of the United transaction: value was assuredly not destroyed, and it looks as if substantial value has been created.

Ironically, the performance of the Shuttle by United—the establishment of which was probably the critical variable in persuading the United board to approve the buyout in 1993—has been quite mixed. Shuttle by United was successfully launched in the fall of 1994 but has been at best a break-even operation. United has substantially reduced the Shuttle's operating expenses, from 10.5¢ to 8¢ per "available seat mile."[22] The Shuttle has proved valuable in building United's long-haul traffic from its California hubs, San Francisco and Los Angeles, taking market share primarily from Delta.[23] However, the cost target had been 7.4¢ per available seat mile and Southwest, its chief competitor in that market, has costs of 7.1¢ per available seat mile. Industry observers, moreover, seem to regard the Shuttle's performance as a disappointment, and the Shuttle's chief operating officer was

22. The "available seat miles" (seats per plane times miles flown) is a standard industry measure of capacity.

23. Susan Carey, "Aided by Its Shuttle, United Air Is Taking Los Angeles by Storm," *Wall Street Journal*, January 16, 1998, p. 1, col. 1.

replaced in the fall of 1995.[24] In the run-up to the employee stock ownership transaction, United had predicted that the Shuttle would eventually account for 20 percent of United's domestic operations; currently, the figure is just 3 percent.

Measured by United's internal yardsticks, the airline has seen significant improvements in morale and productivity.[25] In an internal 1995 survey of employee attitudes, 62 percent of the employees said they had seen positive changes in the company's culture over the past year, 62 percent claimed to believe in the effectiveness of "task teams" (employee-led work groups), 93 percent professed to be committed to improving the way they do their work, and 87 percent said they were looking for opportunities to keep quality high and costs low. These self-generated soft data on employee attitude changes are backed up by some concrete measures of morale and performance. Sick time in 1995 was down 17 percent from the prior year, worker compensation claims were down 17 percent, disability claims were down by 15 percent, and 75 percent fewer grievances were filed. On the performance side, United asserted that "task teams" had produced fuel conservation savings of $30 million annually and aircraft scheduling savings of $25 million annually, and noted significant improvements in on-time performance and baggage handling.

One especially interesting performance comparison is between UAL and Delta, which, as discussed earlier, addressed transition problems through substantial layoffs beginning in 1994, the same year as the UAL employee buyout. Using 1993 as a benchmark, both UAL and Delta achieved substantial labor savings in subsequent years, as shown in table 10-2. Nevertheless, UAL's average annualized stock return of 46.5 percent during the 1994–97 period was substantially higher than Delta's 20.5 percent. Although direct comparisons are difficult to make because of differences in route structure and competitive pressures, the comparative stock price performance of UAL and Delta offers suggestive support for the efficiency of an employee stock ownership transaction in managing a transition. Moreover, despite Delta's positive stock price performance, the Delta board perceived that the job cuts had precipitated a crisis in the Delta "family" culture that caused passenger service to deteriorate and increased union organizing activity. The CEO who initiated the downsizing was

24. Scott McCartney and Michael J. McCarthy, "Airlines: Southwest Flies Circles around United's Shuttle," *Wall Street Journal*, February 20, 1996, p. B1.

25. This information is based on a first-quarter 1996 presentation to security analysts by John Edwardson, United's chief operating officer.

Table 10-2. *Change in Labor Cost per Available Seat Mile*[a]
Percent

Airline	1994	1995	1996
Delta	0.08	−11.20	−6.22
United	0.04	−5.96	−4.30

Source: Computed from Form 41 Data, airline submissions to U.S. Deparment of Transportation.
a. Baseline is 1993.

forced out.[26] This suggests that Delta's layoffs may not have been the optimal transition strategy.

Only tentative conclusions about the performance of United's employee stock ownership transaction are possible at this point. A relatively short time has elapsed since the transaction. Moreover, unusually favorable conditions have prevailed in the air travel market in the period: air travel demand has increased, fuel prices have held steady, safety concerns have slowed the entry of new carriers, and the airlines have avoided rapid capacity expansion and the all-out price wars that have undermined profitability in the past. The real test of the resiliency of the transaction will come when economic conditions worsen or the inevitable fare wars break out.[27]

Midterm Wage Negotiations

From the of fall 1996 into the spring of 1997, United went through wage negotiations with the pilots and the machinists, which revealed both the fragility and the strength of United's employee ownership structure. The backdrop was a term of the 1994 buyout that permitted a midstream reopening of the wage settlement, as protection against the possibility that industry wage levels had changed in relation to prior expectations. The buyout agreement precommitted the parties to arbitration in the event of deadlock, capped the amount of the arbitration award to a 10 percent wage increase in the last two years of the employee stock accumulation period (1998 and 1999), and barred a strike until the collective bargaining agreement became amendable in 2000.[28]

26. Martha Brannigan and Joseph B. White, "'So Be It': Why Delta Decided It Was Time for CEO to Take Off," *Wall Street Journal*, May 30, 1997.

27. For another account and assessment of the UAL transaction, see Oakeshott (1997).

28. Stanley Ziemba, "More United Labor Woes: Mechanics, Technicians, Reject Pact; Ramp Workers and Others Approve It, but New Turbulence Adds to Questions about Employee Ownership," *Chicago Tribune*, January 10, 1997, p. 1.

The company originally proposed a deal significantly better than the arbitration baseline, which included a significant element of profit sharing. Nevertheless, in January 1997 the pilots and the mechanics rejected the company proposal. The pilots were particularly indignant, rejecting the company's "business-as-usual attitude that has no place in an employee-owned company."[29] Although the pilots could not threaten to strike, they did threaten to end the culture of employee ownership: "They can expect no cooperation. . . . They will find every interaction with us equally as difficult as they have made this negotiation."[30] Although the company made moves to submit the matter to binding arbitration, eventually the parties came to an agreement much closer to the pilots' position: a 10 percent wage increase received over 1997 and 1998, the recovery of certain pension benefits, and a guaranteed "snapback" by 2000 to wage levels prevailing before the employee buyout.

The implications of this outcome for the United employee buyout are complex. It shows that employee ownership can transform contracts with strict terms into relational contracts that can be renegotiated in midstream. There is nothing inherently unreasonable about the employees' desire for an extracontractual wage increase. After all, the performance of UAL and the industry generally since the 1994 transaction significantly exceeded the parties' profitability expectations. Projections prepared in connection with the 1994 transaction anticipated a net income of $118 million in 1995 and $244 million in 1996. The labor savings associated with the transaction were estimated to add $250 million to net income in 1995, increasing net income to $370 million the first year, and presumably equivalent amounts in subsequent years.[31] The realized results were significantly better: a net income of $662 million for 1995 and $960 million for 1996, nearly double the earlier estimate. Moreover, the 10 percent wage increase (and remember, it was from a lower base after the employee concession-for-equity deal) is not out of line with the 9 percent wage increase (over 1997–2001), plus stock options, that American Airline pilots received at the conclusion of their difficult wage negotiations in April 1997. Pilot wages at United will still be approximately 15 percent less than comparable wages at American.[32]

29. Mary Ellen Podmolik, "United Pilots Reject Contract; Arbitration Will Follow Lopsided Vote," *Chicago Sun-Times,* January 17, 1997, p. 45.

30. Paul A. Driscoll, "Employee Ownership Threatened by Pilots, United Airlines Dispute over Wages Termed 'Serious,'" *Arizona Republic,* January 10, 1997, p. E8 (AP story).

31. UAL Proxy Statement, 6/10/94, 21–23.

32. Scott McCartney, "American Airlines Pilots Are Expected by Union Leaders to Ratify New Pact," *Wall Street Journal,* April 7, 1997, p. B2.

Nevertheless, the midterm negotiation does represent a new deal, and one that is less favorable to the public shareholders than sticking to the terms of the 1994 deal. There are three possible reasons why management did not assert its contract right to arbitration and, by some notions, may be deemed to have capitulated. The first is a possible loss of the immediate economic benefits of the employee ownership culture. Even though increased morale and productivity are likely to be of some value, as discussed earlier, the factors most significantly accounting for United's unexpectedly favorable results have not been improvements made by the work force, but industry conditions: a growing economy that has led to an increased demand for air travel, which translates into higher fares and a higher proportion of filled seats.[33]

A second possibility is that management capitulated because the employees' governance rights were strong enough to threaten management's ability to run the airline. Gerald Greenwald, the United CEO, was brought into the transaction by the employees, the pilots in particular, and losing the goodwill of the pilots would have been a major blow to his leadership. Moreover, the risk of boardroom conflict seemed very real, in part because of the particular governance regime at United. The company's labor negotiations were orchestrated through its Labor Committee, which meant that directors were involved in an unusually immediate way in the formulation of the company's strategy. (The more common practice is simply for management to present its proposed strategy to the board at the outset and make routine reports along the way unless a major problem arises.) Although the governance structure devolves the board's authority in labor negotiations to the Labor Committee, apparently the directors on that committee felt it was inappropriate not to share information, and perhaps responsibility. The employee directors were present during at least some of the briefings. There are reports that the negotiations changed the "temperature" of the boardroom over several months, even in deliberations on matters that did not have direct bearing on the labor negotiations. Failure to resolve the conflict—first of many to come—obviously carried the risk of a downward spiral in boardroom cooperation that could undermine the company. United management must have been aware that at Eastern Airlines, employee representatives with far less influence over the board's agenda and procedures than was the case at United became vocally disenchanted with the management team and antagonism and havoc spiraled.[34]

33. UAL Proxy Statement, 3/31/97, p. A.6 (Management Discussion and Analysis).
34. Gordon (1995).

The third possibility is brighter than the first two: it may be that management was offering cooperation and flexibility in the good times, expecting these to be reciprocated in the tough times. Historically, the airline business has been highly cyclical. Certainly if United management had insisted too vigorously on enforcement of the contract, bargaining with employees in an economic downturn would have been much harder. If employee stock ownership is to induce a willingness to share economic adjustment costs in the face of new competitive scenarios, then presumably the converse must follow: that public shareholders must share some of the unanticipated rents. Sometimes the challenges of prosperity equal the challenges of adversity.

The United midterm negotiation also demonstrates a weakness of employee stock ownership as an economic incentive, at least when this occurs in the structure of an ESOP. Regardless of the employees' sense of unfairness in the turn of economic events, they had in fact profited hugely on their stock ownership and had more than recouped their investment of forgone wages. By my calculation, the average pilot contributed approximately \$50,000 in forgone wages and benefits over the period from July 1994 to January 1997, the point at which the pilots and machinists rejected the management contract proposal as grossly unfair. The stock received was then worth approximately \$150,000. In the month after the midterm wage settlement was announced, the stock rallied by another 25 percent, adding another \$37,000 to the value of a pilot's stock.

The problem is that the stock appreciation is locked up in the ESOP and is not available for consumption purposes until the employee retires or quits, and many employees were frustrated at being unable to realize the fruits of their investment. Indeed, it seems peculiar that high-level managerial employees in many companies receive the incentive of stock options that (upon vesting) typically have an exercise period of two to ten years, while line employees in the United deal were given an appreciating asset that could not be cashed out until retirement! Several hypotheses are available to explain the common use of an employee stock ownership plan in employee stock ownership transactions despite such "incentive compatibility" problems. A leveraged ESOP has certain immediate tax benefits, which may blind the public shareholders and other parties to the incentive failures of ESOP stock ownership. The ESOP also serves as a convenient way to lock in employee ownership. Lock-in may serve the interests of other parties. In the past such provisions have been used to create a block of employee shareholders who will resist hostile takeovers. On the other hand, lock-in may be necessary if employee ownership is to remain in place and to cement a value-increasing corporate culture, or to give credibility to the arguments of board-level employee representatives. Whatever the reason, the economic benefits to employees of the ESOP form are clearly in tension with its economic limitations.

Conclusion

This discussion has focused on the value of employee stock ownership transactions in solving transition problems in the U.S. setting. However, employee equity ownership can be of use in other settings as well, such as the transitional economies of Eastern Europe and Russia or in the privatization of state-owned enterprises facing a new competitive environment. Insofar as employees start with significant bargaining endowments and unsustainable wage and labor amenity claims, equity can play a role in restructuring the economic claims on the firm. Similarly, significant employee ownership might be valuable in firms under intense competitive pressures—for example, in the high-tech area—and hence in a state of more or less continual transition. Thus the wide dispersal of stock options among Microsoft employees not only acts as an incentive for strenuous activity to increase the value of the firm but also encourages employees to leave after their period of maximum productivity.

However, these potential benefits are subject to the important caveat that a successful employee ownership transaction depends in large part on the details of governance participation and gain sharing. The UAL example illustrates that institutions matter, including the structure of the board, the nomination procedure, and the committee structure. The particular vehicle for holding employee stock affects incentives as well as governance authority. It would be a mistake to take the United precedent as a standard form: after all, other companies will face different information, credibility, commitment, and incentive issues and thus may choose different approaches to gain sharing and governance participation. For example, the field is open for the design of transactional alternatives that might maintain long-term employee ownership while connecting present employee compensation to equity-type returns. More broadly, "employee ownership" is not a unitary thing, but rather a transactional framework that needs to be filled in with key institutional design parameters. Whether United will establish a successful precedent for a new organizational form especially well-suited for industries in sharp transition—the large corporation of mixed public and employee ownership—is still an open question.

References

Blair, Margaret M. 1995. *Ownership and Control: Rethinking Corporate Governance for the Twenty-First Century.* Brookings.

Blair, Margaret M., Douglas Lynn Kruse, and Joseph Raphael Blasi. 2000. "Employee Ownership: An Unstable Force or a Stabilizing Force?" In *The New Relationship: Human Capital in the American Corporation,* edited by Margaret M. Blair and Thomas A. Kochan. Brookings (forthcoming).

Blasi, Joseph Raphael, and Douglas Lynn Kruse. 1991. *The New Owners: The Mass Emergence of Employee Ownership in Public Companies and What It Means to American Business.* New York: HarperCollins.

Charny, David. 1990. "Nonlegal Sanctions in Commercial Relationships." *Harvard Law Review* 104 (December): 373–467.

Earle, John S., and Saul Estrin. 1996. "Employee Ownership in Transition." In *Corporate Governance in Central Europe and Russia,* vol. 2, edited by Roman Frydman and others. Central European University/Oxford.

Gordon, Jeffrey N. 1991. "Corporations, Courts, and Markets." *Columbia Law Review* 91 (December): 1931–88.

———. 1995. "Employee Stock Ownership as a Transitional Device: The Case of the Airline Industry." In *The Handbook of Airline Economics,* edited by Darryl Jenkins, 575–92. New York: McGraw-Hill.

———. 1997. "Employees, Pensions, and the New Economic Order." *Columbia Law Review* 97 (June): 1519–65.

Hansmann, Henry. 1990. "When Does Worker Ownership Work? ESOPS, Law Firms, Codetermination, and Economic Democracy." *Yale Law Journal* 99 (June): 1749–1816.

———. 1996. *The Ownership of Enterprise.* Harvard University Press.

Hyde, Alan. 1991. "In Defense of Employee Ownership." *Chicago-Kent Law Review* 67 (1): 159–211.

Knoeber, Charles. "Golden Parachutes, Shark Repellants, and Hostile Tender Offers." *American Economic Review* 76 (March): 155–67.

Mitchell, Lawrence E. 1992. "A Theoretical and Practical Framework for Enforcing Corporate Constituency Statutes." *Texas Law Review* 70 (February): 579–643.

Oakeshott, Robert. 1997. "Majority Employee Ownership at United Airlines: Evidence of Big Wins for Both Jobs and Investors." Working Paper. Job Ownership Ltd. (July).

O'Connor, Marleen. 1993. "The Human Capital Era: Reconceptualizing Corporate Law to Facilitate Labor-Management Cooperation." *Cornell Law Review* 78 (July): 899–965.

Sabel, Charles. 1994. "Learning by Monitoring: The Institutions of Economic Development." In *The Handbook of Economic Sociology,* edited by Neil J. Smelser and Richard Swedberg, 137–65. Princeton University Press.

Shleifer, Andrei, and Lawrence Summers. 1988. "Breach of Trust in Corporate Takeovers." In *Corporate Takeovers: Causes and Consequences,* edited by Alan Auerbach, 33–56. University of Chicago Press.

Singer, Joseph. 1988. "The Reliance Interest in Property." *Stanford Law Review* 40 (February): 611–751.

Williamson, Oliver. 1985. *The Economic Institutions of Capitalism.* New York: Free Press.

Contributors

Theodor Baums
University of Osnabrück

Margaret M. Blair
Brookings Institution

David Charny
Harvard University

Gregory Dow
Simon Fraser University

Bernd Frick
University of Greifswald

Ronald J. Gilson
Stanford University

Jeffrey N. Gordon
Columbia University

Nobuhiro Hiwatari
University of Tokyo

Katharina Pistor
*Max Planck Institute for Private Law,
Hamburg*

Louis Putterman
Brown University

Edward B. Rock
University of Pennsylvania

Mark J. Roe
Columbia Law School

Michael L. Wachter
University of Pennsylvania

Index